East Dunbartonshire

3 8060 06002 5319

D1795504

My Windows on the Street of the World

433D

MY WINDOWS
ON THE STREET OF THE WORLD
VOLUME ONE

Thomas Walker R.C.A. del.   *David y W W Walker ptr. sc.*

James Mavor

PROFESSOR JAMES MAVOR
from a study in chalk for the portrait in oil by
HORATIO WALKER, LL.D., R.C.A.,
presented by the Artist to the
University of Toronto

MY WINDOWS

ON

THE STREET *of the* WORLD

BY

JAMES MAVOR

Author of " An Economic History of Russia "

EMERITUS PROFESSOR OF
POLITICAL ECONOMY IN THE
UNIVERSITY OF TORONTO

VOLUME ONE

MCMXXIII   LONDON & TORONTO
J. M. DENT & SONS LIMITED
NEW YORK: E. P. DUTTON & CO.

Cook. . . . I find you want
A special service here, an antimasque,
I'll fit you with a dish out of the kitchen,
Such as I think will take the present palates,
A metaphorical dish! . .

  .   .   .   .   .   .

Bring forth the pot, it is an *olla podrida*;
But I have persons to present the meats
BEN JONSON,

Neptune's Triumph for the Return of Albion (1624).

TO

MY WIFE

OUR CHILDREN

AND

GRANDCHILDREN

PREFATORY NOTE

BY

Sir JAMES W. WOODS

PROFESSOR MAVOR's long study of Canada and Canadian conditions, his contact with the varied phases of world politics, his friendship and association with so many men playing a part in world affairs, together with his abilities as a trained observer of economic movements, have all contributed, during the past fifty years, to a most remarkable fund of knowledge.

It seemed, therefore, to a group of Professor Mavor's friends, the most fitting recognition of their esteem for him that they should undertake the publication of these Memoirs drawn from the wealth of this knowledge and experience. A Committee representing associates of Professor Mavor's, both within and outside of the University of Toronto, took action accordingly.

The Committee feels that these Memoirs, which are being published in token of esteem and friendship, will also prove a contribution to historical literature.

(Signed) J. W. WOODS,
Chairman of Committee.

TORONTO, *3rd August,* 1923.

PREFACE

THERE are two ways of knowing the world: one way is to go about it and the other is to allow the world to revolve around a fixed point. In either case we look upon the world through the window afforded by a science or an art, fully mastered or otherwise; and whether we travel or not, we see only what is revealed to us through this window. If we sit still we do so by a tangible opening through which, as well as through the other, we may watch the passing show. Both the *plein-air* method and the cloistral offer advantages. An academic position, involving as it does more or less lengthy vacations, enables the occupant to adopt each of these methods alternately. Since my particular vocation has been the study of economics and especially the comparison of the economical development of different peoples, this is naturally the principal window through which it has been my fortune to look upon the world, although from time to time I have been able, after a fashion, to look through other media.

As for my tangible gateway to knowledge, I have been singularly lucky. For many years I lived in a house some of whose windows looked upon a road along which there passed nearly all tourists who visited the New World as well as nearly every inhabitant who travelled about it. Such travellers find their way to Niagara Falls, and most of them cross Lake Ontario or go round the head of it, and thus arrive at the city of Toronto. All who do so are taken as matter of course to the park in which the University is situated, and so soon as they entered the precincts of that dispenser of learning they had to pass my window. Not long ago they had to pass within a few yards of it; but later, owing to the pertinacious advance of modern science in the shape of chemical and physical laboratories, my window was thrust somewhat back from the passing human stream. Yet the tourist was still visible and audible, for he usually came in a huge sight-seeing automobile equipped with guide and megaphone. By means of this offensive instrument, the guide imparted his ignorance by attributions more or less at variance with the truth. Thus, with unconscious humour, he indicated the Library as the Department of Hydraulics (*hortus siccus* would be a sounder description), or the building of the Medical Faculty

ix

as the Physics Department. Not the misguided globe-trotters who consigned themselves to such a cicerone, but the more discriminating who not rarely, by painful search and many wrong turnings into neighbouring *culs de sac*, found their way to my door, shrouded by summer foliage or concealed behind snow banks, are worthy to be counted, for they really desired to find that which they sought Some of these hardy adventurers did not readily meet with success For example, my good friends, William Poel, who was the first in recent times to put *Everyman* on the stage, and Cecil Reddie, the founder of Abbotsholme School in Derbyshire—one known for research in mediæval drama, and the other for research in mediæval alchemy— were both unsuccessful in their search for my gate They were brought in by scouts sent out to look for them. Dr. Shadwell, the Provost of Oriel, was found wandering in a totally wrong direction, and even so acute and experienced explorers in obscure byways as Mr and Mrs. Sidney Webb achieved only the garden and failed to find the door. Others have been even less successful, probably some of them are still prowling about looking for a gate they can now never find.

From this secluded observation post, for a full quarter of a century, I surveyed the world, save when I sought closer views of some parts of it, obeying an irresistible impulse towards movement It is true, as Peacock observes, that "intellectual progress does not consist in whisking the body about"; but a body which always remains in its accustomed place can only be regarded as a log or a mineral *in situ* Such a body has its interest, but this interest is not of a moving character

It has seemed advisable to explain the double motive of my title as well as to give in the following pages an account of part of the process by which I came to look out of my windows. My general object has been to reproduce such views of life as these windows have afforded over a period of nearly seventy years.

I am fully aware that what follows may fairly be described as an *olla podrida* Those who do not like a dish of that kind may pass it by, it is not for them The publication of this book is not of my own volition. Certain friends of mine suggested that it should be written, and other friends were kind enough to take upon themselves the task of sending it to the press.

JAMES MAVOR

UNIVERSITY OF TORONTO,
Easter 1923

CONTENTS

VOLUME ONE

xi

CONTENTS

LIST OF ILLUSTRATIONS

VOLUME ONE

MY WINDOWS ON THE STREET
OF THE WORLD

CHAPTER I

A SCOTS VILLAGE COMMUNITY IN THE FIFTIES AND SIXTIES

> A faire felde ful of folke
> fonde I there bytwene,
> Of all maner of men
> þe mene and þe riche
> Worchyng and wandryng
> as þe worlde asketh.
> WILLIAM LANGLAND, *Piers the Plowman* (1377).

NEW ABERDOUR, a village in the district of Buchan, Aberdeenshire, lies about eight miles west of Fraserburgh, on the road between that town and Banff, about a mile from the ancient church of Aberdour, and a few hundred yards more than a mile from the Moray Firth. Between Peterhead and Fraserburgh in and on either side of Rattray Bay, the coast forming the north-east angle of Aberdeenshire—a great salient projecting into the North Sea—consists of sand dunes precisely similar in character to those of Holland and Belgium. West of Kinnaird Head, near Fraserburgh and towards Banff, the coast becomes higher and frequent small bays are flanked by eminences. On one of these eminences stands the ruin of the old fortress of Dundarg, one of the strongholds against the attacks of the Northmen. Between Dundarg and Fraserburgh is the fishing town of Rosehearty. Westwards from Dundarg the Old Red Sandstone Conglomerate becomes more and more rugged. The only wide beach in a stretch of twenty miles or more is the Broad Shore of Aberdour. Beyond, the cliffs are shattered into jagged columns and mined into arches, forming a broken and tumultuous coast. Of the numerous headlands, Troup Head and Gamrie Head are the most conspicuous. Near Troup, the fishing village of Pennan [1] nestles in a tiny bay beneath the cliffs. The indentation affording foothold to the village is so narrow that it is

---

[1] *Pen*, promontory; *an*, diminutive ("British," Gaulish and Bas-Breton). Glossary in Chalmers' *Caledonia* (London, 1807), i. 35.

possible to throw a stone from the top of the cliff into almost any chimney. I once rode my pony down the steep zigzag path, to the delight of the children, who had rarely seen so large an animal in the village. Gamrie is known among geologists for its ichthyolites, and among historians of early Scotland as the scene of a sanguinary battle (*circa* 960 A.D.) between the Maarmor of Buchan and Danish invaders. Depressions in the neighbourhood, traditionally regarded as sites of Danish camps, are known as the "Bloody Pits." The skulls of the Danish rovers are said to have been built into the walls of a church erected soon after this engagement. In 961, the Danes landed again, at Cullen beyond Banff, and met there Indulf, King of the Scots and Picts, by whom they were defeated. This battle, in which the victorious king lost his life, is known as the "Battle of the Bauds." [1] How much is fact and how much fiction is not more easy to determine in respect to the early history of Scotland than in respect to any other history ancient or modern. Some importance must, however, be attached to persistent local tradition.

The ancient church of Aberdour is situated near a small stream flowing into the Moray Firth at the eastern end of the Broad Shore. This stream gives its name to the place, for *Aber* in the "British" language means an influx, and *dour* in the Celtic means water.[2] The foundation of the church is attributed to St. Columba. If this is correct, it must have been founded in the fifth century. So little of the existing church remains and the structure is of so simple a character that it is impossible to determine the period when it was built. In the graveyard there is a row of tombstones marking the burial-places of successive Deans of Aberdour before the Reformation.

A solitary house is the sole probable representative of the ancient village which in earlier ages sprang up round the church. The modern village is placed about a mile inland on an alluvial upland. The village is clearly of much earlier date than any of the houses which compose it, and, new as it is relatively to the old village on the lower level, is undoubtedly of very early date, for the system of landholding which characterised it until recently could not readily be applied to the older site and yet was of high antiquity. This system, of which New Aberdour was one of the best, if not *the* best, of recently surviving examples, is known in England as the "open field," and in Scotland and Ireland as the "run-rigg" system. I shall endeavour to describe the case of

[1] There is a cairn in the neighbourhood known as the King's Cairn, and regarded as a memorial of King Indulf. *Cf.* Chalmers, *op. cit.* i. 35. and Pennant's *Tour*, 1769, i. 146.

[2] Chalmers, *op. cit.* pp. 34 and 41. "British" is his expression.

New Aberdour without entering upon the disputed question of the status of the occupants of such lands in earlier times. They may or may not originally have been "free" tenants. Judging from the history of land tenure on the continent of Europe, it seems not improbable that the status of the tenant was subject to frequent fluctuations, and that as well there were variations in the customary law and in the practice in different places at the same period.[1] Wide generalisations about the prevalence of any one type of landholding at a particular time are therefore to be distrusted. The characteristic of the New Aberdour villager was his occupancy of (a) a village lot sufficient for a house and its appurtenances and a garden, all held on a ninety-nine years' lease; (b) four "riggs" or unenclosed fields divided from one another and from the neighbouring "riggs" by unploughed spaces of the width of two ploughshares, the "riggs" being each one-half of the width of the village lot; two "riggs" were situated behind the garden and separated from it by a lane which ran parallel to the village street, while the remaining two "riggs" were situated behind the others and usually separated from them by a transverse uncultivated strip, the "riggs" being held on the same tenure as the village lot and being inseparable from it; (c) pastures usually in more than one place in the village lands and consisting altogether of about seven acres in the hands of each tenant, these lands being held on a nineteen years' renewable lease and being redistributed on the expiry of a term. In addition, the villager had rights of cutting peat in the "moss," a lot in the moss being allocated to each tenant. The most important of these features are the "open field" (the "riggs" or infield not being fenced), the long lease of the "riggs" and the village lot, which gave great stability to the community, and the periodical redistribution of the outfields which in time gave every tenant family an equal opportunity in respect to the quality of the pasture land. The plan of the village showed the perfect regularity of the "riggs," and the somewhat wide distribution of the pastures occupied by the same tenant.[2] The "riggs" were usually cultivated in the following

[1] I have given an account of such fluctuations and variations in the case of Russia in my *Economic History of Russia* (London, 1914), vol. i. *passim*.

[2] Comparison may be made between the case of New Aberdour as briefly described above and that of the village of Hitchin in Hertfordshire, described by Mr. Seebohm in his *English Village Community* (London, 1884). The advantage of studying the system in New Aberdour is that in its essential features it was in full operation within the memory of living persons. I am informed by the factor of the Brucklay Estate that the system has been altogether changed. He is not aware of the date at which the change took place. Probably the system altered gradually as tenants' leases expired.

rotation: oats, barley, fallow or clover. Potatoes, cabbage and other vegetables were sometimes grown upon the whole or a portion of a "rigg." Young stock was tethered on the stubble, or allowed under the care of a herd to graze over the whole of the village field.

The village is situated on the Brucklay Estate belonging to the Dingwall Fordyce family. With the exception of the two inns, the village houses in the fifties were all built of turf and thatched. About 1863 the first two-storied slated stone house was built. The houses consisted of a "but" and a "ben." The "but" was the kitchen and general living-room. There was a large open fireplace with a "crane." Opposite the fireplace was a recess containing a bed. The "ben" sometimes contained a similar recess with a bed; but otherwise it was furnished as a parlour into which distinguished guests might be brought. The "shop" where the occupant practised his craft, if he had one, was usually alongside the kitchen and was entered from it. Each village house had behind it a yard in which were the byre, some-times a pen for pigs, a small dairy, a shed or tool-house for the imple-ments of the farm and garden, and the peat stack. Peat is a rapidly burning fuel and a supply of it occupies approximately four times as much space as would be required by coal sufficient for the same heating service.

The village was highly self-contained. All the primitive industries were represented. Carpenter, smith, saddler, weaver, and shoemaker supplied everything that was necessary. None of these made for stock. They only made to order. Each of these craftsmen had his land and he worked at his craft when occasion demanded. Wool was spun in nearly every house, and the weaver wove the wool so spun into the wincey from which the clothes of the women were made by them-selves. There was no tailor, and the clothing of the men was either obtained at Fraserburgh, which is the nearest town or was made by the women. Ready-made clothing was unknown. On Sundays and at funerals the older men wore frock-coats, a single coat lasting a life-time. For such goods as were imported into the village—tea, sugar, salt and the finer cloths [1]—there were two "merchants." They also managed such exportation as there was. They took a calf, a "stirk" (a year old) or a pig in exchange for the goods they supplied and sold these in the Fraserburgh market. About 1895 a branch bank was established in the village; but in the sixties, to which period the above description applies, there was little need for such an institution.

---

[1] Linen was not spun in Aberdour, so far as I am aware. In New Deer, flax was grown and linen was spun at an early period.

Very little actual coin changed hands. The "merchants" had running accounts with everybody, and the produce they obtained from their customers balanced accounts periodically. The people exchanged commodities, especially meat, with one another, for it was not economical for a small household to kill animals for merely domestic consumption. They usually arranged beforehand for the distribution of a carcass, and they shared with others when they killed. There was a village mill of early date. I am not aware whether or not in recent times there was any obligation upon the tenants of the village lands to have their grain ground at the village mill. Probably such an obligation existed at an earlier period. I have seen in the yards of several of the houses, the "quorn" or hollowed stone for grinding grain in small quantities, although I do not recollect having ever seen it in use. There were baking ovens in more than one house; but owing to the skill of one woman who had learned to bake in Fraserburgh, the villagers in general purchased their bread from her for cash or exchanged it for flour or other commodities.

Itinerant vendors of fish and of ribbons and the like made periodical visits, carrying the gossip of the country. In general little was bought, the individual household production, supplemented as described, sufficed for the simple wants of the people. The soil was fertile, enriched by animal manure, well cultivated, and there was a due rotation of crops. Vegetables and fruit were grown in the garden. Like the people of early England, the village folk were fond of spice; but that was easily obtained from mustard which grew in every garden, the seeds being ground in a bowl by means of a solid iron ball about three and a half inches in diameter. Mineral oil was not in use. Light was obtained either from tallow candles or from rush lights in the "cruisie."[1] The universal fuel was peat. The peat was cut, piled at the "moss," and left there until it parted with some of its moisture, and then drawn either by peat barrow or by cart to the village where it was piled in a stack at the back of the house. The moss was about two miles from the village. My acquaintance with the village began before 1860, and such were the conditions at that date as they had been from time immemorial and as they continued to be for many years afterwards. I have not visited the village since 1880, when I went to attend the funeral of my grandmother.

In the early sixties, society in the village was divided into two well-marked groups—these were the members and adherents of the

[1] An iron lamp of a pattern prevalent in the north of Scotland and in Orkney and Shetlands.

Church of Scotland "as by law established," and those of the Free Church. There was a solitary Baptist, a woman who was not a native of the village. No other sect was represented. The controversies of the Disruption of 1843 were still warm. To my mind these ecclesiastical disputes at once arose out of and contributed to the growth and wide distribution of intellectual activity among the common people of Scotland. The series of controversies culminating in the Disruption disseminated widely a serious habit of thought upon fundamental ideas of the character and functions of the State as well as of the limits of governmental authority and those of the liberty of communities within the nation. The arguments for and against interference in spiritual affairs by the "civil magistrate" (by which phrase was meant the total of magisterial power exercised by executive government and judiciary) were presented in every pulpit and discussed at every fireside. The Moderates defended the State and the Frees defended the Church. It was the old quarrel between the Emperor and the Pope. Two irreconcilable rights divine crossed one another. The Ghibellines and the Guelphs had come to life again in the Scots villages. Recondite and difficult aspects of Erastianism were threshed out in their own way by artisans in the towns and by labourers in the rural districts. The women became ardent partisans. The evangelical point of view fell into the background although there were evangelicals like MacCheyne and the Bonars in the Free Church who expressed that point of view fully. In the Established Church, moderatism or doctrinal toleration was predominant, if not universal. The marrow of the dispute was not religious, it was essentially political. It was a question of the government of the Church in its relation to the government of the State. The question was in the field of political science rather than in that of theology. Such a subject cannot be discussed without some knowledge of fundamental things in the history and theory of politics, and the people, under the influence of the ecclesiastical crisis, threw themselves into the study of these, perhaps without adequate educational preparation, but with an ardour which largely compensated for that absence.[1]

Lord Morley[2] quotes what he well describes as a "deep saying" from a passage by Mark Pattison to the effect that what is important

[1] Dr. Figgis was, I believe, the first to detect in the ecclesiastical disputes of Scotland an important contribution to those perennial controversies. *Cf.* his instructive *Studies in Political Thought from Gerson to Grotius, 1414–1625* (Cambridge, 1907). He was followed by H. J. Laski in his *Studies in the Problem of Sovereignty* (Newhaven, Conn., U.S.A., 1917).

[2] *Recollections* (London, 1917), vol. i. p. 72.

to know, in any age, our own included, is not its peculiar opinions, but the complex elements of that moral feeling and character in which, as in their congenial soil, opinions grow. In the case in question, the really important matter was not the controversy, nor its consequences in the narrow sense, but the quality of the mind and character of the people among whom the controversy arose, and only in so far as the controversy throws light upon these is it of substantial importance. Not merely an enthusiasm for dialectics, quite properly regarded as a characteristic of the Scot, but more importantly a passion for liberty, and in especial, in this case, for the liberty of the religious group, and a determination to resist the domination of the State was at the foundation of the Scots revolt against Erastianism. This revolt was the outcome of a deeply-rooted habit of mind which rejects smoothing over difficulties by the specious plan often suggested in America of "getting together." To the Scots mind, not "getting together," but getting decisively separate on fundamental contradictions, is the right plan. It is the Scots habit to meet difficulties, not to gloze them over.[1] Brougham, who understood nothing of the Scots point of view,[2] told the Scots ministers, "If you wear the collar of the State, you must bark as the State bids you." He made the Scotsmen furious. Their bark, at least, was their own. If statesmen chose to direct it, they knew neither their business nor the limits of the power of the State. Individual liberty was not directly at issue in the Disruption controversy. This issue was delimitation of jurisdictions of two authorities, not delimitation of jurisdiction of either authority in respect to individual liberty.

Chalmers puts the case with precision in two sentences:

"The great battle with us is for the privileges of the Church, as a self-acting and self-regulating body in all things ecclesiastical."

"In things ecclesiastical, the Church should be the uncontrolled mistress of her own doings."[3]

While individual liberty was thus not the point at issue in the Disruption controversy, limitation of the authority of the State aimed at by the Disruption was nevertheless in the interests of individual liberty, and therefore the passion for liberty was aroused and was the source of the driving power of the people behind the ecclesiastics.

---

[1] This accounts, e.g., for the failure of Arminianism and Methodism to effect any serious lodgment in Scotland, and for the enthusiasm for Calvinism.

[2] Brougham was born and educated in Edinburgh; but he went to London in 1803 and remained there.

[3] Chalmers, Thomas, *Remarks on the Present Position of the Church of Scotland* (Glasgow, 1839), p. 47.

While Scotland has experienced moments of ecstasy, the history of religion in that country is rather a chapter in the history of ecclesiastical policy than a chapter in the history of religious enthusiasms.[1]

The village folk were great readers. To one house at least there came a monthly box of books from Mudie's Circulating Library in London, and in winter these books were read aloud at the kitchen fire while the neighbours came in to listen. The village boys were generally employed on the neighbouring farms as herds in the summer; in the winter they were at school. I have often seen a herd-boy hammering away at Ruddiman's *Rudiments* or the *Dialectus* (the two elementary Latin school books of the time) while he was herding cattle, the open-field system rendering herding necessary. I was walking one day along a bridle-path when I saw before me a small pony which I had often ridden. The bridle was looped in the arm of the owner, who walked in front. He was the parish schoolmaster of Aberdour, Mr. James Ironside, and he was reading a book. The book was Homer. Mr. Ironside was a good scholar. Many boys went from his hands to King's or to Marischal College, Aberdeen.

A society of this kind unfortunately carried within it the impulse towards its own disintegration, for the narrow village life offered no future for educated youth. Boys and girls inevitably sought a living elsewhere. Some of them went into professions in towns—especially into the teaching profession; many of them went abroad. New Aberdour was not unknown in India, Ceylon, China, Australia, New Zealand, Demerara, as well as in the United States and Canada, where its youth had gone and prospered. What is true of New Aberdour is true of many villages and small towns in Buchan. Occasionally a prosperous coffee planter returned from Ceylon, or a stockbroker from Shanghai, and settled again in his native place. In one instance, a Ceylon planter took up the remainder of a nineteen-year lease of the farm of his brother who had died. The farm was a few miles from the village and was not upon the Brucklay Estate. The proprietor was not in affluent circumstances, and the ex-coffee planter, who was well off, built, under an arrangement with the proprietor, a new house and farm buildings, and engaged extensively in cattle-breeding. He kept a good establishment and lived as a country gentleman.

Many large farmers were not only expert breeders, chiefly of polled Angus, but were alert students of affairs. One to whom I paid an annual visit in my boyhood, James Lovie of Towie and Nether

---

[1] This is, of course, not the view of the Free Church historians, who lay emphasis upon the evangelical attitude of the leaders in the Disruption.

Boyndlie, had subscribed to the *Saturday Review* from its beginning in 1859. His mother was a delightful old lady. In the grove near the house at Nether Boyndlie, which was on the coast, there were many figure-heads of wrecked vessels. Such figure-heads made gruesome mementos of memorable storms. Among other intelligent and cultivated people in the region at that time (1860–66) and for some years after, until one by one they were gathered to their fathers, there were Mr. George Ironside, schoolmaster of Tyrie, brother of the schoolmaster of Aberdour, and especially Mr. Charles Barclay, a very dear friend of our family, factor for the Brucklay Estate, who lived at Aberdour House. He was a keen Free Churchman, and a benign and amiable influence in the community. The parish minister of my time I do not recall, but his immediate predecessor, Mr. Gordon, had been in his day a well-known character. He must have been a muscular cleric of the type of Parson Jack Radford. Gordon was dining at Aberdour House with the factor, whose name was also Gordon. There he met a young Englishman who contrived to offend him. After a wordy passage of arms, the minister invited the young man to finish the dispute on the lawn, where, taking off his coat and throwing it on the grass, he said, "There lies the minister, and here is the man." The story relates that Gordon exhibited an excellent knowledge of "practical science," and administered what he thought appropriate chastisement.

On the farm "toons," harvest is the time of joviality. The farm hands are then re-enforced by men and women from the neighbouring towns accustomed to farm labour. In the evenings the big kitchen is cleared for a dance, and there is always a fiddler.

The folk of the region rejoice in the rich Buchan tongue. For them any other is an uncivilised jargon. "Thae loons canna speak richt," was the frank criticism of a youngster on hearing my brother and myself speaking in our southern way. The Buchan tongue is perhaps the purest surviving example of the northern dialect of the Middle English language.[1] This northern dialect seems from the thirteenth century to have encroached upon Celtic dialects until it became universal in the Lowlands, and even penetrated into the Highlands of Scotland. It was the official language, and the language of gentry and common people alike, until the end of the eighteenth century, and even in the nineteenth it was still spoken by old-fashioned gentlefolks in all parts of Scotland. The great north-eastern Buchan salient

---

[1] *Cf.* Oliphant, T. L. K., *The Sources of Standard English* (London, 1873), pp. 146, etc.

is precisely the region where the last stronghold of a language might be expected to be found. As Celtic had to retire before northern, so northern has been forced into a corner by southern dialects, especially during the past century. Not alone in survival of words which have disappeared in more southern regions where once they were prevalent, but also in persistence in certain grammatical forms which elsewhere have become obsolete, does the Buchan dialect offer peculiar interest. Above all is the characteristic intonation, which to an acute and accustomed ear presents variations even in contiguous villages.

The Buchan tongue is noted for its diminutives. "Faur's ma fuppie?" (pronounced fuppoy), I heard a driver say, meaning "Where is my little whip?" My younger brother Henry was fond of making caricatures and indifferent about subject or occasion. A piece of gossip was seriously whispered round the village one Monday morning. "The chiel Māvor was drāen in the kirkie," meaning "The Mavor lad was drawing in the little church." Double diminutives are very usual. "Little littleanes," small children,[1] and "wee loonie," very small boy, may be taken as examples of these. "Hit" for it, and "hiz" for us, are examples of old forms that have survived, so also are "pitten" for put, and "gotten" for got.[2]

Dean Alford, afterwards Bishop of Victoria, drove through the village in the sixties and halted for a moment at one of the two inns. He found a domestic scrubbing the doorstep.

A. "Is the innkeeper in?"

Girl. "Na. Hit's oot."

Having so spoken, the girl calmly proceeded with her work. The Dean supposed that this was an example of village ignorance and went on his way without further attempt to find out what manner of people inhabited the place. The girl's answer was not only dignified and correct, it was also a lesson in common-sense grammar. An innkeeper might be either a man or a woman, therefore the pronoun used instead of this word might with propriety be neuter. Moreover, the innkeeper was to the domestic the sign and symbol of authority, and should therefore be spoken of with due reverence. The girl no doubt had in her mind the honorific expression, "Art thou not *It* which hath dried the sea?"[3]

Buchan genders are not always so easily defensible. It is hard to understand, for example, why *kettle* in Buchan is feminine; but all languages exhibit similar perplexities.

[1] Alexander, W., *Johnny Gibb of Gushetneuk* (Edinburgh, 1881), p. 327.
[2] "Gotten" is customarily used in Canada and the United States.
[3] Isaiah li. 10.

The mail-gig between Fraserburgh and New Aberdour had a single wide seat upon which at a pinch two passengers might bestow themselves beside the postman. One day I occupied one of these seats. At a farm-house on the way we picked up a little old lady very neatly dressed in black cashmere and wearing a smart and becoming bonnet. Her features were of the sharp, refined type very usual in the district, and she carried herself with dignity. Had we met elsewhere, I might have supposed her to be at least a countess in her own right. This aristocratic lady seated herself with composure between the driver and myself. We had just started when she embarked cheerfully in conversation.

Old Lady. "That's a fine gyäen [1] pownie [2] ye've gotten, mãn."

Postman. "Aye, Bibby."

Then after a brief pause:

Old Lady. "That's a fine gyäen pipie ye've gotten, mãn."

Postman. "Aye, Bibby, wud ye like a drãã?"

Old Lady. "Aw wud na say."

The postman took the pipe out of his mouth and politely handed it to the old lady, who continued to smoke to the end of her journey, to her evident satisfaction but to the detriment of her conversation, for she relapsed into silence.

Children readily acquire the dialect and intonation of those among whom they live even for a short time. One of my younger brothers when three or four years of age was left at the village for a month or two after the remainder of the family had returned southwards. On his return he was perched upon a chair to give an account of his adventures.

"They pit me in a train, an' it ruggit, [3] an' ruggit, an' ruggit, and brocht me here."

My mother, who had a strong sense of humour, thought the family would be diverted if she brought one of the village people south on a visit. She selected a worthy woman, Jean Robertson. Jean had never been far from the village and had not been familiar with the outer world, yet she bore herself in her unaccustomed surroundings with perfect ease. If her social experience had been narrow it had been intimate, and she was seldom astray in her judgments. Speaking about someone for whom she had acquired a dislike, she used the magnificent phrase, "Deil plenish the heavens wi' the vratch." [4] She did not wait to think that the keys of heaven were not generally understood

---

[1] Going.   [2] Pony.   [3] Past tense of "rug," to pull.
[4] "The devil furnish the heavens with the wretch."

to be in the keeping of the "Deil," or that furnishing heaven so far as was known was not any part of his business. Jean described to us a visit of condolence she had paid to a neighbour who had lost her husband. From an inaccuracy in a scriptural reference occurring during the conversation, I suspect that the neighbour belonged to the Established Church. After some appropriate consolation administered by Jean, the widow said unctuously, wiping her eye with the corner of her handkerchief:

"Aye, Aw ken he's in Bāālzebub's bōzum."

Jean. "Hoot, woman,[1] ye mean Ābraham's bōzum."

Widow. "Weel, weel, hit's yin o' thae fowk onyway." [2]

William Chambers, the publisher, died in Edinburgh while Jean was visiting us in Glasgow. She read the obituary notice. In the account she gave us there occurred the phrase:

"Chām-mers had his early dēvil-op-ment in a dām's squeel." [3]

Like most Aberdonians, the people of the district round Aberdour had a caustic and sometimes merciless wit. A village girl employed as a domestic on a farm was sent with a message to another farm a few miles distant. The farmer's wife, intending to give the girl some refreshment after her long walk, said kindly:

"Jeannie, wull ye hae a piece?" (The piece she intended was no doubt a slice of home-made bread and jam.)

Jeannie (pertly). "Na, thenk ye, Aw had a leg o' a turkey jist afore Aw cam awa."

Farmer's wife. "So Aw see, Jeannie. Aw notice a fedder[4] o't on yer breest."

The girl looked down and saw that a dry mass of porridge had lodged on her shawl. Although Jeannie was caught in a trap of her own contriving, she nevertheless showed very proper pride in the housekeeping of her mistress, and her exaggeration was merely a polite way of intimating that she had no need to go abroad for food.

The village smith, whose name was Bruce, lived outside the village proper. He had a large farm, and in early days had made money. He had two sons. One of them became a journalist, or perhaps a writer for the magazines. He made infrequent visits to his father. I recall him as he was more than sixty years ago—a picturesque figure in loose

[1] Pronounced "wumman."
[2] "Yes, I know, he is in Baalzebub's bosom."
"You mean Abraham's bosom."
"Well, well, it is one of these folk anyway."
[3] "Chambers had his early development in a dame's school."
[4] Feather.

black cloak and soft black felt hat, who went about alone and rarely spoke to anyone.   The other son, of whose personality I have no recollection, was a marine engineer.   Like many Scotsmen of the same profession, he was engineer of a steamer trading on the China coast. The vessel, with a cargo of coolies, was caught in one of those typhoons so much dreaded in the China seas.   The only safe course for a vessel in such a hurricane is to put out to sea, and avoid if possible being driven upon the rocky coast stretching northwards from Swatow to Fuchow.   For some reason the vessel was unable to put out to sea, or having put out was driven back by the irresistible force of the wind.   In order to give as many coolies as possible a chance to save their lives, it was necessary to hold the bow of the ship against the rocks by keeping full steam ahead.   Bruce did so, and with great gallantry sacrificed himself.   He was drowned in his engine-room.

The elder Bruce, the smith, was reputed to be well off and stingy. He had been a widower for years, and had been attended by a man who was his factotum.   One night during a heavy rainstorm the man went to his master's bedroom and complained that water was coming in through a hole in the roof and that his bed was unendurably moist.

"Strike a light, John," said his master.   John struck a light and found that his master was lying in bed under an umbrella upon which rain was falling through a hole in *his* roof.

Bruce (calmly).   "Dinna ye think, John, ye'd better do as Aw do?"

I was told this story in the village shortly after the incident, and years afterwards someone told me of having heard the story told at a camp fire on the veldt in South Africa.   Neither name nor place was mentioned by the story-teller; but some listener remarked, "I knew the man, his name was Bruce."

Among my friends as a boy was Mrs. Craik of the Mill Farm, a pleasantly-situated house between the village and the old church of Aberdour.   I often enjoyed her hospitable board and excellent cellar and listened to her quaint wisdom.   She was a very handsome old lady with precise manners and a pretty wit.   She had not travelled much since travelling became easy.   In earlier years she had gone more or less frequently to Aberdeen—driving all the way (forty miles) in her own "gig."   Shortly after the railway came within about fourteen miles of her farm she decided to make an excursion upon it to Aberdeen. When she arrived at the railway station of Strichen she found that she had forgotten her purse, a convenience which under the conditions of her usual life she had no need to carry.   Much to her surprise, the station-master, who was a new-comer in the district and was therefore not acquainted with her, said he was not accustomed to give tickets on credit. She told me that she thought the arrangement very stupid and a decided defect in railway administration. Her daughter Jemima was a well-educated young lady, very sprightly, and a fearless rider. I used sometimes to ride with her in my boyhood, not without apprehension, for she was in the habit of riding along the top of the cliffs, frequently in dangerous proximity to the edge. She used occasionally to visit us in the south in the winter. Samuel Craik, the only son of the family, went to Australia in 1849, during the gold excitement. I think he became a farmer rather than a miner; but to the village folk, everyone who went to Australia went for gold. One day there arrived at the village, for Mrs. Craik, a heavy box from Australia. Immediately the rumour ran that Samuel had sent a box of gold to his mother. Samuel's filial devotion was applauded; and perhaps visions of a generous distribution began to be entertained. When the box was opened it was found to contain a cheese.

By far the most interesting inhabitant of the village was Peter Walker, dyer. He occupied an old cottage on the Broad Shore, mentioned above as a probable survival of the ancient village. Peter's house was built on the edge of the shingle only a few yards above high-water mark. I once saw Peter bending over his dye-tub or cleansing some dyed stuff in the little stream that ran past his door; but his dyeing days must have been over. When I came upon the scene he already lived in honourable retirement. His house was quite unlike any other in the region. I do not remember to have seen anywhere any precisely like it, although in one feature it resembled the castle of the early Middle Ages, and more recent houses which I have seen in Iceland. This feature was the absence of a chimney. In Peter's house there was a kind of domestic altar—a structure of stone, formed of small boulders rudely squared—about three feet in height and about the same in width. A peat fire was made upon this altar, and the smoke found its way through an irregular hole in the thatched roof in the manner most convenient to itself. The house consisted of two very small rooms; one contained Peter's dye-tubs and I suppose his bed, the other, approached by a passage alongside the first, was his study, his sitting-room and the salon where he received his friends. This room was lighted partly through the hole in the roof above the altar, and partly by means of a window. The window was exceedingly small—only a foot square in total area—and the light it might have afforded was restricted by the continuous absence of glass in one of the four divisions and by the presence of a bundle of rags filling the space. A great pile of well-worn and much-smoked books lay in a heap in one corner. A small table beside the window and three chairs constituted the furniture. Peter received at any time. He never seemed to have anything to do more urgent than to engage in conversation; but he was fastidious about those upon whom he bestowed his time, and still more about those whom he admitted to his sanctum. My father and I used often to visit him together; sometimes I went alone. His invariable practice, no matter at what hour of the day we made our visit, was to go into his other chamber and shortly to emerge with a bottle of old port and glasses which veracity compels me to admit might with advantage have been immersed occasionally in the limpid stream that ran by Peter's door. The port was always good. How much Peter had in his cellar I never knew, probably he reserved his wine exclusively for his particular friends; but each year over a period of at least fifteen years, with the same formality, he poured for us the same wine, each year more matured, into the same glasses, each year more encrusted. Peter had enjoyed a long life of unimpugnable sobriety so far as anyone knew, and his experience led him to avoid alike excess and asceticism. In general, he was a disciple of "the doctrine of the mean"; yet he had his aversions.

It is a singular fact that in Scotland at this time men who practised any of the textile industries were almost invariably infected with heresy both in religion and politics. Why weavers, dyers and tailors should be agnostics or atheists and radicals, I cannot tell; nor can I why carpenters and shoemakers should be generally devout and conservative, and butchers and bakers indifferent alike in religion and in politics.

Peter was not at all shy in expressing his opinions about religion to those to whom he desired to confide his opinions upon any subject. He simply would have none of it. The village, as we have seen, was quite otherwise minded; but that did not influence him in the least. He never engaged in propaganda; and he declined to permit anyone to practise propaganda upon him. He admitted that the establishment of religion had social value. It helped to keep people in order, and in so doing saved the expense and inconvenience of police, therefore Peter went to the parish church once every Sunday and put one halfpenny in the plate. Having done so, he felt himself absolved from further interest in ecclesiastical or religious affairs. His belief, whatever it was, was his own, and no one else had anything to do with it. On one occasion two evangelical ladies who were visiting the village learned about the state of Peter's mind, and with the best intention and the least wisdom called upon him to remonstrate. They were not admitted to his house, and the interview was not prolonged. What Peter said he, being a gentleman, never told; nor did the ladies in detail, but it came to be known that they beat a hasty retreat. They made no further efforts to evangelise in that quarter.

Peter's figure was tall with a slight stoop. His body was well-knit, lithe and sinewy. His keen grey eyes shone from sharp intellectual features. In his youth Peter had been a powerful swimmer; and when he had passed his sixtieth year he was able to swim every day through the surf of the Broad Shore, where indeed no one else customarily swam, to a rock distant a hundred yards or more according to the state of the tide. We knew this as Peter's Rock, for when he reached it, his tall figure surmounted it for a short time. I often lay on the promontory above, after I had had my own more modest dip in the quieter waters of the Boat Shore, and watched Peter having his morning swim.

No one knew who Peter's relatives were, nor did anyone know his early history. Nothing ever transpired to show that there was any reason for reticence excepting that this accorded with Peter's temperament. When he died he was found to have left some money, and heirs made their appearance. Although Peter had, so far as I know, no special knowledge of science, as Edwards, the naturalist, and Dick, the geologist, had,[1] he was a man of similar type—an intellectual peasant who had shrewd and penetrative views of life and independence as thorough-going as his frugality. He showed always a stately courtesy and occasionally something of the grand manner.

Of women of the village, other than those I have already mentioned, two were remarkable for different reasons. One was an old woman who had been in the habit in her earlier years of walking to Aberdeen fish market from the village—forty miles—on one day with a "creel" of fish on her back and out again the next day, and of doing this twice a week. The other was a "witch." The "witch" was shunned by everyone; she had the "evil eye." In her youth she had been brought before the Kirk Session, charged with a lapse from virtue. The "ruling elder," a well-to-do farmer, admonished her more sharply than she relished, and she told him that one day he would suffer for his severity. Thereafter, every night, so the story went, she pronounced upon the head of this farmer one of the imprecatory psalms.[2] Within a year and a half an epidemic of foot-and-mouth disease struck the

[1] Smiles wrote the life of Edwards, and Wm. Jolly that of Dick.
[2] Probably Psalm cix.

district, the polled Angus herd of the farmer was stricken, and he was ruined. Everyone believed that the witch had brought her curse to bear upon him.

Intelligent the people were in many ways, as I have endeavoured to make plain, yet in general they entertained some primitive superstitions. My aunts Elspeth and Mary, who were by no means wanting either in acuteness of mind or in education, have been known to have their churn carried across a running stream so that their butter might be freed from witchcraft. Such harmless gaucheries are by no means the last, and may well be considered as the least, of the evidences of superstition.[1]

My visits to the village were frequent during more than twenty years, and I never heard of a crime being committed in it or in the district round it during that period, nor did I ever see a policeman. There was a coastguard station and men of the "preventive service" watched the coast, for smuggling had been carried on in its unfrequented bays; but so far as I know, no one living in the district was ever implicated in smuggling adventures.

The villagers occupied themselves wholly with their land and their handicrafts; they did not engage in the business of fishing. The nearest fishing places were the small town of Rosehearty to the east and the village of Pennan to the west; the fishermen there were not farmers. The shrewd Aberdonians avoided the amphibious life of the West Highlanders and the people of the west of Ireland, who fish and farm and do neither with skill or success.

Within a small area many picturesque features are concentrated. At the head of the village near the parish church there is the "Knowe," a hill of fifty or sixty feet above the surrounding level and about three hundred above the sea, covered to the top with yellow broom. From this eminence may be seen the Moray Firth stretching north and west. Immediately to the west of the village is the Den or ravine in the valley of the Dour—the stream which gives the village its name.

[1] O l'heureux qui celui de ces fables
Des bons demons, des esprits familiers,

. . . . . .

On a banni les demons et les fées;
Sous la raison les graces etouffées,
Livrent nous cœurs a l'insipidité;
Le raisonner tristement s'accredite;
On court, helas! après la verité,
Ah! Croyez moi, l'erreur a son merite.
                    VOLTAIRE.

I—B

The Den is wooded by birch, beech and other trees and shrubs; in the undergrowth is bracken in extraordinary profusion. West of the village there are the Dens of Auchmeddan, Troup and Gamrie, each well known to botanists and palæontologists. The characteristic features of the coast-line have already been mentioned. To these may be added the Boat Shore, where alone boats may conveniently be kept; the Otter Cave, where tracks of its shy inhabitants appeared at low tide; the Iron Well, where a mineral spring strongly impregnated with oxide of iron oozes from the cliff at the western end of the Broad Shore; and the rocks near it, covered at high tide, where, when the tide was ebbing, we used to gather the most delicious of dulce and whelks of peculiar succulence.

There was little game in the district. The proprietors in the region were not much addicted to sport, and there was comparatively little effort to preserve. We used to go rabbit-shooting in the dunes when we visited our connections the Hendersons at Rattray House, otherwise the only sport was trout-fishing in the streams and sea-fishing in the bay. There were few wild animals, and these were small—stoats, weasels, hedgehogs and the like. Sea birds were fairly numerous—guillemots and puffins were often seen, and sometimes after a severe storm were found dead on the beach.

In the days before steam trawlers worked the Moray Firth and the North Sea fishing grounds, one of the finest sights of the kind was to witness, as the sun was setting, the fishing smacks with their brown sails putting out from the villages along the coast, each village sending its fleet until there were a hundred sail or more in sight from one of the promontories of the Aberdour shore. Slowly as the darkness came, the horizon swallowed the fleets until not a sail could be seen. Beyond another horizon these fleets have passed for all time, and things of beauty as they were, they remain only as a memory. Their successors, the trawlers and drifters and their hardy crews, have amply earned the gratitude of half the world by fishing not for their accustomed catch, but for those monsters of the deep whose depredations, great as they have been, would have been greater still but for the skill and endurance of the Scots fishermen. It may never be known how many submarines and their pirate crews lie at the bottom of the North Sea through the vigilance of these Imperial sentinels.

The funeral customs of the village, although not wholly unique, had features which I have not witnessed elsewhere. On the morning of the day of burial, two chairs were taken from the house and placed in the middle of the village street. Two poles were brought by the carpenter and placed one on each side of the door of the house from which the funeral was to take place. A service was held in one or other of the churches. In the case of all well-known persons, labour in the village and sometimes in the district was wholly suspended. All the men and youths but none of the women attended. The coffin was brought out and placed upon the chairs. The poles were placed under the coffin and held by eight bearers, two on each side of each pole. Then the procession to the graveyard of Old Aberdour began. Every minute or less, a fresh bearer volunteered and stepped silently into the place of one who fell out, the procession proceeded without halting, and during its progress—the distance was about a mile— everyone had an opportunity of acting as bearer. Sometimes the procession numbered several hundred. At the graveyard there was no service, the coffin was silently committed to earth. As is usual in very ancient graveyards, the mould was almost altogether composed of human dust, and the coffin was usually covered with disarticulated bones. On two different occasions someone standing beside me recognised the skull of a relative. Once a man said to me in a solemn whisper, "Thae're ma faither's banes they're pitten in noo." [1]

From these notes it may be gathered that, taking into account the variation of the seasons and occasional losses through epidemics among cattle, the people of the Aberdour region were comfortably off. Their life was so self-contained that they were little affected by the fluctuations of prices in the external markets. There were practically no landless people in the region, and the large farmers were neither rich enough nor numerous enough to compose a separate social class. The same was true of the proprietors. There was thus a real feeling of social equality, although there were both differences and fluctuations in well-being. [2] There was no factory industry, or mining, or forestry to draw into or sustain in the district a proletarian labouring population, while the excess of youths of both sexes drifted off, leaving the community rather unprogressive but highly homogeneous and contented with what nature and industry provided

[1] " These are my father's bones they are putting in now."
[2] This pervasive sense of equality naturally gave rise to a feeling of political independence, even when this characteristic was unusual in Scotland. The proof may be found, for example, in *A Confidential Report on the Opinions, Family Connections or Personal Circumstances of the County Voters*, 1788, where the notes "independent," "very independent," "quite independent," are frequently attached to the names of the 178 voters in the county of Aberdeen at that date. See Adam, Sir C. E. (Editor), *View of the Political State of Scotland*, Edinburgh, 1877.

—a liberty-loving society in a shell in which feudalistic incidents had survived feudal relations.

I have given these details of the position and life of the village of New Aberdour partly because the district had a special character which I think ought to be recorded, and partly because one of my parents was brought up in it and during early boyhood I spent a part of each year there myself. The family of Mavor or Maver, for the name occurs in both forms in the case of even near kinsmen, was before the end of the seventeenth century somewhat widely dispersed in Aberdeenshire and Banffshire. Many youths bearing the names Jacobus Mavor and Gulielmus Mavor appear in the books at King's College, Aberdeen, as "bursars" from the beginning of the eighteenth century. The origin of the name is unknown. There are many Norman family names in Buchan, and it may be one of these. The particular branch of the family to which I belong was settled for a long period in New Deer, which lies about twenty miles south of New Aberdour. It is a tradition in the family that one of its members, as one of a group of fifteen, accompanied Lord Forbes of Pitsligo when he joined the army of the Pretender, and that he remained with him while he was in hiding after the Battle of Culloden.

The only member of the family who achieved notoriety was William Fordyce Mavor, LL.D., Rector of Bladon in Oxfordshire and Vicar of Hurley in Berks. He was born in New Deer in 1758, and was a cousin of my great-grandfather. William Mavor was a member of the Board of Agriculture while Arthur Young was Secretary, and was the author of some of its Reports. He invented a system of shorthand, compiled a spelling-book which had an immense circulation, edited a collection of travels, wrote a Universal History and so many miscellaneous works that altogether some fifty pages of the catalogue of the library of the British Museum are required to contain their titles. The only work of his in which I find any interest is his edition of Tusser's *Five Hundred Points of Good Husbandry*. According to the *Extraordinary Black Book*,[1] the total income from William Mavor's two livings, including the chapelry of Woodstock attached to Bladon, was one hundred and sixty pounds a year. He was thus, like many others of his time, driven to write copiously for the booksellers.

Some more or less distant kinsmen were Fellows of Pembroke and Lincoln in Oxford in the beginning of the nineteenth century. One branch of the family went to Virginia at an early period in the history of that colony, and at later periods others went to Illinois and Michigan

[1] London, 1832, pp. 115 and 661.

as well as to South America and New Zealand. One kinsman was a captain in the army of the East India Company early in the nineteenth century, another became Rector of the Aberdeen Grammar School.

My grandfather, John Mavor, was born in New Deer in 1797. He married Elizabeth Ingram of the same place, and moved to New Aberdour about 1820. His eldest son, Alexander, who died at an early age, had some local reputation as a mathematician. His second son, John, became a teacher and went to North Shields, where he became Chairman of the School Board. He also had mathematical talent. My father, James, also became a teacher, after going to Glasgow at an early age for his education. The youngest son, William, died while a law student at Marischal College, Aberdeen. Among the contemporaries of these youths in New Aberdour was William Henderson, who became Provost of Aberdeen.[1]

My grandmother's family, the Ingrams, had a somewhat similar history. One of her brothers went to Peterhead and became the owner of a fleet of fishing-smacks. His principal business was the exportation of herring and haddock to Hamburg. His son and successor went often in the course of his business to Germany, and on one of these occasions, about 1870, he learned that at one time there had been erected in Berlin a bronze statue of James Keith, Field-Marshal under Frederick the Great.[2] This statue had disappeared. After painstaking researches, Ingram discovered the statue in the basement of one of the public buildings in Berlin. Long negotiations ensued; and by the aid of the British Ambassador, the statue was secured, transported to Peterhead, and erected by Ingram on a granite pedestal in the market-place. Ingram was at the time Provost of the town. Another of my grandmother's brothers emigrated to Canada about 1835, and founded a place which he called New Aberdour on the Saugeen river in Ontario. This Ingram came to visit us in Glasgow in 1865, and recounted his experiences of thirty years before in hewing his way through the Canadian forest to the spot where he settled. Another of my grandmother's relatives went from New Deer to the United States. His son went to China as a medical missionary about

---

[1] Sir William Henderson of Devanha died about 1900. My aunt Ann, wife of John Mavor, was Sir Wm. Henderson's sister. She died in London in 1917 at the age of ninety-eight.

[2] Field-Marshal Keith was killed at the battle of Hoch Kirchen in 1758. He was a son of the ninth and only brother of the tenth and last Earl Marischal of Scotland. The Keiths had been Marischals of Scotland from the year 1010. Their seat was Keithhall, near Inverurie. For eight hundred years this family had contributed many persons of distinction to the public life of Scotland.

1880.[1] Other Ingrams from New Deer and from the neighbourhood of New Aberdour were similarly scattered.

This family history, with its early and wide separations, is by no means unique. It is the usual history of Aberdeenshire families. A spot on the face of the earth to which some Aberdonian has not penetrated would be difficult to find.

[1] I met Dr. Ingram at Kalgan, on the Mongolian frontier of China, in 1910 (*cf.* vol. ii. p. 335).

CHAPTER II

A SCOTS SEAPORT IN THE THIRTIES

> You should have seen, man cannot tell to you
> The beauty of the ships of that my city.
> That beauty now is spoiled by the sea's pity;
> For one may haunt the pier a score of times,
> Hearing St. Nicholas' bells ring out the chimes,
> Yet never see those proud ones swaying home
> With mainyards backed and bows a cream of foam,
> Those bows so lovely-curving, cut so fine,
> Those coulters of the many-bubbled brine,
> As once, long since, when docks were filled
> With that sea-beauty man has ceased to build.
>
> Yet though their splendour may have ceased to be,
> Each played her sovereign part in making me;
> Now I return my thanks with heart and lips
> For the great queenliness of all those ships.
>
> JOHN MASEFIELD, Ships (1912).

THE estuary of the Tay affords a fair anchorage, and thus there grew at an early period a flourishing shipping in Dundee. In the Burgh Laws of Dundee for the year 1550 it is enacted "that no ship be fraughted be privat persons but openly in presce of Prouest or Bailles or than befor the Dean of Gild to pas in merchandice. In France, Flanders, Denmark, Danskine [Dantzig], or any free port without this realme,"[1] etc. Thus in the sixteenth century there was already an active trade between Dundee and the Continent.

The timber trade brought the port into relations with Bergen and Quebec, and the trade in tar with the Swedish and Finnish ports in the Gulf of Bothnia and with Archangel in the White Sea.

In the thirties of the nineteenth century Dundee had become the seat of the linen trade. The industry had passed from the domestic to the factory stage. There were then more than fifty factories producing the staple. This trade brought the port into close relations with the Baltic and especially with Russia, and when the trade in jute began, with India. When China was opened to British trade, Dundee ships went to Hong Kong and Canton.

---

[1] Warden, Alex. J., *Burgh Laws of Dundee* . . . (London, 1872), p. 13.

Dundee ships engaged in whaling and sealing both in the Arctic and the Antarctic regions. So long as the sperm-whale fisheries lasted, Dundee whalers took an important if not even the leading place. Every year the whaling fleet departed on its adventurous voyage for the hunting grounds in Davis Straits or the Southern Seas. By common custom, everyone was interested in these voyages. The people of Dundee have from time immemorial been sailors and ship-owners. The ownership of each vessel, before the days of shipping companies and great "combines," was divided into sixty-four shares. The captain invariably owned one or more sixty-fourths, sometimes the mate owned one also, and their family connections held the bulk of the remainder. When the whaling fleet returned, the "catch" was the universal topic of interest and conversation. The amount of it was signalled from the first available point, and by the time the ships were sailing up the Tay, everyone knew how many barrels of whale- and seal-oil and how many sealskins each ship brought. Already projects for the spending or investment of the profits of the voyage were being formulated.

When a ship was too old or too unseaworthy for any other service, she was sent to Quebec for timber; because with such a cargo she could not sink.

Under the conditions of ownership which have been mentioned, it was naturally common for the shipmaster who was leaving for a long voyage to take his wife and even other members of his family with him. The Dundee folk of this time were thus much-travelled.

My mother's name was Mary Ann Taylor Bridie. Her family had been for several generations sailors and partners in the ownership of vessels sailing from Dundee.[1] Her father, Captain John Bridie, had been in all the branches of the Dundee trade—in the Baltic, in Archangel, in India, in China, and in the Quebec timber trade. He retired from active seafaring about 1840, and up till that time had made eight voyages round the world, some of these extending over two or three years. Thus of Dundee days in the thirties I learned from my mother. She was born in Dundee in 1828. She told me of frequent voyages as a girl with her father, of going by coach to Newcastle-on-Tyne and other ports to meet him after long absences, of the presents he always brought her from foreign countries—furs from Russia, eiderdown compressed

[1] It was customary for captains to have paintings by marine artists of their ships when new. A reproduction of a painting executed at Riga about 1820, of the schooner *Ann*, built for my grandfather and called after my grandmother, is given by way of example.

THE SCHOONER "ANN" IN THE HARBOUR OF RIGA

From a painting in oil (executed at Riga c. 1830) in the possession of Mr. Sam Mavor

in bladders of sheep from Copenhagen, a monkey from the tropics, quaint ornaments from Canton, an ostrich from the Cape, or the skin and feathers of an albatross or a polar bear's skin from Davis Straits. An ostrich excited the household by swallowing my mother's crochet needles and bobbins; a monkey committed havoc with plates, upon which he swooped at unexpected moments and scampered off to enjoy the clatter they made as he smashed them by throwing them on the floor. The animals accumulated to such an extent that from time to time they had to be packed off to Wombwell's menagerie. My mother's only brother, John Bridie, became a captain at twenty-one, and soon afterwards master of an East Indiaman.[1]

Life in those days was a mixture of exciting moments and intervals of waiting for the return of the ship from long voyages. Of the friends of the family at that time I know little. I remember, however, that Michael Scott, the author of *The Cruise of the "Midge"* and *Tom Cringle's Log*, was a friend of my grandfather and an occasional visitor, and that my mother used to go on more or less prolonged visits to the Miss Websters of Balruddery.[2] Mr. Webster was a keen palæontologist. He had found in the Den of Balruddery, in the immediate neighbourhood of his house, fossils which about this time (1840) began to attract attention. The Den had been known locally for its extreme picturesqueness, but it became widely famous for its fossils. Hugh Miller visited Balruddery frequently, and took with him at least on one occasion Sir Roderick Murchison and Dr. Buckland. When Agassiz visited Scotland, Miller took him also. In his *Old Red Sandstone*,[3] Miller gives an account of that visit and of the identification by Agassiz of a huge fossil lobster previously unknown.

In 1839, when my mother was eleven years of age and at a boarding school, her father was sailing his ships in the Baltic trade. In the autumn of that year, while on a Baltic voyage, his vessel was pursued by a pirate. At that time the Baltic was infested by pirates, none of the maritime nations bordering upon the sea having a sufficiently powerful navy to hunt them down. Captain Bridie ran his ship into shoal waters near Narva, where she escaped her pursuer but grounded. He determined to purchase his stranded ship and cargo from the underwriters and to attend to the salvage himself, but the lateness of the season and the closing of the harbour of Narva by ice compelled

[1] He was killed in a railway accident at Kirtlebridge in 1863.
[2] This estate is now in possession of my friend J. Martin White, formerly M.P. for Forfarshire.
[3] Miller, Hugh, *The Old Red Sandstone* (Edinburgh, 1874), p. 158.

him to postpone operations until the spring. Instead of returning to Dundee, he decided to bring his family to Russia to spend the winter. Thus my mother, with her step-mother, Mrs. Bridie, went to Narva and joined her father. During the winter they posted, or went in their own carriage, from Narva first to St. Petersburg and afterwards to Moscow. The railway between the two capitals was not opened until the following year. Through this journey of my mother as a girl, and through her accounts of it to me as a child, I became more interested in Russia than in any other foreign country. On my mother's side I am thus of seafaring folk.[1]

My mother's mother, Ann Taylor, of Forfarshire farming stock, had died in my mother's infancy. Her step-mother, Mrs. Isabella Bridie, was the only mother she knew. Throughout her life, Mrs. Bridie remained a valued member of our family circle.[2] Her maiden name was Barland. On her father's side she was of Dutch extraction. Her paternal grandfather had been a member of the Incorporation of Glovers at Perth. His father or grandfather had migrated from Holland about the end of the seventeenth century. Mrs. Bridie was born in 1805. Her father was a farmer at the farm of Orwell, near Errol in Perthshire. "The dear years" (1802-3) during the Peace of Amiens were past just before she was born; but in her childhood the recollection of these years remained, and prices were still high. Her family was relatively well off, but frugality was necessary. The high duty on salt and its scarcity made carefulness advisable even in so wholesome an article. On being asked for salt, Mrs. Barland [3] (1809 or 1810) answered, "Salt tae yer parritch! Na! Na! I'll learn ye nae sic extravagant habits."

Politics were keen in the first quarter of the nineteenth century. The farmers in the valley of the Tay were in general Radicals, while of course the landed proprietors were Tories. Barland of Orwell was involved in an election exploit (about 1819) which throws some light on electioneering practice at that time. During a hotly-contested election, it came to be known that the Tory agent intended to drive out from the county town to the country with a considerable sum of

---

[1] The seafaring strain came out more in my brothers than myself. In their youth one of these became an officer in the Chilian Navy, another for a short time an officer in the Japanese Navy, another, who ran away to sea, took a voyage before the mast to Rangoon, while another went round the world in a sailing ship as supercargo.

[2] I edited some of her papers and gave a sketch of her life in *Mrs. Bridie*, Edinburgh, 1889.

[3] I knew Mrs. Barland more than fifty years later, and sixty years ago, as a kindly old lady with great determination of character.

money in gold (to the best of my recollection, the amount was several thousand pounds) for the purpose of purchasing votes. Barland and some of his friends waylaid the agent, took his money from him, and sent him on his way lamenting. After the election they returned the bags of gold intact to the agent.

In her early youth Mrs. Bridie had often seen long lines of horses in single file coming from the river into the country with hampers laden with schnapps and brandy smuggled from the Continent. I remember that she told me of having seen Charles X. in Edinburgh in 1830, while he was living in Holyrood Palace. She accompanied her husband to the China Seas about 1835.

I gathered from Mrs. Bridie, that although the outlook upon life in her circle in the thirties was influenced largely by contemporary ecclesiastical controversies (her people were "Auld Licht Anti-Burghers"), the poet most popular among them next to Burns was Byron rather than Scott. This was natural in a community that had set its face against the Tory party and had little sympathy with what it looked upon as an attempt by Scott to embellish Toryism with a halo of romance. They might well have accepted both Scott and Byron on literary grounds, although these sturdy Radicals may be forgiven, for they were impatient with Young, whose *Night Thoughts* afforded a poetic standard for no inconsiderable number of other Scots people of that day.

In the thirties, *Constable's Miscellany* was to be found in many of the farm-houses as well as in the houses of the common people in the east of Scotland. The Tories had the *Edinburgh Review* and the Radicals *Tait's Edinburgh Magazine*, while from London there came into Scotland at this time Murray's *Family Library* and Knight's *Penny Magazine*. I mention these because I have seen them in my own youth on the shelves of farmers and of artisans in towns as possessions of their parents. I recall visiting a slater who had worked at his trade over a large part of Europe between 1830 and 1840. He had saved money enough to be independent, and when I saw him about 1870 he was occupying his leisure in reading through *Constable's Miscellany*. At that moment he was deep in a history of Persia. He was doing what those who remained at home did thirty years earlier. The daily newspaper was a slender affair in the thirties, and those who read, read on the whole good if somewhat heavy literature. Perhaps easy availability and cheapness accounted for this, but some importance must, I think, be attached to reaction against the rubbish which poured from the press in the English magazines of the latter half of the eighteenth century. Writing intended for popular consumption had probably never sunk to so low an ebb as is to be found, for example, in the *Town and Country Magazine*. The change for the better made its appearance about the close of the eighteenth century, when the *Monthly Magazine or British Register* (1791) and the *Scottish Register* (1794) were the forerunners of still better journals.

During visits to Dundee in the early sixties I used to stay at Broughty Ferry. From the high ridge upon which our relatives lived, I watched the ships coming in with the tide—whalers in whose blunt bows and weatherbeaten aspect were the evidences of successful struggles against ice and wind, and smart ghost-like clippers painted white from stem to stern, in whose graceful lines there lay indications of tremendous speed. The whalers were clumsy enough, although they gave an impression of obstinacy and power; but the East Indiamen, as they shortened sail on entering the estuary of the Tay, were the things of beauty described by John Masefield in the motto of this chapter. His river was the Mersey and his city Liverpool; but his description applies as vividly to the River Tay and the city of Dundee; and I can say as truthfully as he can, speaking of the ships of other days in whose sailing my own folk played their part for several generations:

> Yet though their splendour may have ceased to be,
> Each played her sovereign part in making me;
> Now I return my thanks with heart and lips
> For the great queenliness of all those ships.

CHAPTER III

A GALLOWAY TOWN ABOUT 1860

"Oh, wha will shoe my bonny foot?
  And wha will glove my hand?
And wha will lace my middle jimp
  Wi' a lang, lang linen band?

 .   .   .   .   .

" But I will get a bonny boat
  To sail the salt, salt sea;
The sails were o' the light green silk
  The tows o' taffety.

 .   .   .   .   .

" Now whether are ye the queen hersell
  (For so ye weel might be)
Or are ye the Lass of Lochroyan,
  Seekin' Lord Gregory?"

"Oh, I am neither the queen," she said,
  "Nor sic I seem to be;
But I am the Lass of Lochroyan
  Seekin' Lord Gregory."

The Lass of Lochroyan, Old Scots Ballad.

STRANRAER is situated at the head of Loch Ryan. From an architectural point of view, it is a commonplace town; but the isthmus which separates the loch from Solway Firth and the peninsula known to us as the Mull of Galloway, and to the ancients as the Novantian Chersonesus, are both very beautiful, and are, moreover, full of archæological interest. Stranraer is said to have been known to the Romans and to the Novantes, the inhabitants of the region in Roman times, as Rerigoneum [1] or Retigonium; but there is uncertainty about the precise locality to which this name was attached.[2] In the map in Chalmers' *Caledonia* [3] the site of Rerigoneum is placed, not at the head

---

[1] Richard of Cirencester mentions another Rerigoneum which has been identified with Ribchester on the River Ribble in Lancashire. Bohn's edition (London, 1848), pp. 448 and 488.

[2] M'Kerlie in his *Lands and their Owners in Galloway* identifies the village of Innermessan, about two miles from Stranraer, as the site of Rerigoneum (i. p. 185, and ii. p. 207).

[3] Chalmers, George, F.R.S. and S.A., *Caledonia, or an Account Historical and Topographical of Great Britain* . . . (London, 1807), vol. i.

of the loch, but at or near the village of Cairn Ryan, directly opposite Corsewall Point. Roman remains have been found in the immediate neighbourhood of Stranraer, and there are many other antiquities at no great distance.

In the parish of Stoneykirk, for example, on Luce Bay in the Solway Firth, there are at Kirkmadrine what the antiquaries regard as the oldest Christian sculptured monuments in Scotland. One of these stones contains the following inscription:

HIC IACENT SCI ET PRAECIPUI SACERDOTES ID EST VIVENTIUS
ET MAVORIUS.[1]

It has been conjectured that these are names of two of the masons or architect monks who, according to Ailred of Rievaux in his *Life of S. Ninian*, were brought by that saint from Tours to Scotland to build a church for him.[2] That one of these names bears a close resemblance to my own is a matter of curious interest to me.

Much more important, from an archæological point of view, than these monuments, which are not earlier than the fifth century, are the remains of what appear to be dwellings of men of the Stone Age, discovered in the same parish of Stoneykirk after laborious and skilful research by my friend Ludovic Mann. Although he has given an account of the nature of his discoveries, he has with great modesty not indicated the process by means of which he was led to the locality in which his researches were made. I may therefore be allowed to mention at least the character of this process. It should be premised that Mr. Mann had no connection with the district. Proceeding upon the hypothesis that the earliest colonists of North Britain must have made their landfall at some place on the coast, and desiring to find this place, Mr. Mann made a careful survey of the coast-line of Scotland from this point of view. He eventually decided upon Luce Bay as being for many reasons a highly probable spot. It is not a little remarkable that, according to some writers, the Novantian Chersonesus was regarded as the most northerly part of Great Britain.[3] Thus for a time it may have been looked upon as Ultima Thule, and therefore the destination of very early explorers. Having decided upon the spot, Mr. Mann began a series of systematic probings of the soil by means of steel rods about thirty feet long. His industry and skill were rewarded by the discovery at a depth of thirty feet below the surface of a number of

[1] Stuart, *Sculptured Stones of Scotland.*
[2] M'Kerlie, P. H., *op. cit.* ii. p. 161.
[3] Richard of Cirencester, *op. cit.* p. 450.

oval obstacles. The area in which these obstacles were found was then excavated and five piled floors, tooled by stone axes, were discovered. There were evidences of entrances to the structures of which these were the floors on the east side of each oval. The implements and pottery found on the site as well as the tooling of the timber suggest that the buildings belonged to the Stone Age, and that they composed a group or village of workshops, storehouses or shelters. These antiquities are comparable to the piled pits found in the Isle of Wight and in some other places. The evidence seems to show that they were used by people who lived a settled life in villages and had advanced in a certain measure in the arts.[1]

Stranraer is the centre of a good agricultural district. Dairying was highly developed in the fifties and sixties. The farmers were extensive breeders of cattle. Competition of range cattle from the United States and Canada and of frozen mutton from New Zealand had not begun. In general, the farmers were well off, some of them even had handsome establishments. There were no manufactures in the district. Farm labourers and poorer people in towns were, as a rule, Irish who had migrated from the north of Ireland, and there was besides an annual migration at harvest time of Irish reapers, who brought their reaping-hooks with them.

The social contours were sharply defined—the landed gentry, the Earl of Stair, his connections the Dalrymples, Sir Andrew Agnew of Lochnaw, and a few other proprietors on a smaller scale, formed the superior social stratum, while near them came the Cairds,[2] who lived at Baldoon and afterwards at Genoch, Sir John Ross, the Arctic explorer, who lived at North-West Castle, the Alisons, who lived in the town, and some others. Then there came the professional people, and, following them, the farmers, the shopkeepers and the craftsmen, with the Irish farm and town labourers at the bottom of the social mound. In such a society the prevailing political colour was the blue of the Tory party. Some of the elections before the extension of the franchise in the burghs were hotly contested, but extreme radicalism was unknown. I remember a story of an election which occurred about 1860. The contest was a close one, the constituency was not numerically large, a dozen votes would turn the scale on one side or the other. One of the candidates, I forget which, or his agent, decided upon a

[1] Mann, Ludovic Maclellan, F.S.A.Scot., *Excavations in Wigtownshire— Prehistoric Pile-structures in Pits*. A paper read to the Society of Antiquaries of Scotland, May 11th, 1903, and reprinted from their Proceedings, Edinburgh, 1904. For an account of other antiquities of the region, see M'Kerlie, *op. cit.*

[2] Sir James Caird, the well-known writer upon agricultural questions.

bold manœuvre in order to win the election. This manœuvre was, in effect, to kidnap a sufficient number of voters who were known to intend to vote on the other side and to keep them in durance until the election was over. About a dozen voters were invited to dinner at an inn in the country some miles from Stranraer. They were given excellent fare and kept amused for the required period.

There was little unemployment in the district at that time; begging was unusual. I recall only a single instance. One day a servant came to my father and told him that a man was begging at the door who spoke a language she could not understand. My father went to see the man, who promptly addressed him in Latin. He was a Hungarian, and he had been taught colloquial Latin at school as were all Hungarian boys.

In 1850, my father, then twenty-two years of age, was appointed master of the Free Church School at Stranraer. At the same time he married. I was born in that place in 1854. The impressions I have retained of my early years in Stranraer are those of a quiet, agreeable life and of a friendly, mature and cultivated society. The Crimean War and the Indian Mutiny cast dark shadows and left deep traces of a period of national crisis. Whether for that or other reasons, the social atmosphere of that time (1855–62) had a certain sombre hue. The Indian Mutiny made a great impression upon my parents, who named my younger brother after Sir Henry Havelock.

I went to school at the age of four years and six months. In accordance with the practice at that time, I began to learn Latin in the second year of my life at school. The chief concern of contemporary elementary education appeared to be the cultivation of the memory; at all events, this seemed to be the chief concern of mine. In after years Sir William van Horne told me that he had cultivated his memory, which was unusually retentive, by learning the numbers of railway cars as they passed by. The apparatus employed in my case was quite different. It was the *Shorter Catechism*. I am afraid that, considered as a gift of nature, my memory must have been a poor one, for the process of cultivating it was very hard. When a mistake was made in reciting the answers to the compendium of the Westminster Confession of Faith, which was by no means seldom, the additional task was imposed of committing to memory one of the longer psalms or a chapter from Isaiah. If this *pœna* were not properly accomplished, then a hundred lines or more of *Paradise Lost* or portions of Scott's romantic poems were inflicted as a further task. I shall draw a veil over what occurred when these multiple impositions proved to be ineffective. I am afraid that my reverence for the sacred text and for certain masterpieces of literature was not enhanced by their association in my mind with punishment. I am not sure that the method is the soundest that might be chosen; but perhaps for great dullness any other method might be quite fruitless. I think probably the effect upon me was beneficial, although the process was sometimes difficult to endure.

St. Augustine remarks with his customary candour, "I loved not study, and hated to be forced to it. Yet I was forced; and this was well done towards me; but I did not well; for unless forced, I had not learnt. But no one doth well against his will, even though what he doth be well. Yet neither did they well who forced me, but what was well came to me from Thee, my God." [1] I can subscribe to the greater part of this without compunction, for I was not destined to be a saint, and yet was almost incurably dull; but I cannot subscribe to the conclusion of St. Augustine, because so extreme piety to God were impiety to my instructors, the chief of whom was my own father. If any credit is due for even partial success in the employment of force, some credit at least must be given to the human instrument even although the weapon by means of which the force was applied was sometimes wielded with extreme vigour.

The process is not agreeable to experience, but there is much to be said for physical correction. A man who has not been sharply chastised for offences in his youth is generally recognisable in his maturity by undesirable qualities and by the perpetration of offences which bring upon him, or ought to bring upon him, punishment much harder to be borne than physical thrashing.

Although I performed my school tasks with difficulty and under compulsion, I had an insatiable curiosity for what lay outside of these. Before I was nine years of age I had read rather copiously not merely the books customarily read by boys of that time, but more solid books on history and travel. I remember reading with great pleasure Washington Irving's *Mahomet and his Successors*. In 1862 I began to read Gibbon. I did not finish him at that time, but the impression of some of the chapters I read then still remains in my mind. It was my fortune to read him in the original quarto edition. I devoured Gordon-Cumming's African books, and read Speke's *Journal of the Discovery of the Nile* immediately on its appearance in 1863. I read Thackeray's *Four Georges* in the *Cornhill Magazine* (Vol. II., 1860) within a short time after its appearance. In the

[1] From the quaint translation of Dr. Pusey.

I—C

same volume of the *Cornhill* there appeared Ruskin's *Unto this Last*;
but I do not think I read this until somewhat later. I recall being
much impressed by an anonymous poem also in this volume, *Ariadne
at Naxos*. Some years afterwards it transpired that this poem was by
a young man of genius, Thomas Davidson, probationer of the United
Presbyterian Church, who died at Jedburgh in 1870. In addition to
the *Cornhill* and some other magazines, the *Saturday Review* was
available, and I began to read it in the early sixties. Probably I had
rather more opportunity than the average Scots boy of my time to
engage in discursive reading, but my case was by no means unusual.
Of my school-fellows of these early days I retain the vaguest recollection; only one of them, so far as I know, attained distinction. He
came to be known to the world as Sir Leander Starr Jameson. His
father was a Writer to the Signet, and was living in Edinburgh when
Jameson was born in 1853. Shortly afterwards the family removed
to Stranraer, where the elder Jameson became editor of a newspaper.
In my recollection, Mr. Jameson was a man of intellectual aspect
whose neck was encircled by the "stock" of the period. I remember
Mrs. Jameson quite vividly. She was a distinguished-looking, rather
small lady, who often wore, as was then customary, a cashmere shawl.
She had sharp intelligent features, a prim air, and precision in her speech
and manners. Both Mr. and Mrs. Jameson were frequent visitors at our
house; but I have no recollection of their son, although I believe that
he and I were in the same class when we were about six years of age.

Among our other friends in Stranraer were Mr. Charles, the Free
Church minister, and Dr. Orgle, the leading physician in the district.
Both were worthy and intelligent men. The latter was of the type
described with so sympathetic a pen by "Ian Maclaren." [1] Sir John
Ross, who was a son of the parish minister of Inch, near Stranraer,
died in 1856. Of course I do not remember him; but he was a friend
of my parents, who were often at North-West Castle, where they met
the Ommaneys [2] and others who were interested in Arctic exploration.
Sir John Ross used to like to have such people about him. I have before
me two duodecimo volumes bound in calf, each with a simple book-
plate, "Mr. Ross." These little books contain the poetical works of
John Dyer and Ambrose Philips, with lives of the authors by Samuel
Johnson. They were published by Samuel Bagster in 1807, and were
part of a set of the poets in a hundred and twenty-four volumes

---

[1] The late Dr. Watson who was for a time minister of St. Matthew's Church,
Glasgow, and was a friend of my later years.
[2] Sir Erasmus Ommaney was one of Parry's captains.

given by King George IV. to Mr. Ross on the eve of his departure on
his voyage to the Arctic regions in 1829. Ross may or may not have
taken these books with him; but if he did, and if he took them up
to beguile the tedium of an Arctic night, he must have been more
amused by the pungent criticisms of Johnson than by the tiresome
verses of these minor poets. After Ross's death the bulk of the collection came into the hands of my father. In his *Narrative*,[1] published
in 1835, Ross gives an account of his arrival at Loch Ryan, which he
had chosen as the place of rendezvous for his ships, of a mutiny on
board of one of them, and of his departure from the loch on his
northern adventure.

The Stranraer people had long been interested in Arctic exploration. They subscribed liberally to the fund raised for the journey of
Captain George Back in 1833–5.[2] The early interest of our family
circle in the Arctic regions was not confined to the explorations of the
two Rosses (Sir James Clark Ross was a nephew of Sir John, and was
also a Wigtownshire man), or to the whaling voyages of my grandfather.
My uncle, Captain John Bridie, was also familiar with Arctic conditions,
and during an interval between voyages (he was then in command of
the *Kohinoor* East Indiaman) he was sent for by Lady Franklin, who
desired the benefit of his experience and advice. She was then (in
1857) fitting out the *Fox*, which, under the command of M'Clintock,
was sent by her to discover the fate of her husband.

In my childhood, my favourite place of resort was Castle Kennedy.
The formal gardens and terraces were at that time very celebrated.
The old castle is a ruin, and the new Loch Inch Castle had not then
been built. The grounds had been laid out in the Dutch style before
the middle of the eighteenth century. A few years before my time
the head gardener of the Earl of Stair,[3] Archibald Fowler, had begun
to plant conifers systematically. Now these trees must be more than
seventy years old, and the aspect of the place must be very much
changed. One of the features of Castle Kennedy as I remember it
was the avenue of auricaria as well as the numerous individual trees
of this species on the lawns.

[1] *Narrative of a Second Voyage in search of a North-West Passage, and of a
Residence in the Arctic Regions during the years* 1829, 1830, 1831, 1832 *and* 1833.
By Sir John Ross, C.B., etc. London, 1835.
[2] Back, Captain George, R.N., *Narrative of the Arctic Land Expedition*, etc.
(London, 1836), p. 663.
[3] Baddeley, in his *Guide to Scotland*, Part I. (ed. 1889), p. 15, says en-
thusiastically that "Mr. Fowler's knowledge of trees can only be compared
with that ascribed to King Solomon"; but it may fairly be inquired, "Why
drag in Solomon?"

Among indoor games, draughts, chess and backgammon were the chief, at all events in our circle. I do not recall witnessing any card-playing at this time. I have heard of some shopkeepers playing draughts all night, and of leaving their boards only in time to take down their shutters in the morning. In chess, next to my father, my principal instructor was Mr. James Alison,[1] a gentleman of independent means, who divided his time among yachting, bowls, chess and wood-turning. He was always in the mood for a game. Occasionally we were interrupted by the claims of public business, for Mr. Alison was a Justice of the Peace; but these claims were generally met without rising from the table. When the business was finished we resumed our game. The Alisons' house, especially the playroom, was my favourite place of indoor resort as a small boy. One day I was taken to the drawing-room and presented to three beautiful ladies. I was not unfamiliar with them individually, but their collective splendour, dressed as they were in vast white flounces, extended by the enormous crinolines of the period, and their striking beauty, made me shy and dumb. One of these ladies became Mrs. Cochran Patrick, the other two were destined to die within a few years. I felt a childish jealousy of one of these latter (Mrs. Macgregor) because she had taken from me my greatest friend and most loyal playmate, her husband Dr. Macgregor, who as a bachelor had been a constant visitor at our house. He was the headmaster of the Stranraer Academy and my father's greatest friend. Both he and his wife died early.

Golf was not played in Wigtownshire at this time. The habitat of the game was in the east of Scotland; only much later than the time I speak of did the links of Ballantrae become known to golfers. The outdoor games of Galloway then were bowls in the summer and curling in the winter. Farmer, townsman and peer met on the "green" and on the "ice" on terms of inequality only of skill. I used often to go with my father to watch him playing both games with the persons whose names I have mentioned. McDowall, the Free Church minister of Leswalt, not far from Stranraer, a great friend of ours, was a keen curler. One Sunday a sudden fall of temperature afforded an unexpected opportunity too good to be missed. After he had pronounced the benediction, McDowall leaned over the pulpit and said to his congregation, "We'll meet at the ice the morn."

During our Stranraer period we made at least annual journeys northwards. In my early childhood I remember being awakened in

[1] John Alison, brother of James, was the inventor of the vertical boiler.

Glasgow, after our arrival the night before, by hearing a policeman spring the formidable wooden rattle carried by the force at that time and call out in a stentorian but not unmusical voice, "It's five o'clock an' a fine frosty mornin'." On this or on some similar journey about the same time I was taken by my mother to visit friends in the Vale of Leven at Renton. There we called upon the Miss Smolletts of Bonhill, the grand-nieces of Tobias Smollett. These ladies were old friends of my mother. Once we hurried through Glasgow northwards because of an epidemic of cholera.

I have already mentioned the Jacobite leanings of a member of my father's family; on my mother's side there were similar associations. On one of our journeys in 1859 or 1860, I was taken by my mother to visit two old Jacobite spinsters who were distant relatives of hers and possessors of a tiny estate in Kinross-shire. We passed through Perth, and while we were waiting on the platform of the station a train came in from London carrying the Queen to Balmoral. We had a good view of Her Majesty sitting at the window of her saloon and bowing to the few people who were in the station. When we started on our own journey, my mother charged me to say nothing to the ladies we were going to visit about our having seen the Queen. Any suggestion of want of frankness was so unusual with my mother that I forgot all about the warning. On being subjected by the ladies to a catechism concerning our doings, I admitted that I had seen the Queen. The result was a scolding administered to my mother, "Mary Ann, you ought not to have done this wicked thing. You knew what our principles are." My mother, who knew that the Queen was something of a Jacobite herself, took the reproach with good nature. These ancient prejudices have long died out, but even so recently as sixty years ago they were entertained by many people.

During our residence in Stranraer and on occasional visits for a few years afterwards, we walked or drove to many places in the neighbourhood. Inch we went to frequently, for the teacher there was a friend of ours. One holiday of a month was spent at Drumore on the Mull of Galloway, where we went by coach. Drumore is near Kirkmaiden, and the farthest point of the Mull is only a few miles from it. On the other side of the Mull and overlooking the Irish Sea is the bold headland of Dunnan. From Drumore the wide expanse of the Solway Firth stretches away to the east. The whole region is finely wooded until, towards the point of the Rin (or horn) of the Mull, the landscape becomes bare. The shore at Drumore is composed of fine sand and at low tide the beach is of great extent. My brother and

I stayed with the coastguard officer, and we were constantly on the water, watching the mackerel fishers and keeping a look-out for smugglers, who found the region then favourable for their operations, as they had from time immemorial. The Mull is saturated with history and prehistory. Here the Picts are said to have made their last stand in this part of Scotland, and here, the legend has it, they were either driven into the sea or they threw themselves into it rather than surrender. A double line of ancient fortifications extends across the Mull, and near these is the cave chapel of St. Medan, which tradition regards as the dwelling-place of a pre-Christian recluse.[1]

About 1860, the railway between Stranraer and Port Patrick was opened for traffic. While the line was under construction, I made a journey which to a youngster was a great source of delight. My father and I went over the line on a contractor's engine. After the line was opened we made many journeys to Port Patrick, and even after our family had left Stranraer I visited the little port on several occasions up till 1868, when I made my last visit. In the sixties an effort was made after the completion of the railway to establish a mail and passenger service from Scotland and England *via* Port Patrick and Donaghadee on the Irish coast. The width of the Channel between these two points is only twenty-one and a half miles. A steamer was placed upon the route—I think her name was the *Dolphin*—about 1865 or 1866. I went in her upon a trial trip which extended half-way across. The coast is wild, and the narrowness of the Channel causes the tides to flow through it with great force. The Admiralty spent much in building a breakwater; but in the winter of 1867 this breakwater was so severely damaged through a storm undermining a portion of it, that all projects for the further improvement of the port were abandoned and the service to Donaghadee was discontinued. As in some other places exposed to winds from the sea, the windows of the houses in Port Patrick are usually encrusted with brine from the wind-blown spray. Bathing is fine, but not without danger. I remember seeing an elderly lady, one of our friends, dashed with great violence upon the rocks by a wave of unexpected force. There was a pleasant society at that time in Port Patrick. Our principal friends were the family of Dr. Urquhart, the Free Church minister, a man of distinguished appearance and high character, and that of Mr. Shields

[1] Although the cave chapel of St. Medan is on a much smaller scale, it may be placed in the same category as the cave chapels near Wetheral on the River Eden in Cumberland and those at Inkerman in the Crimea.

the teacher, a sterling though somewhat sombre person. His eldest son, who was a lad of great promise, went to the Pacific in the employment of a trading firm. He was stationed at one of the islands in the Torres Straits, where after a few months he died of fever.

One of my latest definite recollections of our residence in Stranraer is hearing the bells ringing on the death of the Prince Consort on the 14th December, 1861. A few months later we left the town.

CHAPTER IV

GLASGOW IN THE SIXTIES

Hail, great black-bosomed mother of our city,
  Whose odoriferous breath offends the earth,
Whose cats and puppy dogs excite our pity,
  As they sail past with aldermanic girth!
No salmon hast thou in thy jet-black waters,
  Save what is left adhering to the tins.
Thus thy adorers—Govan's lovely daughters—
  Adorn thy shrine with offerings for their sins.

  .   .   .   .   .

Yet art thou great. Though strangers hold their noses
  When sailing down to Rothesay at the Fair,
Thy exiled sons would barter tons of roses
  To scent thy sweetness on the desert air.

                CHARLES J. KIRK, "Ode to the Clyde,"
                        in *University Verses* (1911).

THE Civil War in America, in the making for several years, began
with the attack on Fort Sumter and the calling out of the Northern
troops on 15th April, 1861. Four days later, on 19th April, Lincoln
declared a blockade of those States which had joined the Southern
Confederacy. This blockade was the means by which the North
became victorious, for it prevented the South from exporting cotton,
and therefore from obtaining the supplies necessary for the conduct
of the war. The effect of the blockade upon the textile industries of
Great Britain was disastrous. Upon Lancashire the blow fell heavily.
The west of Scotland had been an important centre of the cotton trade
in the earlier years of the nineteenth century, but from various causes
into which I cannot enter here, the manufacture of grey cotton there
had relatively declined, and the trade had been concentrated in
Lancashire. Calico-printing had, however, remained in the west of
Scotland, the grey cotton being brought from England. The calico
printers were thus seriously affected by the scarcity of cotton, and their
workpeople, as well as those engaged in cotton manufacture, suffered
from unemployment. Yet Scotland was much less affected by the
blockade than was Lancashire, because the working force of the people
was more widely distributed over a greater variety of industries; and

at the very moment when the cotton trade was suffering enforced stagnation many of the other industries were even expanding. In particular, shipbuilding and marine engineering made a great leap forward. The development of the steamship had its principal impetus in the decade 1860–70, during the transition from sail to steam and from wood to iron. In the improvement of the marine engine the Clyde engineers played a large rôle. Briskness in shipbuilding meant briskness in the iron and coal industries, and these in turn reacted upon the miscellaneous ancillary trades. Thus in the sixties on the Clyde there was comparatively little disorganisation of industry on account of the Civil War in America.

In July 1862 we left Stranraer and migrated to Glasgow. Soon we began to learn of blockade-running by ships from the Clyde.[1] A special type of ship—swift and of moderate size—was built for the express purpose of blockade-running. The economic reactions of war, especially upon shipping, which had been manifest in the Crimean campaign, now became vividly exemplified.

The change from the semi-rural and compact society of a country town to a city crowded with an industrial population highly diversified and very individualistic was at first rather depressing. In the country, everybody knew everybody else. Everyone had a recognised place in the community. In the town, no one knew or cared to know his next-door neighbour. In the country there was little ostentatious display of wealth, little subservience to it; definite obligations attached to its possession. There are rural districts where the people have become lackeys, but these cannot be held to represent the country as a whole. The sordid peasant is not unknown, but even in his case sordidness is not regarded by his neighbours as a virtue, and it is restricted by a sense of the advisability of keeping on good terms with the community. Over all there is the saving grace of rustic humour. In the town vulgar display abounds; there is much wealth and poverty. Sense of obligation on the ground of social position has little force, commercial keenness is looked upon with approval; and while there is abundance of caustic wit, there is, in general, slender humour. These reflections

---

[1] The following shows the expansion of shipbuilding on the Clyde during the American Civil War, and the check to expansion at the close of it:

1860	Tonnage built		48,000
1861	,,	,,	67,000
1862	,,	,,	70,000
1863	,,	,,	123,000
1864	,,	,,	179,000
1865	,,	,,	154,000

Industrial Rivers of the United Kingdom (London, 1888), p. 104.

have been given a general application; but they may be regarded as being specially applicable on the one hand to the country districts of Aberdeenshire and Wigtownshire and on the other to Glasgow, the commercial and industrial capital of Scotland.

The manners of the city people, if they were more urban, were certainly less urbane and friendly than those of the country folk. I remember as a small boy carrying my books from school in a strap with two boards to keep them in position, standing alone with my back to a wall and defending myself vigorously with my strap-full of books, which was the only weapon I had, against an attack by half a dozen young ruffians. Nor were some of those with whom otherwise we came into contact much removed in spirit from these gamins. In time we found congenial friends, but at first our experience of a provincial centre of commerce and industry was harsh and unpleasant.

My father, now in his thirty-fourth year, had been appointed teacher of the school maintained and controlled by Free St. Matthew's Church, then under the care of Dr. Samuel Miller, who had been, if not a leader, at least a follower of the Disruption party of 1843. St. Matthew's was at that time one of the two fashionable Free Churches in the West End of Glasgow—the other being the Free College Church, whose minister was Dr. Robert Buchanan. The tone of St. Matthew's was one of extreme orthodoxy in doctrine, and its practice in ritual was one of extreme conservatism. There was, of course, no instrumental music, there was not even a choir. The precentor sat in a pulpit on a slightly lower level than that of the minister, and at the quarterly sacrament he reverted to the old Scots Presbyterian practice of reading out each two lines of the psalm before singing them. The singing consisted almost exclusively of the psalms. Very rarely one of the sixty-seven paraphrases was introduced; I do not recollect that any of the five hymns usually bound with the Authorised Version of the Bible was ever sung. Many of the hymns customarily used in churches have little to be said for them either from the point of view of religion or from that of art, while some of the music to which they are sung is associated with emotions by no means religious. One well-known hymn, in itself not without poetry, is usually sung to an equally well-known German students' drinking-song.[1] But many of the hymns and much of the music of the early Christian Church are very fine, and there are many modern hymns of high spiritual and poetical qualities. Yet all of these were regarded as too secular for St. Matthew's. When someone ventured to remonstrate with Dr. Miller about his

[1] Such songs were, of course, sometimes set to religious music.

narrowness in this respect, he said, "When we have exhausted the psalms, we can turn to the hymns." Since he considered the psalms inexhaustible, there was little prospect of ever reaching any other form of religious verse.

Although there were in this congregation, as there are in all communities, many people whose piety was their only impressive quality, and others whose conduct in life bore slender relation to their pretensions, there were also some who were of the salt of the earth. Of these last, there were Dr. Harry Rainy, retired physician, father of Principal Rainy of the New College, Edinburgh. Dr. Rainy sat directly in front of us in the gallery of the church, and as my seat was customarily immediately behind him I became very familiar with the external anatomy of his large and benevolent cranium. His fine face was naturally less intimately known to me, but it was a joy to look upon. Its type was mingled Celtic and Lowland. He had something very like the fire of genius in his fine blue eyes. Near him there sat William Ramsay, retired civil engineer, father of Sir William Ramsay, the chemist, who sat with him until he left Glasgow. Near them also there sat two elderly ladies with their nephew, M. M. Pattison Muir, who had left the High School about the time I entered it, and who, like Ramsay, became a chemist. Among others of the same group were G. M. Grierson and his son, afterwards Sir James Moncrieff Grierson.[1]

The young men I have mentioned, with others of less note, sat together through the same long sermons and endured the same kind of discipline.

In due time I was sent to the High School of Glasgow. The school was at that time situated in a building erected in 1820 behind St. Paul's Church and in the immediate neighbourhood of the old college buildings in the High Street. Like the foundation of the University of Oxford, that of the High School of Glasgow, for many centuries known as the Grammar School, is lost in the mists of antiquity. It is said to have been founded early in the twelfth century, but of its beginnings nothing is known. When the University of Glasgow was founded in 1450 by a bull of Pope Nicholas V., the Grammar School had already acquired a reputation. At the time of the Reformation, the school appears to have passed directly from the control of the ecclesiastical authorities to that of the Town Council. It does not seem ever to have been under the control of the Presbytery. In the

[1] Military Attaché at Berlin, and appointed on the outbreak of war as General of Division. He died in France in August 1914, on his way to assume his command.

sixteenth century the headmaster, John Blackburne, must have been a person of consequence, for he was elected Lord Rector of the University. From about 1685 the school had been definitely regarded as preparatory to the University, and the curriculum seems to have been determined by the Senatus. The rule was established that all instruction was to be given in Latin and that no other language was to be used during school hours. When the rule was changed does not appear; but it must have fallen into desuetude before the end of the eighteenth century. Up till the year 1782, the head of the school had been variously styled master, principal or rector, while the other teachers were known as doctors. At the date mentioned, the office of head was abolished and the teachers formed a small republic in which all were on equal terms. This was the state of matters in my time, though in the interval there had been another rectorial period. From the account-books of an eighteenth-century lawyer in Glasgow, which came under my eye many years ago, I gathered that in the early part of the nineteenth century the customary clothing of the boys, if not their recognised uniform, was the kilt; but by my time this ancient garb had disappeared from the school.

I have not at hand any means of giving a list of High School boys who rose to eminence in after life, even if such a list came within my design; but I may notice that Adam Smith was a High School boy. In his time it was customary for boys to enter the University at about fourteen years of age. Indeed, this remained the rule for at least a century after Adam Smith's time. I remember hearing Dr. Robert Buchanan of the Free College Church say that he had entered the University at the age of fourteen and had become a Master of Arts at the "mature age of seventeen." Nor was the standard of education either at the school or the University necessarily low. Education was more intensive than is now customary. Small attention was paid to modern languages, very little to science, and none at all directly to history. It was assumed that if a boy knew Latin, Greek and mathematics, could write a clear hand and could spell the words of his own language, the whole field of knowledge was before him and he could make his way in it for himself. It was assumed also that foreign languages could only be properly acquired in the countries where they are spoken, and that those who desired to acquire them must go to the countries in question for that purpose.

The masters of the school in my time were not without distinction. The classical masters were James Paton and John Hutcheson. Both had the reputation of being good scholars and good teachers. The

English master was James Bell. The writing and mathematical master was Macnab and the science master was James Bryce, LL.D., father of a son known to fame as Viscount Bryce, who was a High School boy, as was also his brother, J. Annan Bryce, East India merchant and M.P. for Inverness Burghs. The French master's name was Wolski. He was a Polish refugee, whether of the revolutionary movement of 1830 or of some later period I am not certain. Two important elements of education were well taught in the High School— one was to write a round legible hand and the other was to spell correctly. While I was a boy at the school, a gymnasium was established under the care of a Crimean War veteran called Long. From him I learned to fence. High School boys had certain privileges connected with the University. We had special places at Rectorial Addresses and some other functions. I was present when Lord President Inglis gave his address as Lord Rector in, I think, 1867. Of my school-fellows, I remember as a special intimate Duncan Ferguson, who went to the University of Glasgow and afterwards to Oxford. He became a judge in India and died at Rangoon soon after his appointment. He was a singularly attractive youth, of high character and good abilities. Andrew Bonar Law,[1] Alexander Maclay,[2] and James R. MacColl[3] were proximate contemporaries.

The chief delight of my school days had no connection with the school. It came to be my habit, day after day, during the final year of my school life, when I was between thirteen and fourteen years of age, to go at four o'clock to the shop of James White, the optician and mathematical instrument maker, then in Buchanan Street. James White was a Dundee man and an old friend of our family. He allowed me to go in and out of his workshop as I pleased; and, moreover, taught me a great deal about the instruments he was making. There I met, almost every day, Sir William Thomson (afterwards Lord Kelvin), who had one year before completed his great task of acting as electrician for the second Atlantic cable, that of 1865-66.[4] Sir William Thomson was also a friend of my father, who had been a student of his. I had the good fortune to stand beside him while he was giving instructions to the skilled mechanics who under his immediate eye were developing his inventions. After I left school this practice continued as occasion permitted, and under these conditions I witnessed the gradual evolution of the mariner's

[1] Prime Minister, 1922-23.   [2] Now Lord Maclay.
[3] Now of Providence, Rhode Island.
[4] He had also acted as electrician of the first cable, that of 1857-58.

compass, with its numerous needles, invented by Thomson, as well as of the electrical balance, and, most important of all, the syphon recorder, the wonderful instrument by means of which marine telegraphy over thousands of miles of cable is accomplished through the employment of an infinitesimal electrical current. These experiences continued for a period of seven or eight years. Thirty years after they began, I happened to meet Lord Kelvin at some function. With them in his mind, he shook his finger at me with an admonishing gesture and said, "Mavor, you should never have left electricity. You should never have left electricity." Perhaps he was right.

Among the reminiscences of my school days, I may mention a row at the University, which, as I have said, was quite near the school. This occurred, I think, during the winter of 1867. There had been an unusually heavy snowfall, and the students amused themselves by a snow battle in the High Street. The battle assumed considerable proportions. The police were called out, and since the offence had taken place outside the precincts of the college, a number of students—some twelve or fourteen—were arrested and next day brought before the Police Magistrates. At that time there was no stipendiary, and the Bailies (or Aldermen) sat on the Bench in rotation. The magistrate for the day was a certain Bailie MacBean, who was, I believe, a manufacturer of paints. He imposed sharp fines upon the students, and gave them a lecture upon their behaviour. On the following 1st April the students had their revenge. They played upon the Bailie what is known as the Wood Street joke. At an early hour in the morning, goods of various descriptions, including pianos and furniture, began to arrive at the Bailie's house. These supplies continued all day. In the afternoon a funeral equipage came, and last of all a bell-hanger, who said he had received instructions to repair the door-bell. The affair was rather mischievous. It was really a joke upon the unoffending tradesmen who contributed to its success rather than upon the Bailie.

I was the eldest of nine, and the *res angusta domi* rendered it necessary for me to leave school at an early age. I was apprenticed to a drysalter. This ancient expression no doubt originally meant a dealer in those compounds of metals and alkalies with acids known to the chymists of former days as salts; but the business of a drysalter came to be more extensive. The firm was in business in a large way. It dealt in salts like bichromate of potash, Stassfurt salts, Glauber's salts, and the like, but it also dealt in indigo, cutch, annatto, gambier, madder roots, shumac, sulphur, cochineal, galls, logwood, fustic, sanderswood, garancine, gum tragacanth, gum senegal, olive-oil, tin and other natural products. Most of these it imported—cutch from Rangoon, tin from Singapore, madder roots and olive-oil from Smyrna, shumac from Palermo, sulphur from Messina, olive-oil from Naples, Gioja and Zante, garancine from Avignon, logwood from Brazil, galls from China and from Smyrna, and nitrate of soda from Peru. Indigo from India and Guatemala, and cochineal from Mexico and elsewhere, it bought at the dock sales of these commodities in London. The wide connections of the firm gave me a practical touch with foreign trade as it was conducted at that time, and with foreign exchange, bills being drawn upon the firm by its correspondents abroad and accepted payable in London through Smith, Payne and Smiths, who were the firm's London bankers. Most of the commodities I have mentioned, with the exception of those purchased at the dock sales in London, were customarily imported in cargo lots. The ships chartered were usually small sailing vessels, chiefly Italian and Norwegian, carrying from three to five hundred tons dead weight. The sale for these commodities was chiefly to the dyers and calico printers. The firm had a mill in the country to which the dyewoods were sent for the extraction of their colouring matter. The turnover in the year was usually between two and three million pounds sterling. Unfortunately, in the middle of the seventies, the firm relaxed its habitually conservative method of conducting its business and embarked in speculation, at a moment when the markets were declining owing partly to the beginning of the trade depression and partly to the introduction of synthetic dyes, which gradually killed the trade in almost all of the natural products I have mentioned above. The consequences to the firm were ruinous; one of the partners committed suicide. This event affected me deeply, because, in spite of disparity of age, we were upon intimate terms.

Although I had left school, my education went on uninterrupted by my going into business. While I did not have any aptitude for commerce, I have never regretted the experience of world-wide trade which I acquired at an early age. The nature of the business led me into the study of chemistry, and my association, humble though it was, with Sir William Thomson led me into physics.

At this point I feel that I ought to give some account of an institution which was the forerunner of the technical colleges now to be found everywhere, as well as of the Universités Populaires which have been established under that name in Paris, under the name of Universités Libres in Brussels, and under the name of University Colleges, later transformed into Universities, in England. This institution was Anderson's College, founded in 1796 under the will of John Anderson, Professor of Natural Philosophy in the University of Glasgow. Anderson's brother Andrew had been James Watt's school-fellow, and by means of this connection Watt had been brought into those relations with the Glasgow professors which led to their offer of hospitality when Watt was prevented by the Incorporation of Hammermen from carrying on the business of mathematical instrument maker in Glasgow. The University was an *imperium in imperio*, or rather an enclave in the city and beyond the jurisdiction of the municipal corporation. After he had taken up his quarters in the University, John Anderson placed in Watt's hands for repair the model of Newcomen's steam engine, which had been used in the class-room for table experiments. Anderson also gave Watt the use of his library and otherwise assisted and encouraged him. Out of his study of Newcomen's engine and of the problems excited thereby in his mind there came to Watt the idea of a separate condenser, which was his tremendous contribution to mechanical science and to the industrial world. Anderson saw in Watt a type of the Scots youth whose means did not permit them to devote their whole time to study because they had their living to make, but whose abilities entitled them to such educational facilities as they might be able to utilise. He thus began within the University evening classes for young working men and for employers as well; and when he died, he left all his means for the foundation of an institution for the education of both sexes in science and the arts. This institution was established in 1796 and was conducted by a board of trustees constituted under his will until 1886, when it was amalgamated with other institutions, given a substantial subvention by the Government, and continued under the name of the Glasgow and West of Scotland Technical College. In 1909 it had on its roll 10,008 students, 2064 in day and 7944 in evening classes.[1] Since then it has become affiliated with the University of Glasgow.

In 1868, immediately on going into business, I began to attend the evening classes at the Andersonian, as it was customarily called at that time, and continued to attend them for several years. The first year the classes in chemistry were conducted by Dr. Stevenson Macadam, who came weekly from Edinburgh for the purpose. In the following year Dr. Thorpe,[2] then a very young man, was appointed,

[1] My brother Henry A. Mavor was a Governor for many years until his death in 1915.
[2] Now Sir Edward Thorpe.

and I got my chemistry also from him. At the same time I took classes in physiology and anatomy from Dr. George Buchanan and in physics from Herschel, a relative of the great Herschels. All of these were first-rate teachers; and I bear all of them in grateful remembrance. Herschel was an odd personality; but I derived great benefit from him, and used to volunteer to assist him in his experiments. In course of time I set up at home a small chemical and physical laboratory and provided myself with indispensable apparatus. By this means I was able to follow with intelligent interest many of the advances in the physical and chemical sciences which came in increasing volume in the succeeding decade.

When Gladstone's Reform Bill was introduced in 1866, a demonstration in its favour took place in Glasgow. There was a procession of all the trades—an interesting affair led, as is usual in Glasgow, by the carters, whose magnificent Clydesdale horses decorated with ribbons are an impressive feature of such parades. Much fun was made of the Cave of Adullam, the refuge of Robert Lowe and others who, belonging to the Liberal party, were opposed to the extension of the franchise until after an adequate measure of national education had been provided. John Bright came down to make a speech, and I saw for the first time this tribune of the people.

In our family circle during the succeeding five years interest was largely concentrated upon the educational problem of that time. Elementary education under denominational control had done much for Scotland. It produced a type of teacher unparalleled elsewhere. Having been brought up in a school-house, I had ample opportunities of knowing these teachers. They were nearly all—at least, all of our acquaintance—graduates of one or other of the Scottish Universities. Many of them were highly-cultivated men. Some were very fine scholars. More than one of the teachers of our acquaintance took reading parties of undergraduates from Oxford, who received instruction in classics, and not seldom also in the art of fly-fishing, of which some of the country teachers were great masters. I went once trout-fishing with my father in the Mull of Cantyre. During a heavy shower we took shelter in a small school buried in the hills, more than a dozen miles from the nearest town. There we found a schoolmaster of the old type. In his senior class he had four or five fine-looking young Highlanders, who were all going to the University. I was at that time at the University myself, and I was ashamed to find how much farther advanced they were than I was. They were fitted to take a first-rate position when, the following year, they would enter the University.

I—D

It is quite true that so advanced education did not fall into every-one's lap. It cost little positively, but it cost time, and unless the scholar could afford to devote himself to study exclusively he could not avail himself of it. The demand for labour in the industries and the advance of wages had acted as a magnet drawing the youth into employment before even the elements of education could be com-municated, and in the absence of compulsion it was supposed that many who might be susceptible of education were suffered to escape. With the extension of the parliamentary franchise, the prospect of an uneducated electorate became a threat to public security. The teachers were in general strong advocates for national education. Perhaps some of them had reason to be dissatisfied with denomina-tional control, and they hoped that administration by representative public bodies would result in greater efficiency. But, in Scotland, denominationalism cannot be said to have relaxed its grasp upon the educational system. Candidates for the School Boards, which were instituted under the new Act (1870), came forward in the interests of the denominations and in some districts denominational power was intensified and extended instead of being diminished as was expected by optimistic supporters of the measure. Some of the deno-minations made a successful struggle for "the Bible in the schools," and thus the real interests of education were for a time lost sight of in an ecclesiastical squabble. In Glasgow, Harry Long, a freelance preacher, and a violent Orangeman, not without a certain gift of rude eloquence, found himself at the top of the poll in the first School Board election and therefore entitled to the Chairmanship of the Board.

In the following decade, the reactions in an educational sense made themselves felt. The compulsory clauses filled the schools with numbers of children and caused a greatly increased demand for teachers. This demand was coincident with trade expansion, which drew into industry and commerce many of those who otherwise might have constituted the available supply, and many teachers of the older type found it difficult to accommodate themselves to the new conditions in which their independence appeared to them to be com-promised. The consequence was, at least for a time, decline in status of the teaching profession and deterioration of the teaching staffs.

In the country districts, the maintenance of a compulsory system of education, where the population was scanty, became economically very burdensome and in some of the remoter places special govern-ment grants came to be necessary. While state education thus deve-loped a series of difficult problems, the mere extension of the benefits of education may on the whole be said to have justified the measure, although so far as Scotland is concerned the voluntary system had already been widely extended before the national system was introduced. There are difficulties alike in extreme centralisation and in extreme localisation of control.

Since the burning of the Theatre Royal in Queen Street, Glasgow, in 1829, there had only been one theatre of consequence in Glasgow. This was the Caledonian Theatre in Dunlop Street. From about 1826 until 1851, this theatre was under the management of John Henry Alexander, a celebrated actor-manager of his time.[1] I do not remember the name of his successor; but about 1863, when I saw my first Christmas pantomime on its stage, it possessed a stock company. I believe that Henry Irving was then a member of it, or had been a short time before. The starring system had, however, begun, and in the later sixties I saw in that theatre, Irving in *The Bells*, *The Lyons Mail* and *Eugene Aram*, and Toole in Kenny's comedy, *Sweethearts and Wives*. In opera I heard Titjens and Modjeska, Foley, the Irish tenor, and others whom I have forgotten.

Sheridan Knowles, author of *The Hunchback*, lived in retirement at Rothesay in the Island of Bute. He devoted himself during his later years to propaganda against the Roman Catholic Church [2] and to evangelistic labours. My grandmother, Mrs. Bridie, knew him, and frequently spoke to me of the impressiveness of his reading of the Bible.

---

[1] I have before me a curious little book, *Stage Reminiscences . . . during the last Forty Years*, by "An Old Stager" (really a stage carpenter), published in Glasgow (in a second edition) in 1870. There are many interesting anecdotes of actors and the stage between 1816 and 1851.

[2] He wrote a reply to Cardinal Wiseman on Transubstantiation and other controversial tracts. Knowles died in 1862.

CHAPTER V

From day to day, from year to year,
Beneath the college profs. I sat,
And stowed away a store of lere,
With countless views on this and that;
As true and trustful as a lamb
I took their lectures meekly down,
Showing in essays and exam.
How well I made their thoughts my own.

And thus, perhaps half-unperceived,
I have become, in leaf and stem
(It seems too good to be believed),
A fragrant flower akin to them;
And yet, I may presume to add
That, thanks to kind Carnegie's pelf,
The day will come, it is too bad,
When I retire—into myself.

T. L. Douglas, "A Prof. Mixture," in *University Verses* (1911)
(With emendations in the four last lines).

Two important events contributed to economic expansion in Scotland in the period between 1870 and 1875. These were the recovery of the United States from the exhaustion of the Civil War and the war between Germany and France in 1870–71. The first occasioned an enormous demand for railway iron and the second eliminated for a time the competition of Germany and France, especially in the textile markets. The prices of iron soared and the wages of miners and ironworkers followed. Shipbuilding was stimulated by the advance of freights and new lines of steamships were projected. Relieved of the competition of Mulhouse, the calico printers became very busy. The railway companies were able, without much grumbling from traders, to increase their rates through the addition of terminal charges. Industrial districts went full steam ahead. Advances in wages became general, affecting all industries, and migration to the towns went on at an accelerated rate. Rents advanced, quarters of towns inhabited by working people were congested, acute sanitary and engineering problems began to manifest themselves. Private enterprise found manufacture so profitable that it was disinclined to provide capital for public services, which were demanded by the increasing

52

urban population. Public services which had in the main been left to private enterprise came to be inefficiently rendered, because, compared with other forms of investment, they yielded small profits. Public demand for the rendering of these services under the management of representative bodies began to emerge. Water and gas were municipalised.

One of the public services, however, did not at that time attract municipal enterprise. This was urban transportation. Growth of cities, intensive and extensive, in population and area, made manifest the inadequacy of existing means of communication. No one in the municipal councils had vision enough to foresee the importance of the problem of urban transportation from a municipal point of view. No one saw that direction and character of civic development must depend largely upon facilities for movement within cities and between them and their immediate outskirts. For distances of a few miles in certain directions, railways availed, but utilisation of urban fractions of long through lines of railway for local traffic was doubtful economy from the railway point of view, and the mere fact that it was necessary sometimes for passengers to walk a greater or less distance to and from railway stations suggested that some more convenient and readily available system might be provided.

Omnibuses had been introduced in large cities and had been used, together with coaches, for inter-urban traffic. Light rails, known as tramways, had been used for waggons drawn by horses and carrying minerals and merchandise; but the system had not been extensively developed even for such traffic and it had not been applied to conveyance of passengers.

So far as I am aware, the first attempt to utilise the public streets for the laying of tramways and to use upon these omnibuses for the conveyance of the public was made in Paris in the sixties. The Paris experiment was not followed by any immediate developments elsewhere; but in the late sixties an eccentric American, George Francis Train, began a propaganda in favour of urban tramways. He was successful in securing some concessions from municipalities in the United States, and in obtaining capital to construct such lines there. In, I think, 1869, he crossed the Atlantic, and promoted in London the British and Foreign Tramways Company. This company succeeded in making an arrangement with the city of Glasgow, under which tramway lines were to be constructed in that city and a certain amount per mile was to be paid by the company to the city. The lines were constructed in 1870–71. I remember quite well the public feeling upon the project at that time. The success of the enterprise was generally looked upon as very doubtful. Some people thought that if passenger traffic was insufficient to justify exclusive use of the lines for omnibuses, that the lines might be used for conveyance of goods. When the lines were opened, it began to be apparent that there was little justification for foreboding. For some years tramways did not pay; but gradually the habit of using them increased and the profitable character of the enterprise became evident. Before the lines reached a paying basis, they were purchased by a company organised by Glasgow capitalists, and the British and Foreign Company disappeared from the scene. The original lease was drawn for twenty years from 1870. At a later period it was extended by four years, so that the close of the lease came in 1894.

The shrewd Town Councillors thought that they had made a good bargain with the promoters. The arrangement for payment of a rental per mile of constructed line was not contingent upon any profit being made by the company, and thus the city could not incur any loss should the enterprise turn out unsuccessfully. The terms of the lease were, however, provocative of friction between the Corporation and the company during the whole of the period of the lease. The method of payment formed a direct inducement to the company to refrain from extending its lines or to permit extension of them by the Corporation of the city, unless the estimated revenue from the extension was regarded as sufficient to pay the additional rental as well as to give increased returns to the capital of the company. Had payment to the city been based upon the profits of the company or upon its gross earnings, the city would have had to go without any payment for a few years, or would have had to be content with a small return, while in subsequent years it would have shared in the prosperity of the company.

The Town Council of Glasgow in the seventies was composed of men belonging to the smaller merchantry and the smaller manufacture with a slender number of important merchants and engineers. A solitary councillor represented the Trade Unions. Few members were men of great wealth; but in general they enjoyed a comfortable income. Some of them had retired from active business. Their services to the municipality were rendered gratuitously and there was no taint of corruption. The Lord Provost was chairman of the Town Council and was elected by it from among its members. He was not regarded by the public as responsible for the policy of the Council. A tradition of rather more than ample hospitality had gathered round the civic chair, and thus the rule came to be established that none but men of ample means should be elected. When the supply of such men in the Council ran short, as it often did, it was necessary to introduce one into the Council for the purpose. The inducement of a knighthood and in more recent years of a baronetcy usually sufficed to attract a suitable candidate. The burden of civic administration did not fall either upon the Lord Provost or upon the Town Council. The administration of Glasgow at this period was essentially bureaucratic. The Town Clerk, the manager of the Water Works, the manager of the Gas Works and other technical officers were the real administrators and the real authors even of municipal policy. The Council was very reluctant to add to its obligations, and was even slow to permit itself to take the measures urged upon it through increase of population and through extension of civic boundaries, which took place in consequence of that increase.

Under these conditions municipal affairs were conducted with cautious deliberation; discussion was businesslike and brief, and the proportion of their available time occupied by the members of the Council in civic business was not unduly great. The time came when these conditions were changed.

The series of economic movements described above sustained a check in 1873, when owing to the railway crisis in the United States and financial difficulties on the continent of Europe, iron dropped in price and wages fell. In Scotland much of the surplus profit of the preceding period was now thrown into house building, induced by rise of rents and facilitated by the fall in wages. The West of Scotland was further affected during the three succeeding years (1873–76) by the immediate consequences of demonetisation of silver by Germany and suspension of the Latin Monetary Union. The fall in Indian exchange resulting from these events affected a wide range of industries in Glasgow. At the same moment the technique of an important group of industries—the calico printing and dyeing trades—was altered through the introduction of new chemical compounds replacing the natural products, of which mention has been made in a previous chapter. Synthetic alizarine took the place of garancine, aniline derivatives took the place of cochineal and dyewoods. A long list of chemical compounds which had been used in the processes formerly employed almost disappeared from the markets, and a new list made its appearance. Drugs which had been made in trifling quantities for medicinal purposes found uses which compelled their production on a large scale. Simultaneously with these changes there came the Solvay alkali process, which replaced that of Leblanc and altered an important branch of the chemical industry in the West of Scotland as well as in Newcastle-on-Tyne.

These changes coincided with recovery, during the second half of the decade 1871–80, from the exhaustion of the war by Germany and France. Germany especially, after the reaction due to over-speculation, plunged into chemical manufacture with vigour; and Mülhausen in Alsace competed with the calico printers of the West of Scotland as well as with those of Lancashire. During the same period, overbuilding of railways in New Zealand and speculative enterprises in Australia in which Scottish capital had been largely embarked brought heavy losses. Fortunes made in 1868–75 melted away, and the desperate enterprises of some of those who had launched into speculative adventures, instead of conserving their resources brought catastrophe. The failure of the City of Glasgow Bank in October 1878 was the result of these general and special causes. The unlimited liability of the shareholders caused the blow to fall heavily upon them. Only two of the shareholders remained completely solvent. The others had to compromise or surrender everything they possessed to the liquidators of the bank. Credit was restricted, and for three or four years Scottish enterprise was paralysed as it had not been since the beginning of the eighteenth century.

Up till 1875, wages had advanced in industrial towns and had remained stationary in agricultural districts. The rural labourer was beckoned to the industrial town by the prospect of relatively high wages and extruded from the country by the decline of employment. Small market towns in which no industry was carried on remained stagnant, or even declined. When the curve of brisk trade reached its highest point in the middle of the seventies, country districts were found to be denuded of their labourers, and industrial towns choked with them. Thus decline of trade caught especially those who had not yet become completely habituated to urban conditions and those who were not very skilful artisans. It is not surprising, therefore, that in 1876 and 1877 there was observable a certain vigour in emigration. This emigration was not in any way promoted by propaganda or assisted by benevolent or governmental agency, but was wholly spontaneous. From Glasgow at that time large numbers of energetic emigrants, not wholly unprovided with funds, sailed for New Zealand. The ships sailed from what was known as Plantation Quay, and I went down several times in these years to see the ships take their departure and to talk with some of the people who were going in them. They were sailing vessels of the New Zealand Shipping Company, and the voyage out by Cape Horn took about three months. This movement was checked, however, by financial collapse in New Zealand in 1877–78. There was some emigration, not very extensive, to the United States in 1876.[1] At that time Canada was not drawing many emigrants.

To sum up the situation: fall of agricultural rents, decline of wages, losses in foreign investments, and consequent restriction of credit, produced together a diminution of demand for commodities and thus reacted upon prices, production and employment. The long depression of trade, which lasted more or less acutely until 1890, was the outward and visible sign of these phenomena. Such was the economic background in Scotland between 1870 and 1880—a period of three years of abounding prosperity, followed by five years of decline, these being succeeded by two years (within the decade, with more to follow) of distress. I shall endeavour in subsequent chapters to reflect, as nearly as may be, the contemporary moods to which these economical incidents with other contributory causes gave rise.

In 1874, when I was between nineteen and twenty years of age, I entered the University of Glasgow—at once handicapped and advantaged by the years I had spent at business; but not any older than the average of my fellow-students. Unfortunately my health broke down during my course and I was unable to complete it; but I owe a great debt of gratitude to the University for what I gave it the opportunity of giving to me. Adam Smith, in his *Wealth of Nations*, draws a comparison between the University of Oxford in his day and the Universities of Scotland, having in his mind principally Glasgow, at which he had been a student, as well as a professor. He denounces the Oxford system of fixed endowments and applauds the Scots system as it was in his time and long after, by means of which the income of the professor depended upon the number of students he was able to attract to his classes. This method of "payment by results" had much to be said for it. As the numbers of students attending the Universities increased, and as the number of professors did not increase or did not increase in the same proportion, the emoluments of the latter became very large. Indeed for many years the chairs of the Universities of Glasgow and Edinburgh in particular became the blue ribbons of the professions with which they were associated. The fixed endowments of Oxford and Cambridge afforded an income of

[1] The United States labour market was absorbing the heavy German immigration of that time.

only a few hundred pounds, whereas the fluctuating fees of the student attending the Scots Universities yielded incomes amounting in some cases to several thousand pounds a year. For those who only desired a life of learned leisure, such incomes offered no attractions; but good scholars are sometimes ambitious, and the celibacy to which the fellows in the English Universities were condemned, acted as a heavy handicap to these Universities when they entered into a competition for the service of brains. The academic incomes at the English Universities were too small for men without independent means or other sources of income. Large relatively as they were, the incomes of the Scots professors were no larger than those of judges, and not so large as those of successful barristers.

In many of the chairs in the University of Glasgow there had been a notable succession—in the Chair of Greek, for example, Sir Daniel Sandford, Henry Lushington, Richard Jebb up to the period under review, and Gilbert Murray later—a succession such as no other University approached. In 1874 Sir William Thomson (afterwards Lord Kelvin) was Professor of Natural Philosophy, Lushington of Greek, Edward Caird of Moral Philosophy, Nichol of English Literature, Young of Natural History, Allen Thompson of Anatomy, James Thomson of Engineering, John Caird of Divinity. All of these were men of note, most of them of eminence. Ramsay, Professor of Latin, and Veitch, Professor of Logic, were good teachers, but were not men of genius.

Apart from Lord Kelvin, of whom I have already spoken, two of the group mentioned above I hold especially in affectionate remembrance. These are Edward Caird and John Nichol. I saw something of them while I was at the University; but in later years I became intimate with them. Of Edward Caird, I may say at once that from my first contact with him I felt in him a man of very fine genius. This opinion was strengthened by time; but with a qualification. He lectured, through no fault of his, but through a tradition of his chair, at eight o'clock in the morning. Now, no man of genius is ever at his best at that hour, unless it happens to coincide with the climax of a stimulating evening. Nevertheless, his eight o'clock lectures were undeniably fine. There was a curious feeling rather prevalent at that time that Caird's teaching was "unsettling," in other words that it gave rise to doubts about the validity of the evidences of religion. I certainly did not derive this feeling from my father, who was a stout defender of Caird; but I recall being somewhat impressed by it. During the two or three years before I entered the University

I had relaxed my coquetry with science and had read some philosophy. I had for example read some of Kant's *Critique of Pure Reason* and all of Hegel's *Philosophy of History* (I had been studying German from 1870), so that I did not go wholly unprepared; nevertheless, my reading had been desultory and my ideas, such as they were, were rather at loose ends. Caird certainly showed me how to arrange them, however little I may have profited by his instruction and example. A very good idea of Caird's customary lecture is to be found in the introduction to his *Kant*. This is practically as he gave it in his class-room. Caird is usually classified as a Hegelian and he certainly gave colour to that classification himself. I shall not attempt to discuss how far it was justified, but I venture to believe that in Hegel's application of his philosophy to the state Caird did not follow him, and he certainly did not accompany the German Neo-Hegelians in their further development towards the doctrines of collectivism.[1] Caird had strong objections to mechanical views of social action and reaction; and he had sympathy for every means which he considered worthy of spontaneous and co-operative social activity. He was much interested, for example, in what came to be known as settlement work as it was carried on by Canon Barnett at Toynbee Hall, and he assisted in the promotion of a similar institution in Glasgow. Undoubtedly his influence upon the youths with whom he came into contact was thoroughly wholesome in a mental and moral sense. He deepened their view of individual and social obligation and assisted them towards estimating the relative importance of the elements which compose the total of life. His manner was highly sympathetic to those with whom he came intimately into contact; and he was an excellent companion in a walk. In after years, when I lived in the country, about six miles from Glasgow, he used to come out on Saturday afternoon. We took long walks and occasionally took rest or shelter from a shower in country inns where we regaled ourselves with long cigars, of which Caird always carried a good supply of his favourite

[1] I recall Edward Caird's mentioning to me, as an illustration of the decline of German interest in Hegel, that when in 1870 it was proposed to make some celebration in Great Britain on the hundredth anniversary of the birth of Hegel, it seemed to be impossible to excite any interest in the matter in Germany. I am not certain of the precise date of the correspondence; but it was probably in June of 1870, when the Germans were preoccupied with preparations for the war which, as is now known, Bismarck was then engaged in provoking. Even Hegel's own son was wholly indifferent on the subject of celebrating his father's memory, and so far as I remember refused to impart some personal information about his father which those who contemplated the celebration asked him to furnish.

brand, and pots of porter which we obtained on the premises. On one of such occasions he tried one of his Gifford Lectures on me before delivering it at St. Andrews. Yet to some he was reserved and even shy. He found small talk irksome, and if he could not readily find a common ground of intelligent conversation, he was apt to be quite taciturn. This habit gives a vraisemblance to a story which was current about him when I was at the University. The story relates that he invited an undergraduate to walk with him in a constitutional he used customarily to take after his eight o'clock lecture. When they left the college gate, Caird said to the student, "Have you read Gibbon, Mr. ——?" The answer was "No, sir." They then walked about five miles without conversation. As they approached the college gate on their return, Caird said, "You ought to read Gibbon, Mr. ——."

Caird had humour, sometimes even of a sardonic kind; and above all he had humour enough to enjoy a joke against himself. He told me with glee of such a joke. One night he was studying late, after everyone in his house had retired; suddenly there was a sharp ring. He went to the door, and found a student whom he recognised. The young man told him that, being in a state of despondency, he was about to commit suicide and that he had come to inform Caird of his intention. Caird felt at a loss to know what to do; but recalling that his next-door neighbour in the college, John Young, Professor of Natural History, had the degree of Doctor of Medicine, he decided to call him into consultation. Young advised that they should get a cab and take the unfortunate fellow to the lunatic asylum, which was at no great distance from the college. When they arrived at the asylum all was dark. They rang the bell of the residence of Dr. Yellow-lees, the director, who was a friend of both professors. Dr. Yellowlees put his head out of an upper window and cried, "Who is there?" Young answered, "Caird and Young." Yellowlees shouted from the window, "Which of you is bringing the other?"

John Nichol was, undoubtedly, a man of genius. He was a poet, though not perhaps of the first order. As a critic, however, he must be ranked among the first. I do not mean that he could be fairly placed alongside Sainte-Beuve and Bielinsky, for these are un-approached; but it seems to me that in soundness of judgment and in aptness of expression of it, he was at least the equal of any English critic of his time. As a writer he was too exiguous; even his lectures, properly so called, were not numerous. A large part of the time of his class, too large a part for the eager student, was occupied with unimportant matters. When he did lecture, he lectured well.

The gist of his book on Byron in the "English Men of Letters" series
and the whole of the critical part of his sketch of Burns in Paterson's
edition of Burns were delivered to his class. It is true that writing
and speaking or lecturing are two different arts, rarely attaining
excellence in the same person and almost never in the same product.
Yet Nichol's lectures in both the cases mentioned were good and the
books arising out of them are good, although the spoken and the
written words were not quite the same, and perhaps they were both
good for that reason among others. Nichol was a fellow-student at
Oxford of Swinburne's, and they remained friends. The only occasion
when I met Swinburne was with Nichol. In 1875 or 1876 I had asked
John Nichol to come over to Pollokshields to lecture. He came and
brought Swinburne, who was then staying with him. He introduced
me and we exchanged a few words. Canon Scott Holland speaks of
Swinburne's "long arms reaching to the knees, like Buddha's, with
the hands wagging and out-splayed, and the very short legs, and the
short crumpled trousers, ending somehow above the funny boots.
Everything was queer and uncanny until you were close enough to
catch sight of the fine grave eyes above the elusive chin, and the
splendid brow." Although I helped him into his coat, I do not recall
an impression of long arms; but the fine eyes, the massive forehead,
the luxuriant yellow hair and the bewilderingly weak chin linger in
my memory. Some years afterwards I had occasion to write to him
about a young poet, and he replied in a friendly letter; but I never
saw him again.

Nichol told me of a curious adventure in Naples. Nichol frequently
carried a sword-stick which had been given him by a friend, and while
doing so went into a shop with his wife. By some unintentional jerk
he loosened the catch of the slender steel concealed in his cane, and
the presence of the weapon was unfortunately revealed to a policeman
who happened to be in the shop. This functionary at once arrested
Nichol, charging him with carrying, without a licence, a lethal weapon
longer than the prescribed dimensions. Nichol had to remain in
durance while the British Embassy at Rome took the necessary steps
to secure his release; and he had to leave Naples at once as an indispensable condition.

In 1875, Richard Claverhouse Jebb was appointed Professor of
Greek in succession to Lushington, of whom Tennyson said, "his
learning lay on him lightly like a flower." Jebb was in his thirty-
fourth year. He had been a Fellow of Trinity and Public Orator of
the University of Cambridge; his reputation as a classical scholar

was already of the highest. I attended a course of lectures on Greek Literature given by him in his first session. I think that these lectures formed the basis of the volume published by him some years afterwards called *Lectures in Greek Poetry*. In his youth Jebb was somewhat of a dandy. A malevolent and wholly unjustifiable Cambridge joke described him as "devoting to the neglect of his duties what time he could spare from the adornment of his person." One day I was going up one of the steep streets in Glasgow when I saw Jebb bearing down upon me "in full sail." This equipment included a glossy silk hat, smart cut-away coat, lavender-coloured trousers, in vogue at that time, gloves to match, and a cane. Years after this period, I became acquainted with a man who had been Jebb's fag at Charterhouse. His name was Lyndhurst Ogden. Part of his duty was to see that when Jebb presented himself at prayers in the school chapel he was properly dressed. As Jebb left the least possible margin for the performance of his toilet, Ogden had nearly every morning to run after him carrying parts of his clothing which he put on as he ran. Jebb's fastidiousness in person had evidently not been acquired at school; it must have been developed later. Thirty years afterwards when I saw him at Cambridge, crippled with rheumatism and bent with premature age, I recalled the brisk and elegant figure of his youth.

The incumbent of the Chair of Humanity (Latin) at Glasgow in my time and for long after was Professor George G. Ramsay. He was a tall good-looking man, whose distinguishing personal characteristic was the magnitude of his feet. These extremities were indeed somewhat out of proportion to the rest of his figure. One day I happened to go with my brother to our shoemaker to order some shoes. We noticed on a bench a pair of quite unusual size. My brother said, "I bet I know for whom these shoes have been made." "I won't bet," I said, "I know whose they are. They could fit only one man." "That is what I thought," he said. We asked the shoemaker, and found that they had been made for Ramsay.

When I went to the University in 1874 the buildings on Gilmore Hill had not been finished. Indeed, it was not for some years that the spire was placed on the main tower. While the tower was still incomplete, a couple of students mounted it to survey the landscape, a scene of much impressiveness stretching south over the Renfrewshire hills. These young fellows took out their penknives and succeeded in carving their names somewhat deeply in the stone parapet, then almost if not altogether free from such decoration. Their exploit was reported, and Ramsay was appointed by the University authorities to deal with the case. He summoned both the culprits to appear before him in his private room. The first who presented himself halted on the threshold, became suddenly pale and before Ramsay could utter a word of inquiry or reproach, fainted. The professor, seriously perturbed, rang for a college servant, and both with much solicitude proceeded to revive the youth, whom they dismissed without reference to his offence. Meanwhile, unaware of what was transpiring, the other youth had waited his turn for an interview. When he entered, Ramsay, fearing another case of collapse, told the retiring servant to remain within reach. The second offender entered with a jaunty air, and when asked in a very mild and apologetic manner by Ramsay if he had carved his name on the tower, replied defiantly that he had done so, and that in similar places he had seen the names of Scott and Byron and other celebrities carved by them in their youth, and that the public seemed to value these memorials. "No doubt," said Ramsay, "but since you have not yet given sufficient evidence of the likelihood of future distinction in your case, you are fined one guinea. If in future years you become as great a celebrity as those you have mentioned, and if you apply for the money, it may be refunded."

With John Young, although I did not attend his classes, I came to be on friendly terms after I left the University. He was perhaps not a great man of science, but he was versatile and humorous. His sprightly air earned for him the soubriquet of "Cocky," by which he was universally known and was even on occasion impudently addressed by his students *en masse*. Mrs. Young for many years wrote musical criticisms for one of the Glasgow newspapers with acknowledged skill. Her husband used to go to the concerts with her, and to amuse himself by drawing caricatures of the people on the stage and in the audience. He was not the only caricaturist in the University. Mrs. Blackburn, wife of the Professor of Mathematics, was extremely skilful with her pencil and witty in her character sketches. There were two quaint and lugubrious figures in the University in my time. One was Dr. Anderson, Professor of Chemistry, and the other was Dr. Jackson, Professor of Hebrew. Both were perfectly bald alike on face and head. The latter was popularly known as "the Holy Ghost."

In 1873, Jowett, Master of Balliol, came to Glasgow and preached in the college chapel. At this distance of time, nothing remains in my mind of his sermon, which was no doubt beyond criticism; but I remember an incident that occurred at the close of it. The Principal of the University was the Rev. Dr. Barclay, a venerable minister of the Church of Scotland of unexceptional character, rather distinguished aspect and no very distant fame. Towards the end of Jowett's discourse there was a sudden commotion, followed by the evacuation of the pews occupied by the professors and their families. When Jowett concluded, a note was handed to him by one of the college servants. He immediately said, in his characteristically shrill voice, without any attempt at emotion and even in a casual manner:

"I have to announce that the aged person who presided over the University has just died."

No exception could be taken to this. Every word was true and there was no more to be said. To Jowett and to nearly everybody else, the Principal was an "aged person" and nothing more; but to state this literal truth at that solemn moment and in so precise terms was a trifle harsh. Although Jowett was the head of a college with a Scots name and associated with Scotland, he had no special interest in the country, and had, I suspect, a somewhat modified respect for its intellectual products.

A feature of the Scots Universities, unique among the Universities of the world, and an indication of their essentially democratic character, is the election by the undergraduates of the Lord Rector, one of three highest officers in the University. It is true that the office is customarily regarded as purely honorary; but it has not always been so regarded. If the Rector chooses, he may exercise great influence upon the University. When Thomas Campbell, the poet, was elected Rector of the University of Glasgow in 1826, he took a conscientious view of his functions and entered actively into University affairs. While the Rector is entitled to nominate an assessor to represent him in the University Court—the governing body of the University—his personal obligations are now in effect confined to the single task of delivering an address to the students at some convenient time during his three years' tenure of office. The Rectorial election is of a peculiar character. The successful candidate must have a majority in at least three of the four "nations" into which the student body is divided. If two "nations" give a majority for one candidate and the other "nations" give a majority for the other candidate, the casting vote is given by the Principal of the University. Membership of the "nations" depends upon the birthplace of the undergraduate. "Natio Glottiana" comprises those born in the valley of the Clyde and contiguous regions; "Natio Rothesayana," those from the Highlands and Islands; "Natio Loudoniana," those from the Lowlands; and "Natio Transforthiana," those from beyond the Firth. It may happen that a candidate has the largest number of votes from the whole

MRS. JAMES MAVOR
(1828-1896)

THE REV. JAMES MAVOR, M.A.
(1828-1879)

constituency, but a majority in only one "nation," although that is the largest, yet he will be defeated by the candidate who has a majority in each of the three smaller "nations."

The Rectorial contest is usually, but not invariably, conducted on political grounds. An unsuccessful attempt was made in 1874 to break down this tradition by the creation of an Independent party with Emerson for its candidate. An election is always an occasion for much boisterous fun. I recall a meeting of the supporters of one of the candidates—I think Gladstone; the room was the Greek class-room, at that time the largest in the University. The meeting was raided by the opposite party—the supporters of Disraeli—who succeeded in entrenching themselves in the back benches. Armed with pea-shooters and plentifully supplied with ammunition, they bombarded the front benches and the platform. No visible progress was made, and at the end of an hour the floor was thickly covered with peas. In revenge for this invasion of the rights of freedom of speech, the injured party laid a deep plan. They refrained from attempting to enter the room where their opponents were assembled on the following afternoon; but when the meeting had begun they established a blockade by screwing up the door and fastening the windows. Through an opening which they had left for the purpose they threw into the room quantities of burning asafœtida, which had a deplorable effect upon those who were imprisoned. They were following the Greeks with their stinkpots and anticipating the Germans with their tear-gas. Such escapades naturally led to the rule that meetings connected with the Rectorial elections should not be held within the walls of the University. On the evening of the election it was customary to have a torchlight procession through the town and to end by a great bonfire in front of the University buildings on Gilmore Hill.

Some classes were rather notorious for rowdiness; but in general, the Scots students go to the Universities to learn, and their poverty causes them to be frugal of their time.

In the eighties a project was carried into effect in Edinburgh for the provision of residences for students attending the University there, and a similar project was formed for Glasgow. Those of us who were interesting ourselves in the matter found on inquiry that the Glasgow student paid so small a sum for his board and lodging that a considerable annual subvention would be necessary to maintain a college residence in which students could live at a fair standard of comfort. It appeared to be the fact that the students boarded with widows and married couples possessed of small means, who chose

I—E

this method of increasing an already existing income. The effect of this condition was that the students received their board and lodging [1] for little more than the cost of it, while out of the balance the services of their landladies were remunerated at a rate for which specialised service could not be obtained. Students whose families reside in Glasgow do not require a college residence to be provided for them, while those who come to the University from the country are not usually possessed of more means than may enable them to meet the expenses necessarily incurred under the conditions which have been described. The richer families in the country usually sent their sons to the English Universities. The fame of the Edinburgh medical school drew students of medicine there from all ranks of society in Great Britain and even from abroad, especially from Australia, and thus the problem of residences in that University bore a different aspect and offered much greater prospects of success than in the University of Glasgow.

There being no college residence, no common-room, no students' union, no gymnasium, there was thus in my time no opportunity for students to meet as students elsewhere than in the class-rooms. There was a general debating society called the "Dialectic," and there were special class debating societies; but these were not as a rule attended by more than a few, and they had no influence upon the general body of students. The University was thus decidedly deficient in college life. This was so obvious a disadvantage that in later years all the wants save one—that of residences—were supplied. While there was complete absence of general college life, students formed, nevertheless, fairly sound judgments upon the ability of their fellow-students as these disclosed themselves in their classes. The practice of long standing in the University of awarding the class prizes by votes of the class and not by the award of the professor perhaps contributed to this. I have never heard of a case in which the prizes were alleged not to be given in accordance with merit.

Of my fellow-students I remember only a few. Among these was James Lambie, who went to Australia, became a journalist, and during the South African War went as war correspondent of a Melbourne newspaper. He was killed in one of the early battles. Robert Kemp, who gave promise of being a poet, wrote some fine lines on Marlowe and then buried himself as parish minister of Blairgowrie; W. P. Ker, who went to Balliol as a Snell Exhibitioner and became Pro-

[1] The average cost to the student, as we found at that time (1887 or 1888), was 12s. 6d. per week.

fessor of English Literature in University College, London; Wallace
Lindsay, who also went to Balliol, edited *Plautus* and became Professor
of Humanity at St. Andrews; George Dodds, who became Senior
Tutor of Peterhouse, Cambridge; Patrick Smith, who became Sheriff-
Substitute at Selkirk; Kirkpatrick, who became Professor of Theology
at Knox College, Toronto, and Peter Clark, who became a Free Church
minister at Perth, are some of those whom I remember.

Among the lectures I listened to in Glasgow in the seventies (in
1876 and 1877) was one by Fleeming Jenkin on Telpherage,[1] or a
system of communication by means of aerial wires from which small
carriages were suspended and along which they were propelled by
mechanical or electrical power. Jenkin was very enthusiastic about
his system, upon the development of which he had embarked a considerable amount of money. I doubt if the company he formed made
much out of it. Probably some mechanical details remained to be
perfected. Now telpherage is in extensive use. I have seen it in operation in the backwoods of Canada, where it was carrying material across
gorges and bringing ore out of quarries. The same idea has been
applied in the mines at Bilbao,[2] and during the war, in the Italian
campaign on the Isonzo, where telpherage was used to carry guns
and ammunition from the valleys to the peaks, and from one peak
to another.

About this time there was a legal dispute over improvements
upon the dynamo, or Gramme machine, as it was then called. I went
to Edinburgh in order to hear some of the evidence. Young, Shand
and Asher, all afterwards on the Bench, were engaged in the case.

In 1876 I had the good fortune to hear Alexander Graham Bell
deliver one of his first lectures on the telephone. Another significant lecture of this kind was given by Swan of Newcastle upon his
incandescent lamp.

About the same date Dean Stanley came to Glasgow and lectured
upon the Christian Church. Stanley was a diminutive person, extremely
thin, with an active body and an eager face. The vote of thanks was
proposed by Norman Macleod. Macleod was a man of great if not
enormous bulk, and when he appeared in public was habitually
jovial. In moving a vote of thanks, Macleod spoke of Stanley as the

---

[1] Fleeming Jenkin afterwards (in 1884) read a paper on the same subject
before the Society of Arts. This paper was published by Robert Louis Stevenson,
London, 1887.

[2] It is also used on the aerial line extended above the whirlpool at Niagara.
This line was constructed by the same Spanish engineers who built the similar
line at Bilbao, and it was originally financed by Spanish capital.

Dean of Windsor; and Stanley, desiring to correct him, plucked his sleeve, like a small boy endeavouring to engage the attention of a giant. Stanley whispered, "Dean of Westminster." "Of course, of course," said Macleod. "As I was saying, we have listened to an admirable lecture by the Dean of Windsor." Stanley jumped up and again interposed; but when Macleod repeated the offence once more, he shrugged his shoulders and sat still. Whether or not the repetition, or even perhaps the original offence, was a mistake or a piece of mischievous fun I do not know. It is possible that it was a joke.

On some such occasion, I do not remember who was lecturing or what precisely was the subject, although it must have been connected with the utilisation of water power for the generation of electricity, possibly at the Falls of Foyers, Lord Kelvin, then Sir William Thomson, made a little speech which I do not find recorded in any of his published writings. He spoke of the possibility of utilising Niagara Falls in the production of electrical power, and he defended the use of them in this manner against the criticism of those who objected on the ground that the scenic beauty of the Falls would·be diminished or destroyed.   "Think," he said, "what would be the aspect of the Niagara gorge and of the precipice over which the waters now tumble if these waters were altogether withdrawn and permitted to enter the river channel at a lower level. The face of the precipice would soon be covered with aquatic plants giving a splendour of colour which with all their magnificence the·Falls do not now possess, while the pool below would have a quiet beauty instead of its present misty turbulence." I do not recall if he suggested, as he may have done, that the abrasion of the crest of the precipice from the flow of the stream would cease and would only occur very slowly from the milder forces of the atmosphere.

During the crisis induced by the Russo-Turkish War (in 1875–77) Gladstone came down to speak at Glasgow. I took with me to hear him my friend Leo Mélliet, who had been a member of the Paris Commune of 1871. Gladstone was a member of the Cabinet which entered upon the Crimean War, but he had withdrawn from the Ministry upon what appeared at the time to be an inadequate pretext. Goldwin Smith told me that he thought Gladstone never approved of the war, which in Goldwin Smith's opinion had been brought about by the co-operation of Napoleon III., Stratford de Redcliffe, who was British Ambassador at Constantinople, and Palmerston. He thought also that Gladstone had all along been anxious to find an excuse for separating himself from his friends. However that may be, for a long period before 1876

Gladstone had been on the one hand disturbed by Turkish misrule in the Balkans and by the atrocities in Bulgaria, and on the other, largely through the astute diplomacy of Madame Novikov (known as O.K.), he had become very sympathetic with the Russian point of view. Disraeli, who had a certain *flair* for the East, was apparently preparing for war; but the decline of industry in 1874 had resulted in annual deficits in the Treasury, then under Sir Stafford Northcote. These deficits contrasted strongly with the surpluses created by the advance by "leaps and bounds" which had characterised the preceding period. In his speech at Glasgow, after a long passage composed of one of his involved sentences, Gladstone, after the manner of Macaulay, concluded with a short pregnant phrase. "They cannot go to war; they have no money." This was wildly applauded. I do not suppose that there is an instance in history of a nation refusing to go to war for the sole reason that it had no money. Turkey had no money and yet went to war; the finances of Russia in 1876 were not flourishing and yet she went to war. The phrase was a mere sophism, yet it produced the effect it was intended to produce. I asked Mélliet, who was himself one of the most persuasive of speakers, what impressed him most in Gladstone's speech. He mentioned this very phrase. I pointed out that it was not true. He replied, "That does not matter. You noticed that when he said it, he carried his audience with him. That is the point of all oratory." This argument, however, was not convincing. Thoughtless acquiescence in an untenable proposition is apt to result in reaction and in a feeling of grievance at what may be looked upon as an attempt to mislead. I heard many of Gladstone's important speeches at different periods, and it seems to me that his power did not lie in the least in his argument or in his phrases, telling as these sometimes were, but exclusively in his silvery voice, which captivated his hearers. A great tenor may sing in a language wholly unknown to his audience and yet carry it away with enthusiasm by the mere beauty of his notes: so with Gladstone. To hear his speeches was a delight, to read them almost impossible.

Among the orators whom I heard in the late sixties or in the early seventies was Gavazzi, the patriotic Italian priest. To describe Gavazzi as plain would be flattery. He was positively ugly; but he had a fine eye and a mellifluous voice. He spoke in Italian. His speech was translated by a young scholar afterwards known to fame as Sir Henry Campbell-Bannerman. It is well known that Sir Henry was drawn, long after this period, with much reluctance on his part, from his study into political life. I believe that to the end he solaced himself and found recreation from the cares of office in French and Italian literature.

I had my first glimpses of Lord Rosebery in 1873 or 1874. I am not sure of the sequence of two occasions. Probably the first of these occasions was at a dinner of the Dialectic, the students' debating society at the University. Benjamin F. C. Costelloe, who was the crack speaker of the society, was in the chair. The principal speech naturally fell to him. After he had spoken, Rosebery was called upon. He began with juvenile *naïveté* and obvious sincerity, "I wish I could speak like that." He came in his time to speak better, although Costelloe, who was an Irishman, had real oratorical power. Years afterwards, when Lord Rosebery was Chairman of the London County Council, Costelloe was a member of it.

About the same time as the incident I have just described, a Liberal political meeting was held in Glasgow. I do not recall the occasion or the speakers; but I do remember that when these had had their say, there were calls in the audience, "Rosebery, Rosebery." After some moments, in which the calls became more insistent, a figure rose from the extreme left wing of the platform. It was the figure of the Fat Boy in Pickwick. He wore a "double-breasted" jacket and he had his hands in the pockets. The audience laughed involuntarily and cheered because it was amused, while young Rosebery calmly surveyed it. He looked like a boy although he was about twenty-five years of age and he spoke with curious care and precision, as if public speaking were a novelty to him and as if he felt obliged to employ in it a form of language to which as yet he was not accustomed.

Of all the political speakers whom I have heard, I think Lord Goschen was the most convincing. He relied on none of the arts of the orator; but he marshalled his arguments with consummate skill and stated them with perfect clearness. I have heard him address a great audience of working men and carry them with him by sheer invincible logic.

About the end of the decade (1870–80) I was dining one evening with Edward Caird; his brother John, then Principal of the University (since 1873), sat next to me. By way of drawing him out, I asked him whose oratory had impressed him most. John Caird was himself an orator of real power, although he never spoke extemporarily. He replied that he thought Darboy, Archbishop of Paris, was by far the greatest orator he had ever heard. It happened that a short time before I had been catechising my friend Mélliet upon the events of the Commune of Paris, and among other things I said to him, "Why did you shoot Darboy?" He answered, "*We* did not shoot him. He was taken out of our hands by the mob, which had passed from under our control. They shot him. But we made a mistake, we should have shot him ourselves. The reason is this. When we instituted the Government of the Commune, we had two tasks before us: first, to make an indelible impression upon the State by making a Republic absolutely certain and necessary; second, to make an indelible impression upon the Church, by showing that its highest dignitaries are subject to the law. We tried Darboy by process of law. We were satisfied that he ought to be executed, and we ought to have executed him." Then he went on to describe a scene at which he was present. The scene took place in the Cour de Cassation. Accounts of it have been given by others; but it seems worth while to give Mélliet's account of it, because he actually played a part in it and told me about it shortly afterwards. The Judicial Committee of the Commune was composed of five members: Theodore Roussel (who was Chairman), Leo Mélliet, and three others. This committee formed the bench. When the Archbishop was brought before them, Mélliet said that they were all immensely impressed by his venerable and distinguished appearance. On entering the chamber the Archbishop held up his hand and said, "Bless you, my children." Roussel said severely, "You are not before children, you are before magistrates." The interrogation then proceeded strictly according to the form prescribed in the Code Napoléon.

Roussel. "What is your name?"

Archbishop. "Georges Darboy."

Roussel. "What is your profession?"

Archbishop. "Servant of God."

The next prescribed question is "Where do you live?" but since a servant is held under French law to be domiciled at the house of his master, the question properly assumed the following form:

Roussel. "Where does your master live?"

Archbishop. "Everywhere."

Roussel (to the clerk of the court). "Write down, Georges Darboy, servant of one God, who according to the deposition of his servant lives in a state of vagabondage."

It was irreverent of course; but it was also pregnant with meaning. The Church could not be permitted to shelter itself behind an assumption of service to a power not before the court.

After other illuminating details about the Commune, some of which I shall recite later, Mélliet went on to apply the lessons of the Commune to the case of Glasgow.

"For example," he said, "in case of a revolution, it would be necessary to strike at once at the chief centres of the power of the existing order. The personage analogous to the Archbishop of Paris is, in Glasgow, the Principal of the University. However worthy of respect he may be personally, occupation of his office is sufficient to justify his execution, and therefore he ought to be shot." I heard this with mingled horror and amusement.

To return to the dinner table at Caird's, I told John Caird the above story about Darboy; but I refrained from disturbing his peace of mind by telling him the sequel.

The heresy hunt of which Professor Robertson Smith was the victim did not come to its close until 1881; but it was in full cry during the last year of the preceding decade. There had not been an important case of alleged heresy in the Free Church since the trial of Walter C. Smith in 1867 for his sermon on "The Sermon on the Mount." In that case the heresy hunters were defeated; but in the case of Robertson Smith, the heretic was found guilty and dismissed from his chair. Robertson Smith was Professor of Hebrew at the Free Church College, Aberdeen. His alleged offence consisted in his attitude towards the Bible. This attitude may most appropriately be put in his own words: "The Bible itself is God's book, but the Bible as read and understood by any man or school of men is God's book *plus* a very large element of human interpretation"; or again, "The Word (*i.e.* the Bible) is a written word, which has a history, which has to be read and explained like other ancient books."[1] It is, of course, upon this foundation that the Science of Biblical Criticism, if there be such a special science, must rest, but many of the Scots clergy and many of the laity were quite prepared to demand of science of any kind that it should keep its hands off the Bible. They had maintained this attitude in the face of the geologists and the astronomers who had presumed to give an account of the world which appeared on the face of it to be inconsistent with the account given in the Bible, and they were not prepared to admit that scientific historians were more fitted or more entitled to meddle with the sacred text. That the sacred text might already have been meddled with and perhaps seriously altered by editors in various ages, and that it might be important to ascertain the nature and extent of this meddling by means of the application to the surviving text of precise scientific methods, did not enter and apparently could not be intro-

[1] Smith, W. Robertson, *The Old Testament and the Jewish Church* (Edinburgh, 1881), p. 4.

duced into their minds. The attack on Robertson Smith resulted in his being suspended from the duties of his chair in the winter of 1880–81. During this winter he delivered a series of lectures in Glasgow and Edinburgh in which he expounded his position.[1] I attended these lectures, and thus the Robertson Smith case comes into my reminiscences. In the summer of 1881 the case came before the General Assembly of the Free Church, which is customarily held in Edinburgh. On the day upon which the debate was expected to be closed I went to Edinburgh and witnessed the final scene. The Assembly Hall was crowded. On the front benches on either side of the Moderator there sat the leaders of the progressive party on one side, and the leaders of the opposition on the other. On the side to the right of the Moderator there was Dr. Rainy, Principal of the New College, obviously distressed, for he knew what victory of the anti-progressives might mean in its effect upon general ecclesiastical policy. On the opposite side was Dr. Begg, who led the attack in the speech of a tragedian, "Tears in his eyes, distraction in 's aspect."

The final word lay with the accused. It was a very fine performance, candid, well ordered, convincing, with occasional subtle phrases, as for example when he obliquely described Dr. Begg as a "wily ecclesiastic"; but he did not convince the majority of his audience excepting in the sense that he was guilty of heresy. The result was a foregone conclusion. The Highland host had been gathered from every glen and had come to Edinburgh to turn out the heretic. They might have burned him, if the faggots had not been kept from them. It was really an interesting moment, the spirit of the Middle Ages seemed to have revived. After the vote was announced there was a momentary silence, then from the back of the gallery a clear voice rang out, "Ichabod." That voice was mine, and what it said was my sole contribution to the discussion. I believe that, as not infrequently happens, the voice from the gallery interpreted the feeling of the wide public and at the same time stated an essential truth. I do not think that the Free Church has recovered from the self-inflicted blow. At all events, what I said was the outcome of quite deep feeling on my own part. It seemed to me that the Church in which I had been brought up had disgraced itself by expelling one of the few men of genius who were attached to it, and had done so at the dictation of ecclesiastical politicians like Dr. Begg and ignorant fanatics like the Highland host. It seemed to be the victory of intrigue and superstition over the light. The particular opinions of Robertson Smith were

[1] These lectures were afterwards published in the work cited above.

not to my mind at issue; the cardinal question was whether or not
a teacher in a college or university was assumed when he was appointed
to have sold himself body and soul. Colleges would become the abodes
of ignorance and dulness if a proposition of that kind were admitted.
Since tests were abolished in the English universities, there could be
no excuse for their maintenance in the Scots colleges—even in the
denominational colleges—because the students who attend these
institutions have already, as a rule, received their general education
in arts in a "free" university, and may therefore be presumed to have
acquired the power of discriminating between those opinions which
are compatible with their religious beliefs and those which are not.
Immature youths may do harm to the flocks who may pass under
their ministerial care by superficial and inaccurate reproductions of
the views of their instructors; but they may do so in respect to the
most orthodox and conventional of instruction as well as to any other.
When so sincere a man and so profound a scholar as Robertson Smith
stated explicitly, as he did, that he did not consider either his method
of research or the results of it incompatible with his performance of
the duties of his chair at Aberdeen, that ought to have been sufficient
to exempt him from attack. This attack was made not on critical
grounds, but without knowledge as well as without any religious
feeling properly so called.

These reflections had passed through my mind as the controversy
proceeded, and they were confirmed by the final debate. They received
further confirmation by a curious incident which occurred immediately
afterwards. The debate did not close until after midnight. As I had
intended to return to Glasgow by the last train from Edinburgh, I had
not made any arrangements to spend the night. I walked over from
the Mound, where the Assembly Hall is situated, to the New Town,
and in St. David's Street (Hume's street, by the way) I noticed a
light in a small inn previously unknown to me, I think it was called
"The Ship." I went in and engaged a room. As I did not feel inclined
to retire at once, I went into a sitting-room and there found three or
four Highland elders, members of the Assembly, who were discussing
the debate over their pipes and steaming tumblers of whisky toddy.
I joined them in all three diversions. They belonged to the Highland
host, and they agreed in denouncing Robertson Smith. They clearly
knew nothing whatever of Robertson Smith's position or of the merits
of the controversy, yet they had had the impudence to assist in dis-
missing him from his chair. They said he was as bad as Voltaire,
that his opinions led to atheism, and so forth. Their vituperation

grew hotter and hotter as their glasses were frequently replenished.
I had not committed myself to any side of the controversy, and had
confined myself to drawing them out by means of questions. At last,
about half-past two in the morning, I had had enough of it; as I rose
to say good-night, I gave them my mind in a few sharp words. The
old fellows listened with open-mouthed amazement and I left them to
continue their carousal.

Immediately after his dismissal from the Free Church, Robertson
Smith was invited to Cambridge, where he became Lord Almoner's
Professor of Arabic. He also succeeded Spencer Baynes as editor of
the *Encyclopædia Britannica*. It was matter of deep regret to me that
I did not see Robertson Smith in later years; my visits to Cambridge
were generally made in vacation, while he was away. I used often to
hear of him, however, from mutual friends. He was on very intimate
terms with Prince Kropotkin, and different in many ways as were the
two men, there sprang up a deep mutual regard. Robertson Smith
was anxious to secure Kropotkin for Cambridge as Professor of Geography. Kropotkin told me that he did not care to compromise his
freedom by accepting such a position; but he felt very pleased that
Robertson Smith's friendship had prompted him to so generous a
project. Ridgeway [1] also had a great regard for Robertson Smith.
He told me that having written and sent to Smith some articles for
the *Britannica*, in which he expressed views of a novel character,
Smith had submitted the articles to five English scholars for their
opinion. They were unanimously against their publication on the
ground that they contained views antagonistic to those of Mommsen.
When reporting these expert opinions to Ridgeway, Smith told him that
precisely because the conclusions of his articles were antagonistic to
those of Mommsen, they should be printed as they stood. This incident
may also serve to illustrate the exaggerated importance which with
too great generosity and with deficient critical sagacity was at that
time attached by English scholars to German research.

Related to the religious life of Scotland, but removed equally from
the field of theology and from the field of politics, was the "revival"
movement promoted by the two American evangelists Moody and
Sankey. This movement took place in the early seventies. It was
countenanced by all the more evangelical clergy irrespective of
denomination, and it was effective in exciting a great deal of religious
emotion among people of every condition. Moody had been a merchant
who had been "converted," and on this account he felt himself called

[1] Sir William Ridgeway, Disney Professor of Archæology at Cambridge.

to "convert" others. Sankey had a fine if rather overworked tenor voice, and he brought into wide popularity many hymns of no great merit from any point of view. Moody's addresses were forcible appeals, but they were repellent on account of their crudity. Moody professed to expound the Scriptures in a commonsense manner, but it was evident that he knew nothing of exegesis and brought a wholly untrained mind to the task. It may be survival of influence from remote Catholic heredity, but I have always instinctively preferred professional to amateur interpretation of the Scriptures. The movement influenced a great number of enthusiastic young people and caused many of these to prepare for the ministry—a course they might not otherwise have adopted. After the weeding out of those who remained educationally or otherwise unfit, there were some who entered the ministries of the various churches. Apart from this effect, it is doubtful if the movement of Moody and Sankey had any real influence upon the religious life of the community. Moody and Sankey were speedily overwhelmed by the Salvation Army, by which appeal to emotion was made in an even more strident fashion.

Among the working population of Glasgow there was in the seventies a relatively small number who inherited from some of the groups of the twenties and thirties traditions hostile to revealed religion. This small group of "secularists" was as sincere in its propaganda against the churches as the evangelicals were against them. The prophets of this group were George Jacob Holyoake and Charles Bradlaugh. Holyoake I knew slightly. He had been an Owenite; but he fell out with Owen, apparently because both Owen and he desired to monopolise the platform. Holyoake was an early historian—somewhat uncritical, be it observed—of the Co-operative movement. In his later life he attacked the Christian religion with great fervour. He was a man of good character and of sharp wit. He knew something of science. I went once on a geological excursion with him in the Severn Valley and found that he really had some knowledge of geology. Holyoake was a good example of a polemic. Bradlaugh I often heard in his secularist addresses, although I never made his acquaintance. He was a man of immense force of character, and of invincible intellectual and moral probity; but he was not tolerant of opposition. It was his habit after lecturing to invite questions from his audience; but woe betide any rash person who ventured to put a question which implied criticism or contradiction of Bradlaugh's views. He fell upon such a critic like a thunderbolt.

Mrs. Besant used also to come to Glasgow in those days and to address the small "secularist" group upon the questions in which she was interested. She was an extremely persuasive speaker, although she had acquired, through her association with Bradlaugh, a certain stridency of manner. I became acquainted at that time with this remarkable woman. She had been refused admittance to the classes at University College when she presented herself along with the daughter of Bradlaugh. My friend Patrick Geddes, then assistant to Huxley, undertook to instruct both of the young women in botany and zoology. Mrs. Besant went up for examination in the London University and took honours in botany. Afterwards (in 1874) she began to lecture in connection with the National Secular Society and became co-editor with Bradlaugh of the *National Reformer*. She was undoubtedly at her best in the seventies. She had an aptitude for the study of science and she could lecture well on matters she understood. When she passed into the Socialist movement in the next decade she was on less sure ground, and still more was this the case when she passed into the Theosophical movement under the influence of Madame Blavatsky. Her external appearance altered with these changes in her interests. While she was in the "Secular" movement she dressed with exceeding plainness, but not in altogether good taste; when she became a Socialist, the plainness remained, improved in taste; and when she became a Theosophist she assumed, at the beginning of that stage of her career, an almost excessive splendour of adornment, of which the taste was at least doubtful. She was clearly a woman who needed, and at the same time resented, judicious guidance, while defective judgment led her to accept guidance which could not be fairly described as judicious.

Less positive in hostility to revealed religion than the Secular Society was the Unitarian Church, of which Dr. Crosskey, afterwards of Birmingham, and Page Hopps were the ministers. Dr. Crosskey was a man of high character and of no inconsiderable influence. He was free from the acerbity of some of his successors. I recall hearing in his church Moncure D. Conway lecture on Devil Worship—a subject which he had made his own. Many years afterwards I saw Dr. Conway in New York. He had been a friend of Emerson, and was a good representative of the Unitarianism of New England of the nineteenth century. The Sunday Society, which was formed for the purpose of organising concerts and lecture courses on Sunday evenings, had some vogue of a spasmodic character in the latter part of this decade. Good concerts were given occasionally, when the presence of a visiting orchestra rendered it possible to organise them. One Sunday, about

1880, the Hon. Roden Noel came to lecture on Byron. I saw a good deal of him and had some talk with him about Byron, of whom he said nothing which may not be gathered from his very interesting little monograph.[1] Noel was a pleasant, placid, simple-minded man.

Among those who represented liberal tendencies in Scots Presbyterianism in the seventies, Dr. Marcus Dods, of Renfield Street Free Church, was most conspicuous. He gave a series of lectures on Sunday mornings upon the Kings of Israel. Although these lectures might have more appropriately been delivered to a class of theological students, yet the fact that they were actually delivered to crowded congregations, many people being drawn from churches other than his own, was evidence not merely of Dods' skill as a lecturer but also of the wide interest in intellectual treatment of the Scriptures. The lectures were full of pungent psychological analysis. They were written carefully and read closely, and they were not to be followed without attention; they had undoubtedly a great influence upon those who heard them. Dods did not escape criticism from the narrow-minded who smelt heresy in so severely applied intelligence; but nothing came of an attempted attack.

Outside the Presbyterian churches, evidences of liberal views on religion were not wanting. Congregationalism, imported from England, had not taken any firm hold in Scotland; but the amiable personalities of the brothers Pulsford, one in Edinburgh and the other in Glasgow, represented a type of evangelicalism of a mild order, divested of positive Calvinism and suffused by geniality and poetry. One Sunday in the middle of the seventies I heard George Macdonald preach in William Pulsford's church. Macdonald then was a picturesque personality—quite unclerical in appearance and manner. He had a mass of black hair and a black Charles II. beard. The impression made upon my mind by his sermon was not very favourable. He seemed to me witty but shallow. His novels, however, are good, *Robert Falconer*, *David Elginbrod* and *Sir Gibbie* are first-rate stories, and some of his verses have fairly high poetical qualities. He spent his later years in Bordighera and dropped out of sight of people in England.

During this decade spectacular football emerged as a distinct social phenomenon. Cricket had been played by the Scots youth, but somehow they did not excel in it. "Rounders," the predecessor of American baseball, afforded more active exercise than cricket, and became popular in the sixties and seventies. But none of these games attracted crowds of spectators. They were not sufficiently vivacious

[1] *Life of Lord Byron*, London, 1890.

or sufficiently dangerous to excite the public. Some of the engineering and shipbuilding apprentices and young journeymen in Glasgow and in the Vale of Leven at Dumbarton threw themselves with great energy into football, and developed a special technique in marshalling their forces in the game. The consequences were the formation of numerous football clubs, acute rivalry among these, increasing crowds of spectators, exploitation of the game by means of gate-money, and the gradual transformation of it from a healthy athletic exercise by amateurs to a spectacular contest between professional teams directed by professional captains, by whom the tactics of the game were further developed. Among the professional football players and their critics in the newspapers a new language made its appearance. The journals gave increasing space to sport of all kinds, especially to football, and the leisure of the working population came to be largely devoted to witnessing contests in which an insignificant number took any part, excepting as spectators.

In 1873 or 74 I resumed my interest in chess, and in one or other of these years I joined the Glasgow Chess Club. About the same time Zukertort came to Glasgow to play a series of simultaneous blindfold games, and I was asked to call out the moves for him. I think he played twenty-two boards. It was a very marvellous performance. One of the players challenged one of Zukertort's moves. The player had in defiance of all rules been moving about the pieces on his board. Zukertort was not in the least disturbed by the challenge. He repeated the game from the beginning, and then gave the position as it should be. It is needless to say that he was indisputably right and the seeing player wrong.

Within this decade also I became acquainted with Blackburne, with Captain MacKenzie, the celebrated American chess player, and more importantly, with Steinitz, with whom I remained on friendly terms until his death. Steinitz was undoubtedly the greatest chess master of his time, and perhaps of any time. He did not distinguish himself beyond the field of chess, but he had other interests. He had either invented or somehow become involved in an invention in marine engineering. This invention consisted in some alleged improvement in the screw-propeller. I got him some information that he wanted from some of my shipbuilding friends, but I do not think his project came to anything. Much more interesting were his philosophical views which he propounded on various occasions. Curiously enough, he regarded his achievements in chess with great modesty; but he really prided himself upon his powers as a philosopher. I cannot say, however, that there was anything original in his philosophy. So far as I could form a judgment, he was a Spinozist. Among his less well-known writings is a little pamphlet called *The Economies of Chess*, in which he shows for the benefit of the intending chess professional that chess does not pay. This pamphlet promulgates the thesis which he once developed to me *viva voce*: "Here am I," he said, "the most successful chess professional of my time, winner of the most important prizes in chess matches and editor of the most important and re-munerative chess column" (he edited the chess column of *The Field*), "and yet, on the average, I have not received more than the wages of an artisan." Sometimes, in the eighties, I used to play with Bird at Simpson's Divan in the Strand, and occasionally Steinitz used to look on and make caustic comments on the game.

Of the intimate friends of this period, none held a greater share in my affections than Gerald George Challice.[1] Although he wrote none but fugitive pieces, he had a decided poetic gift and keen critical talent. He translated into vigorous English some of the graceful and fiercely propagandist verse of Louise Ackermann as well as some of the poems of Baudelaire.

Among my most loyal and devoted friends also was Donald Cameron, a Highlander from Appin. Cameron was a civil engineer. He afterwards became City Engineer of Exeter, and later went to Vancouver. From Vancouver he sent six sons to the war; one of these was killed in one of the engagements in Flanders.

---

[1] Captain G. G. Challice was at this time (1880) an officer in the Glasgow garrison. He afterwards went to Egypt, and after the Egyptian War to Mauritius. He retired as lieutenant-colonel, and died at Algiers in 1922.

CHAPTER VI

A PRESBYTERIAN JOB

> D'ye mind that day, when in a bizz,
> Wi' reekit duds, an' reestit gizz,
> Ye did present your smoutie phiz
>   'Mang better folk,
> An' sklented on the *man of Uzz,*
>   Your spitefu' joke?
>
>   ROBERT BURNS, *Address to the Deil* (1786).

THE Scots, at least from the time of John Knox, have been shrewd theologians. They have, moreover, usually mingled their theology with common-sense, and have a peculiar affection for those passages of Scripture in which this quality is most conspicuous. The Westminster Confession is the universal *credo* to which appeal may be made. There are many Scots sects, but these are divided rather on questions of Church government than on questions of theology. The divisions of the early nineteenth century—the Auld Licht Burghers and the New Licht Burghers, the Auld Licht Anti-Burghers and the New Licht Anti-Burghers—still subsist under other names, but the divisions are not based on fundamental theological questions, they are all either on questions relating to the interior administration of the Church, or to its relation to the State. If, in an extreme example, a minister elects to pass from the Free to the Established Church, he need change no part of his creed, he need only change his attitude towards the "civil magistrate."

One of the friends of my youth was a certain Rev. Peter M———. He was a most worthy man, full of the inner light of the Spirit, but rather lacking in intellectual force as well as in the social graces. Nature had clearly designed him for tillage, but instruction and ambition made him a "probationer."[1] After a long struggle in this ambiguous rôle, in which a man is neither lay nor cleric, the Rev. Peter achieved a church. The church was in a mining district; but neither the mines nor the church experienced the benefits of war prices for coal, and both remained in a depressed condition. I remember

---

[1] A probationer is licensed by the Presbytery to preach; but he does not have charge of a congregation until he is "called" to one and "inducted."

hearing the Rev. Peter discourse to a slender congregation under the dismal influence of candle-light, for the church was not equipped with the convenience of gas although that illuminant had been invented about seventy years before by an intelligent gentleman called Murdoch at no great distance from the site of the church. The worthy Peter had done his utmost to keep the "ordinances" going; he had remained a bachelor; he had lived on an income less than the minimum of the "sustentation fund."[1] He had struggled hard, without success, to get his charge placed upon it. He had even given of his own slender means to keep his church going. These circumstances rendered it necessary for him to economise beyond the dreams of a Food Controller. For weeks at a time he lived upon "crowdy." I do not suppose that many persons in this luxurious age know what "crowdy" is. I may therefore explain that when a Scotsman is very poor he lives, or lived, exclusively upon porridge; but the making of porridge, or even of "brose,"[2] requires fuel. In every deep there is lower depth. A Scotsman without meal is a dead Scotsman; but if he has meal and cold water he can live without fuel, because he can mingle his meal and cold water, and thus make "crowdy." Such a diet, if not varied, is nourishing. Peter adopted it; and he not merely subsisted on it, he wrote poetry, not about it, but on it. While he was thus gallantly mortifying the flesh, for Peter loved good cheer as much as anybody, he read to me long passages from an epic in the style of *Paradise Lost*. So far as I recall, Peter avoided direct competition with Milton by passing lightly over "man's first disobedience" and really began his epic by plunging into the Flood. His knowledge of human nature, especially on its sordid ecclesiastical side, was of great assistance to him in understanding the kings and prophets of Israel when he came to deal with them, and the vituperative dialectic of which he was a really masterly exponent in the Presbytery at its monthly meetings enabled him to explain to others, either in his poem or in his pulpit, the shortcomings even of the saints. For years I retained in my mind some of the lines of Peter's epic. I doubt if they would readily be accepted as poetry even by a very partial literary judgment. These lines have, however, wholly faded from my memory, and I fear that the poem, as a whole, has crumbled into dust unless the manuscript has been preserved as an heirloom by some of Peter's kindred.

[1] The "sustentation fund" is accumulated by general collections, gifts and bequests, and the income of it is divided among those charges which are on its list. Many of the newer and smaller charges derive no benefit from it. There is, therefore, on their part often a struggle to be placed on this list.

[2] Porridge is boiled meal; "brose" is meal upon which hot water is poured.

In the course of time, the Rev. Peter left his mining charge in the suburbs and came into town, where a brand-new church raised by Peter's self-sacrificing devotion seemed to crown his patient career. I went to the inaugural service of this edifice with a distant relative who admired Peter's pluck and had given him a good subscription. Unfortunately, neither sound theology nor poetic temperament nor capacity of living on "crowdy" availed; the town public did not appreciate Peter, and even "crowdy," the irreducible minimum of subsistence, became difficult to procure.

Probably Peter's want of success and his descent from temporary eminence were facilitated by the hostility of members of his Presbytery who somehow were not among his admirers. Peter had certainly a provoking way with him. Secure in his capacity of living upon "crowdy," while his opponents probably drew the line at "minced meat," he protested against everything in which he did not believe, no matter how injurious his protests might be to his material interests. These material interests were so small that they could not be diminished without extinction. Eventually Peter protested too much, and extinction came. Even "crowdy" was impossible to obtain. Peter did not believe in the maxim of Voltaire, whose very name was anathema to him, "Il n'y a pas d'homme nécessaire." On the contrary, Peter knew that in a corrupt age *he* was the necessary man. In other words, the instinct of self-preservation asserted itself. He could not dig, to beg he was ashamed, and so he resolved to go over to the Establishment. In thus resolving, Peter did no violence to any article of his faith, he merely abjured an opinion which he found untenable, viz., that the "civil magistrate" is not the head of the Church. He came to realise that the Church was, in one of its aspects, a group of professional persons whose maintenance was necessary in the general scheme of social things, and therefore that maintenance came within the duty of the "civil magistrate."

The Established Church of Scotland was at that time somewhat in a decline. The popular preachers were either Frees or United Presbyterians. The theologians were all Frees, as were also most of the heretics, of whom there were not many. The Rev. Peter, though not an intellectual figure, was nevertheless a theologian. From the point of view of ecclesiastical politics, it might have been well to have kept Peter as a distracting influence within the fold of the Free Church, so that he might continue to be a thorn in the side of his Presbytery and an example of the manner in which the "voluntary system," in spite of the repudiation of it by the Free Church, worked out in practice. The Established Church did not, however, adopt this narrow point of view, it opened its arms and took in Peter.

When he assumed the duties of his new office, Peter, for the first time in his life of hardship and sacrifice, had an assured income sufficient for the slender needs to which he had habituated himself. It is not surprising, but greatly to his credit that, having been starved out of one Church and warmly welcomed by another, he should have chosen as the text of his inaugural sermon, "And Peter stood with them, and warmed himself." [1]

[1] St. John xviii. 18.

CHAPTER VII

HOLIDAYING IN SCOTLAND IN THE SEVENTIES

> Nay seek them not, the old belovèd haunts;
> The loch, the islets, and the little boat
> Against whose prow the spray in sprinkling fonts
> Flung forth at every dip a rippled note.
> Find not the yellow sands that like a topaz lay
>   Within the bay
> Sun shimmering; nor tread the ribboned line
> Of velvet turf from the shore's incline
>   Old Time had beat
> Through waving bracken, gold-gowned woodbine.
> 'Tis not for you these store their rich acclaims,
> For you they would but speak some scattered names,
>   Enhanced, sweet.
>
> KATHERINE MANN, "Ode to the Olden Days,"
>   in *Stray Stanzas* (1907).

No city, even London or Paris, approaches the city of Glasgow in its relation to surroundings of natural beauty. On every side save one, near and far, there stretch systems of hills, valleys, rivers and lochs, and in the farther but still no great distance there is the incomparable archipelago of the West Highlands. The one side upon which scenery is deficient is the eastern side between Glasgow and Edinburgh, and between Hamilton and Kirkintilloch. The broad belt of iron and coal forming the mineral reserve from which Scotland has drawn the means of her industrial development and the deposits of millstone grit from which fireclay is manufactured occupies this region, whose importance lies underground rather than on the surface. In every other direction within a few minutes' walk of the municipal boundaries natural beauty of great variety abounds. The city lies on the carboniferous limestone series. In the north there are the Campsie Hills, a mass of stratified trap separated by a great "fault" from the sandstone and conglomerate of the South Hill.[1] Within the Campsie Hills are Ballagan Glen and the cleft of jagged trap known as the Whangie. Farther north than the igneous rocks there lies the

---

[1] For descriptions of the geology of the Clyde Valley, see the writings of two old friends of mine, Prof. John Young, *Geology of the Clyde Valley* and *Physical Geography*, and Dugald Bell, *Among the Rocks round Glasgow*, Glasgow, 1881.

Lower Old Red Sandstone embracing the upper valley of the Forth and its tributary streams; and westwards and north-westwards there lie the schists and slates of the Lower Silurian rising to the round head and shoulders of Ben Lomond, and scooped out in the deep depressions of Loch Lomond, the Gare Loch, Loch Long and Loch Goil. A good walker in a single day can march across the deposits of the most distant geological ages. The roads throughout the region are excellent, but many of the finest points from which the landscape may be observed can be reached only by bypaths on foot. It is thus, or used to be, a practice of Glasgow youths to take long walks, especially on Saturday afternoons, sometimes taking the railway to the outskirts of the city, and then plunging into the scenery. Even before the "Access to Mountains Act" was passed through the persistence of Mr. Bryce (afterwards Lord Bryce), who was himself an ardent walker and climber, the proprietors in the neighbourhood of Glasgow were not intolerant of peaceful pedestrians, especially in proportion as their estates were distant from the city and therefore less frequented by numbers. As for myself, I was accustomed to develop the walk into something like an expedition. During the whole of the decade of which I am speaking and during the succeeding decade it was my habit, when I felt inclined or had opportunity, to start from Glasgow about five o'clock on Friday afternoon, walk for a good part of the summer night, put up somewhere in the country, walk part of the next day and return by train to Glasgow in the evening. On such an occasion I walked from Glasgow to Callander *via* Strathblane, Aberfoyle, and the Lake of Menteith. About midnight, the sky became overcast and the darkness so intense that it was impossible to see the road. The night was absolutely still, there was no sound but my own footfall. I had walked at a good pace, and become rather thirsty. I listened for the trickle of water from some stream where I might refresh myself. On such night journeys I carried a candle, a means of illumination not so heavy as a pocket lantern, for impedimenta had to be cut down to the lowest limit. At last I heard a trickle in a field on the roadside. I went to it, found what I wanted and returned to the road, extinguishing my candle. As I did so, I heard a footfall warily making its way on the other side of the road. I called out that there was no need to be frightened, and a cheerful answer came from the darkness. From the voice I deduced a young man, and although we could not see one another we found we were going in the same direction. We were at the time somewhere between Water of Endrick and Flanders Moss. The young man turned out to be an engineer who was going to visit his parents in the village of Gartmore. I had not intended to go by this village, but to keep to the main road to Aberfoyle, where I expected to arrive about two o'clock in the morning, and to find accommodation in the well-known hostelry where Bailie Nicol Jarvie set the Highlander's kilt on fire with a red-hot "coulter." When we came to the point where the road to Gartmore branches off, my unseen friend persuaded me to go with him to Gartmore and to accept his hospitality. We arrived at the village about one o'clock. His parents, worthy folk, expected him and received me with cordiality. Gartmore is perhaps the steepest village in Scotland. The village street is simply an uncovered slope of Old Red Sandstone. Gartmore House, the only feature of the place, is the ancestral home of my good friend Cunninghame Graham, most delicious of essayists and one of the bravest and quaintest of men. At that time Cunninghame Graham was acting as cowboy on the pampas of South America. In the forenoon I walked to Aberfoyle, and then over the hills through the pass of Aberfoyle past the sombre woods and waters of the Lake of Menteith to Callander.

It is best on the whole to walk alone; companionship can be easily had if it is wanted, and when it has ceased to be companionship it can be shed. A journey undertaken with another is like marriage, it must, unless there is positive rupture, which is disagreeable, continue to the end.

I did not, however, always walk alone. On two long excursions I had a congenial friend. We left Glasgow one afternoon by train to Killin. There we dined, and then about eight o'clock on a fine summer evening we set off to tramp over the shoulder of Ben Lawers into Glen Lyon. It is alleged that Killin should properly be Kil-Fin, for in the village there is a stone which tradition says marks the burial-place of Fingal, the hero of the verse of *Ossian*:

Fingal shall be clothed with fame, a beam of light to other times; for he went forth, with echoing steel, to save the weak in arms.[1]

For some miles the road passes along the shore of Loch Tay, and then at Edramuckie we climbed up on the moor, traversed the high pass and dropped down to Glen Lyon sometime after midnight, for we took our journey in leisurely fashion. Indeed, the dawn was almost breaking when we roused up the minister of Ard, who was a cousin of my companion, and quartered ourselves upon him.

Glen Lyon is the longest and in many ways the finest glen in Scotland. The mountains which tower above it are from 2000 to

[1] Macpherson's *Ossian* (London, 1825), p. 439.

4000 feet high. In its upper reaches it is very narrow, but in many places it becomes a broad valley. There is one loch in the upper part of it, and there are evidences of former lochs at various parts of its course. The lower glen towards Fortingal is justly celebrated for its extreme beauty. There are legends that at one time the glen was occupied by a large population, but there is no record of this having been the case within historical times. The glen stretches from the highlands of Appin in Argyllshire almost to the exit from the High-lands to the Lowlands of Scotland. There are passes at both ends of it. Thus, like all such regions, it must have been the scene of conflicts between Highland and Lowland tribes from remote ages. Fingal is described in a Gaelic couplet [1] as having had twelve castles in the glen, and there are traditions of many battles having been fought in it. A ruin was pointed out to us as the site of a monastery, but·I have been unable to find any confirmation of this attribution. It is probable that the glen may have been denuded of its population at a very early period, for one of the numerous names which have been attached to it in past times is the Deserted Glen.[2]

When we had rested we walked on to Fortingal, where we saw the famous yew-tree which is reputed to be a thousand years old. This corner of Perthshire is the south-eastern limit of the ancient Caledonian Forest, and there still remain in some parts of it many trees of great age. At Taymouth Castle, near Kenmore, there used to be a herd of the white cattle, early denizens of the forest. In the afternoon we walked to Aberfeldy, and then went by train to Glasgow, having been absent only twenty-four hours.

The most extensive of these early journeys was a walk of fifty-four miles in less than eighteen hours, from Dunoon on the Clyde to Connel Ferry on Loch Etive. This famous tramp was accomplished with my friend of the Glen Lyon pilgrimage.[3] We left Dunoon at ten o'clock in the forenoon, and walked by Loch Eck to St. Catherine's on Loch Fyne, where we ferried across to Inverary. In the afternoon we traversed the moor to Port Sonachan, where we dined sumptuously in the excellent hotel, then ferried across Loch Awe and started on our long tramp to Taynuilt. This night walk was wonderful; when we

[1] Quoted in *The Statistical Account of Perthshire* (Edinburgh, 1842), p. 530.
[2] One of the dark shadows of Scottish history lies over Glen Lyon, for it was Captain Campbell of Glen Lyon who was the instrument by which the massacre of Glencoe was carried out. See H. G. Graham in *Scottish History and Life*, edited by James Paton (Glasgow, 1902), p. 130.
[3] Now James R. MacColl, President of the Lorraine Manufacturing Co., Pawtucket, Rhode Island, U.S.A.

emerged from the moor and reached the valley of the Awe, we plunged into dense woods, and the fitful flare of the glow-worm was the only light we saw. We reached Taynuilt about eleven; but we had made up our minds to push on to Oban, which lay about thirteen miles beyond, and therefore we left Taynuilt and its inn behind us after supping. But we were rather spent, and our progress in the darkness was slow. We felt uncertain about the distance which separated us from Oban, refreshment and rest. We saw a light in a cottage, and thinking that someone was awake at that early hour for some reason, we knocked. The door was opened by a Highlander who had evidently just risen. We asked lamely for a drink of milk. This simple and very natural request seemed to act like a blow in the face to the gentleman, who upbraided us sharply for disturbing his rest on so trivial a matter. We apologised and left him to his slumbers, conceiving that he really was under no obligation to be hospitable to strangers in the middle of the night. We continued to tramp on in the darkness and silence. Suddenly I became conscious of a strange musical murmur in the distance. Then I knew precisely where we were. I had never been there before, but I remembered "the murmuring stream of Lora" in *Ossian* [1] and felt certain that this was what we heard. As we advanced the murmur became more distinct until we stood beside the so-called Falls of Lora. This phenomenon is produced by the tide flowing into and out of Loch Etive, an arm of the sea, over a bar which stretches across the narrows at Connel Ferry. The pebbles on this bar, being moved by the incoming or outgoing waters, produce the murmur. We were rejoiced to know exactly where we were, but we were too spent after our fifty-four mile tramp to go farther. We therefore decided to arouse the innkeeper at the "Ferry Inn," and put up there for the rest of the night. Day was just beginning to break. The innkeeper was sleepy and reluctant, but persistent applications of our sticks to his door, and threats of the pains and penalties of the law, which in Scotland in such matters is wholly on the side of the traveller, brought him at last, and caused him to say:

"Ye'll be no shentlemans, or ye would na be walkin' at this time in the mornin'."

We told him that gentlemen walked when and where they found it convenient, and that *his* exclusive business at that moment was to fetch us a bottle of port and three glasses, with some whisky for himself if he wanted it, and then to prepare beds for us without delay.

---

[1] Lora is frequently mentioned in *Ossian* as the "murmuring stream," the "echoing stream," the "gliding stream," etc.

To these indications of habit to command he capitulated and made us very comfortable, putting everything in the house at our disposal, and even sitting up with us for a while listening to the tale of our adventures. In the morning we took the train to Oban, and the steamer up the Sound of Mull to Tobermory. On the steamer we ran across Professor John Stuart Blackie, who was striding up and down the deck with his grey plaid over his shoulder, as was his custom. We joined him in his stride, and he expounded to us his interpretation of the meaning of every place-name in the region. Gaelic, of which I know nothing, must be a language with a meagre vocabulary, for one word seems to do the duty for which, in other languages, half a dozen may be employed. This circumstance gives a large range of choice of interpretation, and of this the Gaelic scholars seem to avail themselves. Two of them rarely agree upon the meaning of almost any word, and they seem thus to exist in a region of surmise and controversy. This feature of the language is not without significance. The Celt probably never knew his own mind, and therefore spoke as he thought, vaguely and without attaching precise and invariable meaning to the words he employed. He is consistent only in demanding extension of poetic licence.

Professor Blackie had Highland blood in his veins, no doubt, but he was a Lowlander. Nevertheless, for many years he was the chief protagonist in Scotland of the Celtic Revival. At the time I speak of (1878 or 1879) he was in his seventieth year, still in the active discharge of the duties of the Chair of Greek in the University of Edinburgh, and urging with all his vigour the establishment of a Celtic Chair in the same University. The chair was founded in 1882, and thus the Celtic Revival in Scotland [1] antedated the similar revival in Ireland, which did not come into being until nearly twenty years later. The Celtic Revival in Scotland was purely literary and artistic. It had no political bearing. In Ireland, the revival has been, so to say, adulterated with politics and religion. Blackie was a copious and amusing talker. As he walked up and down the deck of the steamer in the Sound of Mull, he stopped frequently to re-enforce his sometimes extravagant and already emphatic phrases by thumping me on the back, on the principle, I suppose, of the "whipping-post." Blackie was not merely versatile and entertaining, he had a great fund of good-nature and common-sense as well as not

[1] There was, of course, the earlier revival initiated by the publication of Macpherson's *Ossian* (1761–63). The modern revival of interest in Celtic literature may be said to date from Renan's *La poésie des races celtiques*, followed by Matthew Arnold's *Essays on the Study of Celtic Literature*, 1870.

a little moral energy. Blackie left us at Loch Aline, and we went on to Tobermory. After spending a few days there, in which we boasted about our walking exploit, only to find that there was an old woman in Tobermory who thought nothing of trudging *sixty* miles a day, we went on to Staffa and Iona. This excursion is so much within the ordinary route of the tourist that I need not detail our experiences.

Upon other long walks in Renfrewshire, Lanarkshire, Stirlingshire, Perthshire and Argyllshire, and particularly in Bute and Arran, I need not dwell. Sometimes, as may be surmised, it rained as it can rain in the west of Scotland. Once I remember walking through a heavy shower from Inversnaid to Callander through the Trossachs, in adhering mud up to the ankles or higher; but youth is reckless of these trifles. Somewhere between Inversnaid and Stronachlachar, in spite of the moisture without, I felt intolerably thirsty within, and noticing a cottage at no great distance from the road, I approached the open door, and as I did so there came and stood placidly in it a woman of austere and matronly beauty. I asked for a glass of milk. She brought and gave it me with so mature and gracious ease that I regretted the lapse of time and the change in convention that prevented me from swinging my hat in a wide curve and bowing low after the manner of the Middle Age. Had I acted instinctively and disregarded the anachronism, she would have thought quite as instinctively that I was trying to make a fool of her. I therefore thanked her in a commonplace and clumsily offered payment for my refreshment. This she waved aside with a superb gesture, and I tramped on humiliated as though I had been guilty of gaucherie in the palace of a princess.

Of one holiday of this time, I think it was in 1872, I may give some details because it involved fresh experiences. This holiday was spent with a farmer on the estate of Mr. Malcolm of Poltalloch, near Lochgilphead on Loch Fyne. The Crinan Canal, which connects the loch system of the Firth of Clyde directly with the sea and saves the long detour round the Mull of Cantire, passes near by. The farming of the district is concerned chiefly with cattle and sheep raising. The cattle are for the most part the native Highland stock—small, shaggy, hardy animals, very shy and wild. The sheep are partly of native breed and partly of imported stocks. The less hardy sheep are sent as "hoggs," or one-year-olds, to Ayrshire for the winter, in order to avoid undue loss from the severity of the climate. The farms are sometimes of vast extent. One farmer whom I visited on one of the long drives I took while I was there, had a large tract on the shores of Loch Awe, and had, moreover, several islands. He had a fleet of boats for the purpose of conveying his sheep to and from the island pastures. About 30,000 sheep formed at that time his usual flock. The farmer with whom I stayed had a very large herd of Highland cattle, how many I do not now remember. His farm was called Kilbride, from a chapel dedicated to St. Bride in the neighbourhood. Near it is Carnassary Castle, at one time an important stronghold because it guarded one of the principal passes into Argyleshire. There is a legend to the effect that after a long and unsuccessful siege the fortress was captured through the treachery of a woman, who opened a gate by which the enemy entered. I went with my farmer host to a farm on the east side of Loch Awe, a drive of about twenty-five miles, to buy sheep. We started early and arrived at our destination before noon. Our reception was so characteristic of the place and the people that I must give it in detail. The farm was of moderate size; the farmer was in comfortable circumstances, but had not an extensive flock. On our arrival we were shown into the parlour, and the farmer's wife immediately placed upon the table a bottle of whisky with a number of sherry glasses. Water was conspicuous by its absence. There was a service of whisky all round. Then we went out to look at the sheep, which had been brought into a fold for the purpose of inspection. My farmer spent about half an hour looking them over; then we returned to the house. There was another application of neat whisky, and another and another. Then we went out again and looked over the sheep once more, then we returned for lunch. This meal was quite substantial, accompanied, of course, by more whisky, and also by tea. Then we looked at some more sheep, and afterwards had more whisky. Late in the afternoon we turned our faces homewards. My farmer was about sixty years of age, a sturdy and well-preserved man. Our way had some difficult bits in it, steep hills and sharp turnings; but in spite of the very considerable amount of potent spirit he had imbibed, he took them all without a tremor. I came to the conclusion that there must be definite compensatory affinity between Highland whisky and Highland atmosphere.

On the farm where I was staying there were several crofters' cottages with minute lots of land, upon which garden produce was grown by the occupants. The crofter question had assumed at that time an acute form, but it varied in different places. Here the crofters were employed on the farm, and there was no difficulty, excepting that of immobility, in so far as that might be regarded as undesirable.

There were many interesting and some notable personalities in the district. There was, for example, Sir John Orde of Kilmory. He was a man of eccentric character. I saw him frequently driving about in a peculiar conveyance. It was a kind of glorified baker's van. He drove this waggon himself, and as he disapproved of a dashboard and disliked either to dock the tails of his horses or to permit them to be swished about to keep off the flies or for equine enjoyment, he had them plaited into white manilla rope and lashed to the whipple-tree. Sir John had been a sailor and liked to have everything taut and trim. I drove more than once down a steep and narrow pass between the hills which my driver told me was celebrated as the scene of an encounter between Sir John and a party of tinkers.[1] When two vehicles meet at this place, it is necessary for one of them to draw close to the cliff on one side in order to allow the other to pass. Sir John ordered the tinkers to draw their cart to the side. They refused, and with his customary acerbity he proceeded to emphasise his orders with his whip. But the tinkers were free roadfarers who looked with contempt upon Gringo dignitaries. They had their weapons ready to their hands and they pelted him with tins, drew his horses to the side, retrieved the ammunition, and left him in possession of the field in which he had been defeated. I was told a story of a similar encounter which Sir John had with Malcolm of Poltalloch, grandfather of the present Lord Malcolm, on a similar occasion, with similar consequences for him. In spite of the violence of his temper, Sir John was liked in the district because of his joviality when he had a mind to be jovial.

I need not detail others of my longer holidays in these years of the seventies, at Blairgowrie, for example, which I happened to visit in 1871, at a time when the town was stirred by preparations for the celebration of the hundredth anniversary of the birth of Sir Walter Scott; from there I drove to Meigle where I saw the ancient monuments, then rather ill cared for, but now I believe properly housed, and to Glamis Castle, one of the finest French châteaux in Scotland. Tradition says that in the older castle Malcolm II. was murdered.

One holiday we spent at Alloway in Ayrshire, the birthplace of Burns. We rented the cottage next to Burns's, and took long walks and drives through the whole of the Burns country, visiting the fine woods round Loch Doon and every other beautiful place within reach. We used often to go at night to the ruined Kirk of Alloway, but perhaps, owing to inadequate preparation, we failed to see what Tam O'Shanter

[1] In Scotland gypsies are known as tinkers. They often practise the trade of making and mending tin cans.

saw. Another holiday we spent at Tarbert on Loch Fyne, where we climbed the hills and wandered in the woods of Barmore, and where I used to go out with the fishermen at night, see the whales blowing slender phosphorescent columns as they pursued the "schools" of herring, watch the fishermen trawling in the shallow bays, until the boats were full to the gunwales, and arrive at the quay at five o'clock in the morning covered with scales. I need not detail week-ends during the year at Dunoon, where the surf in the south-west gales is magnificent, or at Skelmorlie in the summer, where the rhododendrons bloom as nowhere else in the world, or at Rothesay, or the Kyles of Bute, or the Holy Loch, or Loch Lomond. The tourist sees little of these lovely places as he rushes past by swift steamer. Their full enchantment can only be absorbed by frequency and leisure; and this enchantment is incommunicable. The impossibility of conveying such a feeling is expressed in the charming little poem by the late Miss Kitty Mann which is placed at the head of this chapter. The same beloved haunts, the boat and the islets were very familiar to me in older days.

CHAPTER VIII

DISRAELI: WITH NOTES ON HIS EARLY LIFE

Who would true valour see
Let him come hither!
One here will constant be,
Come wind, come weather:
There's no discouragement
Shall make him once relent
His first-avow'd intent
To be a Pilgrim.

Whoso beset him round
With dismal stories,
Do but themselves confound;
His strength the more is.
No lion can him fright;
He'll with a giant fight;
But he will have a right
To be a Pilgrim.

JOHN BUNYAN.

THE wave of Liberalism, which had carried Gladstone into power in 1868, had spent itself by 1874. Notwithstanding the great expansion of trade during the six years of Liberal administration, for which expansion the Liberals claimed an amount of credit to which they can scarcely be regarded as entitled, the conservative working man made himself felt at the polls for the first time. He may have been exhibiting a belated gratitude to the Tories for the extension of the franchise in 1866, or he may have disliked Gladstone's bid for the middle-class vote by the promise to abolish income tax, or he may have been dazzled by the mysterious dreams of empire which Disraeli interpreted for him. Whatever was his motive he sent the Conservatives to Downing Street, with Disraeli at their head.

As from the death of Palmerston until 1874 the most important figure in the public life of England was Gladstone, so between 1874 and 1880 the most important figure in the same field was Disraeli. Indeed, with the possible exception of Bismarck, he was the most important political figure in Europe, not merely because he was Prime Minister, but because of his ascendancy over men, and because he gave the political activities of Great Britain a direction determined largely by his personal political ideas.

Disraeli was elected Lord Rector of the University of Glasgow in 1874. He did not deliver his Rectorial Address for nearly two years after his election. For some reason I was unable to be present when he gave his Rectorial Address; but immediately before its delivery I saw him. It is difficult to set down in cold words the impression of that singular figure. His face was deadly pale, a black lock almost detaching itself from his hair came sharply over his brow. His eyes were penetrative and sparkling with intelligence. Clearly he knew what he was about; he was not given to dreaming of mysterious things. His nose was large, but not obviously Hebraic. His upper lip was as if it were chiselled in marble; his lower lip in its mobility suggested a trace of self-consciousness, as if he were aware that he might be suspected of posing. His gait was easy and not in the least infirm. His whole aspect suggested that he might have sinister impulses, but habitually kept himself in leash and controlled them. He might have been taken for a magician, the more easily in his mediæval costume as Lord Rector, a long gown, heavily embroidered with gold lace, and he might have been credited with knowing and practising the Black Art. He looked as if he might have been in Hell, and successful in escaping unscorched and undismayed. He looked as if he might have been in Heaven, and able to endure the evaporation of some of his illusions. In short, he was a figure giving the impression of austere and commanding power—not without moral sense and moral direction, but with intelligence predominating.

Froude lays emphasis upon what he calls Disraeli's extraordinary "cleverness"; but cleverness is too feeble a word. Disraeli's intellect was not disciplined in the academical sense, but it was, nevertheless, an important, if not a great intellect, which such training might have spoilt. The course of his life showed that he had, and desired to have, mastery over men, rather than sympathy with them. We cannot suppose that those over whom he exercised ascendancy were all ineffectual and unintelligent persons; indeed, many of them were precisely otherwise. The influence he exercised over men of great ability, Lord Salisbury for example, implied an unusually powerful intellect on his own part. A merely clever man might have done many of the things done by Disraeli; clever men did them, and did some of them better than he; but only a man of real genius would have done all the things Disraeli did, or could have had the temerity to think he could do them.

The rise of Disraeli to high political position in England began in a period long antedating these memoirs. In general, I have refrained from repeating stories which have come to me at second-hand. It seems expedient to depart from this rule in order to give some details of the early life of Disraeli which appear to me to throw light upon the actual process by means of which Disraeli stormed a fortress regarded as impregnable, and obtained in it not only a footing, but a mastery. This fortress was the political power, held for nearly two centuries by one or other of two not very numerous groups, each very jealous of intrusion into its ranks by anyone who was not entitled to admission by birth, by fortune, or by brilliant ability shown at the public schools, and at Oxford or Cambridge. Disraeli was not only lacking in all of these qualifications, but he belonged to a race which on the ground of its traditional faith had been excluded from Parliament. Yet he succeeded in surmounting the enormous difficulties by which his pilgrimage was beset at the beginning of his career. The first steps were necessarily by far the most arduous. Whether or not the incidents I am about to relate were known to the biographers of Disraeli I am not aware. They may have been considered as too trivial for detailed narration. I do not take this view. It is impossible for me to vouch for the accuracy of the narrative. I can only tell it as it was told me, omitting merely those details which are well known. Circumstances have not favoured my making researches which might have led to confirmation or rejection of some parts of the narrative.

About 1888, my friend Sir David MacVail [1] told me that some years earlier he had met, at the town of Alnwick in Northumberland, a lady who had been an early friend and confidante of Lady Beaconsfield. I suppose that he must have mentioned the name of this lady; if he did, her name has not remained in my memory.

The story begins with the menage of Mr. and Mrs. Wyndham Lewis. They made their living by means of a haberdashery shop in the East End of London, and they lived in the premises behind the shop. Their income was no more than sufficient for simple needs. One morning Mr. Lewis received a letter from a solicitor informing him that if he would be good enough to call upon him, he would learn something to his advantage. Mr. Lewis lost no time, and discovered that the "something to his advantage" was a legacy from an uncle, who had bequeathed his fortune to him. When the estate was finally realised, it was found to consist of about £80,000 and the singular asset

---

[1] Physician in Glasgow and member of the General Medical Council. He died in 1917.

I—G

of four hundred feather beds, which were not immediately saleable. In what manner and for what reason the deceased uncle had accumulated so luxurious a domestic equipment does not appear; but it may be surmised. Mrs. Lewis was a sprightly person, whose attendance at the haberdashery counter was an affliction to be endured rather than the occupation of her choice, and she naturally proposed that her husband should retire from retail commerce, and with his fortune in his hands, devote himself to other pursuits. Mr. and Mrs. Lewis were not experienced in the ways of any other than their own small world, and since they—or rather she—aspired to pass beyond it, she resolved to seek counsel from someone who possessed a wider experience than their own. Mrs. Lewis sought this counsel from a lady who had been a school-fellow of hers, and who had been fortunate enough to acquire some touch with the great world. There was no doubt in Mrs. Lewis's mind about what she wanted. She wanted to enter the great world herself in order at least to see what it was like. She saw very well that through the newly acquired means of her husband, an entry could be made; but there must be a right way and a wrong way to set about it. In order that she should become a lady, it was obvious to her that first her husband should become a gentleman. So she invited her friend to make her aware by what process her husband could most speedily become a gentleman. Her friend advised her that one of the recognised methods, and also one of the speediest, was for her husband to enter at one of the Inns of Court, eat his dinners, and become a barrister-at-law. Provided he had a good digestion the process was certain and reasonably quick. Mr. Lewis failed not in respect of digestion. He ate his dinners, and he became a barrister-at-law and legally a gentleman. But Mrs. Lewis was still in the outer world. Her position as a lady must in some manner be formally recognised. She consulted her confidante on this delicate point. The confidante was equal to the occasion.

Confidante. "It is necessary to install yourselves in a good house in a fashionable quarter where you may entertain suitably."

Mrs. Lewis. "That is very easy; but how am I to get the people to suffer themselves to be entertained?"

Confidante. "That will come later. First you must get yourself invited to some of the houses of the great, then you can invite them to your house."

Mrs. Lewis. "How can I manage that?"

Confidante. "There are noble and impecunious ladies who for a consideration might be willing and able to arrange invitations for you."

Mrs. Lewis. "Can you tell me of one?"

Confidante. "I can"—and she did.

The name of the lady was revealed to me, but discretion does not permit me to mention it. I will call her the Lady Flora C——. Mrs. Lewis waited upon the Lady Flora and cautiously disclosed her mission. Lady Flora acknowledged the possibility of obtaining such invitations as Mrs. Lewis desired, but permitted herself to say that they would cost a good deal of money.

Mrs. Lewis. "How much?"

Lady Flora. "A thousand pounds."

Mrs. Lewis. "So be it. I will give you a thousand pounds if you get me the invitations I want during the season."

The Lady Flora was as good as her word. Invitations came duly and were as duly accepted. Towards the end of the season Mrs. Lewis repaired once more to the Lady Flora.

Mrs. Lewis. "Everything has gone very well. Now I want you to get your friends to accept *my* invitations."

Lady Flora. "That is another story. It is one thing for them to ask you to their houses, it is quite another to induce them to go to yours."

Mrs. Lewis. "Could it be arranged for another thousand?"

Lady Flora. "I think so; but on one condition which I hardly like to mention."

Mrs. Lewis. "What is it?"

Lady Flora. "My friends, without exception, like you very much. Your conversation amuses them, and there will be no difficulty so far as you are concerned; but they cannot tolerate your husband."

Mrs. Lewis. "What then?"

Lady Flora. "I would suggest that when you give your reception your husband should be indisposed."

Mrs. Lewis. "There will be no difficulty about that."

There was not. Mrs. Lewis gave her party, Mr. Lewis was indisposed, and the party was a success. Mrs. Lewis was now fairly launched upon her career as a great lady; but she was not yet satisfied. She conceived the idea of getting her husband into Parliament. There was a difficulty. Mr. Lewis was not dumb, and yet he had no power of speech. This defect might not be observed when he became a member, but in a candidate it was anomalous. For Mrs. Lewis, difficulties existed only to be surmounted. Again she consulted her invaluable ally. This lady told her that, just as there were impecunious and noble old ladies who might be made useful, so there were impecunious and clever young men who might be made useful also. "Find me one," said Mrs. Lewis. One was found, who undertook to do the speaking for Mr. Lewis and to promote his candidature otherwise as he could. The impecunious and clever young man was Benjamin Disraeli. He was introduced to Mrs. Lewis by Lytton Bulwer "at particular desire." Disraeli's account of the lady does not lack sharpness—"A pretty little woman, a flirt and a rattle—indeed, gifted with a volubility which I should think unrivalled. She told me she liked silent, melancholy men. I answered that I had no doubt of it."

The appearance of Disraeli at this time is familiar from the drawing by Maclise—partly, no doubt, a caricature—an artful pose, over-dressed, Eastern accessories in his room, billets thrown on the mantel-piece with ostentatious negligence.

The constituency of Maidstone in Kent aroused the interest of Mrs. Lewis. A vacancy occurred in one of its seats and, with the aid of Disraeli, Mr. Lewis won the election. Disraeli was himself defeated at High Wycombe, but later, when the second Maidstone seat became vacant, he was able, through the influence and assistance of Mr. Lewis, to secure it.

In 1838, a year after Disraeli entered Parliament, Mr. Lewis died, and his widow married his colleague. The task of engineering the haber-dasher-barrister-gentleman-member of Parliament had been loyally performed, but it had been very hard. A ball and chain upon her dainty ankle would have impeded Mrs. Lewis's movements less than Mr. Lewis impeded her ambitions. Yet she carried him up with her so far as he had wit enough to suffer himself to be carried. He was good-natured and irreproachable, but embarrassing and disappointing.

The engineering of Disraeli was a totally different affair. Mr. Lewis had the mind and the ambitions of a haberdasher. Disraeli was a man of genius and his ambitions were boundless. He had already made his mark in the House of Commons. He had written some novels and some verse. He was well known if not famous, and he was somewhat feared because on occasion his tongue could be harsh. Of adherence to political principle he could scarcely be accused. He was opposed to the advance of democracy, because he had united himself to the country party, yet later he "dished the Whigs " by outbidding them in reform of the franchise. Essentially his politics consisted first in such measures as might force him into high office, and second in making England—of which he aspired to be Prime Minister—as great and powerful as he could. In this sense he was patriotic; but his imperial aims cannot justly be dissociated from his desire to exercise power. This power when he attained it was, however, never exercised otherwise than with benevolence; and, confident in the purity of his motives, and in the superiority of his mind over the minds of his colleagues as well as over most of the minds of his political opponents, his manœuvres were never petty, and he was by no means implacable in his antagonisms.

Mrs. Disraeli before her marriage had acutely discerned Disraeli's powers, and had reason to know how the exercise of these was impeded by debts, which were the inevitable consequence of his position and not of any irregularity in his life. Her first husband's money had made life wide and interesting for her, and she now determined to use her money for the purpose of making life still wider, and more interesting both for herself and her more promising second.

It is well known that Mrs. Disraeli made up her mind soon after her marriage that she would make Disraeli Prime Minister. To this adventure she bent her whole energy. How was it to be accomplished?

The ruling class in the England of the time was slender in numbers and very exclusive. The great offices of State belonged to this class as of right. The tradition of the class rendered the service of the State in the army, in Parliament, or in the Church at once the duty and the privilege of its members. In entering upon careers which promised pecuniary returns, insignificant in comparison with those of commerce, manufacture or law, those hereditary servants of the State regarded the distinction of office as equivalent to emolument. They regarded such prerogatives of influence as they possessed as on the whole justly earned and properly employed for the maintenance of social order and national prosperity.

The Whig and Tory parties were alike dominated by the members of this ruling class in their respective ranks. A change in Government thus meant no subversion of the social order, although political orators lashed themselves into furious rhetoric in describing the risks involved in change.

Neither Disraeli nor his wife had any idea of altering these things. They were accepted. They were indeed necessary for advancement. Neither Disraeli nor his wife had been born in the ruling caste, and neither had any tangible connection with it. The atmosphere in which it lived, the language its members used, the work of it, and the sports of it were all unfamiliar, although Disraeli in his earlier novels had allowed his fancy to play about them. The fortress of caste had now to be stormed for a more serious purpose than writing about it in a novel; it had to be stormed moreover not for destruction but for command. Mrs. Disraeli had found that there is at least one right and

effective way of acting, and many wrong ways. She was in the habit
of choosing the way that gave the greatest promise of being the right
way. Even if she had been endowed with greater wealth than her
fortune afforded, there was much to be done that could not be done
by money. Besides, even her fortune was now restricted. The capital
amount had been reduced by the costs of bringing Mr. Lewis into
public life, and the income of the balance was all that Mrs. Disraeli
had to depend upon. Even this amount was somewhat reduced by the
arrangement to liquidate the debts of Disraeli. It was thus necessary
to leave the house at Grosvenor Gate, where the Lewises had lived,
and to occupy one of less pretensions. The Disraelis sold the furniture
of the larger house, and installed themselves in the new one in the most
frugal manner. They chose a house with two large and some smaller
rooms; but the two large rooms were not furnished. They contemplated, and afterwards carried into practice, the design of hiring
furniture and servants for the occasions when they entertained their
friends. They elected to live very simply in the smaller rooms, as Mrs.
Disraeli had done in her haberdashery days, the material difference
being the employment of a single domestic. There was another and
more important difference of a spiritual character. The purpose of
the economy was a high purpose. Their means economically employed
made them independent of patronage and indifferent to fluctuations
of political fortune. In this simple menage the lady to whom I am
indirectly indebted for these details was a frequent visitor. She told
how Disraeli dined when at home on a steak and a pot of porter,
brought from the nearest chop house; and how Mrs. Disraeli, before
she went abroad to dine, took a simple dinner at home in order to
be able to concentrate her mind upon the conversation of the table.
This indeed was part of her plan. Although she and her husband were
admitted to the society frequented by the political leaders, they
suffered the disadvantage of being outsiders. They did not know and
could not know, without deliberate and continuous learning, the
social ramifications that played so important a rôle in the drama of
politics, and by means of which the ruling caste exercised its influence
and maintained its position.[1] The "rattle," with all her "volubility,"
had ears and an excellent memory. Contemporary memoirs describe
Disraeli as silent but observant in company. Together the Disraelis
did not fail to learn much.

[1] Plutarch says that Cicero "made it his business to commit to memory not
only their names, but the place of abode of those of greater note, what friends they
made use of, and what neighbours were in their circle."

Mrs. Disraeli was a martyr to neuralgia, and after an important social function would throw herself on a sofa and dictate to her friend (the lady above mentioned) the details she had gathered. These details were not heedlessly set down, but were systematically recorded in a social ledger under specific headings. Disraeli, whose mind was not systematic, and whose temperament predisposed him rather towards vehement assault, than the careful scientific sapping which Mrs. Disraeli's system involved, may at times have regarded her meticulous proceedings with indulgent amusement. Yet when a political crisis occurred the social ledger yielded surprising results. Well-recorded conversations threw a light, unrecognisable when they took place, upon later political movements, and the interior relations of groups were found to be set down in black and white.

As Disraeli rose into a position of power, the shrewd management of his wife did not relax. After an exhausting session, some time between 1874 and 1878, Disraeli was bordering on nervous prostration. He was captured by the Duke of Northumberland and carried off to Alnwick Castle. The local Conservatives were anxious to get him to make a speech upon the political situation. They urged the Duke to ask Disraeli to speak; but the Duke absolutely refused, saying that Disraeli needed rest, and that he had brought him to Alnwick in order that he should have it. The deputation departed discomfited; but on their way down the avenue they met Mrs. Disraeli (now perhaps Lady Beaconsfield). She was evidently there for the purpose of way-laying them.

"Well," she said, "what did he say?" The deputation told her the result of their interview with the Duke.

"Go back," she said, "and tell the Duke that Mr. Disraeli is quite able to speak and that I think he ought to do what you ask."

They went back, and the arrangements were made forthwith.

The details in this sketch have been drawn from the narrative of the confidante of the wife of Disraeli. No doubt there will be those who declare that there is no word of truth in them. This is possible; but if they are an effort of the imagination, the effort is not mine. I have simply written them down as I received them, and thus far I am prepared to vouch for them, errors and omissions excepted; and these, after a lapse of years, are not improbable. Whether or not the rise of Disraeli was achieved at least partly by the means above described, it is evident that that rise—amazing as it was—was neither miraculous nor accidental, and that some method must have been employed with more or less system to enable him to achieve the position towards which his ambition directed him at a very early stage in his career. English society has undergone metamorphosis since eighty years ago, and the conditions of success in political adventure are not what they were. Whether the new phase is in any sense an improvement upon the old one remains to be seen. The possibilities of change are not exhausted.

CHAPTER IX

THE FRANCO-PRUSSIAN WAR AND THE COMMUNE OF PARIS

> Son aigle est resté dans la poudre,
> Fatigué de lointains exploits,
> Rendons-lui le coq des Gaulois;
> Il sut aussi lancer la foudre.
> La France, oubliant ses douleurs,
> Le rebénira, libre et fière.
> Quand secouerai-je la poussière
> Qui ternit ses nobles couleurs?
>
> P. J. BÉRANGER, *Le Vieux Drapeau* (1820).

THE phase of British foreign policy represented by Palmerston closed abruptly with his death in 1865. A rather widely spread contemporary view was that the policy of Palmerston involved too much interference in the political affairs of the continent of Europe on the part of Great Britain, and that a respite in which domestic affairs should occupy a larger share of public attention was highly advisable. During the Franco-Prussian War of 1870–71, an anonymous article upon the war appeared in the *Quarterly Review*. When Gladstone published his *Gleanings of Past Years*, he acknowledged that he had written this article by publishing it in his collection of papers on foreign affairs. He stated in the article that when Prussia was exerting the pressure upon Denmark which led to the conquest of Schleswig-Holstein, Palmerston had urged Napoleon III. to co-operate with England in protesting, and in armed intervention if that should be necessary. Napoleon, apparently on the ground of friendship with Austria, refused to undertake an enterprise against Prussia and Austria combined. Undoubtedly this course of events had been foreseen by Bismarck. To invite the co-operation of Austria was to silence both France and England; and the alliance with Austria might afterwards be dissolved. The victorious campaign ending with Sadowa actually dissolved it. France refrained from intervening between Prussia and her victim; and thus a second time prepared the way for her own *débâcle*. After the defeat of Denmark, a policy of armed intervention in European affairs on the part of Great Britain became almost impossible. She had on the Continent no effective ally. There was as yet no United Italy; there were murmurings of revolution in France and the Second Empire was already showing symptoms of dissolution. It is doubtful if Palmerston would have been supported by British public opinion in an Anglo-French attack upon Prussia in 1864. The question of the Duchies was too complicated. The conduct of the Danes was by no means susceptible of unqualified approval. The interest of Great Britain was not direct or obvious. Yet the thesis might be maintained that Palmerston was right, that his political instinct was sound, and that the ambitions of Prussia ought to have been checked then, rather than at a later stage, when owing to her conquests Prussia became almost invincible.

When these moments passed without intervention, and when Prussia gained the prestige resulting from two brief and skilful campaigns, the external situation as well as the internal mood of Great Britain rendered for the future intervention under any circumstances very difficult. Thus when Prussia struck and crippled France in 1870, Great Britain stood aside, although while the controversy was still in its diplomatic stage Lord Granville, who was then Foreign Minister, did everything in his power to prevent a conflict by persuading Prussia to secure the withdrawal of the Hohenzollern candidature for the crown of Spain, as well as later when the question of guarantees was advanced by Napoleon III. and Grammont.[1] When war became inevitable, partly through the fatuous indecision of Napoleon and partly through the conduct of Bismarck, the only action Great Britain permitted herself to take was the safeguarding of Belgium, thus forcing Prussia and her German allies to attack France through Alsace and Lorraine. Even had he desired to do so, it is wholly unlikely that Gladstone could have created such a state of feeling in Great Britain as would have enabled him to go to the rescue of France at that time. The Second Empire was not popular in Great Britain. There was a not inconsiderable body of opinion favourable to France and the French people, but the Emperor was looked upon as somewhat of a charlatan. Indeed, his real capacity for international politics was probably unduly undervalued. There should also be taken into account the fact, not then widely known, that behind the Emperor there lurked a revolutionary movement which might gain overwhelming force at a critical moment.

---

[1] Cf., e.g., Correspondence, etc., France, 1870 (Blue Books Nos. 28 and 30). While the actual steps which led to war were taken on the one hand by Napoleon in insisting upon guarantees and on the other by Bismarck in his alteration of the Ems dispatch (avowed by himself with cynical candour) as well as by his manipulation of Prussian public opinion through the press, the real motive power which made for war lay in the hands of the Prussian and French people respectively. Even had either Government desired to draw back in the final stage of the diplomatic controversy, neither people would have permitted withdrawal. Their blood was up.

If such a revolution had occurred while British troops were in France for the purpose of assisting that country in its defence, they might have found their own position seriously compromised. I do not know whether such a contingency presented itself to the minds of our diplomatists and statesmen or not; but if it did not, it ought to have done so.

I was not personally aware of the details of this revolutionary movement while it was in progress, but I became aware of some of them shortly after the close of the Franco-Prussian War. As these may be new to some people, I venture to include them in this sketch.

In the late sixties there were still alive many who had taken part in the revolutionary movements of 1848; there were even some survivors of the Revolution of 1830. It cannot be said that any great influence was exercised by these "old men" of the Revolution. Louis Blanc, for example, who was one of these "old men," was actively engaged in conspirative movements in Paris in 1866–70; but his activities were fruitless. Younger and more energetic elements quietly brought his efforts to nought. By way of illustration I may narrate a story which was told to me some time in the seventies by one of my French revolutionary friends. Early in 1870 Louis Blanc had secured a small supply of pistols from London, which he designed to distribute by a simple plan. The pistols were to be carried in canvas bags by revolutionists, who were to sit on public seats on the boulevards. When they rose to leave, they were to abandon the bags they carried, and these bags were to be appropriated by confederates, who in this way would secure their supply of arms. It soon became known that in almost every case the confederates failed to connect with one another, and that the bags containing the small-arms had disappeared. The fact was that the young men of the Revolution had made up their minds that the moment for an outbreak had not arrived and had determined to save the "old men" from the consequences of their precipitate and clumsily executed plots. They therefore appropriated the arms and put them out of harm's way.

But the young men were by no means idle. They were nearly all professional men—lawyers, engineers, teachers, and the like—and they were also in general addicted to intellectual pursuits apart from their professional interests. These pursuits led them to the study of the very numerous French writers upon social philosophy, and particularly of Fourier.[1] In the late sixties there were in Paris a large

[1] About the same time the influence of Fourier upon the Russian revolutionary movement was very important.

number of Fourier Clubs in which social questions were discussed chiefly from Fourier's point of view. In one of his works Fourier draws an elaborate analogy between the relation to one another of elements of human character and the relation to one another of numbers. Thus he attaches a special value to numbers—*one* is the symbol of individuality, *two* society, *three* power, and so on. The relation of the important elements of character is thus expressible in ratios. In these Fourier Clubs it became customary to speak, partly in genuine adherence to this quasi-mathematico-social formula and partly in a vein of delicate humour, of the ratios of individual members. Thus one of my friends, who was a member of a club of this kind, told me that he was in the habit of escorting from the club to her home a lady who was the wife of another member of the same club. Although both husband and wife met frequently at meetings of the club, they did not usually meet otherwise; in fact, they lived apart. My friend, who was on equally good terms with both, ventured to suggest to the husband that perhaps he might prefer to escort his wife rather than leave this duty to another. "Why?" said the husband. "Do you not find her a very charming woman? It is not possible that she bores you." "I find her most charming," was the answer, "and it is precisely this that makes me wonder why you do not find her society so agreeable that you should wish to escort her as you have every title to do." "Ah!" said the husband. "My wife's ratio is as 7 to 11 and mine as 5 to 9."

While Fourier's idea of housing social groups in *phalanstères* did not have many adherents, although it had some, his general view of communism was somewhat widely accepted by the French intellectual groups. This attitude on the part of these intellectual groups was undoubtedly due to reaction against bureaucratic centralisation and incompetence and the banal commercialism which had developed throughout France under the Second Empire, as well as to the decay of art which permitted and promoted the Haussmannisation of Paris. There was also growing a feeling of internationalism, due on the one hand to the acceptance of the communism of small groups in place of nationalism and still more in place of imperialism.

The International Working Men's Association was originally a French idea. After a conflict for the control of the International between Mazzini, who desired to utilise it for the purpose of assisting his political movement in Italy, and Marx, who desired to dominate it personally—a conflict in which Marx was victorious—the International had a brief moment of success through its patronage of a strike among Paris workmen; but otherwise it had little influence in France, and Marx had never any popularity there among the leading figures. This perhaps to some extent arose from the fact that Marx owed at once his collectivist and his communist ideas, confused as they were in his writings, to the French Socialists of the period between 1830 and 1848, and that he had never made adequate acknowledgment of his indebtedness.[1] Socialism, at almost any period of its history, might fairly be regarded as chaotic, because the profession of it may be, and is customarily, made by persons of the most widely divergent views—from the reactionary collectivism of Marx to the complete social disintegration of Bakunin. In the late sixties Socialism, as it was then understood by the intellectuals, had not yet even begun to penetrate the minds of the urban proletariat, and the interior divisions in the intellectual groups professing Socialism rendered these groups ineffectual. The French peasant has never been addicted to Socialism in any form, any more than the *petite bourgeoisie* of the provincial towns. Peasantry and *bourgeoisie* alike have always been strongly individualistic in character; and they have consequently in general been reluctant to trust too much to the bureaucracy. They had had experience of harsh officialism under the Republic. Thus, although there was an undertone of highly intelligent Socialism rising sometimes to eloquence and giving the French Government of the late sixties many anxious moments, there was as yet no effective organisation or sufficiently intimate *rapport* between the Socialist leaders and the working masses to make even a Paris Revolution possible. Yet the conditions which make for revolution were rapidly reaching maturity; and it is highly probable that a revolution in Paris would have taken place some time in the seventies had there been no Franco-Prussian War.

In the autumn of 1869, an active propaganda conducted by intellectual groups had already familiarised the Paris proletariat with communist ideas. Many unauthorised meetings were held at which orators, especially those of the Fourier Clubs, addressed audiences sometimes numbering four or five thousand persons. These proceedings were well known to the French Government; but it was in no hurry to precipitate action against those who were promoting the meetings. Undoubtedly, in presence of a possible war with Prussia, prosecution of the communists would have disclosed domestic weakness which might indeed have precipitated an attack. A Liberal

---

[1] Marx's friend and ally, Engels, had borrowed in the same manner, and also without adequate acknowledgment, from French writers such as Buret, for instance.

ministry came into power in France in the beginning of January, and apparently conceiving that there was less likelihood of an aggressive movement by Prussia while its own intentions were pacific, the new Government decided to take action where its predecessors had been reluctant. In February 1870 a few orators at propagandist meetings were arrested. Among these was my friend Leo Mélliet, then about twenty-six years of age and a member of the Paris Bar. Immediately after his arrest, being well known to the Paris magistracy, he was liberated on his own recognisances, and on his promising to appear before the court a fortnight later. A day or two before the fortnight expired, Mélliet went to the clerk of the court, with whom he was on terms of personal intimacy, and told him that an infectious disease had broken out in the house in which he lived and that he must be quarantined for some time. This excuse was accepted as sufficient, and Mélliet's case was postponed for a fortnight. Taking care always to report either personally or by proxy once a fortnight, Mélliet succeeded in evading proceedings in his case for two or three months. Meanwhile several of his friends, less shrewd or less fortunate, were languishing in prison, where they were luxuriously supported by means of the contributions of their friends, with whom the Government thought well to avoid interference.

Eventually for some reason the authorities determined to bring up Mélliet's case imperatively, and it was fixed for a certain day. Mélliet did not put in an appearance. He changed his lodging and succeeded in evading arrest. One day on the boulevard he encountered the Prefect of Police, to whom he was well known.

Prefect. "What are you doing? Do you not see that I have only to lift my finger and you will be immediately arrested? "

A policeman stood a few yards distant.

Mélliet. "I know; but gentlemen do not lift their fingers in such cases. Instead, you and I will go into this café and we shall discuss the question over an *apéritif*." They did so, and a similar incident happened on a subsequent occasion. In June, foreign and more important affairs distracted the attention of the Government and Mélliet was forgotten. On 19th July, 1870, the French Foreign Office intimated to Bismarck in a dispatch that France and Prussia were "in a state of war."

The defeat of the French armies, the discreditable surrender of Bazaine,[1] and the speedy collapse of the Empire, revealed the fact

[1] Robinson, who was correspondent of *The Daily Telegraph* in Metz during the siege, told me that Bazaine was in an almost continual state of intoxication at this time.

that although the social revolutionary movement of which I have been speaking had made little progress, the political revolution had been in the making for a long time.

The peace gave the social revolutionaries their chance. They succeeded in the Paris municipal elections of February 1871 in getting themselves elected as *maires* of a number of the city *arrondissements*, and their superior talents, despite their youth and the smallness of their numbers, gave them at once a predominance in the civic council. An opportunity thus arose for putting into practical effect some of the ideas they had imbibed from Fourier. They attempted, in short, to supplement the political revolution by a social revolution, and at the same time to give the political revolution a new direction. There were many conditions which rendered the success of these attempts possible. The concentration of political power in Paris, which has already been noticed as the traditional policy of successive French Governments from the beginning of the eighteenth century, had produced in the provinces a reaction in favour of return to the measure of local autonomy which had preceded the policy of concentration. The social revolutionists could not appeal on economic grounds to the peasantry and the *petite bourgeoisie* in the provinces, but they could appeal to their desire for local autonomy. They proposed a measure too drastic for the times, and perhaps too drastic for the national spirit of the French people at any time—they proposed what amounted to elimination of the State and division of France into autonomous communes with the most slender of administrative association. In short, at a moment when above all it was necessary for French society to unite itself for the purpose of enabling it to recover from the disasters of the war, the Commune of Paris, guided by the Socialist or, rather, Fourierist group, proposed a formal disintegration of the nation. It might be held that a real unity might have developed and that a national organisation of a new character might have been brought into existence; but this was too hazardous an experiment to conduct at a moment of national crisis. If it had succeeded, it is doubtful if France would have been even as strong as she has shown herself to be in attempting to repel a second German invasion. As it was, the Commune of Paris was defeated by Thiers and the coalition he had succeeded in effecting; and France became a Republic, controlled, as the character of French society rendered inevitable, by the *bourgeoisie* and the peasantry, rather than by the intellectual social idealists or by the urban proletariat.

In a previous chapter I have referred to Marx's relation to the

Commune, and I have also given some personal notes which I owe to Leo Mélliet, who was a member of the Judicial Committee of the Commune. Mélliet was a refugee living in Scotland for nearly thirty years. After the complete amnesty of the participants in the Insurrection of the Commune, he returned to France and became a deputy for one of the southern constituencies. Later he retired to a small property of his in the south of France. According to him, Paris under the Commune was incomparably more closely invested than during the German siege. Food was much scarcer. Immediately on conclusion of peace at Versailles, Paris had been victualled largely from England; but there had been no time to accumulate reserves, and at the beginning of the second siege stocks were very low. The effective circumvallation of the Paris of that period required a larger number of troops than the Germans had at their disposal after providing for the maintenance of their lines of communication, and thus during the first siege food was smuggled through the German lines to some extent. During the second siege, the whole forces of the Versaillists were devoted to the investment of Paris, and smuggling became almost impossible. Desperate expedients had therefore to be resorted to. Mélliet received from one of his friends an invitation to dinner. The invitation-card bore the legend, "We have a dog." After dinner, the host remarked with feeling, "Poor Jacko, how he would have enjoyed those bones!" The bones, of course, were those of Jacko himself, who had fallen a victim to the premature attempt to realise a social and political ideal.

Towards the end of the siege Mélliet was appointed commandant of Fort Bicêtre, one of the circle of forts defended by the Commune. In order to encourage the men who were serving the guns in the fort, Mélliet found it advantageous to offer rewards for accurate artillery practice, and therefore devised a system under which premiums up to a hundred francs were offered for direct hits. It seems that even under the Commune individualist motives were not wholly unrecognised. When it came to be necessary to abandon the fort, Mélliet sent his men into Paris and then alone made his escape in the same direction. He entered the city and found the streets occupied by Versaillist troops. He made his way by narrow passages for some distance and emerged upon a thoroughfare only to find two bodies of soldiers, one to the right and the other to the left. He took shelter in a recessed doorway, hoping to elude observation, at least for the moment. The instant he did so, the door opened and he was dragged into a room which he saw at once was that of a working shoemaker. The shoemaker, without loss of time, tore off Mélliet's coat, hung over his shoulders his own long leather apron, and set him down on a stool, placing between his knees a shoe in course of repair. Immediately there came a thundering knock. The shoemaker opened the door without delay. "Someone has just entered your door. Where is he?" said an officer, who was accompanied by several soldiers. "There is no one here excepting my companion and myself." "We must make a search." "By all means," said Mélliet, rising from his stool and assisting the officer to search the house. Of course no one else was found. The officer went away; but it was impossible to remain in case he might return. Mélliet therefore went out by the rear of the house and proceeded to jump over the palings and garden walls of houses in the vicinity, hoping in this way to arrive at a place of safety which he had prepared in view of such a contingency. He was observed by some soldiers who were posted on the housetops and was fired at several times. His movements were sufficiently rapid and irregular to enable him to avoid being hit, but the situation was precarious. He noticed an open window and walked into a house. "They are shooting the ambulances," he said. "Can you conceal me here for a short time?" The people of the house did so, and at night a young girl bravely volunteered to show him the way to his place of refuge. He reached it without further adventure, and then he proceeded to make plans for his escape from Paris. He knew very well that nothing could save him if he remained. He was too full of life to abandon it without an effort. The house in which he lived was in an important thoroughfare and the street was continually patrolled by troops. It was impossible for him to open the blinds. He had worn a full jet-black beard, and his first business was to get rid of it. When this was accomplished it was necessary to disguise the fact that he had just been shaved, and he therefore with great caution exposed his pale face to the sun as it came in at the edge of the window-blind. This involved time, but it had to be done. Meanwhile he put into practice other elements in his intended disguise. He had been accustomed to walk with his arms rather closely held by his sides. It was essential to alter this habit. He therefore fastened a number of corks together and, inserting a bundle into each of his armpits, practised walking with his arms held somewhat out from his body. He had been accustomed to wear dark clothing; he procured a supply of light-grey suits. Then there was the question of a passport. He succeeded in getting into communication with General Chanzy, who in happier times had been a friend of his, and by means of passport, new name, new profession, new genealogy

I—H

and, so far as he could devise, new personality, he was ready for his adventure.   He left his lodgings boldly, went to the Gare St. Lazare, and asked for a first-class ticket to Brussels.   The station was not without agents of the police, watching for insurrectionists attempting to escape.   Mélliet knew many of these men by sight, and as Mélliet they knew him also; yet none of them recognised him.   He had arranged to meet at the station some of his friends who were not under suspicion, and before the departure of the train he walked up and down with them, speaking of the incidents of the Commune and defending the insurrection with sufficient but not too great vigour.   Mélliet had the idea that all policemen are stupid, and that they would quite naturally suppose that a man who could speak in that manner about the insurrection could not possibly have been concerned in it.   If he had been, he must know that he was running a grave risk, and, from the police point of view, no revolutionary would do that now that the insurrection had been put down.   Mélliet departed from Paris safely, but his risks were not yet over.   At the frontier station the passengers were informed that a mistake had been made about the examination of passports, that they would require to return to a station they had already passed in order to have their passports examined there, and that they would be unable to go to Brussels until the next train from Paris arrived.   Mélliet had made acquaintance in the train with a Spanish merchant, and he proposed to this man that together they should go to the police-inspector at the station and offer to go back with anyone appointed by the inspector, carrying with them the passports of all the other passengers in order to avoid the inconvenience of the return of the whole group. This was agreed to, and Mélliet with his Spanish friend collected the passports, went to the place where the documents ought to have been examined, and submitted themselves for inspection.   This formality was soon over, and while waiting for the train for Brussels Mélliet had a pleasant chat with the police-inspector.   "Are you much troubled by insurrectionists attempting to escape from Paris?" said Mélliet.

"Yes and no," said the inspector.   "We were told that the Communards were escaping disguised as priests and as women, and that we should be on the look-out for any ill-favoured persons in disguises of that kind.   Two days ago we arrested a priest whom we thought ill-favoured enough, and he turned out to be bishop of this diocese.   I received a scolding from Paris, and since then I have arrested nobody."

Next day Mélliet sent in his card at his hotel in Brussels to his Spanish friend.

Mélliet was a friend of Courbet the painter, for whom he entertained a great admiration. On my asking Mélliet why it was that the Commune took the trouble to pull down the Vendôme Column,[1] he told me that this was done at the instance of Courbet, whose argument was as follows: If the spiral bronze reliefs are good, they should be placed in such a manner that the public may see and study them if it wishes; if they are not good, they should not be set up in any way. Moreover, the whole affair is not a work of original art, but is an imitation, and therefore of doubtful artistic merit. Courbet suggested that since it was possible that some of the reliefs, whose position at a great height rendered their detail invisible, might possess artistic value, care should be taken in pulling down the column to preserve them from injury. The Place Vendôme was packed to the depth of several feet with straw manure and the column was pulled down by means of ropes. The operation was so skilfully conducted that the bronzes were not damaged in the least. Courbet also suggested that if on examination the bronzes were found to be of inferior artistic qualities, they should be melted and coined into money. They were, however, preserved and re-erected many years afterwards.[2] Courbet was a fine artist, although his forest pictures with deer smack of the studio rather than the forest. Many of them were, indeed, painted in the prison in which he was interned after the suppression of the Commune. The French Government purchased these and other pictures of Courbet from his widow. Courbet was a large, stout man of imperturbable good humour and with the air of a small tradesman.

In the course of my interrogations I asked Mélliet why the Commune set fire to the Tuileries, pointing out the danger to which this operation must have subjected the priceless collections of art in the Louvre. Mélliet said that the connection between the two buildings had been carefully severed so that the Louvre should not be damaged. " As for the Tuileries, we destroyed that building on the principle that

[1] The Vendôme Column was erected by Napoleon I. in commemoration of his victories in Germany in 1805. It is an imitation on a scale of 1 1–12th of the Column of Trajan at Rome. The bronze bas-reliefs which embrace the stem of the column between the base and the capital represent the victories of the French, while those on the pedestal represent the conquered Germans. The reliefs were cast from 1200 pieces of Russian and Austrian cannon. *Galignani's New Paris Guide for* 1855.

[2] When I was in Paris in 1878 I saw them standing in rows on the ground at the old Palais des Beaux-Arts, opposite the Pont des Arts. The column was re-erected later.

if their nests are destroyed, the rooks will not return." Certainly, though half a century has passed and there have been many crises in French politics, the "rooks" have not returned. I also asked Mélliet to explain the ground upon which the Hôtel de Ville was burned, because the same argument could not be applied in that case. He insisted that the Government of the Commune had not ordered the destruction of that building. I pressed him on this point, remarking that there was a widespread belief to the contrary. He said that he was perfectly certain about it. He was one of the *maires d'arrondissement* and he was present in the Hôtel de Ville when it was set on fire by the mob, much to the disgust and annoyance of the Government of the Commune, although it was then in its last hours.[1]

[1] Compare this statement with that of another equally competent authority, vol. ii. pp. 119, 120.

CHAPTER X

Sometimes, with secure delight,
The upland hamlets will invite,
When the merry bells ring round,
And the jocund rebecks sound
To many a youth and many a maid
Dancing in the chequered shade.

.   .   .   .   .

Towered cities please us then,
And the busy hum of men,
Where throngs of knights and barons bold,
In weeds of peace, high triumphs hold.

> JOHN MILTON, *L'Allegro* (1633?).

But let my due feet never fail
To walk the studious cloister's pale,
And love the high embowèd roof,
With antique pillars massy-proof,
And storied windows richly dight,
Casting a dim religious light.

> JOHN MILTON, *Il Penseroso* (1633?).

PART I.—BELGIUM AND HOLLAND IN 1874

HAVING acquired a fair knowledge of the greater part of my own country, I decided in 1874 to go abroad for my vacation. I spent a day or two in London, and then crossed to Antwerp. Some old friends of my mother had invited me to visit them in Amsterdam, and that city was my ultimate destination; but I wandered about Belgium and Holland on my way thither. Realising that the traveller possesses himself of that, and that only, which he can see from his window, and that the character of this window determines for him the character of his travels, I prepared myself for the journey by careful study of Motley's *Rise of the Dutch Republic*, which I took with me, as well as of other histories of the Netherlands, including Schiller's *Revolt of the Netherlands*; so that I had some idea of the historical background. I had also read Schlegel's *Description of Paintings in Paris*

117

and the Netherlands in the years 1802–1804.[1]   This I found useful as a guide to the works of art.   I had become familiar with the Dutch and Flemish schools so far as they were represented in the admirable collection in the Glasgow Gallery, formed by McLellan and bequeathed by him to the city in 1854.   There was at that time (1874) no catalogue of these paintings.   Indeed, it was not until 1882 that Robinson, H.M. Surveyor of Pictures, reported upon them and first made widely known the great importance of the collection.[2]

Antwerp in 1874 was a sleepy mediæval town.   Belgium had not recovered from the series of economic and political struggles by which her development was arrested and the commerce of her cities ruined.[3] Begging was universal alike in towns and in country villages.   In some parts of the towns pedestrian traffic in the streets was even impeded by groups of professional mendicants, and in some villages all the children assailed every passer-by for alms, presenting tin cups into which contributions might be dropped.   In certain streets of Antwerp tufts of grass made their appearance between paving blocks; docks and wharves were slenderly occupied by shipping.   Churches alone were thronged by devout and indolent groups.   In Bruges and Ghent there was a feeble domestic industry, principally in lace, and there was a similar industry in the houses of the religious orders, as for example in the great Beguinage at Ghent, which contained within its walls eighteen convents with about seven hundred nuns.   An exhibition of their work was being held when I was there; but it was impressive chiefly from its amateur character, and from absence of traditional art.   Cultivation in rural districts was indifferent.   The people were very poor, and were accustomed rather to rely upon the doles of tourists than upon their own industry.   Wages were low, as was also the cost of living.   I lived at many small inns, where I paid customarily not more than five francs for bed and breakfast, including a candle which always made its appearance in the bill as a separate item.

One portion of Belgium alone gave any signs of industrial activity. This was the province of Liège.   At Seraing, a suburb of the provincial city, an Englishman, John Cockerill (a kinsman, by the way, of Samuel Pepys, the diarist), had founded, in 1817, extensive iron works and

[1] Translation, London, 1849.
[2] An excellent catalogue has been issued in successive editions since 1882.
[3] An interesting contribution to economic history has recently been made by a Spanish writer who has undertaken to prove that in the printing trade at least the Duke of Alva conferred a benefit upon Antwerp by promoting there the printing of Spanish books, and thus contributing to the establishment of an important printing industry in the Low Countries.   The Spanish printers seem to have been annoyed by the competition.

engineering shops.   In 1874 these works employed about 9000 men. Every branch of iron manufacture and engineering was carried on in the establishment—locomotives for the Belgian and even for other railways were built in large numbers.   Another important centre of industry in the same province was Verviers, which had long been celebrated for its cloth manufacture and had become known for its yarns—especially for the finer numbers of woollen yarns, of some of which it had even acquired a monopoly.   The water of the River Vesdre, upon which Verviers is situated, is said to be specially suitable for the manufacturing process to which finer yarns are subjected.   I was told by some Verviers yarn merchants that water had been transported from the Vesdre to Yorkshire for experimental purposes, but that the Yorkshire spinners had not been able to produce the numbers of which Verviers retained the specialty.

With exception of this region, the economic background of Belgium in 1874 was depressed and depressing.

The King (Leopold II.) acceded to the throne of Belgium in 1865, and soon afterwards began the policy of pulling down ancient buildings, making wide streets and erecting modern dwellings and new public offices.   In 1874 the heart of Brussels was still antique, or at least had an antique aspect.   But the changes had begun to take effect.   The new Bourse was just finished, the Palais de Justice was still in the hands of the builders.   Both were fresh and clean in their newly quarried yellow and blue stones; but their Late Classic Renaissance style and the banality of the lines of the Palais de Justice made the modern archi- tecture look tawdry and cheap beside the fine Gothic of the Church of Ste. Gudule, or the buildings of the Grande Place.

The Grande Place is one of the finest survivals of the golden age of the city state.   The Hôtel de Ville and the façades of the Guild Houses [1] bear witness to a time when municipal and trade corporations were rich enough to buy princes, and sometimes powerful enough to defy them.   The Grande Place remains to a large extent the centre of the life of Brussels.   Civil marriage is performed in the Hôtel de Ville, [2] and at this function may be seen various types of the Brussels popula- tion.   The concerts frequently given in the Place in the summer attract all sorts and conditions, and on Sunday morning the old-clothes market which is held in it affords good opportunity of seeing Brussels types.   For others, the Bois must be frequented on Sunday afternoon.

[1] The Maison du Roi, opposite the Hôtel de Ville, is mostly of late date and without interest. In front of it stands the monument of Counts Egmont and Horne.
[2] I am not certain when the civil marriage was instituted in Belgium.

In 1874 the Brussels gallery of old masters was housed in L'ancienne Cour, a building which for a time was the seat of the Austrian Government of the Netherlands. The gallery was not large, and it contained little of first-rate importance. It did not compare in any respect with the gallery at Antwerp.

Nowhere else can Flemish art be studied to so great advantage as in the Antwerp gallery.[1] From Jan van Eyck and other primitives to Rubens and Van Dyck, the successive influences—German, Italian and French—which have played upon the art of Flanders may be recognised.

I recall that on this first visit to Belgium I was immensely impressed with the art of the Van Eycks, from the examples which I had the opportunity of seeing in Antwerp, and also in the Academy at Bruges and in the Cathedral of St. Bavon at Ghent. Another artist whose not very numerous paintings can really only be seen in Belgium —Hans Memling —interested me at that time, and has continued to do so ever since.

The principal places at which I stayed on this journey besides Antwerp and Brussels were Bruges, Ghent, Namur and Liège. Of course I went to Waterloo and walked over the whole of the field between the village of Waterloo and Braine l'Alleud. The scale of a hundred years ago is not the scale of to-day, yet from the point of view of the number of casualties, Waterloo must be regarded as having been one of the most sanguinary of battles. There are differences of opinion about the numbers engaged on 18th June, 1815, but it is probable that the Allied forces, exclusive of Blücher's army, were about 75,000, and the French, exclusive of Grouchy's army, were about 90,000. Apart from a slight superiority in numbers, Napoleon had a superiority of artillery of almost two to one. The number of guns was about 300 on the French side and 150 on the British. The casualties were enormous; about one-third of the total forces engaged were killed, wounded, or captured.

The south of Belgium, especially the south-east, is extremely beautiful. The valley of the Meuse, e.g. between Namur and Liège, is charming. There are few places in Europe so picturesquely situated as the little town of Huy, overlooking the river from the high northern bank upon the edge of which it is perched. Liège has been much modernised since 1874. Then its principal feature was the Palace of Justice, formerly the palace of the Prince-Bishops of Liège. The low

[1] The Musée was at that time in the heart of the town. A new Musée was built (1879–90) in the Place Leopold de Vael.

arcade had interesting columns with quaint capitals. This episcopal palace played a great rôle in the history of Liège. Sometimes the Bishop was arrogant and regardless of the liberties of the people, at other times he assisted the Liègeois to defend these liberties against threatened encroachments by their neighbours. The city stands, and has always stood, at a strategic point, alike in commerce and in war. Through Liège there passed the rich stuffs transported by the overland route from the East. From Liège they were distributed to the Flemish towns. Woollen manufactures grew up in connection with this transit trade, for by the exportation of the products of their looms the Liègeois paid for the stuffs they imported. Throughout the later Middle Ages Liège was thus an important commercial and industrial centre. Standing as it does in the gap between the ridge called the Petersburg and the system of hills which forms the right bank of the Meuse, Liège commands the entrance from the Rhine valley to the plains of Flanders and Northern France. The liberties of the city were thus often threatened in past ages, as well as in our own. The people could not fail to have been subjected to a process of natural selection, and they have clung with tenacity to their communal freedom. There is a significant symbol of this in one of their civil monuments which appears to have escaped the notice of compilers of guide-books. Opposite the Cathedral and the Hôtel de Ville there stands a structure known as the Perron de Liège. On this flight of steps there is a bronze column sustaining on its top a fir-cone. The fir-cone is an ancient symbol of community and independence. In remote ages this monument or its predecessors was the Seat of Justice. When the Liègeois were Christianised, they added a cross to the cone, and Christian judges dispensed justice as their pagan predecessors had done. Under the ægis of the Perron, there arose in the eleventh century in Liège the Tribunal of Peace. The Bishop of Liège presided over this tribunal. On the appointed day, those who complained of acts of violence were required to strike the copper ring on the door of the episcopal palace and to lodge their complaint. The accused person was obliged to answer. If he was unable to clear himself from the accusation, he was sentenced by the Bishop to banishment and loss of his goods, if he was a "free" man; if a "serf," to the loss of his right hand. But he had the right of appeal to the ordeal by battle, that is, to the judgment of God. If he appealed, he dressed himself in red armour and fought his accuser in the "Bishop's Meadow," which lay between the Cathedral and the episcopal palace. The right, recognised by local law, in this manner, of appeal to ordeal by battle,

was very important because it removed from the Liègeois the obligation to submit themselves to the more dreadful ordeals of water
and fire. Thus, compared with many other feudal communities, they
had a dignity and independence of which they were very proud
and very tenacious.[1] The "Sens du pays de Liège" was a peculiar
manifestation of the will of the people through an ancient representative assembly.[2]

The opening up of the water route to the East and the consequent
decline of the overland route diminished and gradually ruined the
transit trade of Liège, and for a time depressed its manufactures.
Exploitation of the coal which underlies the city, and the establishment in its vicinity of engineering works, restored its prosperity in
modern times.

From Liège I crossed the border into Holland to the old Roman
town of Maastricht for the purpose of making an excursion to the great
cavern of the Petersburg. The Petersburg is a ridge extending from
Maastricht to the neighbourhood of Liège. It is composed of a light
yellow-coloured sandstone of very fine grain. The stone is so soft
that on the quarry face I made without effort a deep indentation
with my thumb-nail; and it becomes so hard when exposed to the air
that carvings in it, easily executed when the stone is new, become,
when weathered, practically immune from damage. In the mason's
sheds, where the stone is made into required sizes, hand-saws such as
are used for cutting timber are customarily employed to cut the stone.
The great cavern, which extends for several miles in the interior of the
ridge, has been used for centuries as a quarry out of which this remarkable stone is procured. Visitors, who I gathered were not extremely
frequent, were permitted to go under care of a guide from one and a half
to two miles underground. There is one long corridor and subsidiary
passages. In the deep recess of the ridge there is a large chamber—
about 1000 square feet on the floor, and about forty feet in height.
In the centre of the rock roof there is the top of the trunk of a tree
with branches spreading in all directions, while directly beneath there
is the vestige of the base of the trunk about three feet high. The
intermediate stem has disappeared. Constant dropping of water from
the roof had worn a cavity in the top of the base. Imperfect as it is
through the absence of the greater part of the stem, the tree is one of
the finest fossils in existence. There were many inscriptions on the
walls. One was pointed out to me by the guide, who said that it

[1] Cf. Mdme. I. Gatti de Gamond, Histoire de Belgique (Brussels, 1880), pp. 95-97.
[2] Ibid. p. 149.

belonged to the twelfth century. This is possible; for the aspect of the cavern and its similarity to others which I have seen elsewhere suggest the use of the cavern at an even more remote date. Stone has been quarried from the ridge from time immemorial; but there is no obvious advantage in extracting the stone from a lateral mine rather than from an open quarry cutting. It is extremely probable that quarrying was incidental, and not essential to the original purpose of the cavern. Similar excavations on a great scale exist in the Pyrenees, in Brittany and in Kent, as well as elsewhere. The age of these works is not known. Some of them may have been excavated first in early palæolithic times, and the excavations extended in later ages. Their purpose was probably the shelter of their occupants from human or other enemies. In the Petersburg cavern I did not see any holes in the roof by means of which entrance could be obtained—such holes are to be found in Brittany and in Kent.[1] If the practice of bombarding peaceful populations from the air becomes general, these will be compelled to become troglodytes once more. In such an event the ancient caves would again be inhabited.

From Maastricht I made my way back to Antwerp, and then set out for Rotterdam. When I reached the Maas Diep, it was necessary to leave the train and take a ferry-boat to the city, for the great bridge over the Maas was then in course of construction; the longer bridge over the Hollandsch Diep had already been finished.

In Holland the economic atmosphere was wholly different from that of Belgium. There were no beggars, and there was a brisk business-like air. The Boompjes, or wharves, are so called because of the trees which are at once useful and ornamental, for their roots strengthen the foundations of the quay dykes and their foliage decorates the surface. The reasons for the absence of beggars will appear more fully later when I give an account of the beggar colonies of Holland, which I visited nineteen years afterwards (in 1893); but among these reasons was undoubtedly the prosperity of the Dutch East India Colonies. These colonies were not directly a source of revenue to the Dutch Government, but they were large sources of income to the Dutch people.

Although Holland exhibited signs of economic activity absent in Belgium, some of these were quite recent; indeed, at that moment Holland was really in a state of transition. I have mentioned that there was in 1874 no continuous railway communication between

[1] For a note on the Kent caverns and for those in the Crimea see vol. ii. p. 375.

Rotterdam and Antwerp. The bridge over the Hollandsch Diep had quite recently been opened. Before it was available, traffic was either conducted by steamer to Rotterdam from Moerdyk, or sent round about eighty miles of a detour by Breda, Boxtel and Utrecht. There was thus only one through line between Holland and Belgium, and practically only one through line between Holland and Germany, the north through route from Amsterdam to the valley of the Ems being too roundabout for great traffic.

In spite of the signs of active trade on the Boompjes, Rotterdam was still a mediæval town. The streets were narrow and congested, as were also the numerous canals. The primitive character of the municipal administration impressed itself upon me immediately after my arrival. On my first evening there was an alarm of fire in the neighbourhood of my hotel. Like Charles Lamb, I never could resist the temptation of a fire. I found that an oil store in a narrow street was blazing furiously. The street was crowded by people gazing helplessly at the conflagration. After a time the fire engines arrived— or rather one engine made its appearance at the end of the street at some distance from the fire. With much difficulty a way was made for it through the crowd. The engine was of a type which even then was archaic. It was a manual pump with space for about half a dozen hands on each side. It was intended to pump the water from the neighbouring canal. So many eager hands volunteered, and so many onlookers pressed upon it as a new centre of interest, that it was impossible to get it into operation. Everybody shouted advice and instruction and no one directed. Meanwhile the fire had burned up the available oil, and as there seemed to be nothing else combustible in its vicinity, it very naturally expired of its own accord.

Holland in those days was quaint and in many ways still mediæval. In the University of Leyden, lectures in the Faculty of Law were delivered in Latin as they had been since the foundation of the Faculty. They continued so to be given until about 1889. The women wore their beautiful gold skull-caps with the dainty lace caps of their respective provinces over them. In the morning there were to be seen in Rotterdam, and in other Dutch towns, domestics wearing these really becoming examples of ancient headgear while they were squirting water from the long syringes with which they cleaned the windows. When I went to stay with my friends at Amsterdam, I found that the maids waited at table in these fascinating caps. I was told that they were all heirlooms, and how when needs must the spiral gold wire attached to them on either side, and hanging down like ringlets, was clipped with a pair of scissors in order to make a necessary payment —hence the word "skilling" or clipping, from which our word shilling is derived. Alas! these beautiful things have left the heads they appropriately adorned and rightfully belonged to and have gone into museums or into the possession of rich collectors of such ethnographical objects. Twenty years after the date of which I am speaking, I saw one or two of these head-pieces in remote places in the north of Holland, but they were not very fine examples, and they had a modern air. I was told of an old lady who had a very fine and very ancient one which she obstinately refused to part with, although she had been offered fabulous sums for it.[1]

From Rotterdam I went to the Hague, which presented an aspect much less antique than Rotterdam, saw the pictures in the gallery, and visited the places customarily visited by tourists. Then I went to Amsterdam, where I found my friends living in a very nice house on the Amstel. Mr. Croal, my host, was a Scotsman who for many years had been general manager of the Royal Netherlands Steamship Line. He told me an amusing incident that had just happened. A ship was being built for his company at one of the yards on the Clyde. Detailed drawings were sent over to Amsterdam for approval. One of these drawings depicted the Royal Arms of Holland, which were to be placed in the saloon or in some other part of the vessel. The artist had made the design from a blazon in which he found, or ought to have found—for these are the Arms of Holland—*Azure: semé-de-lys, a Lion rampant argent, debruised by a Bend gules.* The arms in the drawing were correctly rendered, excepting that the artist had drawn the lion rampant in the same manner as he would have drawn it for the arms of Scotland, while the head and mane of the lion are drawn by the Dutch heraldic artists in a distinctive manner, different from that in which the lion is drawn by Scots heralds. Mr. Croal objected to the design and informed the firm in Glasgow that they must have a Dutch and not a Scots lion in the arms. The firm answered that they were not familiar with the Dutch lion, but if a cage containing one was sent over they would have it accurately represented.

In Amsterdam I heard some very fine music in a concert-hall near the Amstel Hotel. At that time the picture gallery of Amsterdam, known as the Rijksmuseum, was housed in the Trippenhuis. There were to be seen many of the great pictures of the world: among

---

[1] Robinson (father of Mary F. Robinson) told me that he had seen one of these head-dresses for which £2000 had been offered.

these were the "Night Watch" of Rembrandt and his "Five Staal-meisters of the Guild of Clothmakers." Thackeray, who was not an ill-natured critic of art although he exhibits little knowledge of paint, while consumed with admiration of the Hague Rembrandt, "The School of Anatomy," speaks rather slightingly of the "Night Watch." He says that it is "magnificent in parts, but on the side to the spectator's right, smoky and dim." [1] Maybe Rembrandt chose to paint a group as it appeared at night by the light of a smoky lantern. Why not? and why should Rembrandt not paint dim smoke? Perhaps after two hundred years the picture was not precisely as Rembrandt painted it. Colour is a delicate affair, especially such colour as Rembrandt put in his chiaroscuro. But there it is, and such as it is we may be thankful for it. I see it now in the eye of my mind, although it is forty-nine years since I saw it in paint. I should not presume either to give the jejune impressions of extreme youth or to use these impressions as the basis of more mature judgment. The common consent of the world has placed the "Night Watch" where it is, and there let it remain. I think that it was Millais who said, apropos of the Glasgow Rembrandt, "The Man in Armour," that it looked like "a black cat in a coal-hole." It is certainly true that it was for years impossible really to see that picture; but the grime of two centuries has long ago been removed from it, at least some of the delicacies of the superb shadows have been recovered, and it is possible now to see it more or less as Rembrandt expected it to be seen. Painters have three enemies who attack and undermine their immortality; these are chemical reaction, changes in temperature and humidity, and the unskilful restorer. The casual critic may be likened to the fly which lights upon a few spots on the canvas and then disappears. In the Trippenhuis might also be seen, hanging opposite the "Night Watch," the huge canvas (6 ft. 19½ ins. by 18 ft.) of Bartholomew van der Helst, "The Banquet of the Civic Guard." This feast was held to celebrate the Peace of Münster in Westphalia (1648), which marked the close of the Thirty Years' War. The civic military companies and the guild and civic corporations were the chief patrons of art during the sixteenth and seventeenth centuries. The rise of the democratic spirit had diminished alike the influence and the revenues of princely patrons, and had these public bodies not taken their places as fosterers of art, painting would have perished through lack of sustenance, for the Dutch and Flemish merchants, collectively wealthy, were rarely

---

[1] *A Roundabout Journey*, first published in the *Cornhill Magazine*, vol. ii. 1860, p. 637.

so individually, and their capital was involved continually in commercial adventures.

One Sunday, after attending the Scots Presbyterian Church in the Begyn Straat, I was taken by my friends by rail to Haarlem. The railway passes by means of a dyke to the north of the Haarlemmer Meer; but between the railway and the Ij, an inlet of the Zuyder Zee, there is another dyke upon which there were strung in an imposing and picturesque line some two hundred windmills erected to pump out the waters of the Haarlemmer Meer, which at that time was in course of being drained. Not for some years was this process completed, and then followed an interval until the excess of salt in the bed of the inland sea could be eliminated and the land made fit for cultivation. The neighbourhood of Haarlem is celebrated for its country houses with their parks and gardens. There more than anywhere else could Dutch horticulture be seen to advantage. We drove from Haarlem through miles of hedges, parks, gardens, formal and otherwise, to Zaandvoort and the sea. At Haarlem there happened to be a *kermess*, or fair, in progress, which gave us an opportunity of seeing the country folk. In the Cathedral we heard the magnificent organ and saw the models of ships formerly common in the Dutch churches. Unfortunately many of these models have been wrenched from their appropriate habitat and have been put in cases in museums and in the houses of private collectors, where their historical setting is customarily ignored.

PART II.—PARIS AND THE RHINE IN 1878

International expositions of the products of industry and art have, or ought to have, a great interest for the professional economist. They contain in concentrated form at least suggestions of the stage of contemporary economic development and, not less important, indications of the contemporary phase of architecture and the other plastic arts. The first International Exhibition was held in London in 1851. The reports of the juries were published in a bulky volume.[1] They constitute a really valuable document in economic history. Nowhere else is there to be found in so exact and comprehensive detail the means of forming a judgment upon the economical situation throughout the

[1] "Exhibition of the Works of Industry of all Nations, 1851. Reports by the Juries on the subjects in the thirty classes into which the Exhibition was divided." London, 1852.

world in the middle of the nineteenth century. The second International Exhibition was held in London in 1862. A similar series of reports was published afterwards, the most valuable being the report upon chemical industries. The third International Exhibition was held in Paris in 1867, and the fourth in Philadelphia in 1876. The fifth was held in Paris in 1878.

In 1878 Paris had wholly recovered from the economical effects of the war of 1870–71. Indeed, so rapidly had France revived, that there was a sufficient amount of uneasiness in Germany to lend colour to the accusation current in 1875 that Bismarck was anxious to provoke another war. Bismarck has denied the truth of this accusation.[1] His denial would not of itself be convincing; but the interior condition of Germany in 1875 was not favourable for a renewal of hostilities. This became manifest in 1876 and still more in 1878. In 1876 the German financial and commercial classes encountered a sharp check in the collapse of the indiscreet speculations into which they had been led by the intoxication of the easy victory of German arms over France in 1870–71. In 1878 the Socialist movement became aggressive, and the German Government found it necessary to adopt serious and continuous means of dealing with that movement. Thus in 1878 France had no reason to be otherwise than *en fête*. Paris had recovered from the war, although traces of it and of its consequences remained. The blackened walls of the Tuileries had not been wholly removed. The Colonne Vendôme, the removal of which by the Commune in 1871 has been mentioned in a previous chapter, had not yet been replaced.

I spent some time in the Café de la Régence, the traditional home of chess in Paris, and played at a franc a game with the old fellows who used to be found there, especially on Sunday. It was always easy to get a good opponent. The pieces were characteristic. They were very large and the habitués usually set them down with a vigorous bang as if to announce the decisiveness of their moves. I went to the Opéra Comique and to other theatres, but I have the impression that nothing of a notable character was on the Paris stage at that time. I used to go down to the Marche aux Halles in the early morning to see the country people come in with their vegetable carts, and used to breakfast on quite fair bouillon and quite execrable wine in the small *estaminets* in the neighbourhood, having meanwhile a

---

[1] See Bismarck, *The Man and the Statesman; Being the Reflections and Reminiscences of Prince Otto von Bismarck*, edited by A. J. Butler (London, 1898), ii. p. 189.

causerie with proprietor or customer, generally puzzled over my presence and sometimes suspicious. Had I told them the real truth, which was that I was there in order to see what manner of people they were, and for no other reason—that I was not a novelist or an artist, but only a disinterested observer of life, they would have exploded with laughter. What a fool I must be to imagine that shrewd people like them could be taken in with so bald a fiction!

I made tours of the Boulevards, which took some time, as I sat in many cafés, sampled many vintages, and consumed endless *mazagrans* and *amers*. On Sundays I went to the Louvre, where I often ran across clerical schoolmasters from the suburbs with groups of youngsters to whom they were endeavouring to expound the works of art, sometimes in a rather artless manner.

It was, I think, Frédéric le Play who suggested, and it was Patrick Geddes who elaborated into a schematic whole, the theory of the topography of Paris by which Paris is seen to be a complex of *ronds-points* or places of rendezvous for hunters in a forest. In short, that Paris is a forest city. The Louvre—or Wolf's Grove in which wolves could always be hunted and found—has near it the principal *rond-point*, and all the others are connected with it by radial avenues. It is true that the plan here suggested is the plan of the roads in the forests round Paris. The forest round St. Cloud exhibits the plan precisely. What importance is to be attached to original impulse towards such a plan and what importance to the obvious military advantages, whether for defence against external attack or internal revolution, would be hard to determine. Very likely both were equally important. The original *rond-point* plan would have been abandoned if it had not been convenient to continue on military grounds.

The buildings of the exposition were by no means so fine or so interesting as architectural experiments as those of the exposition of 1889 (which I did not see) or of 1900, of which later I shall give some account. I was, however, much interested in the chemical section, of which I made a careful study. Germany exhibited many chemical products, and I determined to go to Germany in order to make inquiry into what was going on in that connection as well as to see the Rhine. I went from Paris to Strassburg, where I climbed the cathedral spire. The delicate tracery in the upper part of it is quite fine, and the view of the surrounding flat country excellent. From Strassburg I went to Mülhausen to see chemical works, and on the same errand to Frankfurt-on-the-Main. In both of these places I found the beginnings of the chemical industries which were soon to assume

I—I

such large proportions. I did not derive a great deal of detailed information, indeed it was not my purpose to seek it. I only wanted to gather in a general sense what was the nature and extent of the movement. I met a number of the leading people in the industry, and I was struck by the fact that almost none of those whom I met were young men—nearly all of them were men of highly mature years. It struck me at the time that many of them must have left other employments in commerce or finance to go into the chemical trade. It appeared to me that for their apparent size the businesses were somewhat overloaded with non-technical directors.[1]

One of the works which I visited was that of Meister Lucius and Bruning at Hoechst, a suburb of Frankfurt-on-the-Main. It was a small affair then. Within a few years it had expanded greatly and acquired a wide celebrity. I went to Wiesbaden, where it occurred to me that I might call upon Fresenius, the chemist. Strangely enough, although he had extensive fame outside Germany, I experienced difficulty in discovering where he lived. I found his house, but unfortunately he was away from home. Wiesbaden was at that time a favourite resort of the English people, who went there for the cure. There was a kursaal and gardens and the usual appurtenances of such a place.

Frankfurt was just beginning to transform itself. A part of the Judengasse had just been pulled down, but the old Rothschild house was still standing as well as other houses of the same period. I went to Worms because of its historical interest, to Mannheim and to Heidelberg, where I saw the castle and its tuns, and the fine view of the Neckar from its terraces. On the opposite bank of the Neckar is the inn where the Heidelberg students went to fight their duels. From Heidelberg I went to Mainz. Apart from its monuments and historical associations, Mainz was interesting to me because it was the home of my friend Henry Ettling, the master drummer. Ettling was a merchant in wines—the light wines of the Rhine—and he plied his trade in England in happier times before the German megalomania. Wine gave him a living; but his real *métier* was that of a musician. He was by common consent of those who knew the greatest drummer of his age. Everywhere he was in demand, and he used to play the big drum at every big concert in Europe. He beat his drum for the mere joy of it.

---

[1] I was unable to account for this phenomenon at the time. Not for years afterwards did its real significance dawn upon me. The youths in the scientific departments in the universities and technical colleges were being exploited by the financiers, who were represented by the directors whom I saw. By means of this co-operation of financial power and scientific intelligence the huge structure of German business was built up.

Ettling was besides a first-rate amateur conjurer. One evening at my house, after playing some classical pieces on the piano, he asked for a large clothes-brush, and with this implement he executed some astonishing *jeux d'esprit*. Then the brush disappeared before our eyes. It was found later in some remote part of the room. He was especially skilful in palming coins. His art lay in extraordinary rapidity of movement. Placing a coin in his open palm, he was able, by a motion too quick for the eye to follow, to throw it into his hair, of which he had more than abundance—a trick I never saw any professional conjurer attempt. He told me of two tricks he played upon professionals. One of them was played upon one of the "Doblers" or "Hermanns," *i.e.* one of the men to whom some well-known conjurer sold the use of his name. This man was performing in a provincial town somewhere in Europe. Ettling happened to be there, and attended the performance. A confederate of the man on the stage sat down beside Ettling and clumsily inserted into the pocket of one of the audience a coloured handkerchief, obviously in preparation for a trick. Ettling immediately abstracted the handkerchief, and put it in his own pocket. When the trick came on the handkerchief could not be found. Ettling left it at the box-office with a note advising the performer to be more careful in choosing his confederates. The other occasion was when Ettling attended the performance of a conjurer who did a trick that Ettling could not follow. The conjurer happened to be staying in the same hotel as Ettling, and Ettling invited him to a game at billiards. Before the game began, Ettling complimented him upon his performance and offered him half a sovereign for an explanation of the trick he could not follow. The conjurer told him how the trick was done, and Ettling produced the half-sovereign. When the game was over Ettling said, "By the way, did I pay you for that trick?" "Yes," said the conjurer. "Are you sure?" "Yes, of course, you put a half-sovereign into my hand." "No doubt," said Ettling, "but I also took it out again. Here it is."

As the steamer approached Cologne, the lofty spires of the cathedral made their appearance. At that time the south spire was enveloped in scaffolding, for it was not yet finished. It was destined to be completed ere long, for the last stone of the south spire was put in position in August 1880, two years after I saw it. Apart from its great size and the height of its spires, the cathedral of Cologne is not remarkable. Although the design is old and although it is a fair example of Gothic architecture, it has been largely built in recent times. Considered as a work of art, it cannot be compared with either the cathedral of Rheims, which the Germans have wantonly destroyed, or the cathedral of Amiens, which ran risk of destruction at their hands.

At Cologne I sat down in the Dom Hof at a table where a young priest was already seated. He courteously asked me to share his wine. I found that he came from Glasgow and was leaving Cologne that day. So was I, and we travelled together so far as Aix-la-Chapelle. This friendly young cleric became, many years later, Dr. MacGuire, Roman Catholic Archbishop of Glasgow.

At Aix-la-Chapelle, as the French called it when it was theirs, or Aachen as the Germans call it, I saw some chemical works and people of no great importance, and went to the basilica to see the simple stone in the pavement upon which are inscribed the magic words *Carlo Magno*. It was here that at nine o'clock in the morning of the 28th of January, 814, Charlemagne died. There were legends that he was buried sitting upon his throne, with his crown upon his head and his sceptre in his hands, as if some day he might be expected to resume sway over his wide empire; but the hard historical fact is that he was placed recumbent in a coffin like ordinary mortals. Yet Charlemagne was not an ordinary mortal. When his coffin was opened in 1861, measurement of his skeleton showed that he stood six feet four inches, nearly a head taller than a tall man of his or of our own time.

PART III.—ROTTERDAM, THE RHINE, THE MOSELLE, ITALY AND
SWITZERLAND, 1881

In the summer of 1881 I sailed from Leith, as the guest of a captain of a cargo steamer, with a friend who was on his way to Brussels. After a somewhat stormy passage we drew up at the Boompjes in Rotterdam. Seven years had wrought great changes. The bridge over the Maas Diep had been finished, a great clearance of ancient houses and streets had been made, and there was a new railway station in the heart of the city. There were signs of commercial activity everywhere. Rotterdam had been profiting by the trade movement in Germany, and particularly by that of the lower valley of the Rhine. We did not delay in Rotterdam, but soon made our way to Antwerp. There seven years had wrought even greater changes. The reconstruction of the quays and docks had begun in 1877 and was proceeding. The effect upon the shipping trade of Antwerp of the growth of

German commerce was obvious, and not less so the effect of the growth of Belgian industry. The manufacture of light iron beams for the construction of buildings had been rapidly developed, and the skill and ingenuity applied to this industry gave Belgium for a time a practical monopoly in light girders. The British iron manufacturers had devoted themselves to the production of the heavier iron products, and their machinery was specially adapted to this work. Up till 1873 they had been overwhelmed with orders, and they had not yet turned their attention to other forms of demand. Moreover, the iron ores of Luxemburg, which formed three-fourths of the ores manipulated in the Belgian furnaces, were specially suited for light iron manufactures. Thus during a period of trade depression throughout the world Belgian iron manufacture increased rapidly because the Belgian product met the demand for structural material. This material was required for the building of industrial and other dwellings under the conditions indicated in a previous chapter. In 1881 Belgium exported heavily to Holland, Great Britain, the French Colonies, and even to the United States, whose great iron development had not yet begun.

In Brussels also the years had wrought changes. The process of widening the main avenues and rebuilding was going on apace.

From Brussels I went to Cologne, and from there up the Rhine to Coblenz. From Coblenz I had intended to sail up the Moselle, but it was not possible. The summer was unusually hot, and the river had sunk to a tiny stream. Nevertheless, the scenery as viewed from the railway is very picturesque. There is indeed no more beautiful valley in western Europe than the narrow valley, almost a gorge in places, through which the Moselle flows to the Rhine. At Treves I found the magnificent Roman villa which had comparatively recently been fully exposed.

From Treves I went to Luxemburg, whose position on an abrupt ridge rising out of a valley approaching it on all sides renders it one of the most picturesque of cities; and from Luxemburg I went on to Metz. I took the opportunity of walking round the outskirts of this celebrated fortress, and of looking with the eye of an amateur upon the system of forts by which it was surrounded. From Metz I went direct to Basle, and so found myself in Switzerland. I spent a short time in Geneva, where I went to see the point where the white waters of the Arve loaded with the mud of the glaciers join the blue waters of the Rhone, filtered as they are by passing through the great basin of Lake Leman, and amused myself by putting a sheet of paper between the rivers at their juncture, so precise is the line of demarcation.

From Geneva I went to Lausanne and thence to Villeneuve. From the head of the lake I went by rail to Vernayaz, and then past the Gorge de Trient to the point where the road from Martigny joins the Vernayaz road and passes over the Col de Balme to Chamounix. Near the small village of Salvan I was trudging along with my knapsack on my back when, much to my surprise, I heard my name shouted from the hill above. There was a flutter of a coloured skirt, and in a few moments a young lady jumped down upon the road. She was a friend of my sister's at school at Lausanne in the winter, and spending her vacation in a secluded châlet. At the village I found a fête in progress. There was a fiddler and a jovial company. The peasants were dancing in the inn, their huge boots making a violent clatter, and outside were

> many a man and many a maid
> Dancing in the chequered shade.

I watched them for a while, and then marched on towards Chamounix. Great masses of dark cloud wrapped the mountain-tops completely within their folds. Suddenly, as I approached Argentières, the loftier cloud masses separated, and there appeared, hanging like a cathedral in the sky, the spire alone of the Aiguille du Dru, a wonderful effect of light and darkness.

At Chamounix, before engaging a guide, I decided to make a short excursion on my own account, for I felt at home in the hills. I therefore walked up to the Montanvert early in the morning, had breakfast there, and proceeded to explore the lower part of the Mer de Glace. I was amusing myself jumping about on the ice when I saw a party consisting of two guides and two travellers leave the Montanvert and come in my direction. I waited, and they came up to me. At the same moment there came down from the direction of Le Jardin another party of guides and travellers. The two parties, as is customary, stopped to exchange greetings, one on one side of a crevasse and the other party on the other side. The home-going party had been attempting the ascent of the Aiguille Verte and were full of their experiences. As the two parties separated, one of the outgoing travellers spoke to me in German, I answered in the same language, and then the other traveller, whom I at once recognised as an Englishman, joined in the conversation, and very politely told me that they were going up to Le Jardin, and that if I chose to go with them they would be glad to have my company. I replied that I should be delighted, but that I had only my alpenstock and no supplies for the day, as I had had no intention of going so far at that time. They consulted their guides, who thought there was sufficient in their packs, and so we went on. The English traveller then very courteously began to translate into German for my benefit the information which had been given by the Aiguille Verte party. I listened for a short time and then undeceived him. He told me his name—he was Dr. Theodore Williams, of the Brompton Hospital for Consumptives. We had a very pleasant excursion. When we reached the Glacier de Taléfre, with its blue ice pinnacles and tumbled ice masses, we had a little bit of rather hard going, and our companion, the young German, told us that he was played out and could go no farther. There was nothing to be done but to send him back with one of the two guides and to go on with the other. The alternative was for the whole party to return without reaching its objective. The expedition was not in the least dangerous or difficult and there seemed no reason to doubt the wisdom of going on. We reached Le Jardin comfortably and rested. As everyone knows who has been in it, Le Jardin is a little oasis in a wilderness of ice and rock. In it the gentian and the ubiquitous bluebell give a note of vivid colour. Towards the south there rises the magnificent amphitheatre of the Grandes Jorasses, to the west there is the Col de Géant, and north-west the round summit of Mont Blanc, while to the north there is the peak of the Aiguille Verte. Indeed, from Le Jardin there is by far the finest view of the Alps in the Chamounix region. We lingered perhaps rather too long enjoying the superb prospect. Late in the afternoon we began to descend. We had not proceeded very far when Dr. Williams slipped on an ice hillock and twisted his ankle. This accident delayed our progress greatly; and the evening was beginning to close in before we were able to cross to the west side of the glacier. Then indeed our troubles began. We found that a wide crack which we had easily jumped over in the morning had developed into a chasm, which without a ladder and in the disabled condition of one of our party was quite impassable. We had, therefore, to climb the precipitous rock flanking the glacier in order that we might get round this crack. This was a really difficult business. However, our guide was vigorous and skilful, and he hoisted us one by one from ledge to ledge, where this was necessary, until we reached the top. I have climbed much since; but I always look back upon that first climb in the Alps as being by far the most risky experience I have ever had. It is not a pleasant sensation to cling in the dark to a ledge an inch or two in breadth over a chasm of unknown depth. However, we survived it and reached the Montanvert without further mishap. After some other excursions I went from Chamounix by the Tête Noire to Martigny, walking down at night through the tall trees of the forest on the east side of the pass, the stars shining with unusual brilliancy between the tree-tops, for these contracted the area of light and the tall trees acted almost like a huge telescope. As I approached Martigny the sky became overcast, and I entered the town in inky blackness. I heard voices which I inferred were those of guides or villagers sitting on the bench before the inn, and proceeded towards them. Next day, under a broiling sun, I walked up the valley of the Drance to Orsières, where I had my siesta and then in the cool of the afternoon continued. As I passed through the villages in the evening the goatherds were driving in their goats from the pastures, and children were watching for the goats of their households as they came along the village street, rushing to them, throwing their arms about the necks of the animals, and dragging them into the lower storey of the châlets in which they were housed.

I fell in with a peasant driving an empty char-a-banc upon which he had carried some produce to Orsières, and got a lift from him. When he left me at his châlet, I tramped on. Ere long I was overtaken by another peasant mounted on a mule, and leading another which he was taking from his lower pastures. I mounted this spare animal. No one who has never ridden a mule bareback knows the full discomfort of such a mode of locomotion. The mule is an invaluable animal for draught purposes, although he has a mind of his own and understands very well how to use it to the discomfiture of his employer if need be; but the articulation of his vertebral column is too much like a cross-cut saw with large and sharp teeth to render riding upon it an experience of pleasure. My mule was perfectly amiable and willing, and he was not responsible for his anatomical structure. After some time I felt more fatigued with the riding than I thought I should be with walking. I therefore dismounted and tramped along with the muleteer. We had a pleasant chat about the mountain pastures, the weather and other topics. Every now and then the valley was lit up by noiseless flashes of summer lightning. Ere long we came to Bourg St. Pierre, where my muleteer lived. He invited me into his house. The living-room was dark save for the light of a minute lamp on the table which revealed the faces of the family at supper. In the centre of the table was a bowl out of which each helped himself or herself by means of spoons. I cheerfully joined them in this primitive repast, had a gossip with the family, and then set off in the darkness for La Cantine de Proz. I had intended to go on to the monastery, but rain began to fall heavily and the path came to be difficult to distinguish. The narrowing pass was filled with ghosts. Cæsar passed this way from Rome and Napoleon's soldiers dragged their cannon over this pass to Italy. I decided to spend the night in the village. Readily I found a châlet where travellers were received, supped on bread and honey, and next morning, although it was still raining heavily, continued my way up the pass until I arrived at the Monastery of St. Bernard. I was soaked to the skin. There were no other travellers, and the monks gave me with great cordiality their exclusive attention. I had sent on my baggage by post to Zermatt, and was travelling with a minimum of impedimenta. The good-natured monks supplied me with a change of garments—not the habit of a monk, which indeed, under the circumstances, I should have been quite willing temporarily to assume, but more secular garments. Meanwhile, my clothes were taken to the kitchen to be dried near the enormous ovens in which the good fare of the monastery was prepared. I went into the kitchen after a time to retrieve my belongings, and found it occupied partly by the monastic cooks, and partly by the enormous dogs for which the monastery is celebrated.

The monks belong to the Order of St. Augustine. I spent some time in the library, and made the acquaintance of the librarian. The library is, I imagine, unique among monastic libraries, because, in addition to the theological treatises which might be expected in such a collection, there was a really fine scientific library, containing series of the transactions of the chief among the learned societies of Europe. These series were kept in excellent order. I am not aware if any continuous or important scientific work has been accomplished at the monastery apart from meteorological observations, but the monks have through the generosity of the learned societies the opportunity of keeping themselves *en rapport* with the growth of all branches of science. At the midday meal a number of Italian peasants who were crossing the pass from the Val d'Aoste made their appearance. The meal included meat, of which I had not partaken since I left Chamounix, and to which I expect the Italian peasants were not habituated. Large flagons of good red wine gave an appropriate air of monastic cheer.

Norman Macleod, in a couple of amusing letters which are printed in the *Life* by his brother, describes his impressions of St. Bernard. He writes to his wife bidding her farewell and telling her that he has made up his mind to become a monk. Next morning he repents, and gives the reason for his change of intention.

The life of a monastery has attractions and perhaps even advantages for a certain type of mind. The cloister permits a concentration upon mental labour or upon mere reflection, together with indifference to economical considerations; but its very detachment from the organic life of the world is its undoing. Human life cannot be at once solitary and sane. The rare successes of the cloister cannot be set against the numerous instances of sheer inertia.

Nevertheless, with some reluctance I left the hospitable and friendly monks and walked down the mountain towards Aosta. In the pastures and cultivated plots in the neighbourhood of the châlets I saw very numerous cases of goitre. Indeed, I recall one field in which about half a dozen peasants were working. Each of them had a large pendulous goitre, some of them had a terrible aspect. This disease was said at the time to be more prevalent in the Val d'Aoste than anywhere else. I could readily believe this to be the case.

Aosta (*Augusta Prætoria* of the Romans) is a wonderful relic of the ancient world. It is true that the town is secluded in the mountains, but it commands one of the two important passes over the Western Alps, the other corresponding town being Susa, which commands the pass of Mont Cenis. It was over the pass of the Little St. Bernard near the greater mountain that Hannibal fought his way through to Italy; but it was Cæsar and Augustus who made the Great St. Bernard a military road. Then Aosta became an inner gateway of the imperial system. The remains of that epoch are ample—a fine though not large triumphal arch to Augustus, a theatre, a gateway and a bridge. Otherwise Aosta is, or was in 1881, a mediæval town, substantially as it was when under the feudal dominion of the Princes of the House of Savoy. The streets are very narrow, and the projecting balconies of the houses approach one another so closely that from the top of the diligence it is possible to touch them on either side. The streets were lit by oil lanterns, suspended by means of a rope from wrought-iron brackets, some of fine design. The system of sewage was very simple. The narrow street inclined towards the centre and into the channel thus formed everything was thrown; in the evening a stream of water carried away accumulations and discharged them into the river. Towards the afternoon, especially on warm days, the stench of the streets, though it did not seem to trouble the noses of the natives, became hard for those of visitors to endure.

From Aosta I took the diligence to Chatillon, and then climbed up the Val Tournanche. On the west side of this beautiful valley, in the upper part of it, there is to be seen stretching in a long line on the side of the enclosing mountain the extensive remains of a Roman aqueduct which brought water direct from the hills to the settlement or camps in the valley below. Late in the evening I arrived at the Matterhorn Hotel, a hostelry upon which there frown the Matterhorn, the Little Matterhorn, and the Lyskamm. The view of the Matterhorn from the Italian side is not so imposing as that from Zermatt, yet its abrupt precipices give it an almost terrifying aspect. While looking at the mountain from the balcony of the hotel in the late evening I saw a cloud mass accumulate round the summit, and then after a while detach itself and roll down the cliffs. It approached rapidly, enveloped the hotel in its folds, and then passed down the valley. Its definite contour and white flexible, billowy mass gave it the appearance of a gigantic feather-bed. Meantime flashes of lightning played about the summit of the mountain.

About three in the morning, after an ice-cold bath and breakfast, I started with my guide, whom I had engaged at Chatillon. We reached the cabane at the top of the pass between seven and eight, and met shortly afterwards a party which had just come down from the Breithorn. They said that it was very stormy, and advised us to wait until the next day. However, neither my guide nor I was inclined to postpone our excursion, and, well roped together, we started and easily made the summit of the mountain about eleven o'clock. The view from the Breithorn is superb. It is very similar to that from Monte Rosa, and it is preferable to that from the Matterhorn, because it includes the Matterhorn itself. Towards Macunaga a thick white fog lay among the hills and obscured the landscape in that direction, but in every other, bright sunlight lit up the peaks—the Jungfrau and the Matterhorn most conspicuously, then the Grand Paradis, the highest mountain in Italy—while fold on fold the mountains towards the Mont Blanc range formed the western horizon.[1] Far beneath lay the Gorner Grat, the Riffel Berg and Zermatt, the broad expanse of the Breithorn, the Théodule and the Gorner Glaciers stretching between.

As we went up and down the arête, the steep ice slope which must be negotiated to reach the summit, I noticed an interesting meteorological phenomenon. This was the sharp stratification of the air currents. At the foot of the arête the wind blew with some violence, although not sufficient to impede our progress. Towards the middle of the slope the wind ceased abruptly, and on the top of the mountain there was not a breath of air. When we descended, we encountered the air current at precisely the same place from which we had passed out of it. Towards the foot of the arête we left the ice

---

[1] A member of the Alpine Club has related that he saw the Pyrenees from the top of the Breithorn. I am not in a position to dispute the statement.

steps we had cut during our ascent and glissaded to the snow field, carefully avoiding a crevasse we had noticed on our way up. The ascent of the Breithorn is one of the easiest in the Alps, and it is one which more than amply repays the climber.[1] The immense amphitheatre of glacier beneath the summit of the mountain gives space in the foreground and produces a panoramic effect in which the proportions of the mountains can be seen to advantage.

When we returned to the cabane we found a French party newly arrived from Zermatt. In this party was the President of the Alpine Club of Lyons and his wife. While resting before our descent of the glaciers I played a couple of games of chess with the lady.

From the cabane we dropped during the afternoon to Zermatt. The view from Zermatt of the amphitheatre of mountains is wholly without parallel in Switzerland. Chamounix is surrounded by high peaks, but there is no intermediate foreground by which the spectator can thrust them back so that they can be seen. Before Zermatt there is the vast glacier system of the Gorner and Théodule Glaciers by which Monte Rosa, the Breithorn, the Lyskamm, the Little Matterhorn and the Great Matterhorn are extended in a mighty panorama. Each of these mountains has a characteristic form—Monte Rosa, round snow-capped summit; the Breithorn, a snow cornice which seems to overhang precariously; the Lyskamm and the Little Matterhorn, needle-like peaks; and the Great Matterhorn, the form of a rearing horse according to Ruskin, or a sphinx according to some.

I found that the indications of heavy weather on the Matterhorn which I had noticed from the Italian side were those of a storm which had raged upon the mountain for several days. The people in Zermatt were in a state of anxiety on account of Mr. Campbell, the blind Alpinist, who had begun the ascent of the mountain four days before, and who, with his guides, was practically marooned in a cabane near the summit. He had sent back some of his guides for food, and these had relieved anxiety about the fate of the party. Mr. Campbell had great courage and perseverance, and his Alpine exploits were conducted by him in order to show what blind men could do; but it is a question whether the good he did by this particular kind of adventure was not offset by the unnecessary risk he imposed upon his guides. I believe, however, that no mishap of consequence attended his expeditions. Next day I learned of an accident on Monte Rosa, in which a traveller, a guide and a porter had lost their lives. I had

[1] The height of the Breithorn, according to the Swiss Trigonometrical Surveys, is 13,685 feet.

intended to climb that mountain, but the weather conditions were not inviting.

From Zermatt I walked up the Visp Thal and the Nicolai Thal to Brieg. I believe that a railway has since been constructed through these charming valleys. At Brieg I took the diligence over the Furca, past the pinnacles of the Rhone Glacier from which the River Rhone takes its primary waters, and on to the junction with the Gothard road from Italy. At that moment the Gothard Tunnel was being constructed, but no part of the line had been opened. The journey by Hospenthal, Andermatt and Goschenen past the Devil's Bridge and on to Fluelen and Altdorf occupied about thirty-six hours. My only travelling companions were a young French gentleman, very culti- vated and intelligent, a kinsman of General Moreau, celebrated in the Napoleonic wars, and an American family of no interest. From Fluelen I went by steamer to Lucerne, climbed the Rigi, saw Pilatus, and then journeyed by Berne to Paris.

CHAPTER XI

> Trim, naked Speed!
> Speed, and a victory
> Snatched in the teeth
> Of the Masters of Darkness.
> For the antient, invincible
> Spirit of Man,
> Stern-set, adventurous,
> Dreaming things, doing things;
> Strong with a strength
> Won from tremendous
> And desperate vicissitudes,
> Out of unnumbered,
> Unstoried experiences.
> W. E. HENLEY, *A Song of Speed* (1903).

THE salient features of economical development in the west of Scotland during the decades 1861–70 and 1871–80 as they envisaged themselves to me have been briefly recounted in former chapters. The opening years of the new decade had a heavy inheritance from its predecessor. The financial catastrophe of 1878 had staggered the people of Glasgow. The situation was on the whole well managed by solvent banks, which lent money on deposits with banks in liquidation and took risk of recovering advances. Benevolence did something to mitigate individual hardship and generosity provided collective funds. Helen Faucit emerged from retirement and Henry Irving came with her to read to a great audience for the benefit of ruined shareholders. For the moment enterprise was arrested; not for three or four years did commercial and industrial life resume even average activity.

To the causes of economic dislocation indicated in a former chapter there should be added others of longer standing and of more gradual influence. These were (*a*) decline of cereal cultivation in Great Britain owing to diminished profit resulting from competition of farmers of the United States and the Argentine Republic with British farmers; (*b*) relatively diminished production in Great Britain of cattle and sheep owing to greater ease and cheapness of production on a large scale on the plains of North and South America and in Australia and New Zealand; (*c*) decline of agricultural rents arising from these

142

movements and diminished employment in agriculture; and (d) general fall of prices from numerous primary and secondary causes, producing dislocation in the mechanism of industry and commerce.

In spite of miscellaneity of industries, Glasgow was heavily smitten; but this very characteristic of miscellaneity it was which enabled the district to recover with comparative rapidity from general depression and from blows which had been especially injurious to its credit. Yet this recovery was not wholly effected until after the close of the decade 1881–90.

The fall in prices which from various causes had taken place during the trade *malaise* stimulated demand; and thus, though wages were low and profits reduced to a minimum in many of the staple industries, movement of goods increased. A consequence of this increased movement of goods was rise in ocean freights. This led to demand for ships, shipbuilding became very active in 1882. The additional demand proved to be readily satisfied and the briskness was only temporary. Stocks of iron were large, prices continued to be depressed and many furnaces were put " out of blast "; 1883–86 were years of great depression.

The coal-miners had attempted to improve their position by strikes, but stocks of coal were ample enough to meet restricted demand without fresh production, and coal-masters were able to defeat the strikers with comparative ease. Under these conditions, it became apparent to miners' leaders that no strike could succeed so long as heavy reserves of coal were available. They therefore proposed to work for a time at the customary wage, but to diminish output by working half time. Adoption of this plan meant that customary earnings of miners were cut to the extent of one-half, and that stocks of coal at the pit mouth and elsewhere were gradually depleted until reserves which enabled coal-masters to resist demand for increased wages were exhausted. This plan, known as "restricted darg," involved great hardships to miners. I made some inquiries at the time into the situation in mining villages. "Restricted darg" resulted in practical elimination of meat from the miner's diet, in practical elimination of clothes from his budget and in piling up of debt. Many shopkeepers in mining districts assisted materially in "carrying" miners over the crisis so far as food was concerned, and clothing was to some extent provided by charitable agencies. The main burden, however, fell upon miners' families. They voluntarily reduced their consumption for a time in order to place themselves on another level afterwards. The short "darg" endured, so far as I remember, for eighteen months. These were eighteen months of great hardship. On the whole, it may be said that the policy was successful. When turn of the tide came, as it did, miners were enabled to benefit by it probably some months sooner than otherwise might have been possible. Yet cases in which a policy of restricted production can be of general benefit to society are not numerous. They can occur only when production has been lopsided and when demand for certain commodities has declined while production has been sustained until accumulated stocks become excessive.

Through the interest of Glasgow capitalists in chemical industries, originating in the latter part of the eighteenth century and extending greatly in the nineteenth century, reduction of copper ores had become a great industry. Copper was imported chiefly from Spain, where it was exploited mainly by Scots capital. This industry led to development of a group of metallurgical chemists in Glasgow who devoted themselves to improvement of processes for extraction of metals. Their investigations, though primarily concerned with copper, were naturally not confined to that metal. In the early eighties attention was widely drawn to extraction of gold from inferior ores through exploitation of the Transvaal mines. It was found that by means of then existing methods of extraction a large amount of gold in the aggregate was left in the ore because its extraction did not pay. Several new processes for extraction of gold from inferior ores were brought forward in obedience to obvious demand. In developing these processes, Glasgow metallurgical chemists took a principal share. One of my friends, J. D. Macarthur, mentioned to me that he had some ideas on the subject, and I encouraged him to set them out in a paper. I was able to arrange for publication of this paper in a technical journal, and it immediately attracted the attention of a group of capitalists who had been induced to embark in another process and had been disappointed in the results of experiments they had conducted. They made an arrangement with Mr. Macarthur, the ultimate result of which was development of the Macarthur-Forest or cyanide process for extraction of gold which wholly revolutionised the industry. This process undoubtedly contributed to immensely increased production of gold which began to take effect in the late eighties.

I cannot in this place undertake to sustain the thesis that the increase in production of gold was the most important single factor in stimulation of industrial activity which put an end to the trade *malaise*. It needs, however, no argument to show that had this increase not taken place, a series of hazardous experiments in currency must have been forced upon commercial nations.

In the perspective of forty years, the conspicuous feature in econo-

HENRY ALEXANDER MAVOR (1857–1915)
Electrical Engineer
From a photograph by Annan

mic development, especially within the ten years 1881-90, is growth
of speed. Transport had to be organised for increasing quantities, and
the most economical systems of transport had to be devised because
of depression of prices. Concentration of population in industrial
areas induced new methods of local transport. Mechanical began to
supersede animal traction—the urban tramways introduced in the
preceding decade were improved—cable and electrical power took the
place of horses, and vicinal railways intensified in many regions facilities for local communication. Passenger trains became faster and
steamships were fitted with engines of greater power. The struggle
between iron wheel and propeller commenced. About 1881 the Age
of Speed may be said to have had its effective beginning.

Greater speed meant evolution in industrial technique, and in this
evolution the Clyde took an important share; for it was on this river
that the marine engine had not only its birth, but its adolescence
and even its maturity. The triple-expansion engine was followed by
the quadruple- and quintuple-expansion engine on the Clyde during
this period.

Another scarcely less important contribution was adaptation to
the mercantile marine of principles of naval design emerging from
experiments of Mr. Henry Froude at Haslam. On the Clyde Messrs.
Denny began the use of the experimental tank,[1] and Lord Kelvin
developed the theory of waves, which together led to improvements in
design. So also the interior combustion engine was advanced a stage
by Mr. Dugald Clerk, whose gas engine was one of the products of this
time. Although the results of his investigations and experiments were
not published until after the close of the period, the application of
electrical propulsion to vessels by my brother Henry A. Mavor[2] may
be said to belong essentially to the same epoch of scientific activity.

Thus during this period, the greater part of which was characterised
by stagnation in trade, there seemed to arise the leisure necessary to
prepare the way for further progress.

This leisure arising from absence of demand for immediate production on a large scale, and utilisation of the leisure by assiduous
brains, resulted in gradual organisation of those mighty combinations
of mechanism controlled by science, and of industry exercised by

[1] My brother, Ivan Ingram Mavor, who had been an apprentice with the Fair-
field Shipbuilding Co., was employed by Messrs. Denny in connection with these
experiments. He afterwards became outside manager of Armstrong, Mitchell
and Co.'s Low Walker Yard, and later manager of Hawthorne, Leslie and Co.'s
Yard at Yarrow-on-Tyne. He was killed at Liverpool in 1886.
[2] Henry Alexander Mavor died in 1915.

I—K

skilful hands that we know as shipbuilding yards and marine engineering shops. It was by no accident of fortune that the Clyde became by far the greatest shipbuilding river in the world. Miles of shipyards and formidable clangour of power rivetters are feebly described by any such word as titanic. The collective energy of brain and muscle is yet to be expressed in some fitting phrase. ·

Among great engineering works in the field of transport, carried out in Scotland in the eighties, the Forth Bridge is pre-eminent. Designed by two Englishmen, Sir John Fowler and Sir Benjamin Baker, this notable work was executed by a Glasgow man, Sir William Arrol. It was my good fortune to know well all of these remarkable men. I visited the bridge at frequent intervals during its construction from beginning to end. I went down into the caissons upon which the piers are built before they were put into position, and I often went up to tops of the towers and to ends of the great cantilevers while they were being constructed. On one occasion I followed Sir John Fowler, then about seventy years of age, hand over hand, up a ladder of three hundred feet to the top of the north tower of one of the cantilevers; and many times I went over the works with Sir Benjamin Baker and Sir William Arrol.[1]

Some of the American engineers of the time derided the immense factor of safety which was involved in the design; but time had its revenge. One of the most scornful of these critics designed an important bridge which collapsed with great loss of life. The report of the investigating engineers showed that an insufficient margin of safety had been provided in the design. The conditions under which the Forth Bridge was built demanded even an excessive margin. The Tay Bridge had collapsed and its deficiency in respect to margin of safety had been demonstrated. Public confidence in great bridges would have been destroyed by another disaster. Therefore the utmost precautions had to be taken to build a bridge that should withstand *any* strain to which it could possibly be subjected. Elaborate and very interesting experiments were made on wind pressure at the site of the bridge; and every other problem of a complicated series was grappled with in the same thoroughgoing manner.

A great deal of nonsense has been written upon alleged deficiencies of Great Britain in technical education.[2] Those who were actually

[1] My brother, Alfred E. Mavor (died 1921), was engineer in charge of the extensive installation of electric light at the construction works.
[2] I am sorry to say that one of the offenders in this respect is my friend Dr. H. B. Gray, formerly Headmaster of Bradfield. His book *Eclipse or Empire?* seems to me to present the case for technical education with gross exaggeration.

IVAN INGRAM MAVOR (1860-1885)
Shipbuilder
From a photograph

engaged in doing the things, some of which I have undertaken to record, were too busy to engage in controversy, and thus the nonsense passed in general without rebuke.   Besides, even nonsense has its uses, and if exaggeration served the purpose of stimulating the mind of the public and of the authorities to further effort, it was not altogether without advantage.

The war made manifest the latent powers of British industry and of British science; but the powers were there all the while. The occasion to exercise them came, and they were not found wanting.

I should not have had the temerity to speak so positively on a matter not strictly within my field, had I not had unusual opportunities during the period from 1886 up till 1892 of making myself acquainted with the development of technical industry in Great Britain.   These opportunities arose through my connection with *Industries*, an engineering paper established in 1886.   Shortly afterwards I became Assistant Editor, and in this capacity visited frequently all the chief engineering centres in Great Britain and Ireland.   I was therefore in a position to know what was going on and to appreciate the enormous mental activity which was being applied during a period of comparatively dull trade to improvements in industrial technique. It is quite obvious that there must be a close connection between the utilisation of technical ability and the general course of trade. I have suggested that development of technical skill was one of the causes of the trade movement which put an end to the depression. In the large sense, therefore, not deficiency in technical ability or even in technical education, but rather deficiency in those general trade conditions by means of which these can be availed of and supported lay at the root of the matter.

In short, not absence of supply of technically trained persons, but variability of demand involving at times serious deficiency of such demand for such persons is the real difficulty. What is necessary, therefore, is education of the organising capitalist or of his professional director where private enterprise is concerned, as well as of the public and their representatives where public enterprises are in question. If there should happen at any time to be a deficiency in supply of skilled technicians, this is soon corrected. The continuous stream of chemists and engineers from Great Britain to the United States during past years has shown that organisation of capital or reluctance of capital to pay a sufficiently attractive price to keep technical skill at home is an important factor.

When I come to describe the industrial conditions which I found to exist in the United States at a somewhat later period, this aspect of the relation between technical skill and capital will become more vivid.

Two industrial movements, one indigenous as regards the working class and the other derived by it, but owing its growth exclusively to that class, made great progress in Scotland in the eighties. These were the trade union and the co-operative movements. Both of these affected, although not uniformly, the general mass of working people. During this period I endeavoured to make a critical study of both of these efforts towards industrial combination. I attended the Trades Union Congresses and visited with some frequency Trades Councils and some local branches of trade unions. Debates in the Congresses were sometimes at a high level; but speakers were embarrassed by the circumstance that votes of members of the Congress were determined before the debate and that no matter how convincing might be their arguments, they could not hope to influence the result of the vote. The method of delegation with instructions formerly in vogue in parliamentary representation had been adopted by the Trade Union Congress at an early stage in its history. The adoption of this method did not, however, prevent a great deal of "lobbying" directed towards future contingencies and policy rather than towards the immediate vote.

A very noticeable feature of Trade Union Congresses of this period was that while resolutions of a thoroughgoing collectivist order were passed sometimes almost without debate, members of pronounced socialist views were never elected to offices—they were, for example, carefully excluded from the Parliamentary Committee which was practically the executive body of the trade union movement. The general body of trade unionists seemed to be quite willing to adopt very drastic resolutions, but very unwilling to entrust guidance of their movement, especially in Parliament, to men who were extreme. The consequence of this policy was that resolutions were deprived of any importance, because no one expected the Parliamentary Committee to do anything whatever to give them effect. The members of this committee at that time were worthy men; but they could not properly be regarded as representatives of wage-earning people. They had been themselves wage earners, otherwise they could not have become trade unionists; but they had long ceased to earn wages by labour. They had been elected to trade union secretaryships and afterwards to Parliament, and their mode of life as well as their points of view were hardly distinguishable in essence from those of the middle class. When they travelled they lived at the best hotels, and in general, in spite of absence of early education, and in spite of a certain awkwardness, they effected an entry into a class to which as workmen they had been unaccustomed. This condition, although not originating in this epoch (1881-90), developed rapidly in it; and it is not therefore surprising that a subsequent period should be characterised by reaction in the ranks of labour against trade union officials and by the growth of a labour party outside the official trade union movement.

While on some questions the trade union movement presented an united front, as, for example, on the question of recognition of unions, on others there was much difference of opinion. Some trades were in favour of an eight-hour day and some were not. So also occasionally there were more or less serious disputes between closely allied trades. Ship carpenters and ship joiners had, for example, a prolonged quarrel arising from the action of carpenters during a strike of ship joiners. The trade union movement during the decade pursued a policy rather of consolidation than of aggressive action. It was in the next decade that it came to be influenced by collectivist ideas.

The real labour difficulties of the eighties arose in the unorganised trades—in dock labour, *e.g.*—and quite as importantly in low-paid domestic industries, chiefly carried on by women—paper-bag making, umbrella stitching and the like. I made at that time some inquiries into the first-mentioned of these, and I found women working in their own wretched houses sometimes till long after midnight making paper bags at incredibly low rates. A strike of umbrella stitchers, an industry at that time carried on by women at home, revealed also very un-desirable conditions. Exposure of these conditions led to the organisation of a woman's trade union and to improvement in the position of certain groups of female workers. I became convinced at this time that the chief reason for the relatively low rate of women's wages under *laisser faire* conditions was that earnings of women were to a large extent supplementary rather than substantive, while the standard of comfort to which they were accustomed and beyond which large numbers of them did not aspire, led them to accept a very low scale of remuneration. This low scale of remuneration reacted upon their work which was not very efficient. Women's work was thus involved in a vicious circle.

Alongside of the trade union movement there had grown in Scotland and in the north of England the co-operative movement. The earlier history of co-operation had made plain the fact that organisation of purchases and sales in retail distribution was much more easily accomplished than organisation of manufacture. After some unsuccessful experiments in co-operative production the strength of

the movement had been thrown into retail distribution. Especially
in the west of Scotland this had developed into an enormous business.
There were some social reactions. In small towns shopkeepers had
formed a stable and effective group in the community. During periods
of industrial crisis they had rendered important assistance, while their
competition with one another had in general prevented exploitation
by them of the working people who were their customers. The co-
operative store prevented in many towns the growth of this class and
in some caused its elimination, perhaps on the whole to the detriment
of the social groups.

The success of the co-operative society in retail distribution led
to the development by the wholesale societies of productive enterprises, not on the limited scale previously attempted by small groups
of workers with insignificant capital, but on a large scale, amply
supplied with capital and with a market for the product already
secured through the distributing societies. Individual distributing
societies also embarked in similar, although smaller, local enterprises.
In 1888, this movement had become very active and a number of
difficult problems had arisen in which the leaders of the movement
in Scotland thought that some advantage might be derived from
external criticism. They therefore asked me to give a series of lectures
to co-operative societies upon problems arising out of co-operative
production. In this course I learned a great deal more than I com-
municated to the people. I found that the matter which occupied their
minds principally was the distribution of the profits arising from
production. Did these profits properly belong to the members of the
society which organised the enterprise and provided the capital or
to the workers employed by it in the productive process, or should
the profits be divided between these groups in definite proportions?
An example will make clear the practical bearing of this problem. One
of the places which I was invited to visit was Neilston, a small manufacturing town in Renfrewshire. Cotton spinning, weaving and bleach-
ing had been established at Neilston before the end of the eighteenth
century. Practically the whole population of the parish had worked
in the mills in successive generations for a hundred years. The co-
operative society monopolised the retail trade and a few years before
my visit embarked in certain productive enterprises. I think they
started a small shoe factory, a bakery and other minor industries.
Moved by enthusiasm for co-operative production, the members of
the distributing society determined at the outset that they would
distribute among the workers employed by the society a generous

proportion of any profit that might accrue in the experiments in production. Affairs must have been well managed, because profits did accrue, and these were duly divided according to agreement. But unexpected consequences ensued. The community was a small one; everybody worked either in the mills or in the co-operative workshops; but those who worked in the mills had simply their wages, while those who worked in the co-operative workshops had wages plus profits. These profits were considerable enough to enable those who received them to raise their standard of comfort above the general level of that of the mill workers. New hats and smart costumes made their appearance on Sundays, and it speedily became obvious that the bonused co-operators who, after all, were the employés of the mill-workers, were about to become a class socially superior to their employers. The unity and uniformity which had characterised Neilston society for a century were thus in peril. There was nothing to be done but to withdraw the bonus; and at the next meeting of the society the bonus was withdrawn. In larger industrial centres the same consequences were not so obvious as in a small compact group such as that of the Neilston society, but the difficulty of mingling profit-sharing ideas with those of the wage earner pure and simple became more or less evident everywhere.

A few private firms in Glasgow organised profit-sharing schemes, but in general these were looked upon with disfavour by trade unionists. These schemes seemed to militate against mobility of the workman by giving him a special interest in a particular firm, thus tying him to it and rendering him reluctant to take action against it when the general interests of his trade or of his class demanded. The trade unions entertained the view that all sums due to workmen should be paid in wages and that contingent benefits should have no place in a wages system.

CHAPTER XII

I see a great land poised as in a dream—
Waiting for the word by which it may live again.
I see the stretched sleeping figures—waiting for the
kiss and the reawakening.
I hear the bells pealing, and the crash of hammers,
and see beautiful parks spread—as in toy show.
I see a great land waiting for its own people to come
and take possession of it.

EDWARD CARPENTER, *Towards Democracy* (1883).

SINCE 1890 industrial conditions have experienced material changes, some of which I may hope to consider in their proper sequence; but looking back upon this now distant time and endeavouring to give to the main facts of it, so far as I have been able to recall them, their due perspective, it seems to me that the explanations of the most important economic phenomena of the present moment (1920) are to be found precisely in the period between 1877 and 1890. To put the case quite briefly and simply, the working people suffered so much during that time that they made up their minds that they would not suffer like hardships again if by any means they could avoid them. Great revolutionary movements do not occur during periods of famine or even of low wages. They usually occur later, when the subjected people have gained somewhat and have energy enough to determine to gain more. The spectacle of distress during that period affected profoundly many who were not wage-earners in the strict sense, but who either themselves felt the pinch of want or from natural human sympathy shared the feelings of those who did. Emotion and determination on the part of workers and their friends would, however, have been quite unavailing had not technical conditions of industry and commerce favoured their action. I have already endeavoured to show that during the period of depression the foundation was laid for greatly increased production and greatly increased mobility alike of men and things. Thus the material and moral forces which effected the social changes of the past twenty years and may effect changes yet to come had their origins in the long

152

depression. Then also had their origins, so far as comparatively recent times are concerned, those social propagandas which may fairly be called subversive, since they aimed at a more or less complete bouleversement of society. These propagandas, although they failed to accomplish their direct object, were significant because they reacted upon the situation and contributed towards some of the changes which have taken place.

During the long depression, as wages fell and employment became more difficult to secure, the workers were compelled to diminish the standard of comfort they had previously enjoyed. They were obliged to move into smaller houses and even to concentrate to an unsanitary extent. The wageless crowded into the narrowest of quarters, many of them living in a state of congestion almost incredible. Four families have been known to occupy one room—one corner to each family. Some found refuge in cellars not normally occupied by human beings. Nor was suffering confined to those who had no means. Many people who had been living at a fairly high standard of comfort came to be in want, many who were not actually in want were racked with anxiety as to the future of their families or themselves. Frugal people reduced their consumption to the lowest minimum. This distress did not affect equally the whole working population. For the bulk of the workers life went on with diminution of comfort, but their means of life were not completely destroyed. Those who suffered most acutely had been under normal conditions always hovering on the verge of absolute destitution.

I do not wish to overload these pages with lugubrious details; but in order to make clear what follows, it seems to be necessary to indicate, at all events, the kind of detail which "sprang into the eyes" of everyone who lived through that time, and who took the trouble to keep his eyes open.

The literature of the subject so far as concerns Great Britain generally and London in particular is well known—the *Report of the Commission on the Depression of Trade of* 1885,[1] Mr. Charles Booth's remarkable series of volumes on London,[2] General Booth's *Darkest England*,[3] may be taken as examples. It is, however, to be observed that the long period of depression—1879 up till 1891—was approaching its close before the first-mentioned made its appearance, and was actually over when the last two were published. So far as

[1] First volume published London, 1891.
[2] London, 1891.
[3] The *Reports on the Housing of the Working Classes,* 1882 and 1885, ought also to be mentioned.

concerns Glasgow, contemporary records of the depression are scanty. No systematic inquiry was made by any competent person, and those who were actually engaged in various activities for alleviation of distress were too much occupied with these activities to trouble about describing them for the benefit of posterity. A vast amount of useful and self-sacrificing work was accomplished without record of any kind.

One form of social agency, in operation at all times and quite active during this period, was district visiting in connection with churches. However well-intentioned, as it was perhaps universally, its efficacy was very variable and there was much overlapping. A visitor told me that she was received in the following manner:

"Now please go away and don't trouble me. I've had six religions up this stair to-day already; and I haven't been able to get my work done."

The churches did what they could with the means available to them; but in general they felt rather helpless—the problem lay in a large measure beyond them. After the depression had lasted about ten years, the Presbytery of Glasgow (that of the Established Church of Scotland), on 5th December, 1888, appointed a Commission composed of ministers of that Church and of laymen for the purpose of investigating a particular phase of the question, viz., the "housing of the poor." The Commission extended its inquiry over about thirteen months, taking the evidence of various persons, and after some delay produced an interesting and valuable report.[1]

This Commission was succeeded by a Committee of rather wider scope as regards membership and reference; and in 1892 the Committee issued a Report upon the German Labour Colonies considered as remedial agencies for the unemployed.[2] I am not aware that any practical measures resulted from these investigations directly; but they were very informative to those who took part in them, and they made clear the magnitude and complexity of the problems they endeavoured to attack. This lack of definite result was due largely to the fact that the depression, with its attendant unemployment, had begun to pass away by the time the Reports were issued.

Meanwhile the problem of housing had been approached in another manner and by other groups of people.

The cities of Scotland, and especially Glasgow, Edinburgh, Dundee

---

[1] *Report of Commission on the Housing of the Poor in Relation to their Social Condition.* Glasgow, 1891.

[2] I was a member of this Committee and also of the Sub-committee which went to Germany for purposes of inquiry.

and Aberdeen, have experienced an urban evolution of a character somewhat different from that of cities of corresponding size in England. In Scotland, the ready availability of good building stone led at an early period to construction of substantial houses, and the ease with which superstructures could be built upon substantial foundations led to the construction in Scotland of tall buildings long before steel and re-enforced concrete came into use.[1] The social conditions in Scotland in the seventeenth and eighteenth centuries led to the building by landed proprietors and prosperous merchants of town houses of highly permanent character and in many cases of considerable dimensions. The growth of the towns in the nineteenth century resulted in these town mansions being surrounded by premises erected for warehouses or for factories. For a time the proprietors or their descendants remained as occupants of these mansions; but the surroundings became distasteful, and the mansions were evacuated by them, new houses being built on the outskirts. Owing to their substantial character, the mansions were not pulled down, yet they could with difficulty be adapted to industrial purposes. Thus they came to be occupied by families of a social class inferior to that of their former occupants, and through the pressure of demand for houses in the immediate neighbourhood of factories, they became overcrowded. Houses built for occupancy by single families at a time when sanitary conveniences were by no means ample even for such occupancy became highly insanitary when their large rooms were cut up by lath-and-plaster interior walls and their wide passages divided in the same manner. By means of these divisions, accommodation of a kind was provided for forty or fifty families in place of one. In those cases where such houses had been surrounded by gardens, the ground came gradually to be covered by buildings of inferior construction, and thus there were frequently to be found rows of houses separated from one another by very narrow spaces situated behind the original mansion, which alone enjoyed the advantage of frontage upon a street. Thus upon the space formerly occupied by a single family there came to be housed a population numbering sometimes many hundred people and a congested area made its appearance. Such congested areas rapidly became slums, partly through pressure of demand and partly through the character of the people. Rapid increase of urban population had been achieved through migration to towns of country people, unaccustomed to town life and unable at once to adjust themselves to changed conditions. In

[1] *Cf. infra*, vol. ii. p. 159.

the country, fresh air and space render attention to sanitation less necessary; in the towns, density of population involves either great risk of epidemics or the closest individual attention to observance of the laws of health.

In 1866, during the depression following the close of the American Civil War, the Corporation of Glasgow embarked upon an extensive scheme of city improvement under which it expended, over about twenty years, upwards of two million pounds. The execution of the scheme involved clearing away narrow streets of old and insanitary houses and opening wide streets in the heart of the city. Buildings erected upon reconstructed areas were adapted partly for business purposes and partly for dwellings; but these latter were necessarily more costly for their occupants than the wretched hovels which had been removed, and they therefore came to be occupied by a class of tenant different from that which had inhabited the areas previous to reconstruction. The new dwellings were for the most part built by private enterprise upon cleared land purchased from the Corporation. The Corporation, however, built some tenements, the rents of which, with one exception, were beyond the reach of poorer tenants. The consequence of these clearances was that former inhabitants of slums were dispersed to the outskirts, there to create new slum conditions, or forced into regions in the neighbourhood of cleared areas, making such regions more congested than before. After twenty years' operation of the Improvement Trust, the housing question was as acute as ever. In November 1888 Dr. J. B. Russell, the Medical Health Officer of Glasgow, delivered a lecture on "Life in One Room; or, Some Considerations for the Citizens of Glasgow,"[1] in which he gave startling details of the state of matters.

There had been in existence for some time a society known as the Kyrle Society, having for its general object promotion of sympathetic relations between the well-to-do and the struggling, not by means of charitable doles, but by means of instruction and advice. Classes in hygiene, care of infants, etc., were organised by this society. Dr. Russell's lecture stimulated the members to further efforts, and adopting methods introduced in London by Miss Octavia Hill, they secured from a sympathetic proprietor a tenement occupied by poor tenants, undertook collection of their rents, organised a club-room for them, and looked upon themselves as being responsible for the general welfare of this small group of people. This experiment was so instructive in making plain some of the conditions of the complicated question of social amelioration that it seems advisable to describe it in detail. When the small committee in charge of the matter assumed control of the tenement, they made a careful survey of it and of its inhabitants. They found that while the human population numbered about forty, the insect population was so enormous that it was difficult to understand how the creatures subsisted unless they lived upon one another. The plaster was literally in motion like an over-ripe cheese. Under these conditions, the first thing to be done was to persuade the people to leave their wretched houses for at least forty-eight hours to permit the sanitary officers of the city to deal with the plague of insects. This was not altogether easy to manage. The people were unfortunately so habituated to the company of insects that they thought we were crazy to trouble ourselves on their behalf. Arrangements were made to accommodate the families in the neighbourhood, and the process of fumigation was carried out. After it was completed and the tenants had returned, I called on an Irish woman who occupied one of the rooms. She had just come in and her belongings lay wrapped in a filthy bundle in the middle of the floor. I said that I hoped she would now be more comfortable. She answered that she did not know, that she had already noticed that what had been done had "made the bugs livelier than they were before." I fancy that some of them had accompanied her in her vacation and returned with her. They may have been invigorated by change of air. By fumigation and other means, and by constant supervision, great improvement was undoubtedly effected in a short time. One result of this experiment was conclusive proof that deterioration of such tenements in the absence of supervision was so great that even relatively high rents rendered their ownership uneconomical. In other words, the actual cost of housing the poor was relatively higher than the cost of housing the well-to-do and careful. Another result was proof that the cost of collecting rents was excessive. They had to be called for frequently. If tenants were permitted to fall behind, they were apt to disappear. In order to meet these conditions, the committee devised a scheme by which those tenants who kept their houses clean, did no damage to property and paid their rents punctually, received a rebate of two weeks' rent at midsummer. This scheme worked extremely well. It was afterwards adopted by the Glasgow Working Men's Dwellings Company, and I believe that it is still in operation. In arranging for extension of the work of the society we surveyed a great many tenements, choosing, of course, those that were reported to us as needing supervision, or as being available for our purpose. In course of these investigations we became aware of the

extent of the problem. In some tenements tenants were so mobile
that rents were collected daily by agents of the proprietors, an enormously expensive method.   In others, poverty and carelessness of
tenants caused them to use as fuel the woodwork of the houses.
Shelving, wooden slats of box-beds, and panels of doors were found
to be used in this manner. Complete absence of furniture of any kind
was not unusual. An empty box was not rarely the only seat as well
as the only table. In one house which we visited we found a strapping
young Irish woman with a small baby. Her husband was, she said,
looking for work. There was nothing in the room but an empty box,
a broken jug, and a pile of rags on the floor by way of a bed. The
woman was quite cheerful and good-humoured. In another very old
and miserable tenement, built like a fortress, the former residence of
a Glasgow magnate of the seventeenth century, we found a woman
whose face was copiously decorated with sticking-plaster. I said to
her, "Dear me, woman, whatever have you been doing to yourself?"
"Hush," she said with great delicacy, lowering her voice to a
whisper, and pointing to a woman who was at the end of the
passage just beyond earshot, "that lady put my head through a
window last night."

Before mentioning some of the general conclusions to which these
experiences led, I must recount here some incidents of a similar
experiment conducted at the same time in Edinburgh by my friend
Miss Mary Hill Burton, sister of John Hill Burton, the historian.
Miss Burton determined to purchase one of the worst tenements in
the Canongate of Edinburgh and make an attempt to improve the
tenants. The house she obtained had been well known as the Saracen's
Head. It was a tall substantially built tenement; but it had been
suffered to fall into disrepair, and the occupants were among the
poorest in the neighbourhood. She began as we did by thoroughly
overhauling the premises. She had the windows glazed with plate
glass and gave her tenants lectures on the virtues of cleanliness and
carefulness. One family consisted of a mother and a son. The youth
in a moment of exuberance amused himself by throwing empty bottles
through the newly-glazed windows, demolishing them completely.
Miss Burton waited until the following Saturday afternoon, expecting
that she would find the culprit at home. Then taking with her two
young nephews, clad in working clothes and carrying a supply of
glass and putty, she superintended the replacing of the windows,
without reproach of any kind. The youth observed this proceeding
with amusement, while the mother told Miss Burton that she thought

that a wealthy lady like her ought to provide her nephews with better clothes than they were wearing.

One afternoon I met Miss Burton in the Canongate near her property, she was carrying what used to be called a reticule. She said to me, "You can't guess what I have in this." Knowing her habits, I answered, "I think I can. You have a scrubbing-brush and soap." "You are quite right," she said, opening her bag. "I am just going to scrub a woman's floor for her. She won't do it herself."

I said, "When you have finished, come and have tea with me and tell me all about it."

When she came, she told me that she had scrubbed the woman's floor while with great good-nature the woman read the evening newspaper to her. Later, I learned from Miss Burton that she found the child of this woman ill with measles and occupying at night the basket which during the day the mother used to peddle oranges. Continuance of this practice was prevented; but the floor remained unscrubbed. After enduring with exemplary patience repeated *lâches* on the part of her tenant, Miss Burton turned the woman out and, locking the door of the room, put the key in her pocket. Next day she found the woman camped in the passage, in which she had spent the night, very penitent and urgently desirous of remaining. This faithfulness was too alluring. One Saturday night Miss Burton went down to inspect, as she conceived to be her duty. As she arrived at the door of her "land" (as such houses are called), there issued from it one of her tenants—a screaming woman with an irate and drunken husband in hot pursuit. Miss Burton committed a mistake that nearly proved fatal. With characteristic gallantry she intervened between the husband and wife and received the blow intended for the latter. She was rather severely injured; but she had the satisfaction of knowing the husband was appropriately conscious of the heinousness of his offence, and that probably the wife escaped subsequent violence.

In my *Economic History of Russia* [1] I have described a movement in that country during the years 1873–76 known as the *V Narod*, or "To the People" movement. The underlying idea was that the intellectuals and the peasantry, or the mass of the people, occupied separate worlds and that neither really knew the other. Social progress in so non-homogeneous a society was impossible. Therefore the intellectuals, as the smaller group, must go to the larger and must *be* of the people. Under the influence of that idea, cultivated men and women

[1] London, 1914, ii. pp. 103–113.

became carpenters and teachers, etc., in villages, living among the peasants and in the same manner. The consequences of the movement were much disillusionment on both sides, a certain breaking down of the social barriers, and prosecution by the autocratic government. In 1885, inspired by similar ideas, although so far as I am aware without knowledge of the Russian precedent, my dear friend of many years, Patrick Geddes, gave up his house in the New Town of Edinburgh and went to live in the Lawnmarket. He certainly lived among the people. The experiment was interesting and not destitute of a practical side; but it did not afford the vital touch of the Russian example, because the "intellectuals" did not establish organic relations with their surroundings. They revived the eighteenth-century traditions of the Lawnmarket, but these fitted in rather awkwardly with those of the close of the nineteenth.[1]

The conclusions which forced themselves upon all of us who engaged in the Glasgow experiments and investigations accompanying them, of which I have given an account, were in the main the following. Within the general category of the poor there is a class in large industrial centres habitually living at an extremely low level, and yet more or less content to do so. Many of this class have never known any condition other than that of extreme poverty. The instances quoted illustrate the insouciance of such people. They do not believe in miracles and they regard with amused scepticism middle-class efforts to improve them. From them I have never heard words of bitterness nor have I ever noticed in them signs of subservience. They have no conception precisely corresponding to the "class consciousness" of the Socialists; but they have very positive ideas about sharp social distinctions within their own order. For example, I knew the wife of a blacksmith who was very scornful at the suggestion that she might visit the wife of a chimney-sweep who was a near neighbour. Within the smaller group there is much fraternal feeling and sympathy in spite of occasional quarrels arising out of excessively close proximity. They lend one another freely articles and money; but they have also sharp notions of ownership, and I have never detected any indication of a tendency towards community of goods. They are rather apt to despise people who have risen from their own ranks or even from those which they recognise to be above them, while they are often very friendly with those who have never felt "the chill of poverty in their bones." Yet they are sometimes intolerant of ignorance of the social etiquette of their group when it is betrayed in forms of speech to

[1] See notes on Patrick Geddes in a subsequent chapter.

which they attach peculiar importance. They are also very sensitive to ridicule; and they can on occasion be very suspicious that some sinister design lies behind efforts on the part of others to improve them. Some of them would rather be left alone. I did not meet many who had dropped into the group of the "very poor" from the superior classes. Of those whom I did meet, some were quite disposed to be permanent dependants upon the bounty of sympathetic strangers, while others were defiantly independent even in extreme poverty. One striking instance of the latter order came under my notice at a Salvation Army shelter in London. He was an old man who had evidently seen better days. He made his living, such as it was, by copying music. He paid for his night's lodging at the lowest rate, viz., one penny, for which he had only a bench; he spent about two-pence for his supper and apparently had a strong disinclination to be made the subject of comment or sympathy. He evidently considered that if he chose to live in that manner it was his affair.

We also came to the conclusion that the labour of this group was probably, in general, below the average level of efficiency, and that therefore, other things being equal, their wages would in general remain below the average wage in their employment. Even where members of the group belonged to trade unions which insisted upon a uniform wage, their total annual earnings were less than the total annual earnings of efficient workers because of the greater fluctuation of their employment. It was thus necessary to provide house accommodation for them at a rate commensurate with their ability to pay. A higher rate would tend to exclude them. It is true that in attempting to provide the opportunity of living at so low a level we were on the one hand facilitating exploitation of their labour by their employers, and on the other contributing to their own contentment with an extremely low standard of life. It seemed to be within our power, however, to raise this standard without at the same time raising the cost of it to them and thus secure immediate improvement in their condition, leaving to other agencies the prevention of unfavourable reactions.

We decided that any scheme which might be devised for the provision of sanitary dwellings at the lowest practicable rate should not only be self-supporting, but should aim at being sufficiently remunerative to draw into it or into similar projects a sufficient amount of capital to provide accommodation for the whole of the social group whose benefit was our primary concern.

We also considered the question of the competition of our scheme

I—L

with private enterprise, and decided that if we were able by means of supervision to diminish deterioration and by means of collection of rents by voluntary agency and the bonus system above mentioned to diminish the cost of collection, our action would tend to impose similar plans on the part of private owners of inferiorly rented property. We also hoped to give an example to them of improvement in such property and of the economic importance of improving it.

In 1890, chiefly through the energy of Mr. D. M. Stevenson [1] and Mr. John Mann, Jnr.,[2] the Glasgow Social Union was founded for the purpose of co-ordinating the efforts of the various agencies then engaged in promoting social reform. An almost immediate outcome of the foundation of this union, the Glasgow Working Men's Dwellings Company, was promoted with a proposed capital of £50,000. The bulk of the capital was quickly subscribed and the company was launched. Mr. John Burnet [3] was chosen as architect, and he and Mr. Mann at once began a careful study of the experiments in housing which had been carried out in other parts of the country, *e.g.* in London, Liverpool and Edinburgh. It was thought by some that the Corporation of Glasgow, which had, not altogether undeservedly, acquired a reputation for enterprise, should undertake the work proposed by the company, or at all events should co-operate with it. The corporation was, however, quite immovable and the company pursued its own course. This was a great advantage, because the operations of the company gained in flexibility and also in freedom from municipal politics. Sir James King, who had been Lord Provost and who was chairman of the Caledonian Railway Company, made an admirable chairman of the Dwellings Company.[4] The company, which has now been in existence for more than thirty years, has undoubtedly fulfilled the modest purpose of its promotion, viz., to point by way of example towards some of the measures by means of which sanitary dwellings might be provided for those tenants who are able to pay only minimum rents. The operations of the company have been fully described in its annual reports and other publications.[5]

[1] Afterwards Lord Provost of Glasgow and Sir D. M. Stevenson, Bart.
[2] Now Sir John Mann.
[3] Afterwards Sir John Burnet.
[4] I had a seat on the Board of Directors until I left Glasgow for Canada in 1892.
[5] The history of the first ten years of the company is described in *Sane Experiments in Housing*, Glasgow, 1901.

CHAPTER XIII

POLITICS IN THE EIGHTIES

Cleon loq. O Demus! has any man shown such a zeal,
Such a passion as I for the general weal?
Racking and screwing offenders to ruin;
With torture and threats extorting your debts;
Exhausting all means for enhancing your fortune,
Terror and force and intreaties importune,
With a popular, pure patriotical aim;
Unmoved by compassion, or friendship or shame.

ARISTOPHANES, *The Knights* (424 B.C.).
(Translated by J. Hookham Frere, 1840.)

ALTHOUGH Scotsmen have borne no inconsiderable share in imperial administration, perhaps for that very reason they have not usually fallen victims to the glamour of imperialist rhetoric, and thus the imperialist movement of the seventies headed by Disraeli found Scotsmen as a rule unsympathetic. The wave of Liberalism which swept over the country in 1880 was probably due to reaction against imperialist ideas rather than to any positive policy of a novel character offered by the Liberal politicians. In the field of the technique of politics, it was due also to superior organisation on the part of the Liberal party and to defective organisation on the part of their opponents. The Birmingham Caucus was not met by equal organisation on the other side. A Tory agent told me that when Sir Stafford Northcote came down to Scotland, as he did occasionally, he contented himself with listening to reports made to him by the party agents; only when Lord Randolph Churchill made such political tours were evidences demanded of activity in registration and in propaganda. But Lord Randolph's activities were rather spasmodic, and the genial confidence of Sir Stafford Northcote was more generally characteristic of the attitude of the party leaders towards organisation.

Three circumstances contributed to emergence in the late seventies of special interest in Ireland on the part of the Scots public. These were influx into Scotland, during the high-wage period of the early seventies, of a large number of Irish labourers, the crofter agitation, and advance of urban rents. The two last-mentioned brought the question of land-ownership sharply into relief, while the first-mentioned gave in certain constituencies an Irish vote which had to be reckoned with and diffused an acquaintance with the current of Irish affairs. To these circumstances may be added the presence of Irishmen in Glasgow who had acquired influence there either through their character and talents, like John Ferguson, or through active advocacy of Irish views.

The question of Home Rule for Scotland had been little more than mentioned. It was never regarded with any enthusiasm, because everyone who thought about it realised that so long as Scotsmen were able to retain the share in the government of the United Kingdom acquired by them in the eighteenth century, and tenaciously held ever since, there was no real need for Home Rule. From the Scots point of view, Home Rule for Ireland stood upon a different footing. The prejudice against England which Scotland shared with Ireland in the eighteenth century had disappeared in Scotland while it remained in Ireland; and although this prejudice seemed to the Scots rather unreasonable, they thought that probably the Irish were likely to be able to manage their own affairs at least as well as the English could manage them. This view of the Irish question was re-enforced by the anti-imperialist views which, as I have suggested, were prevalent in Scotland at that time. The Irish question was thus looked upon in Scotland as partly but not exclusively an economic question, and the aspirations of a large number of the Irish people towards the erection of an Irish nation were regarded with active sympathy. The same optimism which led the Scots to discard the imperialist views of the Conservatives and to accept the vague and less positive policy of the Liberals induced them to believe that the Irish people would at once abandon their hostility to the British as soon as their nationality within the empire was recognised.

In a subsequent chapter I intend to give an account of the origin and direction of the movement known at the time as the Land Restoration movement. Here it may suffice to notice that the persons who were interested in the land question were naturally much exercised about Ireland, where the land question had been thrust into the foreground by the Land League and where the root of the political difficulties seemed to lie in the system of land-ownership. The Land Restoration movement had no political influence, but it had a somewhat wide effect in stimulating interest in the land question.

There was thus in Scotland in the late seventies a deep and extensive sympathy with the agitation of the Irish Land League and with the movement for Home Rule. Parnell, Dillon and other Irish leaders were always sure of a good reception from a Glasgow audience, and they often came at critical moments to deliver speeches. When coercive measures were taken by the Government, these were in general regarded with disapproval, and when the circulation of certain Irish and Irish-American newspapers was forbidden, these newspapers continued to be circulated in Glasgow by surreptitious means. I received these suppressed journals regularly during the periods of their suppression. The sympathy of the Scots people, and especially those of Glasgow, was undoubtedly with Ireland in 1880. A rude jolt was given to this sympathy by the Phœnix Park murders. Once more in her history the annals of Ireland were stained by a crime. I do not believe that anyone who was acquainted with the Irish leaders associated them in any way with the murders or attached any importance to the attack afterwards made upon them by *The Times*. Some at least felt, however, that these murders revealed the existence in Ireland of an element in the population averse from order of any kind, and that even under Home Rule the strongest measures would have to be taken to deprive this element of the power of mischief.

Looking back over the forty years which have passed since then, it is permissible to believe that had Great Britain refused to be diverted by the hands of the murderers, and even if necessary forced the Irish Parliamentary Party of that day to undertake the government of Ireland, the fate of Ireland would not have been worse than it is now. It is possible that an Irish Government would have been more coercive than any English Government ever was, and that agrarian crime would have been put down by it with a stronger hand than any English Government ever dared to use.[1] If this result had not followed, no stable Government could have existed; but the pride and the political ability of the Irish leaders of that period might have been counted upon to see that the result did follow.

The conflict between Catholicism and Nationality—one of the great conflicts of the modern world [2]—would have been waged between the Church and United Ireland instead of between the Church and the United Kingdom. The disruptive influence of the Church might

[1] This chapter was written in 1917. The events in Ireland since then have amply confirmed this anticipation.

[2] The conflict between the Papacy and France, the emergence of Sinn Fein in Ireland, the anti-conscription movement in Australia and Quebec and similar although less·obvious movements in the United States, as well as the ecclesiastical and educational intrigues in the Balkans, are recent incidents in this wide conflict, all intimately connected together and all bearing definitely upon the causes and the course of the Great War.

have been exerted to wreck Irish nationality, as it has been exerted to wreck nationality elsewhere; but the forces of modernism would have been, as they must still be, in favour of Ireland, and with high probability Ireland would have won.

As the most remarkable political figure of the seventies was Benjamin Disraeli, so the most remarkable political figure of the eighties was Joseph Chamberlain. A political figure must be measured in terms of his political activities, rather than in terms of his personality. The activities of Chamberlain began in the seventies with a shrewd attack upon the Birmingham Gas Company, while he was Mayor of Birmingham. The object of this attack was the acquisition of the gas company by the municipality in order to secure for the public a profitable enterprise, with the promise that the profits from the manufacture of gas would relieve taxation. To the superficial point of view prevalent at that time it did not appear unfair for the users of gas to be specially taxed in respect to their use of it; nor did those who made the promise of profit stay to consider that profit is an uncertain element depending upon many conditions, some of them beyond the control of the management of the enterprise. Chamberlain, the putative father of the scheme, was neither more nor less superficial in his examination of its reactions than were those about him or others of his time; but the apparent success of his experiment in municipal ownership carried him into Parliament and became the lever by means of which he forced himself into a position where he exercised his political activities in a larger field. By the aid of a competent lieutenant, Schnadhorst, Chamberlain reconstructed the Liberal party machine and won the election of 1880. This feat gave him an invincible claim upon the party, although the methods of his new organisation were not approved by many of the leaders whose ideas of political ethics were less highly developed than his in certain directions. An organisation without a policy to urge must be a sterile organisation; it was thus necessary for the Chamberlainised Liberal party to find a policy, and it was the task of Chamberlain to find one.

The Liberal party had committed itself to the extension of the electoral franchise and to nothing else. The attitude of the party towards international questions was one of non-intervention in European politics and, towards imperial questions, one of opportunism. A military revolt in Egypt compelled the Liberal Government to engage in a war which some of its members loathed, and in spite of itself, it found imbroglios which were not of its contrivance in South Africa as well as in Egypt. Alike from lack of training and experience

Chamberlain had little knowledge of affairs outside of England, and even outside of the life of a provincial municipality. It appeared to him that the important matters were not those distant and complicated imperial and international affairs, but those matters touching more closely the life of the people in the cities. It was by no accident but by very natural means that he turned his attention to the projects of social change which at that time were assuming vague form in the public mind. Again, he was fitted neither by temperament nor by training for close study of these projects. Their recondite origins did not, and could not, interest him. Their importance for him appeared to lie exclusively in the fact that the public mind was affected by them and in the idea that this fact might be utilised to party advantage. This is, undoubtedly, an evidence of political sagacity—in a minor— yet from the point of view of party interests an important sense. The first steps taken by him in this new direction were taken almost immediately after the public mind had settled down on the conclusion of the Egyptian campaign, and when it was wearied with imperial issues. He launched in 1884 his radical programme in a series of speeches. One of these speeches was delivered in Glasgow.

There he propounded his doctrine of "ransom," while rich landowners and manufacturers like Sir Charles Tennant, the mainstay of the Whig wing of the Liberal party, writhed upon the platform. Some of these experienced men no doubt consoled themselves with the reflection that the fulminations of the speaker were due merely to the exuberance of slightly belated youth and were likely to be forgotten when power brought balance. Others must have been alarmed at the prospect of the fiery words sinking into the minds of the people and of their being remembered by them long after the orator had changed his mind.

I may relate an incident associated in my recollection with this speech, although it must not be supposed that I attach undue importance to the incident considered by itself. One afternoon I was seized on the street by a man whom I knew slightly. He was Morrison Davidson, the author of an amusing and clever book *The New Book of Kings*. Davidson was an unique personality, often amazingly brilliant, always irresponsible, sometimes incoherent.[1] Although we were in a crowded thoroughfare Davidson insisted upon delivering to me a long discourse upon the land question. He was not well versed in economic literature, but he had some knowledge of economic subjects, and he was able to bring to bear upon them his capacity for

[1] Davidson's brother, Thomas, who lived in the United States, was a philosophical writer of real originality and distinction.

pungent polemics. About a fortnight later Chamberlain delivered his Glasgow speech. As he proceeded I was astounded to find in it the same general ideas, the same phraseology, the same superficial treatment of the subject as those of the open-air discourse of Morrison Davidson a fortnight before. I mentioned this circumstance on the day following the speech to my friend Wm. Craibe Angus, who was, I knew, acquainted with Davidson. He remarked that there was no mystery about it, that Davidson to his knowledge had been coaching Chamberlain in the land question for months. I do not blame Chamberlain for utilising the brains of Morrison Davidson; but the episode suggests the explanation at once of the suddenness of his enthusiasm for the land question and of the brevity of its duration.

Under whose guidance Chamberlain acquired the first phase of his point of view of the Irish question I do not know; but here also it is evident that the subject had taken no real hold upon his mind, and that his attitude towards it depended not upon carefully digested knowledge, but upon superficial examination of those elements in it which were related to the political exigencies of the moment. It need not have been matter for surprise, and I am bound to say it was no surprise to me, that Chamberlain should have elected to turn his back upon his past and his party and to throw his influence, such as it was, upon the other side.

Rumours came to me at the time that Chamberlain thought that the psychological moment had arrived when, owing to the increasing age and waning influence of Gladstone, he could make a bold stroke for the leadership of the party, and could carry it with him wherever he chose to go. These rumours cannot be confirmed or rejected until memoirs of the period are forthcoming more intimate and candid than any which have yet appeared.[1]

I did not enjoy the advantage of personal acquaintance with Chamberlain, and I am quite prepared to believe all that Lord Morley says about him in so far as that relates to the impression made by Chamberlain upon Lord Morley's mind. It is possible, however, to deduce character from public activities. So far as his public activities are concerned they suggest that Chamberlain possessed great force of character, but lacked knowledge of political history and of the temperament and nature of the people with whom he came into contact. The educational background which furnishes the statesman with the critical apparatus applied by him to the problems with which he

[1] Whether through excess of generosity or of knowledge or through deficiency in the power of judging men, Lord Morley's *Recollections*, interesting as they are, throw little light on this particular point.

has to deal was not Chamberlain's to utilise, and therefore he approached these problems with a native vigour, but with a rawness and uncertainty which reflect themselves in his frequent changes of attitude on fundamental things. Nevertheless, throughout the eighties and the nineties, Chamberlain was a real force; his very deficiencies throw this force into a stronger light. Yet the danger incurred by a nation which entrusts itself to the unchecked vagaries of a strong, but ill-instructed politician, is after all the most conspicuous lesson of his career. Both the United States and Canada have afforded, and continue to afford, examples of a type of vigorous but unreliable politician which Chamberlain's strongly resembled.

About the year 1881 a great meeting was held in Glasgow for the purpose of re-enforcing the movement for female suffrage, then carried on by an association of which Miss Lydia Becker was secretary, with headquarters at Manchester. The meeting was attended by four or five thousand women. All the speakers were women. Indeed, apart from the newspaper reporters, there were only two men in the audience —W. Craibe Angus and myself. We were permitted as a great privilege to take our places with the reporters because of our known sympathy with the cause. So far as I remember, the principal speakers were Mrs. Charles Bright, daughter-in-law of John Bright, Mrs. Cady Stanton, a fine old lady with silvery hair, who edited the Women's Bible in which the passages adverse to the "monstrous regiment of women" are omitted, Mrs. Stewart, who, like Mrs. Stanton, was from the United States, Miss Mary Hill Burton, who appears elsewhere in these recollections, and a lady whose name I do not remember who was an acolyte of Miss Helen Taylor, the step-daughter of John Stuart Mill. Miss Taylor was, I think, to have been present, but was prevented by illness. The best speech was made by Miss Burton. She was an excellent public speaker. She had a fine voice, and much latent fire beneath her normal restraint. Miss Taylor's acolyte delivered an impassioned oration addressed especially to the wildly applauding younger women. I met this lady after the meeting with Miss Burton at Craibe Angus's house. Her fiery speech had probably excited her unduly; for this reason, or (this is a vague recollection in my mind) because she had suddenly been made aware of waning affection and interest in her welfare on the part of Miss Taylor, she gave way to a violent fit of hysterics which was with difficulty assuaged by the means customarily adopted in such cases. The scene was sufficiently amusing; but it gave rise to the uncomfortable anticipation of a lady Speaker in a co-elected House of Commons having a hysterical fit in the Chair on some lady member protesting against her ruling, and of the Ser-jeant-at-arms, messenger girls and lady members soothing her with smelling-salts and eau de Cologne.

A crisis in the female suffrage movement occurred in 1886, when the problem emerged—Ireland or the suffrage? If Ireland was to take precedence of everything, the suffrage must be postponed. If the suffrage were pressed, Ireland must wait. The majority of the leaders in the suffrage movement, after a sharp struggle in which there were rumoured hysterical incidents, decided in favour of Ireland; and thus the movement remained in a state of stagnation for many years, until it was roused into vigorous and even violent life by the militant suffragettes led by Mrs. Pankhurst.[1]

In the late seventies a society was formed in Glasgow which for many years played a remarkable rôle in the political education of the youth of the city. This was the Parliamentary Debating Society. The debates were conducted precisely after the model of the House of Commons, the members chose constituencies by the names of which they were known, there were divisions in the manner of Parliament, there was a Government and there was an Opposition, Bills were introduced and passed through their successive stages, Budgets were presented, and ministers were subjected to questions—in short, it was a Parliament *in petto*. Many members of the House of Commons and some Cabinet Ministers, including, for example, Mr. Bonar Law, had their early training in political debate in that society. For many years the Speaker, whose name was Turnbull, presided over it. He gradually acquired a very intimate acquaintance with parliamentary procedure, and became a real authority on the subject. Turnbull was a remarkable man. In his youth, fired with enthusiasm for liberty and love for adventure, he had gone to Italy and enlisted in the army of Garibaldi. I played a modest rôle in the society.

[1] I had just (December 1917) laid down my pen after finishing the above sentence in these recollections, when the following weirdly significant incident and coincidence occurred. My telephone sounded with more than usually insistent vehemence and the following colloquy ensued:
"Yes."
"It's *me*."
"Where are you?"
"At the polling-booth."
"Well!"
"The place is all confusion. They are hauling me about. What am I to do?"
"Come home."
"But——"
"Come home."
"All right."

CHAPTER XIV

THE SOCIALIST MOVEMENT IN SCOTLAND IN THE EIGHTIES

> . . . Therefore, well in thee
> To look, not on eternity, but time:
>
> .   .   .   .   .   .
>
> And yet a mortal glance might pierce, methinks,
> Deeper into the seeming dark of things,
> And learn, no fruit, man's life can bear, will fade.
> ROBERT BROWNING, *Balaustion's Adventure* (1871).

In the seventies of the nineteenth century the study of political economy was in a stage of transition. It is necessary to discriminate between the extent of interest taken in a science by the non-professional public and the extent of activity in pursuit of it exercised by special students. In the first field there had been for nearly three-quarters of a century a period of wide public discussion of economic questions. This discussion, especially in its earlier stages, had been by no means confined to practical or political issues, but had been directed even to abstract points of view in respect to rent, wages and interest. By the seventies, practical and political questions such as free trade, the position of trade unions and the like, as well as the theoretical questions in which the non-professional public took some interest, were regarded by it as *settled*. The controversies upon them had lasted for about seventy years, and there seemed to be no more to be said that was new. For the instruction of youth in accepted doctrines there was available the excellent work of John Stuart Mill, and beyond or behind its conclusions it was deemed unnecessary to go. Up till about 1880 this was the general frame of the public mind.

In the universities, political economy had been, to say the least, neglected. In Scotland, where in the eighteenth century Adam Smith had given it an importance scarcely inferior in academic studies to that of moral philosophy, it had not acquired the status of a subject of special instruction by a professor appointed for the purpose. In the seventies of the nineteenth century the Town Council of Edinburgh established a chair of political economy on tentative conditions, tenure of office being for seven years instead of for life as was the tenure

of other chairs.   In Glasgow the subject remained as an appanage
of moral philosophy, and lectures were delivered upon it by the professor of moral philosophy only biennially. In Aberdeen and St. Andrews
political economy was not taught.   In the English universities, lecture-
ships and professorships in political economy had been founded, but
their foundation had not led to recognition of the subject as one of
academic importance, nor had incumbents of these offices done more
than perform their duties in a somewhat perfunctory manner.   This
condition was due partly to the sterilising influence of an accepted
economic *credo*, and partly to indifference of the public, an indifference
undoubtedly to be associated with the sterility of the professional
economists.   Into this stagnant atmosphere there was injected a new
element by Jevons, who approached political economy with the
scientific mind of a chemist, and who showed that Mill was wrong in
regarding the last word upon value as having been pronounced.
Jevons' early death deprived economics of a most invigorating influence, and the technical character of his writings prevented their
importance from being speedily grasped by the wide public.   Thus
the conclusion of the decade of the seventies found the subject of
political economy still in a stagnant condition, while economic problems
of the most vital character were pressing for examination. The professional economists were, so to say, calmly reciting the economic
litany as if the economic world had a kind of spiritual existence remote
from the world of daily experience.   Perverse, ill-trained, and wrong-
headed as the heretics of the past and of the present might be, they at
least were living in the tangible world, and were urging their several
propagandas advocating changes in it with enthusiasm.   It is no
wonder that those ardent spirits who sought light upon problems
that were thrusting themselves forward turned to the enthusiastic
heretics instead of to the passionless economists.

   In preceding chapters I have endeavoured to describe certain
phases of the public life of Scotland during the decade 1881–90.   I
now come to the description of the propagandas which during this
period attempted to influence that public life.   It is always difficult
to discriminate between ephemeral and lasting movements, and at
this time this task was peculiarly difficult.   The question of Pilate,
who must have been one of the rarest of men, a philosophical politician,
"What is truth?" was perhaps never put in a more critical epoch
than precisely at that moment when the economical policy of *laisser
faire* may be said to have attained its high-water mark.   It is true
that many invasions had been made upon the policy in the preceding

decade; but there was as yet no demonstrable change in widely accepted principles, because these invasions had been accomplished by people who had not been actuated by any conscious tendency towards collectivism. My friend Albert Métin[1] gave an excellent name to the attitude of mind which produced this movement towards collectivism in practice. It was really *socialisme sans doctrine*. Municipalisation of water, gas and electricity had familiarised the public with collectivist method without familiarising it with collectivist theory. Step by step public services had been brought under public control without any definitive doctrine. Indeed, many enthusiastic protagonists of collectivism were horrified at the suggestion that their steps were steps towards Socialism. They knew nothing of the history of the subject, and they were influenced wholly by what they considered as practical considerations. I have already mentioned the reasons for the extension of civic enterprise in places like Glasgow and Birmingham. These developments excited little interest among those who looked at the question from a point of view rather broader and deeper than did the members of the town councils. Thus, parallel to the projects of municipalisation, but altogether apart from these, there grew projects of a wider character involving profound changes in industrial organisation. These projects germinated in Scotland in a peculiar manner.

There survived in the early eighties a few men who had been active in the Chartist movement in Glasgow in the thirties;[2] there were some who were interested in the crofter question either personally or sympathetically; and there were still more who had been profoundly disturbed by the phenomenon of unemployment during the Long Depression. Some or all of these groups had been reading the literature of social movements, and had come to be acquainted with the doctrines of various schools of social reform and social revolution. Such books as Patrick Edward Dove's *Theory of Human Progression*[3] and other writings of the Scots Physiocrats[4] were more or less well known.

The Irish land question and the crofter movement had excited

[1] Minister of Labour in the French Government. Died at San Francisco while on a mission to Australia in 1919.
[2] The tendency of the Glasgow Chartists was towards what was called Christian Chartism as opposed to physical-force Chartism.
[3] The edition I have was published in Boston in 1851.
[4] The most important of these was Wm. Ogilvie; but I doubt if his *Essay on the Right of Property in Land* (London, 1782) was known at this time to any of the groups above mentioned. I did not detect any influence of Robert Owen, although his writings were known.

hostility to certain landowners. Into a soil thus prepared by the experience of life and by the results of study there fell the seed sown by Henry George. *Progress and Poverty* was first published in San Francisco in 1879.[1] Towards the end of 1880 an English edition appeared; before the end of 1881 it had come to be widely known. The idea of the nationalisation of the land was new to many people, and to many of those to whom it was not new it was an attractive idea. In short, land nationalisation came to be regarded by large numbers of people in England and in Scotland as a panacea for many, if not for all, economic difficulties. Land Restoration Societies were founded both in England and in Scotland. The movement took especial root in Glasgow, probably because in that city the crofter question and the Irish land question, as well as the questions of unemployment and trade fluctuation, had been forced into prominence by events. *Progress and Poverty* is a verbose and humorless book, and yet it seized and for a long time retained the attention of the public. It leaned upon classical economic doctrines because its author knew no other and had digested these somewhat indifferently; but it placed these doctrines in a fresh light and drew startling conclusions from them.

The Land Restoration movement had in its ranks many who had been supporters of the secularist movement, and who had been disappointed at its obviously negative tendencies. Such people broke away from Bradlaugh, whose denunciations of everything that made for Socialism were nearly as vehement as his anti-theological utterances. Land Restoration also drew into its ranks disciples of Ruskin, whose *Unto this Last* anticipated many of the points of *Progress and Poverty*. Many who were not disposed to regard land nationalisation as a final solution even of the land question, much less of the complicated questions of trade and industrial fluctuation, joined the movement, because in its ranks only did there appear to them at that time any sympathetic relation towards either economic study or action of a vital character on economic questions. All of these groups had come to be dissatisfied with both political parties and impatient with the conventional political speeches, even of the party leaders. The absence of a definite social policy was conspicuous in both parties, and neither their traditions nor the initiative of the leaders suggested the possibility of disappearance of the placid opportunism which characterised the politics of the time.

[1] Henry George told me that he knew nothing of the Physiocrats, either French or Scots, until after he had written his book.

Henry George visited Scotland in 1882; but he added neither to his own reputation there nor to the strength of the movement his writings had induced. He was found to be even more imperfectly acquainted with the literature of the subject than many of his hearers, and he was found also to look at the whole question as exclusively in terms of conditions in America as classical economists had looked at it in terms of conditions in Great Britain. There were not many working men in the Land Restoration movement; but to those who were in it, George appeared to be dominated by middle-class points of view, notwithstanding the fact that he had himself been a working man. Those who looked upon land nationalisation as a mere stepping-stone to something else, whatever that might be, were disappointed at the finality of George's views. In general, while the Land Restoration movement continued to exist for some years, the visit of George did not contribute to its permanence. I met George at this time and shared the prevalent disappointment. The claim set forth in express terms by George in his *Political Economy*, that he had recast the subject, is of course destitute of foundation; what he did do, and for that he is entitled to full credit, was to contribute to the stimulation of public interest in economic questions. He contributed nothing to economic doctrine.

The Land Restoration movement had no importance in itself, and it cannot even be held to have prepared the way in any important sense for the drastic changes in land taxation which came in later years, but it indicated clearly that there was gradually arising among the people, especially in Scotland, a feeling of hostility to both political parties and a contempt for the negative character of their domestic policies. Neither party had grappled with the economic causes which were supposed to underlie the political situation in Ireland,[1] and neither party had shown any real disposition to grapple with the causes of fluctuation in trade and industry.   On these vital questions there was evident only an attitude of mental indolence. Nationalisation of the land might not be found eventually to be a sound solution, but at least serious discussion of the economic situation was indispensable. Impatience induced by the deficiency of the politicians characterised, I think, most of those who threw themselves into this campaign, in substance abortive, but nevertheless productive of some gain in education of the people.

Limited as was its range, the Land Restoration movement implied

[1] It is now evident that the economic causes were uninfluential compared with the racial and religious factors.

a breaking down of the antagonism to economic action by the State which characterised the period of *laisser faire*, and in that sense it prepared the way for the Socialist movement which began about 1884 among groups of people of a character similar to that of the groups which were affected by the Land Nationalisation propaganda, and indeed very many passed from one movement to the other.

"There must be a constant effort to correct the prevailing tendency of things."[1] This is what I felt strongly at that time (1884). There was a definite tendency to treat with contemptuous indifference the Socialist ideas of various complexions which were then beginning once more to thrust themselves upon the people of Western Europe. Such ideas had had their vogue in the last days of the eighteenth century, again in the early thirties, and again in 1847–49. They were preached with vehement passion, and were sometimes propagated by sanguinary assaults upon the social structure. They might be answered by grape-shot, it were better that they were answered with reasoned argument. Above all they must be understood, and the background of the social conditions in which they were accepted by groups of thoughtful persons must be understood also. The validity of the various interpretations of history and of the various economic theories promulgated by various types of Socialists was not so important to discuss, because these were often contradictory; the questions of real importance were the fact that ideas adverse to the existing order of society were beginning to be widely entertained, and the reasons for that fact. When Socialism became, as it did become, prevalent—when it was accepted as if it comprised a consistent series of co-ordinated scientific statements—it became not less incumbent upon thoughtful persons to examine into the reasons for its prevalence. To quote Amiel again, "The various *isms* of the present are not fruitful principles: they are hardly given explanatory formulæ. They are rather names of diseases, for they express some element in excess, some dangerous and abusive exaggeration."[2] So much the more reason exists for investigating the diseases of which the various *isms* are the names. Perhaps even they may not be specific diseases, but only symptoms of diseases which lie deeper even than their names suggest.

The Socialist movement of the eighties was not indigenous in Scotland. Even the tradition of Socialist elements in Owenism and in Chartism, both of which had taken root in Scotland, although they

---

[1] Amiel's *Journal Intime*, 27th June, 1880.
[2] *Ibid.*, 6th July, 1880.

had both been introduced from England, had been almost altogether lost. The new impetus was of distinctly German origin. That is to say, it came from Marx through disciples of his, such as Hyndman. The originality of Marx's views has often been challenged. His indebtedness to the French Socialists as well as to William Thompson of Cork has frequently been pointed out in detail. Yet the acceptance of Marx by the German Social Democrats has given a German stamp to his doctrines from which it would be impossible justly to separate them. Through the friendship of Marx and Hyndman, the Social Democratic Federation was formed in London in 1884. This body was composed of groups that, diverse from the beginning, speedily proved to be quite discordant. There were convinced Marxists like Hyndman, who had recently returned from India, where he had been engaged in some financial business, skilled working men like John Burns, who had acquired some knowledge of doctrinaire Socialism, and at least one continental Socialist, Andreas Scheu, who had been implicated in Socialist agitation in Vienna in the seventies. Scheu was a furniture designer, and was well instructed in the development of Socialism on the Continent. More important from many points of view than any of these was William Morris, who was, I believe, induced by Hyndman to become a member of the Federation. Morris's position in the social movement of the eighties [1] was unique, and therefore I must consider it apart from the sectarian organisations whose origins and character I am at present endeavouring to indicate. A slight acquaintance with Hyndman on the part of one or two young men in Glasgow led to the formation there of a branch of the Federation. The original membership of this branch consisted of a few working men, one or two designers in cast iron and calico, and a few clerks—one of these in the office of a stock-broker. None of them had previously read much Socialist literature, but under the stimulus of the time they were beginning to do so. Hyndman came down from London, gave a Socialist speech, and weekly meetings of the branch began to be held in one of the smaller halls in the city every Sunday evening. I joined this branch, not because I found myself in entire sympathy with the doctrines of Marx, but because I felt that the Social Democrats were at least thinking seriously on social questions and because I recognised in the movement at the beginning of it an educational force of an important character. The Glasgow branch had hardly got under way when a schism occurred in the London body. Others are more competent than I to describe in detail the events which led to this

[1] See chapter xvi. *infra*.

schism. My knowledge of it was confined to the communications of Hyndman and others to the Glasgow branch, and to accounts of it given to me by those who took part in it, and principally by Morris. Although the quarrel had its immediate origin in an accusation of espionage made by Hyndman against Scheu, which Morris was convinced was quite unfounded, it appeared to me at the time that the quarrel had a deeper root. The autoritarian character of Marx had revealed itself on many occasions throughout his career as well as continuously in his writings. He had been a member of many Socialist organisations, and in all of these he had been a disintegrating force. This had been especially observable in the International, where he had endeavoured to exercise a dictatorship. When, for example, the Commune of Paris was fighting for its life in the spring of 1871, Marx, who was then in London, issued fantastic orders which he had no power to enforce and the members of the Commune no disposition to obey.[1] Marx's autoritarianism infected Hyndman, who tried to play the same rôle in the Social Democratic Federation as Marx had played in the International. The result was the same. As Bakunin and others had refused to tolerate Marx in the International, and had broken away from it, so Morris and others found it impossible to tolerate Hyndman and broke away from the Social Democratic Federation. While the controversy was going on in London an incident of no importance occurred in Glasgow. I was formally expelled from the branch there, ostensibly on the ground that I had expressed approval of the propaganda of the land nationalisers, but really because it was known that I was on the side of Morris against Hyndman. I felt very sure of my ground, because I had met Hyndman and his dictatorial manner had convinced me that he was a Marxist *pur sang*. When the split occurred, the branch rescinded its resolution regarding me; but I paid no attention to this action, and when Morris formed the Socialist League I became a member of it. I have narrated these matters at some length, partly because they came within my experience, but chiefly because they illustrate a fundamental weakness in Socialist organisations and because they also illustrate an important truth to which I have already alluded, viz., that opinions are of little account; what really matters are the soil in which they grow and, as an important constituent of this soil, the character of the people by whom they are held. Opinions may change, but character does not change. A dictatorial person who adopts Socialist instead of indi-

[1] This information I received from Leo Mélliet, who was a member of the Communist Government and also of the International.

vidualist opinions remains a dictatorial person, and his difference
of point of view renders him even more obnoxious, because of the
pretence of public interest in which his dictatorship is disguised.

The only Social Democrat with whom I have found it possible
to remain on terms of amity is John Burns, for whose uprightness
and strong common-sense I have the greatest admiration. The Social
Democratic Federation of that and of the immediately subsequent
time was not a revolutionary body, it was essentially a political sect
composed of bigoted adherents of Marx, willing to adopt any scheme
of political chicanery in order to bring his doctrines into prominence.
This was made fully manifest when the Federation came to coquette
with the Conservative party organisers, and to run Socialist candidates in the hope that the Liberal vote would be split and the Liberal
candidate defeated. The Federation never recovered from the discredit in which these enterprises involved it. The direction of the
Socialist movement which it might have had was lost by it, and it
continued to exist without influence.

The Socialist League organised by Morris and his friends was composed of men of a different type from that of those who constituted
the surviving remnant of the Social Democratic Federation. The
nucleus consisted of Morris, Belfort Bax, Scheu, and a few others.
With the exception of Scheu, they were nearly all men of letters; and
with the exception of Morris, they may be said to have belonged to
the "intellectual proletariat." Bax, perhaps alone among the Englishmen, had read much economic literature,[1] and perhaps he alone had
become more or less deeply acquainted with the writings of Marx.
Morris had tried to read Marx, but had not grappled with him in any
serious fashion. I do not know, but I imagine it was owing to the
suggestion of Bax that soon after its formation the League issued
as a kind of manifesto an English translation of the Communist
manifesto which Marx had written in 1847. There was a certain
appropriateness in this, for Marx's manifesto contains a violent denunciation of the German Socialists of that period. Nothing could be
more appropriate for a body of seceders from a Marxist group than
to use Marx himself as a club wherewith to smite their opponents. This
manifesto and the writings of the original members of the League were
clearly intended to indicate the Communist tendency of their propaganda as opposed to the Collectivism which dominated the Federation.

Soon after the formation of the League in London, Morris came
down to Glasgow to address a meeting and to float the branch formed

[1] Bax edited an edition of Adam Smith's *Wealth of Nations*.

there by the small group of sympathisers. There was a large meeting (about a thousand people) attracted by Morris's reputation. It was held on a Sunday evening. I had been asked to take the chair. Before the meeting began, Edward Caird, who was in the audience, came to me and said if there was any difficulty about procuring a chairman that he would be glad to take the chair himself. I put this generous proposition before our small committee; but they decided that the arrangement they had made should be carried out because the meeting was intended for the purpose of propaganda, and this purpose might not be served if the arrangement were altered. As was customary with him, Morris read a carefully prepared speech in which he gave his reasons for his belief in Socialism. Two young men whom I knew came to me at the close of Morris's address and asked to be introduced to him. Neither at that time nor at any other had they any interest in Socialism, although they were both affected by the discontent with social conditions which the Socialist movement indicated. They were John Cramb, many years afterwards to be known as the author of *Germany and England*, and John Davidson, the poet, whose *Fleet Street Eclogues* and other poems of great charm brought him a wide reputation. Although the membership of the Glasgow branch of the League remained insignificant in numbers, it was composed of a loyal if small group, and its frequent meetings were well attended by the general public. Morris came often, and Edward Carpenter came once to deliver an address. My friend Leo Mélliet gave at least one impassioned oration. Mélliet had been a young advocate in Paris during the last days of the Second Empire. He became a member of the International, and for a time was infected by Marxism. His leanings were, however, at this time anti-Collectivist, and it was with genuine enthusiasm that he threw himself into the insurrection of the Commune. He became a member of its Judicial Committee, and took an active part in the defence of Paris against the Versaillists. He was well versed in the controversies of continental Socialism, and was an orator of real power.

In 1886 an incident occurred which led to my dropping out of active participation in the doings of the League and to severance of my connection with it. The commencement of the Soudan Campaign induced Bax and some others, including Morris, to issue a manifesto denouncing the Government. A chief point in this manifesto was a charge against missionaries for having instigated the Government to attack the Soudanese in order to convert them to Christianity. This charge was made without a vestige of evidence; it was, indeed, on the face of it quite preposterous, and it indicated a complete absence of knowledge of the events which led to the campaign and lack of penetration in respect to its causes. I should have protested against the issue by the League of a document so irrelevant to its aims, and so palpably indefensible, had I known that it was to be issued. When it appeared I was astounded to find that the writers had coolly signed my name to it as well as their own names. I wrote a letter of protest to Morris, who sent me a long letter of explanation. He had, of course, nothing to do with the signing of my name. I made no public disclaimer, and allowed the affair to pass; but I gradually ceased to interest myself in the League, although I maintained the warmest friendly relations with Morris until his death in 1896. Sometime after its formation the Socialist League was joined by a group of irresponsible and impatient anarchists with whom it became impossible for others to act. I was not surprised that Morris had himself to withdraw from the League in 1890. In his interesting and penetrative little book on Morris, Mr. Clutton-Brock speaks of the main quarrel in the League as arising out of a dispute on method between "the two sections, parliamentary and anti-parliamentary, which are pretty much commensurate with the Collectivists and Anarchists." These are Morris's own words; but they do not really account for the quarrels either in the Social Democratic Federation or in the Socialist League.

I felt at the time that these disputes were due not to difference of opinion, nor even to variations of opinion, for the first always existed and the latter were constantly occurring, but to fundamental differences in the character of the people who were concerned in the disputes. Morris used to say, truly, that so far from Socialism being likely to result in uniformity, it was likely, if a judgment could be formed on the ground of the characters of those who were drawn into the movement, to result in extraordinary diversity. These differences in character and temperament led to differences in doctrine and method, and these led to the disputes which again and again produced the rupture of relations among the members of these bodies and resulted in schisms. The Socialists appeared to be less sociable than the individualists.

Years later than these events occurred I was visiting a group of people who were practising Communism. Everything they possessed they held in common, and their earnings went into a common fund. One of these people said to me, "I wish we could live as you do, in the world outside. You seem to live good-naturedly with one another, and to give and take without recrimination. In our community we are always quarrelling and upbraiding one another."

I am not sure that he was right about the peace of the outer world, but I am quite sure he was right about the want of peace in the Communist group.

Anything which belongs to the deep affairs of life—to religion, to family interests, to social organisation — induces differences of opinion, and these differences are accentuated and more or less forcibly and offensively expressed in all of these deep affairs according to the character and temperament of the people concerned. Thus religious schisms, family separations, disintegrations of society are occasioned through differences of opinion resulting from differences of character.

Great stress was laid at this time upon the idea that economic power lay at the root of political power. The prevalence of this idea showed that, in spite of extension of the franchise and diminution in relative political importance of the propertied classes in consequence of that extension, there was in the minds of those who entertained the idea slender faith in the potency of political power considered as a special form of energy. The prevalence of the idea showed also a tendency towards a dualistic conception of social life—as if there were two demons by both of which society must be served, and as if it were inevitable that one of these demons should direct the other. From this point of view there arose the notion that instead of the economic demon being the dictator of the political demon, as was supposed to have been the case, the political should control the economic demon. This dualistic conception has found its concrete expression in those struggles between *economism* and *politicalism* in which in all countries those groups of people which for a time unite in social propaganda have found themselves involved.

Philosophical economists from Locke and Adam Smith and practical economists like Ricardo had recognised that economic processes were subject to social laws of a character analogous to the law of the expansion of gases and the law of gravitation. Neither social laws nor physical laws may ever have been expressed in unimpugnably accurate terms; but such laws were nevertheless held to exist and to be alike insusceptible of infringement, whatever modification in the formal statement of them might be found to be necessary. Formal statements of the sequence of economic processes were often made which were not entitled to be regarded as statements of absolute social laws, but were rather to be considered as statements of sequences depending for their validity upon the coincidence at each stage of the process with which they were concerned, of certain social conditions and of the conditions assumed in the hypothesis. Such formal statements are thus to be regarded as relatively but not necessarily universally true. In this category may be placed, for example, the so-called laws of rent, of wages, and the like. The utility of these hypothetical laws in the elucidation of economic phenomena cannot be denied. The objection to them, if it be an objection, lies in difficulty of ascertaining the point at which disturbing elements in the calculation by means of which they are applied to actual conditions can properly cease to be eliminated. If after the inessential elements in a given range of economic phenomena have all been discarded there still remain some elements discordant with the hypothesis, it is time to revise the hypothesis. The chemical investigations of Ramsay into the constitution of the atmosphere may be regarded as an analogous case. The separation of the known constituents of the air being accomplished, there remained an element or elements which had not previously been known to exist; and the formal statement of the constitution of the atmosphere previously accepted had to be altered. Science is not discredited but rather vindicated by such discoveries. If social science is not regarded in the same light, it is because it is so continuously subjected to vituperative attacks by those who have imperfectly grasped its progress and meaning, and perhaps because at times its professors are reluctant to admit the effect of social changes upon traditional formal statements of the laws of economic sequence.

Up till and including the eighties of the nineteenth century, Socialism in Great Britain and on the continent of Europe could not be fairly regarded as in any serious sense a proletarian movement. Its force, such as it was, lay in the adherence of "intellectuals" drawn from all classes, and thus the movement did not have a class complexion. It was a social movement in the strict sense, notwithstanding the influence upon it of the doctrines of Marx, who did not himself belong to the proletariat. These doctrines had two principal implications—one was the materialistic basis of history and the other was the evolution of the proletariat into a conquering class. While the first of these implications seemed to have a certain weight in the eighties, the second had none. The proletariat had not evolved as yet a definite "class consciousness," while the "intellectuals" were experiencing disillusionment regarding the supposititious special virtues of the proletariat. In visions of a society of the future the proletariat had been idealised by those who never had any real knowledge of, or contact with, the working masses; but the closer view which the Socialist movement afforded dispelled the idea that society could be improved by a simple bouleversement in which the proletariat would take the place of the bourgeoisie, unless the character of the proletariat came to approximate more closely to the ideal cherished by the intellectuals.

The international character of the Socialist movement, upon which Marx had leaned, was compromised by the historical, racial and economical differences between the proletariat of one country and that of others. In France, *e.g.*, the bourgeoisie had replaced the aristocracy by the simple process of wiping it out of existence by killing or expatriating its members. But the bourgeoisie were too intelligent and too numerous to permit the proletariat to wipe it out after the same manner.[1] In Great Britain the middle class gradually absorbed the aristocracy and extinguished its separate influence. Here also the middle class was too intelligent and too numerous to permit itself to be conquered by the proletariat, which up till the present has exhibited neither the power nor the will to conquer. In Germany, on the other hand, the aristocracy survived and the middle class had come to be wedged in a precarious situation between it and the proletariat, rapidly increasing through the absorption into its ranks of large numbers of the agrarian population. The German middle class was dominated politically by the land-owning aristo-cracy and economically by the same class through its influence in the State. A species of State collectivism under agrarian domination developed rapidly, and the proletariat found itself rendered economic-ally prosperous and politically and morally depressed by this domina-tion; while the commercial and professional middle class, including the organisers of industry, found themselves increasingly drawn to social democracy because they saw in it a means of gaining the political power of which they were deprived by the agrarian magnates. In Russia the situation was much less highly developed. There was no middle class. The aristocracy survived, but remained politically and economically powerless. The State overshadowed aristocrat and peasant alike, while the proletariat was not yet sufficiently differen-tiated to be reckoned as a distinct social class.

The class contours were in different countries thus varied and the class evolution was by no means co-incidental. For this reason inter-national Socialism was a mere phantasy without relation to realities.

The Marxists had little reason to object to the classical economists on the ground of adherence to *a priori* methods, or of neglect of the facts of social life. The Marxists were themselves not less guilty on both counts.

[1] Since this was written the same process has been employed in Russia, and carried farther than it was carried in France, for the bourgeoisie, small as it was in numbers, was also wiped out.

CHAPTER XV

RUSKIN AND THE POLITICAL ECONOMY OF ART

No, that's the world's way (keep the mountain-side,
 Make for the city!);
He knew the signal, and stepped on with pride
 Over men's pity;
Left play for work, and grappled with the world
 Bent on escaping:
"What's in the scroll," quoth he, "thou keepest furled?
 Show me their shaping,
Theirs who most studied man, the bard and sage,—
 Give!"—So, he gowned him,
Straight got by heart that book to its last page:
 Learned, we found him.
 ROBERT BROWNING, *A Grammarian's Funeral* (1855).

AMONG those who were dissatisfied with the existing social order and dissenting from the accepted maxims of the classical economists I have incidentally mentioned Ruskin. Although we had many friends in common, it was not my fortune ever to meet him. Of those friends I should mention especially Robert Caird of Greenock, who stayed with Ruskin for some time in Florence and who came to be penetrated alike with Ruskin's views on art and with his views on social progress. Caird was a remarkable man, unproductive in a literary sense, but nevertheless highly cultivated. He had gone from Florence and Ruskin to polar opposites—to Chicago and Pullman, the introducer of the variety of travelling couch, or rather bunk, which bears his name. Pullman had been a cabinet-maker, and he developed his idea of a railway sleeping-car from the point of view of his craft, in the same manner as the early designers of gas chandeliers and brackets had developed these from the candlesticks and oil lamps which they had been accustomed to design and as the early designers of electric light fixtures had designed these from gas lamps. The method was natural and frequent in the evolution of design, but it was stodgy and was due to lack of invention. Caird was with Pullman when he developed another idea, well intended but lacking in insight into human nature— the idea of housing his workmen in sanitary but similar houses with formal gardens of deadly uniformity. From Chicago Caird returned

to Greenock to take charge of the shipbuilding yard which was the
possession of his family.

Other friends of Ruskin and of mine were the Tullochs of Kirn,
near Dunoon on the Clyde. Tulloch had been a stonemason and had
early become a devoted adherent. Later he and his wife became
friends of Ruskin. They corresponded with him frequently and paid
occasional visits to Brantwood. They were not cultivated people,
but they had affectionate dispositions and a great fund of common-
sense. Ruskin acquired a liking for them both.

Ruskin does not properly come within the scope of these recollections, yet it is necessary to mention him in this place because of the
direction which he gave to the criticism of art and of life. Someone
has said of William Morris that when he touched anything he somehow
altered its history. The same might be said of Ruskin. Before his
time there was much writing upon æsthetics from a philosophical point
of view; but the philosophers knew nothing of the technique of painting, and in general floundered when they attempted to criticise works
of art. The painters were not used to express themselves in any medium
other than paint, and in general were unable to explain the nature
of the standards they applied in criticism of their own works or the
works of others. There was an equally wide breach between the man
of science and the artist. They did not express themselves in the
same language—to one another they were quite inarticulate. Criticism
of artistic products, such as it was, was left to writers with slender
qualifications for such a task. No first-rate man of letters adequately
equipped for the exercise of the special function of criticism of art
had made his appearance. "Literary criticism" thus became a byword
among artists. They learned nothing from it, and they found in it
only ignorance of the methods, possibilities and purposes of painting
as well as of the plastic arts in general. Into such a field Ruskin came
equipped up to a certain point. He was a good draughtsman and a
competent critic of line. It is true that he was probably deficient in
colour sense; but he had an intimate knowledge of structure and
much experience in detailed examination of numerous buildings and
paintings acknowledged by many generations as great masterpieces.
Behind these purely technical qualifications in regard to the plastic
arts Ruskin had a certain knowledge of science and at least some
knowledge of philosophy, especially in the department of æsthetics.
Added to this equipment he had the great gift of expression. If his
style sometimes lacks restraint, if it is occasionally marred by in-
artistic excess of splendour, it is always lucid. Moreover, at a moment

when the world of art was either dominated by mere commonplace or by meaningless imitation of motives of the Late Renaissance, Ruskin brought to bear upon the criticism of works of art an enthusiasm for the Gothic and a vivid interpretation of it. Above all, Ruskin not only intellectualised the criticism of art, he did much to intellectualise art itself. In so doing he touched the social value and position of art.

The artistic tradition which survived among the peasantry of some of the European countries had disappeared in the whirl of modern industry. Ruskin found the explanation of the depression of life under industrial conditions in the artlessness of it—in the drudgery of mechanical reproduction of things of ugliness instead of invention of new and beautiful things. This artlessness was due, he thought, to the conditions under which production took place, to the system of the organisation of industry for profit, involving exploitation of the workers and depression of their lives to a point at which artistic emotion and artistic invention were alike impossible.

Ruskin found the classical economists unsatisfactory guides in studying the economic aspects of the social problem as it envisaged itself to him. He therefore mapped out for himself a theory of wealth which if not wholly new had new elements. This theory may be found in *Unto this Last* and others of his writings. In these Ruskin may be said, so far as his hostility to exploitation is concerned, to be a follower of Saint-Simon, with whose *Nouveau Christianisme* he was evidently acquainted. In his views on value Ruskin in effect returned to the mediæval idea of a "just price"; and in his views on interest he reverted also to mediæval ideas. Ruskin was probably the first among his contemporaries to emphasise and develop the implications of the idea of the unity of life—an idea by no means neglected by the ancients. Ruskin showed that the fine arts are integral parts of life, are indeed the visible manifestation of the higher forms of it, and are the means by which we recognise and record them. The philosophers and some of the poets had expressed the same idea after their own fashion; but their language was not that of the people, and their views had no wide influence. Ruskin came as an intermediary. He played the rôle of Interpreter and gave emphasis to those elements which seemed to him to need emphasis at his moment.

From the beginning of the nineteenth century it was fashionable for writers on social progress to lay great stress on "conditions"—on the circumstances by which any individual member of society found himself surrounded. It was supposed that all men were equal and that if they were "free," that is, released from external pressure, and not enslaved by society or by a part of it, that all would at least have the opportunity of being equally happy. This is not the place to develop the theoretical relations between the extreme views of Godwin and Robert Owen, the speculations of Darwin, the Utilitarianism of Mill and the views of Ruskin. The theories of life involved in these various speculations are more remarkable for their resemblances than for their differences. They all, for example, lay more stress as determinants of character upon the "conditions" under which the individual exists than they lay upon the inherent tendency towards variation in the character of the individual.

The Stoics and the Epicureans both maintained the opposite thesis. Apart from the ancients, it is a commonplace of modern biology that the character of the response to a stimulus of any kind depends upon the character of the stimulated organism and not upon the character of the stimulus. The same stimulus will produce different effects upon different organisms; and an organism may at one time be excited into violent activity by a stimulus, while in the presence of the same stimulus at another time it remains inert.

The tendency of biological speculation during the past thirty years, if such speculation can be described as having a tendency, has been towards emphasis of the importance of the inherent factor, and therefore towards a readjustment of views regarding the influence of conditions upon individual characters.

At the moment when the societies of Western Europe were in transition from relatively small self-contained communities to large interdependent industrial groups, conditions external to these small communities and to individuals migrating from them were necessarily thrust into practical and speculative prominence. Molecular movements in society which constituted the transition involved changes alike in individual characters and in social conditions by which individuals were surrounded, and incidentally threw an increasing strain upon organs of government. While social systems were in a state of flux, and while, especially after the peace of 1815, the populations of Western Europe were on the whole increasing rapidly, the imperative needs of the hour were economic needs. A new and much enlarged industrial, commercial and financial organisation had to be evolved. This was evolved predominantly by spontaneous private effort, sometimes supplemented and sometimes thwarted by political action. During a period of this character it is not surprising that, save in rare individual instances, the general mind should be bent upon provision for economic needs in the narrow sense and should be distracted from provision for the less obviously imperative spiritual and intellectual needs. The effect of such a situation upon the finer minds of an age can readily be understood; but this effect seldom makes its appearance in an impressive manner until the close of such an age of transition. Only then can the finer minds acquire their necessary audience, and even then the finer minds never go into politics.

The conditions which formed the background of Ruskin's theory of society were already passing away when he began to write.

The acutest phases of the transition had passed before 1850; the Factory Acts and, more than all, the great increase of industrial production and the increased mobility of labour and of goods had, with other factors, carried society over many critical points in the transition—yet the effects of the changes had not become completely manifest. Increase of production and mobility of labour and goods had been attained by means of concentration of capital in the exploitation of raw materials, in manufacture, in railways and steamships. Conditions had been rendered more endurable by the very means that met with Ruskin's disapproval. The character of the industrial organisation spontaneously developed by labourers had been that of a self-contained community. A society wholly composed of such communities had been almost destitute of science, quite ignorant of the fine arts and wholly governed by tradition. The political control of such a society was very easy, so long as those who inherited or secured the control were able to maintain it without increasing the traditional burdens of taxation. A reformer who proposed a new system of education, new regulations in respect to public health, or other measures aiming at the benefit of the community from his point of view, was necessarily looked upon as a public enemy unless he were prepared to sustain the cost of these reforms out of his own pocket. Even if he did so he was looked upon as a person of more or less unbalanced mind.[1]

In the new "Capitalistic" society art was developing rapidly. New schools were growing up in England. Constable and Turner made their appearance.

The industrial revolution in Western Europe was carried out not by the members of self-contained communities, but by people who

---

[1] Chadwick and Richardson, for example, who fought the battle for public health against public indifference, were looked upon even by intelligent persons as mere cranks.

withdrew from them through motives of ambition or who, through
pressure of population, found themselves extruded from the communities. For more than two centuries the self-contained communities
in England and Scotland formed the reservoir from which urban
industry drew its recruits. Gradually these communities were reacted
upon or were absorbed by the industrial groups in their neighbourhood, until their self-contained character disappeared.

While village life was simple and to the sophisticated point of
view of an artist sometimes full of interest, the art in that life, if
there was any, was wholly "unpremeditated" and was therefore in
the strict sense not art. The furniture of the village houses was made
for use and durability; but there was seldom any novelty in design.
The traditional forms had a permanent hold. There was thus a slender
amount of artistic invention and slender appreciation of it when it
made its appearance.

During the two hundred years of the transition—that is, from the
middle of the seventeenth century to the middle of the nineteenth—
art was in general produced in the towns and was economically sustained by them. Thus the art of that period had, as it were, an urban
flavour. Even the rural landscape was formulated in a cabinet picture.[1]
Only in the towns were to be found the emotional and intellectual
stimulus and appreciation which facilitated, although it did not necessarily cause, artistic production.

All of the great artists must have had in their minds, first, the
demands of their art, and only secondarily the requirements of those
"persons of importance in their day" who were to have the privilege
of paying for it. A few may have had visions of future generations of
unimportant but knowing persons whose appreciation was more to
be valued than that of their own contemporaries because it was more
enduring, because it even meant immortality.

Thus, although some conditions may justly be regarded as more
favourable to the growth of art than others, art may be regarded as
being independent of conditions, and as being dependent in the strict
sense exclusively upon the inherent powers of the artist himself. Even
education does little for an artist; he must himself draw out his own
powers in his own way. Not only is it often the case that the best
work of an individual artist is done when he is poor and his indifferent
work when he is prosperous, but sometimes artists have worked best
under the pressure of exploitative dealers who have kept them alive
but kept them producing to the limit of their powers. Works of

[1] As, e.g., by Constable.

art of the finest order have been produced by slaves as by free-men, by hereditary dependents of Daimios as by free citizens of an Italian republic.

The fact seems to be that artistic production depends chiefly, if not altogether, upon the irresistible and unquenchable fire of genius. It seems to do so irrespective of contemporary social conditions. These social conditions may, at the most, contribute stimulus or deny it; they cannot of themselves produce the germ which may respond to the stimulus or may contrive to live without it.

There is a deep pathos in the sacrifice of genius to its product; but such a sacrifice may lie as much in the nature of things as that obscure law which prevents certain creatures from surviving the exercise of their instinct towards reproduction.

I have seen in a dark and filthy cellar in Fuchow an almost nude Chinese weaver, with the pallor of death in his face and a weird sparkle in his eyes, clearly in an advanced stage of tuberculosis, the very personification of human misery, weaving a silk fabric of un-questionable beauty. It may be that he had a joy of his own; it may be that he looked upon his work as torture; but in the best-equipped co-operative or State factory in which the unexploited workers might work under ideal conditions, or in the studio of an artist-weaver who rejoiced in direct public demand for his wares, it is hard to conceive of any more artistic work being done than was being done there in Fuchow under conditions almost indescribably loathsome. Art is a form of expression; but a work of art does not always explicitly tell the story of its produc-tion. The most acute connoisseur could not find in the graceful lines and perfect workmanship of a silk fabric offered him in Regent Street any relation to the dismal house where it was woven or the dying artist who wove it.

While I venture to doubt the soundness of Ruskin's views on the relation of art to society, I do not on that account undervalue the importance of the stimulus he gave to the discussion of the subject or the value of his contribution towards serious and intelligent criti-cism of works of art. It seems to me that artists have in general rendered him scant justice. They have chosen to find in his writings only the ratiocinations of a literary person about art, rather than the helpful guidance of a critic and teacher. At the same time they have insisted that art cannot be taught, that it is a craft which must be learned by the craftsman himself and that he can learn only by per-sonal experiment. There is a good deal in this point of view; and perhaps for those artists who do not desire, or who are not able, to look at the moral and intellectual aspects of art, neither Ruskin nor any other writer can be of service. But there is as wide a gulf between the criticism of Ruskin, literary as the artist finds it, and the naïve judgment of the unenlightened as there is between the latter and the conception of the artist. Ruskin thinks, to some extent at least, in terms of paint or line and endeavours to explain how these express certain meanings to him, while the unenlightened looks at a picture without seeing either the one or the other. The unenlightened is interested in a portrait only if he is interested in the person, in a landscape only if he knows the place or if it is associated with something in his mind. Ruskin at least suggested that a painting should be estimated in terms of the art of which it is an example and that a seeing eye must have a cultivated instinct. He also suggested that art in a high sense could never develop as a factor in common life unless people in general held views of life other than those of the society of his time. He may, as I have suggested, have been wrong in regarding the fine arts as being dependent upon social conditions, but he could not be wrong in desiring social improvement.

Ruskin was thus led through the theory of art in relation to society which was at least of doubtful validity to a sound appreciation of the need for social change; and he was right in believing that since social change involved a change in life as a whole, it must react upon that part of life which we know as art. Yet an age of comfort and universal well-being is not necessarily an age of art. It is even possible that in order to distribute well-being more widely, much of the energy which is now devoted to the fine arts may have to be devoted otherwise.

The war has brought us face to face with many facts of life to which people in general were previously blind. It has shown, for example, most vividly that the worth of a thing is not its price in the market but its availability for the satisfaction of human need. Not merely Ruskin but also the economists have always insisted upon this, but it has been a hard fact to drive into the public mind. It has needed a great war and food control and rationing to hammer it in.

CHAPTER XVI

WILLIAM MORRIS

Stand still, true poet that you are!
   I know you; let me try and draw you.
Some night you'll fail us: when afar
   You rise, remember one man saw you,
Knew you, and named a star!

   .   .   .   .   .

Meantime, I'll draw you as you stand,
   With few or none to watch and wonder:
I'll say—a fisher, on the sand
   By Tyre the old, with ocean-plunder,
A netful, brought to land.

Who has not heard how Tyrian shells
   Enclosed the blue, that dye of dyes
Whereof one drop worked miracles,
   And coloured like Astarte's eyes
Raw silk the merchant sells?
              ROBERT BROWNING, *Popularity* (1855).

WHILE William Morris owed much to the stimulating influence of Ruskin's social ideas, he approached the subject from a different angle. He was quite as discontented with the society of his time as Ruskin was; but his temperament was different. Ruskin was not averse from controversy when controversy seemed to him to be necessary; but he was essentially peaceful, although he did not like his peace to be disturbed. Morris was the reverse of placid. His extraordinary activity of mind, amounting to restlessness, and the vehemence of his likes and dislikes led him into an attitude of almost chronic pugnacity. Ruskin was as anxious as Morris to reorganise society on a finer basis; but he had not the constructive genius to attempt reorganisation. Morris to the vision of a poet added the practical sagacity of a craftsman. He left recondite discussion of the relation of the individual to his environment to those who had a mind for such matters; what he was concerned with was how he as an individual could produce with the speed imposed by the limits of human life the maximum result in leading or pushing society in the direction he thought society ought to go.

Bagehot has pointed out that the craftsman, accustomed to the exact correspondence of intention and result in manipulating the materials with which he deals, expects when he has to deal with human materials a similarly exact correspondence and a response to effort precisely corresponding to the effort. It is possible to find in Morris's views a reflection of this standpoint of the craftsman. A mechanical view of the social organism which such a standpoint implies is by no means confined to craftsmen, and it would not be difficult to discover illustrations of it in Bagehot's own writings. Indeed, the habit of mind of the craftsman might fairly be regarded as going no farther than the fundamental postulate of science, viz., that like causes produce like effects. The difficulty lies in making certain that the causes are really precisely alike.

Morris's point of view was that of the artist who experienced the greatest joy in production, as also in possession and use of works of art; and he found everywhere about him people who experienced no such joy. The problem was why? Morris's answer was, in brief, similar to Ruskin's, namely, that under the exploitative conditions of modern industry it was impossible for the worker to have joy in his work. I have already noticed the inadequacy of this answer, and suggested that there is no historical justification of such an answer. Under conditions where there is no exploitation, we do not necessarily find any high development of artistic powers or any joy in production, while we sometimes find both under conditions of the most severe exploitation. A sounder answer would be that joy in production, possession or use is a function of the person concerned and is not dependent upon the form of his economical life or upon the constitution of the society of which he is a member. To such an argument Morris would probably have replied, "That does not matter. Society is all wrong anyway; and after we have put it on the right track, we shall see what will happen." Undoubtedly the pulverisation of society had no terrors for Morris's mind. He really did not appear to regard society as a growth, but rather as a mechanical structure which might be smashed to pieces or wholly scrapped, and a new society constructed in the place formerly occupied by the old.

It may be urged that at certain moments such a view might be advanced without disadvantage to social progress. Even if the analogy between society and an organism be pushed very far, it must be allowed that, like all organic structures, society has some of the characters of a mechanism. It may be that the removal, even by violent means, of mechanical excrescences upon society, having apparent association with its cardinally organic structure, but forming no really integral part of it, might be effected without imperilling the progress of society and might even promote such progress.

As in all surgical operations, the danger lies in the delicacy of the organism upon which it is proposed to impose mechanical pressure. Mere annihilation of a society could by no means be regarded as an incident of progress.

While thus Morris's propaganda, like the previous propaganda of Ruskin, cannot be considered as having other than an extremely shaky philosophical foundation, both rendered service in disturbing even to the point of irritation the complacent optimism current in their time. Social progress may take a direction quite different from that imagined by either of them; but none the less, the society of the future will owe much to their idealism.

I have already described the circumstances under which I became acquainted with Morris about 1884. Morris was then fifty years of age, stout almost to the extent of rotundity, with a rolling gait not unlike that of a sailor. In his youth Morris had been fond of sailing, and had probably acquired his roll in that way. One of my children, a serious little boy of about three years, was so struck by Morris's gait that he followed Morris as he walked up and down the room, imitating his roll with painstaking fidelity, evidently not for the purpose of making fun of Morris but for the purpose of acquiring the roll. Morris's hair and beard were ample and were dark grey; not yet was there a suggestion of white. His hair was rather coarse, and the hairs of his beard when he was excited seemed to stand out as if they were affected by an electrical discharge. In spite of his bulk, Morris's physical activity was boundless, corresponding, as it seemed, to the restlessness of his mind. He almost literally rushed from one end of Great Britain to the other, lecturing on Socialism; and from London to Merton Abbey looking after his business. Meanwhile he was writing prose copiously, poetry more exiguously, and translating the *Odyssey*. These literary labours were generally performed at Hammersmith or at Kelmscott Manor in Gloucestershire, where he sometimes spent week-ends; but very largely while he was travelling. His custom on a long journey was to secure a first-class compartment where he could be alone, and to work steadily. Early one morning I called upon him at a hotel in a provincial town. We were going somewhere to breakfast. I found him in one of the public rooms working on his translation of the *Odyssey*. This feverish activity which enabled him to work at will under almost any conditions, thereby disproving his own hypothesis, was not accompanied by the will to rest or by the power to rest at will, and this defect probably contributed to the shortening of his life.

One evening in Glasgow, I think it was in 1886, after dinner at the house of Bruce Glasier, Morris pulled out of his pocket a copy of Mark Twain's *Huckleberry Finn*. He had, he said, read a little bit in the train, and if we did not mind he would go on from the point he had reached. He read to us for six or seven hours, that is, till between two and three in the morning. When I saw him early next day I naturally said that I hoped he had rested well, apologising for keeping him up so late.

William Morris. "I rested well enough when I did get to sleep; but I had to finish *Huckleberry Finn*."

James Mavor. "When did you finish him?"

William Morris. "About five o'clock."

There is a sequel to this incident. Mark Twain's seventieth birthday was celebrated by his friends in New York. They gave him a dinner. In replying to the toast of his health he made a characteristically humorous speech. In the course of it he mentioned that he had been told by someone that Darwin had read and enjoyed some of his books. When the *Life of Darwin*, by his son, was published, he had procured it immediately and examined it in order to see if there was in it any reference to himself. There was; this was it: "Towards the close of my father's life, when his mind was somewhat enfeebled, he spent some of his time reading trashy American novels." I had seen Mark Twain in London, at a *soirée* of the Royal Society; but I did not know him. On the strength of this slender tie, and desiring to administer balm to any wound of the spirit which might have been experienced in spite of appearances to the contrary, I wrote to Mark Twain and told him the story of Morris and *Huckleberry Finn*. I was glad I did so, for he liked it very much and wrote me a charming letter, in which he said he had placed mine among his treasured possessions.

Morris was not a great reader, and least of all of minor literature. He regarded a book, if it was a fine piece of caligraphy or of typography, as a thing of beauty to look at, to handle, and sometimes to work upon. If it was a book of great moment in a language he knew, he looked upon it as a fit subject for transmutation into his own language. He was thus drawn to early manuscripts and to early printing because they contributed ideas for designs; and to the Norse sagas and the Homeric poems because he might weave these afresh into fabrics of his own—into his own mellifluous prose or verse.

He had no more regard for commentators than Swift had, and he was not interested in controversies over nice equivalents in translation. For convenience, and in order to save himself the trouble of consulting the bulky Liddell and Scott or other Greek dictionary, he sometimes used a commonplace crib. Nevertheless, especially in those passages of the *Odyssey* where the author describes textiles and other products of handicraft, Morris's interpretation is certainly as subtle and probably infinitely more accurate than any other, because he knew what the poet (or poetess) must have meant to say. In short, the fire, sometimes burning with great intensity, at which Morris warmed himself was kindled by his own genius and not by the genius of other ages.

Walter Crane, in writing to me after Morris's death, remarked that Morris "never had the chill of poverty in his bones." This was true; and it is possible that, had Morris not been from the beginning possessed of ample means, the course of his life in his earlier years might have been somewhat different from what it was. Yet, given Morris's heredity and personality, deficiency of fortune would have been speedily remedied by him. He knew very well the value of the possession of the means of life, and he would have set himself to acquire these with the same industry he employed to amplify the means of life for others. With his practical genius and sagacity Morris could under no circumstances have remained for any length of time a poor man, no matter what buffeting of fortune he might have experienced.

There was in Morris a curious example of what might be called inheritance of an acquired habit and the exercise of it without any need for its exercise. Morris's father was a bill-broker. In the bill-broking business it is necessary not merely to have a large capital but to hold large sums available for instant use. If a bill-broker is not able to discount sound "paper" on the instant, he might as well close his doors. He must therefore keep a large credit at his bankers. Morris was never in his father's business. His father died when he was a boy at school. Neither Morris's own business nor his personal requirements rendered it necessary for him to keep in the relatively unproductive form of bank credits any considerable sums of money, yet he habitually did so. Indeed, he kept in that way sums of money bearing a large proportion to his total fortune, and thereby his income from investments, had his money been shrewdly invested, was less than it might have been. Morris thus did not derive the advantage from his wealth which he might readily have derived.

I think it was in 1885 that Morris came to Glasgow, partly to lecture to the Socialist League and partly to give readings from his own poems to a fashionable audience. It was intended that the net proceeds of the latter effort should be devoted to the maintenance of a reading-room for the members of the League; but unfortunately the expenses were conceived on too generous a scale and there were no net proceeds. The readings were a great success. John Nichol took the chair and introduced Morris in an affectionate and appreciative speech. Some of the items in the programme were suggested by Nichol, for example, a portion of *The Death of Jason*, which Nichol thought Morris's finest poem. Other items, such as a passage from *Sigurd the Volsung*, were suggested by myself. Morris's reading was decidedly not that of the ordinary platform reader. He read in an even, rather sing-song voice wholly in keeping with the narrative character of his verse. His reading had a haunting charm; it brought out the rhythm of the poetry, but it had no dramatic quality. His poetry did not possess and could not educe in reading the quality of drama.

On many occasions Morris read to me passages from his poems, and he always brought to my mind that he was a Welsh bard reciting, in language and rhythm peculiarly his own, the ancient legends that had come down to him. The illusion would have been perfect had Morris's reading been accompanied by the plucking of a string.

In 1889 Morris published *The Roots of the Mountains*. When he showed me the proofs of the first pages he asked, "How do you like the type?" The type was the same as he had employed for *The House of the Wolfings*, published in 1888. It was not designed by Morris, but was selected by him and Emery Walker from a number of old types which were available. To my mind the type was too small for the length of the line used in *The Roots of the Mountains*. I therefore answered that I did not like it.

William Morris. "Why?"

James Mavor. "Because it hurts my eyes."

William Morris. "Damn your eyes."

James Mavor. "Damn your type. Your type in itself is not bad; but the line is one-third too long. My eye, which has a normal range, requires to adjust itself after reading two-thirds only of the line. To read your type is therefore unduly fatiguing. Your type should be larger, or your line shorter."

I don't know that Morris was convinced at the time; but he did not use the type again. He proceeded to design types which were founded for him, and thus gave the world the superb products of the Kelmscott Press. The decorative qualities of Morris's type are indisputably fine; but since each page is considered as an integral decorated

William Morris

From a relief (1886) by J. Pittendreigh MacGillivray, LL.D., R.S.A.

space—one and indivisible—Morris's books, things of beauty as they are, may be better looked at than read; because reading implies analysis of the page and even of the line.

One evening in Edinburgh in 1889, while the National Association for the Advancement of Art was holding its second meeting, Morris was present at the Symposium Club. Those who were present included Patrick Geddes,[1] Thomas Carlaw Martin,[2] William Renton, Belyse Baildon and a few others. They were critical rather than sympathetic, and Morris was clearly not quite at home. He spoke well and vigorously, but with a certain defiance, making little effort towards persuasion. He probably looked upon them as a group of minor writers about whom it was unnecessary to trouble himself. They were, however, very quiet and respectful, and the evening passed without incident.

It was otherwise on, I think, the following evening, which was spent at the house of the Rev. John Glasse. Glasse was a sincere and well-instructed Socialist and at the same time a liberal-minded Christian and the minister of Old Greyfriars, one of the parish churches of Edinburgh. Besides Morris and myself there were, so far as I remember, only Walter Crane and Patrick Geddes. Geddes was vivacious and suggestive as always. His general standpoint on social questions was that of Comte, although he had many original views on such questions as on all others he touched with his acute intelligence. I do not remember at this distance of time what it was he said that roused Morris to fury. I thought at the time Morris did not quite understand Geddes's point. He was certainly not familiar with Geddes's elusive style or with the philosophical and scientific background which Geddes presupposed. I ventured to try to explain Geddes's position, and, in doing so, no doubt in some degree advocated it. Morris turned upon me with a roar, shaking his fist at me across the table, and blazing with magnificent leonine passion.

"You!" he said. "Geddes knows no better; but you! you know; and yet you say these things."

I roared with laughter, and after a while Morris calmed down.

In moments of leisure Morris was fond of telling stories and of listening to them. On the day after the evening just described, Morris, Walter Crane, Emery Walker and I were travelling from Edinburgh to Glasgow. Morris was in high spirits, Crane and Walker were, as was their custom, quiet. Morris slapped me on the knee and said,

[1] Then Professor of Botany in University College, Dundee.
[2] Then editor of *The Scottish Leader*, afterwards Sir Thomas Carlaw Martin, Curator of the Scottish National Portrait Gallery.

"Mavor, tell us a story." Probably I did; but only on condition that Morris followed with another; and so we passed from the region of controversy into the region of fairy tales.

On two sides Morris's attitude, considering him as a true-poet, puzzled me very much. One of these was what in anyone else might have been regarded as an affectation; but in Morris this supposition was impossible—an absence of knowledge of and interest in music. Morris once told me that he scarcely knew the difference between "God Save the King" and "Old Hundred"; that, in short, he had no musical ear. On my remarking that this was strange, he said, "Maybe; but Swinburne's is another case of the same kind."

Years afterwards I spoke of this to Arnold Dolmetsch, who knew Morris well. Dolmetsch had taken to Morris, as he did to me, his viol da gamba and his viola and played upon them the mediæval music written for them. Dolmetsch said that Morris was fascinated, as well he might be. Dolmetsch thought that while Morris had had no musical training, he was not interested in modern music simply because it did not appeal to him; but when he found an opportunity of hearing mediæval music—the outcome, as it was, of mediæval art— he understood it and enjoyed it.

The other side of Morris which puzzled me was what appeared to be his deficiency in appreciation of natural beauty. I went with him once up Loch Goil on the Clyde. The scenery is by no means the finest that Scotland can afford, but it has to my mind a certain charm. Morris had been talking about other things, and I ventured to direct his attention to the things about us. He was not impressed. Pointing to a Scots pine that stood alone on the brow of a hill, well rooted but finding the strong south-west gales almost more than enough for its sturdy frame:

William Morris. "Look at that. It is ugly. It gives a bad line."

James Mavor. "Well! Well! Tell me of some scene which you think really beautiful."

William Morris. "The view of London from Richmond Hill. That is real beauty."

As I write these lines in the Island of Orleans in a quiet garden whose terrace is laved by the waters of the St. Lawrence, I look across the mighty river, sparkling in the sunlight, to the citadel and ramparts of Quebec, or turn to the north towards the lovely contour of the Laurentian hills and the tumbling foam of Montmorency, and think that beauty is in many kinds and that some of these are not inferior in potency to the beauty of London.

In a certain high sense Morris's temperament was anarchic. If he had lived in a pagan society he would not have made fun of the gods, as Lucian did, he would have revolted fiercely against them. He was by nature hostile to forms of authority; above all, he despised the arts of the politicians and regarded the authority acquired by them over other men as mere usurpation. He believed that one day men would pull down the usurpers and simply destroy the political fabric they had erected as a fortress for the maintenance of their power. One afternoon we were passing by the Houses of Parliament:

William Morris. "Ere long there will be a dungheap in place of that pile."

Perhaps Morris's most characteristic feature was his reserve. He was frank and sociable; with his friends he was affectionate and sympathetic, but to everyone there lay, not far in the background, an impenetrable region. Aloofness may arise from consciousness of superior birth or breeding or intellectual powers; but it may also arise from consciousness of emotions pitched, as it were, on an individual key, to which the natures of others do not absolutely respond.

Morris appeared seldom to trouble himself about forming considered judgments of men. He was indifferent to most of the people whom he met. He passed them by because they did not interest him—that is, because they did not seem to be worth the emotional strain involved in friendship. Hence his judgments of men were sometimes abrupt, and often really unsound. For instance, he said to me of Edward Caird, "He is a dull man." Caird was by no means dull, and he had a much more penetrative appreciation of Morris than Morris had of him. Even of his friends Morris gave at times curt and incomplete judgments. Of Rossetti he once said to me, "Sometimes Rossetti was an angel; and sometimes he was a damned scoundrel."

On one of his visits to Glasgow in 1887 or 1888, on the suggestion of Francis Newbery, I was able to induce Morris to give a lecture on the Gothic to the students of the Glasgow Art School. The lecture was delivered in the Corporation Art Gallery then adjoining the buildings of the School. The Gallery was really worthy of the occasion. Morris stood in front of the superb "Enthronement of the Virgin," a large panel attributed to the school of Bellini, on one hand was "The Woman taken in Adultery," one of the finest pictures of Giorgione, on the other the "St. George and Donor" about whose painter there has been endless controversy (a picture Morris admired intensely), and before him was "The Man in Armour" of Rembrandt.

While walking down to the Gallery Morris inveighed with his

customary vehemence against classicism. On the University hill we passed a church in the Classical style, by one of the best of our Scots architects, who is by no means inappreciative or unaffected by the Gothic spirit. The church has simplicity and refinement, even if it is classic. I challenged Morris on these points. He glanced at it and grunted. In the course of his lecture he left his manuscript for a moment, and, with mischief in his eye, told how I had endeavoured to seduce him from the true faith in the Gothic by calling upon him to admire a Classical building.

While on one side of it Morris's artistic and social propaganda was essentially destructive, and while he used often to say that little could be hoped from a new art or a new society until after a period of mere barren simplicity, in which buildings should be reduced to bare necessary walls and life in general should be stripped of adventitious finery, the most important side of Morris's propaganda was after all its constructive side. Morris could not wait for the destruction of the society he condemned. He imagined it was already destroyed, and, in advance of his time as he was, he showed how a new art could be made to grow; and how from immediate surroundings outwards—from private simplicity instinct with artistic feeling—there might emerge a new public magnificence which all might share and enjoy. In this sense Morris's vision was not only realisable, it is in a large measure already realised. He condemned, and even urged the destruction of, the art and of other elements in the social structure of his time, but he planted the seeds of a new art and a new society of which the new art must be the natural expression. Above all, Morris's aims had nothing in common with the narrow materialist aims of the Socialist group by which for a time he was surrounded. He was an idealist who dreamed dreams and knew how to make his dreams come true.

CHAPTER XVII

LITERARY AND ARTISTIC MOVEMENTS IN SCOTLAND IN THE EIGHTIES

Know, the great *Genius* of this land
Has many a light aerial band,
Who, all beneath his high command,
        Harmonioufly,
As *Arts* or *Arms* they underftand,
        Their labours ply.

They SCOTIA'S race among them fhare:
Some fire the *Sodger* on to dare;
Some roufe the *Patriot* up to bare
        Corruption's heart:
Some teach the *Bard*, a darling care,
        The tuneful Art.

                    ROBERT BURNS, *The Vision* (1786).

IT is at once the gain and the loss of Scotland that she exports largely her human product; in more romantic phrase, "She casts abroad her gifts of gold." The sketch which I have given above of an Aberdeenshire village explains the reason. She sends abroad her educated youth because she is too poor to keep them at home. Their value in the markets of the world is higher than she can afford to pay. I do not mean that Scots men of genius have a keener eye to the main chance than other folks, although malevolent tradition may have it so. They are fitted for a wider world than Scotland, and they pass into it. The Scotsman is an example of an animal inheriting and retaining strongly-marked characters, but nevertheless becoming readily adapted to fresh surroundings, partly by yielding to their influences and partly by compelling the surroundings to yield to them. Not merely by pressure of population are Scotsmen driven out of Scotland. The census returns show that the emptied places are filled by others. There are, I am told, more people of English birth in Scotland than there are of Scots birth in England.

London is a huge magnet, drawing its men of letters, its artists, its men of affairs, and its politicians from the provinces of England and her sister kingdoms, from the British colonies and from foreign countries.

Subsidiary though sometimes important centres have been established by groups of people who have resisted the temptations of the

Great Centre, or who, having experienced the stimulus of it, have returned to communicate this stimulus to others; but such groups have usually been too small to be self-perpetuating. Thus in the eighteenth century an intellectual group in Edinburgh — consisting of David Hume, Adam Smith, Robertson the historian, Monboddo and others, with Robert Burns as an occasional and Scott as a young member — made Edinburgh famous; and a similar group, of which Adam Smith also was a member while he was professor in the University, together with Simson the mathematician, and Black the physicist, caused Glasgow to be recognised about the same period as an intellectual centre. Similarly, sporadic growths appeared from time to time in several English provincial towns, as in Manchester, where the group gave a certain tone to English commercial policy, and Norwich, where a group of artists developed a distinctive note in painting. So also in Ireland, a remarkable group of men of original genius made its appearance in Cork in the early part of the nineteenth century.[1] Yet none of these local groups became permanent, owing partly to smallness, temperament, and exclusiveness to rising talent,[2] unless the particular direction of the talent coincided with theirs, and partly to the tendency towards political, social and intellectual centralisation, manifested especially during the period of the decay of the municipal spirit and the increasing Chauvinism, corruption and banality of municipal life. These characteristics were somewhat modified after the reform of the municipal corporations in 1835, but their effects survived and the stream towards the centre continued. The uncritical habit of mind of the local public prevented adequate recognition of native talent unless recognition were first accorded by London, and thus the power of the magnet was re-enforced.

Although centralising forces in Great Britain were very powerful, they were never quite so omnipotent as during the same period they were in France. There, Paris drew to itself all social, intellectual and political life, and the French provincial communes lost their distinctive character. The process began in the early years of the eighteenth century, and continued under the First and Second Empires, only to be checked in some measure in recent years under the Republic.

[1] Wm. Thompson, disciple of Bentham and originator of many ideas which afterwards came to be incorporated in Marxist-Socialist doctrines, was a member of this group. In a recently published encyclopædia I find no mention of this William Thompson, although an article is devoted to a person of the same name who was a pugilist (1811–80), an indication of the advantage of metropolitan over universal reputation.

[2] George Moore says (in his *Vale*) an intellectual movement consists of five persons who habitually quarrel with one another.

Throughout the nineteenth century the stream towards London and abroad of Scots aspirants for fame continued, and thus Scotland was almost denuded of her intellectual proletariat. The agricultural regions could not retain their educated young men, and the social atmosphere of the industrial and commercial regions was repugnant to similar groups within their borders. Intellectual youths became more and more odd birds in their home nests. Even when these nests were homes of cultivated people, ambitious youth did not always find them congenial. Thus from various internal and external causes the process of social disintegration proceeded, and new communities were built up elsewhere out of the proceeds of this disintegration. Scots men of letters left Scotland for one reason or another, and built up their reputations elsewhere.

Bagehot observes in one of his caustic essays that what Scotsmen write is not quite English. In the sense that the evolution of the English language in Scotland has been somewhat different from the evolution of it in England, and probably somewhat slower, this observation is true. Indeed, the writing of Scots men of letters has a distinctive character which differentiates it from the writings of Englishmen, and therein precisely lies its merit. The writings of American men of letters have also a distinctive character, differing from that of English and Scots writers alike. The Union of Scotland and England and increased means of communication toned down the differences which had developed during centuries of hostility and separation, while the American Revolution as well as distance contributed to the differentiation of the English of America from the English of the south of England. English is cardinally a flexible language; but much of its variety is due to the wide separation and the versatility of the communities in which it is spoken and of the men of letters by whom it is written.

It is possible that if the forces of centralisation had been less strong than they were, the nineteenth century would have witnessed development of a type of Scots letters of a character much more distinctive than that recognised, with snobbish contempt, by Bagehot. If, for example, Robert Louis Stevenson had been of less delicate build, he might have remained in Edinburgh and contributed to concentration there of a group of Scots men of letters; if Andrew Lang had been content to live for a while on " a little oatmeal " he might have assisted; if Barrie had been of robuster physique he might have done so also—and so on. But Stevenson went to Samoa, and Lang and Barrie went to London. The two last became anglicised, and though none of them entirely lost his Scots accent either in speaking or in writing, they remained Scots with a difference.[1]

The constitution and character of the Scots Universities were favourable to growth but not to recognition of individual genius, for like careless ducks they left their broods to sink or swim. A personal tradition of letters grew up about the versatile Blackie, the Berkleian Campbell Fraser, and the erudite and genial David Masson in Edinburgh, the Cairds and John Nichol at Glasgow, and Alexander Bain and William Minto at Aberdeen. Many youths were stimulated by these instructors, but in the absence of fellowships or other means of retaining for a time within the walls of the University promising youths who had completed their undergraduate career and who had talent to justify further assistance towards their development, the Scots Universities could not collect about them even the nucleus of intellectual groups. The abler youths thus went to Oxford or Cambridge with scholarships, where, equipped as they were with education at a Scots University, they had a great advantage over English boys younger in years and fresh from the public schools. After they took their degree a large proportion of Scots students gained fellowships, and then either remained in the Universities pursuing special studies for an indefinite number of years, came to be appointed to professorships in home or colonial universities, or achieved some other distinction. Cosmo Lang, whose father was minister of the Barony Parish in Glasgow and afterwards Principal of the University of Aberdeen, went from Glasgow to Oxford, took orders, and became in succession Rector of St. Margaret's, Oxford, Bishop of Stepney and Archbishop of York. In Cambridge many Scotsmen have made their home and have identified themselves with English letters and science. Sir J. G. Frazer, Fellow of Trinity, author of *The Golden Bough*, and undoubtedly one of the first anthropologists of our time, is the son of a druggist in Glasgow and a graduate of Glasgow University. Mollison, Master of Clare, is an Aberdonian. Robertson Smith, whose name has already come into these reminiscences, was a Scotsman, so was Jebb. Sir Donald Macalister, now Principal of the University of Glasgow, and formerly Senior Tutor of St. John's, Cambridge, was born in Argyllshire. It is not necessary to recite the names of others, some of these find mention elsewhere in these memoirs.

The non-academic group of expatriated Scots men of letters was

[1] George Bernard Shaw, who dislikes everything Scots and who has never been in Scotland, finds his model for standard English in Sir Johnstone Forbes-Robertson, who is an Aberdonian. This is not due to perverse humour but to rare perspicacity.

much larger. Many Scotsmen of an older generation had found their
way to Fleet Street, and were still to be found prospering in it or
hovering on its borders. Among those who went in the late seventies or in the eighties were William Sharp, John M. Robertson and
John Davidson.

William Sharp was a man of extraordinary personality. Indeed,
he has not unjustly been regarded as an instance of double personality;
for he acquired two literary reputations, one under his own name and
the second under a pseudonym. Sharp came very near being a man
of first-rate powers. His industry was astounding, and he was very
modest about it. He wrote literally every day several columns—
from three to five, and occasionally even seven—for daily newspapers,
chiefly for the *Glasgow Herald*. This alone, as anyone who writes for
his daily bread must realise, means colossal labour—means, in short,
from three to seven thousand words every day. Nor was this meagre
fare. It was, on the contrary, good solid matter—not literature of a high
order, but extremely good journalism. In addition he wrote some
novels in his own name and some books—a good one on Rossetti, and
an excellent little book on Browning in Scott's Great Writers Series.
I stayed with him in London while he was writing the last-mentioned.
He wrote it, if I remember correctly, in twenty-eight days, at the
same time maintaining his contributions to the newspapers, and
besides he was good enough to bestow some of his time upon myself.
Whether or not as Fiona Macleod he wrote anything during that
month I do not know, but that was the period during which, as Fiona
Macleod, he was most productive. This pseudonym, although the only
one which came to be well known, was by no means the only one he
assumed. In 1889 or 1890 he published what purported to be the first
number of a small magazine. It was really a pamphlet of forty-eight
pages. This pamphlet was called *The Pagan*. It contained about twenty
articles signed by twenty different names. Each of these names was
unusual. They had each a curious imaginative suggestion. They were
all invented, and Sharp had written all the articles. In short, Sharp
had the strange idea of masquerading in the literary world under
various disguises. The complete success with which he concealed his
identity with Fiona Macleod must have been a secret source of grati-
fication to him. He took elaborate precautions, and none of his friends
knew, although many suspected, the truth. The only important
parallel case in literature of which I am aware is that of Salmasius,
who wrote under more than one *alias*, but in his case this identity
was inadequately concealed, although there is uncertainty about

the authorship of some of his alleged writings.   A more celebrated,
though more doubtful case, is that of Bacon.   If the researches of
Captain Stirling can be trusted, Bacon had a similar propensity for
assuming disguises.

Sharp had elements of great dramatic power, but he did not cultivate them.   The enormous extent of his labours prevented these from
being intensive enough to produce any highly artistic product.   He
was an excellent critic of modern literature as well as of art, although
he was not a scholar and his literary standards were based rather upon
instinct than upon systematically acquired knowledge.   So far as art
was concerned, he knew a good deal about paint, although his criticisms of paintings were rather those of a literary man than of an art
critic in the serious sense.   His personality was very charming.   He
was a most genial and companionable fellow.   I stayed with him
several times in London, and he came once to stay with me at Busby
in Lanarkshire while I lived there.

Of an almost entirely different order of Scotsman is John M.
Robertson, now a Right Honourable, and formerly a junior member
of the Government.   Robertson, while a student at the University of
Edinburgh, was a member of the Symposium Club.   He wrote one of
the monographs published by several of its members under the title
of *The Round Table*.   Robertson went to London soon after he took
his degree, and became assistant to Charles Bradlaugh in the editorship of the *National Reformer*. He was like Sharp in one characteristic,
viz., his amazing industry.   But Robertson's industry took, for many
years at least, a form different from Sharp's—he read voraciously.   I am
afraid that he would not be recognised by the academic scholars as
one of themselves, but he had plunged into theological writings and
into biblical criticism with extraordinary vehemence.   I often thought
about Robertson that he was a Calvinist standing on his head.   He
saw precisely the same things as the most rigid Calvinist, and he
expressed himself about them with the same vigour and dogmatic
assurance as the Calvinist did, but he saw them upside down.   In spite
of the stridency of the school of Bradlaugh in which Robertson served
his literary apprenticeship, he retained the gentleness of disposition
which was natural to him, and he practised the intellectual virtues
with a pure exaltation of mind.   When Bradlaugh died, Robertson
went into Parliament.   In some measure he may be said to have played
there a rôle similar to that played by John Stuart Mill a generation
earlier.   Robertson's points of view were different from those of Mill
on many things.   He had no leanings towards Comte as Mill had in

his earlier, or towards Socialism as Mill had in his later, years. Yet he had the same courage in expressing his convictions, and the same avowed hostility to conventional theology. He was even to a considerable extent a Utilitarian in Mill's sense. Moreover, like Mill, he had the Scots fondness for dialectics. Unlike Mill, he was no admirer of Carlyle. He wrote a diatribe against him, pointing out two quite true things about Carlyle—one that he was a peasant, and the other that he was bilious. Carlyle could hardly have been regarded as responsible for the first, and it may be that he even owed the second as much to heredity as to his choice of food and his manner of living.

I remember William Morris saying to me that, contrary to the usual impression, Mill had been a real success in Parliament. He was always heard with respect, and when he spoke he always contributed to the debate something of moment. Mill was the only member of Parliament of whom I ever heard Morris say anything favourable. I fancy that what he said about Mill might be said of Robertson. He may sometimes have been formal and dull; but I am sure he was always sincere, and perhaps sometimes deep. At all events, his success was sufficiently recognised to secure him a place in the Government and a seat in the Privy Council. I bear him in affectionate remembrance for the kindness he showed to me during frequent visits to him in London in my earlier years.

John Davidson was of a type essentially different from that of the two friends whom I have just sketched. His father was a Presbyterian minister in Greenock; I have forgotten to what denomination he belonged. In his youth Davidson became a teacher in a small private school at Crieff in Perthshire. He had not been there very long when he and a fellow-teacher had a quarrel with their employer, the head of the school. They left in indignation, and for a time Davidson went to live with his parents. He had already written a novel, *The North Wall*. There was in it a certain crude vigour, but it had little merit otherwise. While he was in Greenock he wrote and published, with his own name as publisher, his *Scaramouch in Naxos*. This is a work of real power; but here, as in others of Davidson's writings, there is the lack of restraint and of critical sagacity which characterised Davidson's work and prevented him from reaching the eminence to which the vigour of his genius entitled him. Davidson published his *Scaramouch* in a very small edition, and it was quickly exhausted. He seems not to have preserved a copy for himself, for when he wanted one to enable him to publish another edition a few years afterwards, he wrote asking me to send him one of the two copies I had bought from him, as he had not a copy from which it might be reprinted. I mention this because, although I think that Davidson had a certain consciousness of his powers, he was by no means obsessed by this consciousness. Indeed, lack of absolute confidence in his genius was characteristic of him. When he published his drama *Bruce*, he gave me a copy to give to Morris. Morris put it in his pocket, but he said, "I never read minor poetry." I doubt if he ever opened it. If he did, the Scots flavour of it would probably have repelled him. Davidson threw himself into the maelstrom of London in the late eighties. He could find no sale for his wares under his own name, and he was thus driven to a desperate expedient in order to make a living. He acted as a "devil," and wrote some novels which appeared under the name of a popular novelist. For these products of his pen he received the magnificent fee of thirty pounds per novel. Davidson told me the fact, but he very loyally refrained from mentioning the name of the putative parent of these children of his brain. I introduced him to Sharp and to some others, with the hope of rescuing him from so precarious and little creditable employment. I believe that Sharp was very kind to him, and through his own industry he succeeded in acquiring public recognition. He buried himself somewhere in the outskirts of London, and for years worked hard with his pen. His constant friend of these, as of his earlier years, was John A. Cramb, who had become Professor of History in University College, London, and who was thus another literary exile. One afternoon in the summer of 1900 Cramb and Davidson came and spent an afternoon with me in the Savile Club. I find a note in a book of engagements—"Cramb and Davidson to tea—Confounded Imperialists."

It was the moment of South Africa. Cramb's was the stronger character, and Davidson's mind was bent by it in a Jingo direction, although he had little interest in or taste for politics. Cramb's best-known book, *Germany and England*, was written before but was not published until after the beginning of the Great War. The substance of it had been delivered in a course of lectures. Beyond a very limited circle Cramb's personality had no influence, and his views had not sufficient individuality or sufficient differentiation from the views of other Jingoes of his time to attract any wide attention until after the publication of his book. Yet Cramb was a man of sincere mind and of strong convictions. He had come to the conclusion that either the British Empire must develop its latent military strength and prepare for onslaughts by other powers, or must submit to disintegration, with all the consequences to its diversified peoples that such disintegration must involve. I do not remember if either Cramb or Davidson even mentioned Germany in 1900. Their imperialism was of a positive character. If it did not explicitly mean world-dominion, it meant something so near to this that I felt the danger of their views as strongly as they apparently felt that the adoption of them was necessary to save the empire.[1]

Of a more characteristically academic type than any of the Scotsmen in London I have just mentioned is W. P. Ker, Professor of English Literature in University College, London. Ker was a fellow-student of mine at Glasgow. There he had a brilliant career. Clearly Ker belongs to the "aerial band." Within his special field, Middle English, he has few rivals. The only objection to him which it is possible to offer is his immobility. It is true that much may be understood in the cell of a hermit in London or elsewhere, but little can be seen either of the world or of mankind from its narrow windows. Also of an academic type, and also somewhat, although less, of a recluse, is James Bonar, who had preceded Ker both at Glasgow and Oxford, and who in the eighties was in the Civil Service Commission at London.[2] Bonar is a too exiguous and restrained writer. With the exception of Henry Sidgwick, he has had undoubtedly the best equipment in philosophy of any professed economist of his time.

In the late eighties what came to be known as the "kail-yard school" was just emerging. Barrie was publishing sketches in the *British Weekly* under the encouragement of Robertson Nicoll. Although these early sketches attracted wide attention, they rather offered a promise for the future than any actual realisation. Barrie showed in them imaginative power, but they were crude.[3] It was evident that, to use a phrase the authorship of which I have forgotten, he was committing "the indecency of educating himself in public."

Ian Maclaren (Dr. Watson), who had been one of the successors of Dr. Miller at Free St. Matthew's in Glasgow, was more mature than Barrie, although he never developed the sprightly fancy for which Barrie afterwards distinguished himself. Ian Maclaren's character sketches were free from the romantic extravagance of some of Barrie's and were truer to nature, although his style lacked the graceful turns of phrase which characterised Barrie's later phases. Some years after

---

[1] Cramb's historical novel, *The Rule of Might* (Napoleon at Vienna in 1809), is a brilliant piece of imaginative writing.

[2] In 1906 he became Deputy-Master of the Mint at Ottawa, and on his retiral from that post in 1917 returned to London.

[3] I published one of them in the *Scottish Art Review* in 1889. The sketch afterwards found a place in *The Little Minister*.

this period Dr. Watson came to Toronto and lectured upon Scots humour. I then discovered in him a really subtle vein which I had not previously suspected. He had an audience, with only a sprinkling of Scotsmen, composed for the most part of the rather dull people who at that time in general composed Toronto audiences. In the course of his lecture he told a story to illustrate French humour. Two friends were one day driving along the Champs Élysées, one of these was telling the other a long and tedious tale without point or visible end. The listener endured with patience until, noticing at some distance a man seated on the side of the boulevard stretching out his legs and yawning unreservedly, he remarked: "Hush! We are overheard!" When Watson had finished his story, he waited for a moment to discover if the point of it had been grasped. There was no response whatever. Watson then went on: "When I have ventured to tell this story in Scotland I have not found an explanation of it necessary. I see that I shall have to explain it." This he proceeded to do. It was a good and deserved stroke; besides, it conveyed as no argument could have conveyed the similarity in point of subtlety as well as pungency between French and Scots humour.

In general, the "kail-yard school" was a disappointment. None of its members were sufficiently accomplished men of letters to utilise as they might have done the enormous wealth of material which the Scots life of that time afforded—a time when the self-contained community was passing out of existence, and when the individuality of its members was still observable. The "kail-yard school" was anxious to tell the simple observed truth, but the members of it had too slender experience of the external world to observe their own accurately, and with due sense of the special character of observed facts. In their hands the material was in the main wasted and the moment allowed to pass.

Literary energy in Scotland at this time was mainly directed by force of circumstances into two channels, Encyclopædism and Journalism. The *Encyclopædia Britannica* had been born in Edinburgh, and there it continued to have its periodical reincarnations. The Ninth Edition was edited to begin with by Spencer Baynes at St. Andrews, and was edited later by Robertson Smith at Cambridge. Although its contributors were drawn from a wide field, a large part of the *Britannica* was written by Scotsmen. It did not afford an economical basis for the support of a corps of professional literary men, but it drew many such men together. Less important in the history of letters were the Cyclopædias of Chambers and Blackie;

but the editors of these did succeed in keeping about them a number of writers, some of them being men of letters, not merely of industry, but of distinction. Similar enterprises of a later date were the *Dictionary of the Bible* and the *Cyclopædia of Religion and Ethics* edited by Hastings. It was by no accident that encyclopædism should have taken especial root in Scotland. It came by direct descent through the close association of Hume and Adam Smith with the French encyclopædists of the eighteenth century. Among the Scots encyclopædists of the eighties of the nineteenth century there should, I think, be specially remembered besides Baynes and Robertson Smith, who edited the *Britannica*, Patrick who edited *Chambers's*, Patrick Geddes who contributed copiously to both, writing most of the biological articles, Mortimer Wheeler,[1] who is an Englishman, and James Cappon.[2] The two latter wrote the greater part of *Blackie's Encyclopædia*.

The place occupied by Patrick Geddes in Scots life and letters is unique. He was not a normal academic product, and yet he has done more than anyone else for Scots University life. He did not trouble about taking a degree, but pursued his own course in his own way.[3] He became assistant to Huxley at University College, London, and, whether through his association with Huxley or not I am not prepared to say, became rather a disciple of Lamarck than of Darwin. It was a singular though by no means unprecedented occurrence, that while in the sixties after the publication of the *Origin of Species* Darwin was denounced in nearly every pulpit, and especially in the Scots pulpits, before twenty years had elapsed the theologians had in general become reconciled to Darwin, while the biologists were becoming sceptical about some of his conclusions, and many of them were executing a strategic retreat towards Darwin's predecessors and especially towards Lamarck.[4] In the middle of the eighties I attended a course of lectures by John Cleland, Professor of Anatomy in the University of Glasgow, in which he developed and maintained a vivacious attack upon Huxley and all that was his. Geddes was milder but even more positive in his opposition, especially to the later Darwinians. He used to say that Darwin's hypothesis of evolution

---

[1] Now London representative of the *Yorkshire Observer*.
[2] Later Professor of English Literature, Queen's University, Kingston, Canada.
[3] I do not know that this is the best course for everyone to pursue, although for some it has advantages. It was not an unusual course in the Scots Universities at that time and earlier. I followed it myself, although my doing so was rather the result of accident than of design.
[4] *Cf.* chap. xxiii. *infra*.

through natural selection accounted for our survival by explaining the death of our uncles and aunts, and that it was consequently rather a theory in necrology than in biology. Geddes's own views are fully developed in his articles in the *Britannica* and in *Chambers's*, as well as in his *Evolution of Sex*, which grew out of these articles. Early in his life Geddes had fallen under the influence of Comte, although he was not impressed by the curious cult of Comte which developed in London, Liverpool and Newcastle. What impressed Geddes most was Comte's scheme of the sciences, and his attempt to arrange in an orderly fashion the great departments of human knowledge and to show their relations to one another.

Geddes is not a poet, although he has a fecund imagination, and almost invincible eclecticism. He was in many ways nearer in his points of view to Morris than either he or Morris realised.[1] I have already mentioned Geddes's social experiment.[2] He left his chambers in Princes Street and took a "flat" in one of the tall houses in James Court in the Lawnmarket. There he and Mrs. Geddes did their best to associate with the strange society in which they found themselves. The court was filled with a population belonging to the lower ranks of skilled labour—shoemakers, or rather cobblers, blacksmiths, etc.; there was even a sweep who occupied a portion of an ancient palace that formed part of the court. The houses were substantially built. They presented a front of about nine storeys towards the valley which lies between the old and the new towns, and another of about five storeys towards the court. The people were curiously immobile. On one of my frequent visits to Geddes I met a woman who had lived in the topmost storey of one of these lofty tenements. She was a widow with one daughter. When her daughter came to be old enough to be sent downstairs for the daily requirements of the small household, this duty was imposed upon her, and the mother was relieved of the necessity of going to the street. She therefore remained like a disabled eagle in her eyrie, although she had no physical disability whatever. Only when the house caught fire was she with difficulty persuaded to abandon her perch. She had not left it for thirty years. The people, I believe, looked upon the advent among them of the Geddes family with amusement, not altogether unmingled with suspicion. Some of the younger people more or less enjoyed the receptions the Geddeses gave, and the infinite patience and loyalty to her husband's ideals of Mrs. Geddes must have had a good influence upon them. In course of time the court began to assume a new aspect. Partly by force of

[1] *Cf.* chap. xvi. [2] Chap. xii.

example and partly through judiciously exercised pressure by means of influence with the sanitary authorities, the court was cleansed and even decorated. The Geddeses had furnished their house with good examples of Scots furniture of the eighteenth century. They brought some of the beauty and the joy of life into a spot where unredeemed squalor had reigned for at least half a century. Yet the experiment of bringing culture and science to the wage-slave could not be regarded as an unqualified success. The idealism of Geddes seemed fantastic to people who did not speak his language, and who had no inclination to learn it. These things did not discourage Geddes. He formed the ambitious design of resuscitating the ancient splendour of the old town of Edinburgh, and with James Court as a centre he proceeded to carry out his idea. There is perhaps no vision of urban beauty quite so fine as the view from Princes Street of the long line of roofs from the Castle down the Lawnmarket and the High Street towards Holyrood as it appears in the dusk gradually becoming silhouetted against the eastern sky. In that long line of houses the tradition of Scots wit, letters, politics had been maintained for centuries, and only within recent years had this classic ground become a slum. If the people could not be raised out of the mire, the mire might be removed, the region might be swept and garnished. So Geddes set himself to this sanitary office. He formed the project of acquiring gradually, either in his own name or in the names of others who sympathised with his idea, ownership of a great mass of deteriorating property which lay between the Castle and Holyrood. Lord Rosebery and Dr. Barbour acquired some tenements on the suggestion of Geddes, and he acquired on his own account several more. By these means the White Horse Inn, Bailie Waddell's house, and other old buildings were rescued from the ravages of inferior and uncontrolled tenantry, rendered habitable by their former occupants or others on terms of decency, or converted into students' residences. In many cases the interior architecture in French fireplaces and ceilings of the seventeenth century was revealed in an astonishing state of preservation, in spite of the treatment to which it had been subjected by people who had actually lived in these houses without knowing that they were surrounded by things of beauty.[1] Geddes was really on the same track as Morris. With scarcely inferior practical sagacity, though with greatly inferior material means, Geddes had done something to bring back the surroundings of the period before the factory system had divorced the fine arts from production. Geddes had found one place where beauty still existed, over-

[1] An incidental proof that the determination of character by surroundings is a fallacy.

laid as it was by the débris of two or three generations of people who cared for none of these things, and he had at least shown the way by which the lost threads of artistic tradition could be recovered. Geddes's theory was, however, different from that of Morris. He did not believe in razing society to the ground in order to rebuild a new society in its place. His biological training was of value in revealing to him, through the hard experience of direct social experiment, that, important as surroundings might be, the inherent factor was not less important, and that the degradation of surroundings was an index of the degradation of the people who inhabited them. Geddes's schemes were further developed by the acquisition of Ramsay Lodge, the residence of the Scots poet, Allan Ramsay. This beautiful property occupied a large piece of ground on the slopes of the Mound, immediately to the north of the Castle. Here Geddes built a group of studios and chambers for artists and students. He also acquired a tower, built to accommodate a camera-lucida, in which could be seen the promenade of Princes Street far below as well as the surrounding landscape. I happened to be with Geddes when the idea came into his mind. One day in a moment of leisure we paid our coppers and ascended the tower to look at the passing show as it appeared in this huge periscope. He found that the tower was purchasable for a relatively small sum. With characteristic decision and energy Geddes immediately bought the tower, retained the camera-lucida as its crowning glory, and furnishing the lower rooms with maps and other aids to the study of the region of Edinburgh, named the building appropriately Outlook Tower. It was indeed symbolical of a new outlook upon life from the point of view of an Edinburgh encyclopædist. It is for this reason that I have included under the head of encyclopædism an account of this portion of Geddes's activities.

Not in any way connected with encyclopædism, but associated in my mind with Geddes, was Henry Drummond, the author of a book which in its time made some impression upon the religious public.[1] Drummond was not conspicuous as a scientific man, but he took an interest in science and he "professed" it in the Free Church College at Glasgow. He came to be known as a writer of much charm, especially through his short tracts such as his *Pax Vobiscum*. He attempted to carry out in Scotland the methods of Canon Barnett at Toynbee Hall, and he assisted in establishing both in Glasgow and Edinburgh similar houses where theological and other students might come into touch

[1] *Natural Law in the Spiritual World.*

with working people. Drummond, though not a man of genius, was a man of high character, of great charm of manner, and of intense religious enthusiasm.

I have already hinted at a close similarity between the movement initiated in England by Arnold Toynbee and in Scotland by Patrick Geddes and Drummond in the eighties and the movement of the seventies in Russia known as the movement "To the People," or *V Narod*. So far as I am aware there was no tangible connection between them, but both movements were inspired by the same idea. This idea naturally arose in widely separated regions, under similar circumstances, to the minds of men of similar type. The joys of scientific research and of the society of people of cultivated intelligence seemed arid when all around were people whose outlook upon life was sordid and miserable. It was evident that no change in external conditions could be counted as an advantage from the point of view of life unless it was accompanied or even preceded by altered mental horizon of the spiritually depressed groups.

"What right had I to these highest joys" (original researches into the influence of the polar ice-cap) "when all around me was nothing but misery and a struggle for a mouldy bit of bread?"[1] Prince Kropotkin wrote these words in reference to the attitude of those who went "to the people" in Russia, and the same expressions might have been used by those who went "to the people" in Whitechapel and in Edinburgh. The Russian movement had a wider field and a greater number of participants than either the English or the Scots. In both the "toiling masses" were idealised, and in both there was an undue confidence in the value of middle-class knowledge and conventional manners. The fact is that the "toiling masses" have a knowledge, even a science of their own, and a code of conduct of their own also. The idea that they should be induced or compelled to adopt another kind of knowledge and other manners depends upon the presumption of the superiority of the latter kind of knowledge and manners, and therefore both movements handicapped themselves at the outset. They did not really contribute to break down the inequalities of social classification, but perhaps even in some degree tended to increase these inequalities, or at least to make them more apparent.

The second channel in which through force of circumstances the literary energies of Scots youth were directed in the eighties was journalism. The older tradition of Scots journalism, in which the important name of McCulloch, editor of the *Scotsman*, and by far the

[1] Prince Kropotkin, *Memoirs*, p. 240.

most accomplished economic writer of his time,[1] should not be forgotten, had been carried on by Russell, also editor of the *Scotsman*, an
energetic and famous personality.

In Russell's day the *Scotsman* was a great power, corresponding
in influence to *The Times*. After Russell's time personality in journalism ceased to count for so much simply because his successors were
either deficient in personality or deficient in capacity for journalism.
The reigns of Wallace and Couper at the *Scotsman* and of Jack, Russell
and Wallace at the *Glasgow Herald* carried on the tradition of good
journalism without impressing the public with the editorial office
as a personal force.

Some time in the eighties Thomas Carlaw Martin left the service
of the Post Office and became editor of the *Scottish Leader*. The
Scotsman had become Unionist, and had therefore ceased to satisfy
the Scots Liberals, who determined to issue an organ of their own.
Organs of this kind seldom succeed as commercial enterprises, and
fate was unkind to the *Leader*. Nevertheless it was an ably-conducted
paper. Upon it my friend Robert Aitken, who had been practising
for some years as a lawyer, but whose talents clearly pointed towards
literary criticism, made his début as a journalist. He had special
aptitude for writing short leaders. Those who are interested in this
particular form of editorial writing might well consult the files of the
defunct *Leader*. There may be found the pithiest and most pungent
paragraphs to whose composition Aitken brought a really deep scholarship, unusual felicity in concocting epigrams, and a most delicate
humour. One of the tragedies of journalism is that such things, even
though incomparable in their kind, are almost invariably lost and
their writers forgotten. Mortimer Wheeler, who also wrote for the
Leader, had a somewhat similar aptitude. The range of his accom-
plishments was wider than Aitken's, but he was more whimsical,
and therefore less certain in his literary product.

It cannot be denied that, in spite of a few notable instances of the

---

[1] I mean precisely writer; Ricardo was a much greater thinker. Ricardo's
writings, valuable as they are, were issued as leaflets and only later were collected in such a manner as to compose a more or less systematic treatise. McCulloch's *Literature of Political Economy* shows that he was a greater master of
economic learning than any other economist of his period. The catalogue of his
library which I have before me shows that, like Adam Smith, he was "a beau
in his books." The nickname "MacCrowdy" (for the explanation of the meaning
of this expression see chapter vi. *supra*) applied by Carlyle to McCulloch affords
an example of the merciless type of Scots humour of which I have given other
instances. McCulloch's intelligence and his grasp of economic questions deserved
at least justice at Carlyle's hands. I suspect, although I do not know, that Carlyle had some personal grudge against him dating from Carlyle's Edinburgh days.

contrary, Scots journalism of this period was commonplace. The over-worked reporter and the conventional, if reliable, leader-writer really wrote almost all that was written. The newspapers had occasional contributors—clergymen and others who did not depend upon jour-nalism as a means of livelihood—who assisted in maintaining to some extent in at least three or four of the Scots newspapers a certain standard. The absence of a sufficiently numerous literary group was conspicuously felt. Scotland was continuously producing the men; but dispersal of the Scots, like that of the Jews, gave other countries the benefit of their talents.

In the late eighties a gallant attempt was made to found a Scots journal on the model of the *Saturday Review* or the *Spectator*. This attempt was made by Fitzroy Bell, who in 1889 began the publication of the *Scots Observer*. Unfortunately the plans were not well laid, and from the beginning the weekly journal had a precarious existence. The fundamental difficulty was the slenderness in point of numbers of professional literary men who might be counted upon to supply from week to week articles sufficiently vigorous and appropriate to attract public attention towards a new venture in weekly journalism. The desirable number of reliable contributors in such a case is in-definite, but probably five-and-twenty may be regarded as an irre-ducible minimum. No such number was at that time available in Scotland, although so many might have been recruited with pains and time by drawing upon Scots men of letters in London and else-where. I have already noticed the paucity of personalities among the Scots journalists in the eighties, and the fact that the writing of news-papers was confided chiefly to the overworked and, I may add, almost invariably inadequately equipped reporter. An experienced Scots man of letters, adequately equipped for the editorial chair of a weekly critical journal by education, training and sociable relations with his fellows, might have been found in London or elsewhere. Only such an editor could possibly have established a journal to compete with the *Spectator*, then in the most competent hands of Richard Holt Hutton. If the new journal did not make at least a good second to the *Spectator*, with the added advantage of a decisively Scots flavour, there seemed to be no reason for attempting its establishment. Somehow or other these indispensable conditions of success did not appear to occur to the initiator of the enterprise. The circular announcing the advent of the *Scots Observer* shows this clearly. The list of those whose con-tributions were expected to fill the pages weekly and to attract public attention was composed largely of members of the Scots nobility.

The Duke of Argyll, Lord Rosebery, and other eminent personages whose names were on this list, had no doubt flirted with literature, but they had not as yet acquired reputations as writers to be trusted for the production of certain columns of appropriate matter week by week. The captaincy of this distinguished crew was entrusted to an experienced reporter drawn from the staff of the *Scotsman*. Under these inauspicious circumstances the *Scots Observer* was launched, admirably printed by the great house of Constable. Certainly it was a Scots production, but there was no evidence in it either of Scots sagacity or of the vigour of Scots letters. Three weeks had scarcely run their course before the inevitable happened. The ink-wells of the eminent personages ran dry, the minds of the eminent personages were diverted towards other more insistent engagements, or mere mental exhaustion supervened. The editor knew no others to whom to appeal for contributions, and the public had scarcely become aware that a new weekly journal had entered the field. In this distressing crisis I was invited by my friend Walter B. Blaikie of Constable's, best of printers, and one of the best and most loyal of men, to assist in procuring immediate relief. I did so to the best of my ability, and succeeded in collecting together hastily a small group of writers to tide over the dead point until adequate measures could be taken to set the journalistic machinery in motion afresh. Meanwhile it had come to be evident that a personality in the editor's chair was really an indispensable condition. A personality was discovered. He was William Ernest Henley. Henley was an Englishman, but he had had some relations with Edinburgh. He had undergone a serious operation in the Royal Infirmary, and had been obliged to remain prone there for a year and a half. During this period Robert Louis Stevenson had made his acquaintance and had become interested in his vivacious conversation and aggressive opinions on literature and art. Henley had a much wider acquaintance with English and French letters than Stevenson ever possessed. His imaginative powers did not approach those of Stevenson, but he greatly excelled him in critical capacity, although his literary and artistic judgments were often whimsical, and these judgments invariably found expression in more or less merciless language. Henley wrote in 1886 the Catalogue of the French and Dutch Collection of Pictures in the Edinburgh Exhibition of that year, and in that way had been brought into relation with Edinburgh for the second time. For some time before his appointment to the *Scots Observer* Henley had been editing the *Magazine of Art* and contributing to the *Saturday Review*.

As editor of a Scots weekly journal Henley was an angular peg in a round hole. He was an Englishman *pur sang*, to whom everything Scots was unknown or abhorrent, excepting the Scots romanticism of the early days of the nineteenth century. Personality is indispensable in an editor of the first order, but the personality must be that of an editor. An editor who injects his personality into everything which appears in his paper by the simple process of rewriting all the articles by whomsoever they are contributed must soon find that it is not necessary to re-write. He must write every article himself. Contributors will tolerate the rejection of articles, they will not tolerate mutilation of them with their names attached to the mutilated remnants. If an editor finds it necessary to re-write the work of his contributors, he has simply been unsuccessful in his choice of these. His function lies in initiation of topics and in dexterous choice of the pens to deal with them. If he does otherwise, he may make a brilliant splash, but he cannot establish a newspaper. Essentially a newspaper is a co-operative enterprise, and it will be successful only in so far as this is realised by its guiding hand.

Henley had great abilities and enormous industry in spite of his physical infirmity. Both of his feet had been amputated. His temperament rendered co-operation with anyone very difficult, although those who tried to work with him made heavy allowances. Either through excess of conscientiousness—the charitable view—or through perversity of humour, Henley seemed to reserve the most savage of his attacks for those who had in some way rendered him service. Thus he pounced upon Robert Louis Stevenson with a vehemence which Stevenson did not deserve at his hands. In the same manner he pounced upon my friend John M. Robertson. Henley had published his first book of verses, but it had not attracted wide attention and his name was barely known. Robertson reviewed the little volume for me while I was editing the *Scottish Art Review*. His article was more than appreciative, it hailed Henley as a newly arisen poet. Henley asked me who the author of this laudatory review was, and I told him all about Robertson, of whom previously he had not heard. A few months later Henley became editor of the *Scots Observer*. One of the books sent to him for review was Robertson's *Essays Towards a Critical Method*.[1] Henley reviewed it. To say that the review was unfavourable would not describe it. If Robertson had been Henley's worst enemy he could not have stung him more viciously. Robertson regarded the treatment of his book as unjust, and protested in a letter which Henley

[1] London, 1889.

published. It should, of course, be recognised that anything that savoured of science or of what Henley regarded as academism was repugnant to him, and therefore he was prejudiced against Robertson's whole thesis. Nevertheless, a less vituperative and savage review of a genuinely able book might well have been written.

I find it difficult to forgive Henley for his attacks upon others of my friends. He invented the word "bleat" to stigmatise the writings of Morris, Crane, and others upon art and social progress. Henley's attitude towards all such writings was one of extreme hostility. This hostility arose quite naturally from Henley's reactionary political views; but the virulence with which he expressed it deprived his arguments, if such they may be called, of any value. The gentle spirit of Walter Crane was on one occasion stung into a reply, but I doubt if it was worth while. Both Henley's attack and Crane's defence are alike forgotten.

Henley was undoubtedly a true poet. Many of his early verses are very fine, and some of his later poems must be placed high among modern English verse. For example, his poem *Speed*, from which I have drawn a few lines to serve as a motto for the chapter in which I treat of the industrial development of the eighties, to my mind interprets the mood of that period more intensively and in more appropriate versification than any other poem of that time. Henley's prose had the merit of individuality, but it consisted of series of explosive phrases and of thrusts as with a bayonet, as if the subject were an enemy to be exterminated. During his editorship of the *Scots Observer* Henley published many articles of real merit, although there was always to be found an acrid undertone. Liberalism in any sense was assailed with fury, and at a time when the prevailing opinion in Scotland was in favour of Home Rule for Ireland this portion of Liberal policy was denounced with especial fervour. When the Parnell Commission reported on *The Times* charges, Henley published anonymously the verses, afterwards acknowledged by Kipling, entitled *Cleared*, and he also published those anonymous imitations of Day's *Sandford and Merton* in which Mr. Gladstone is satirised as "Mr. Barlow." These things were clever enough, but they were abusive and in the main unjust.

After all, the most notable and interesting thing about Henley is that Rodin did a bust of him. Rodin had a good model in Henley's leonine aspect, although the bust was modelled at a period in Henley's life when he had not developed this aspect to the full.

I feel constrained to place here, as a Scots journalist, James Keir

Hardie, because although he was known rather as a member of Parliament and a Socialist, his real function was journalism. When I first met him, about, I think, 1879, he was an alert, good-looking young man —reddish hair, ruddy complexion, honest but ecstatic eyes, average stature, very fastidious about his dress. Jägerism did not become popular until after this date, but Hardie had independently adopted the light brown finely woven materials which the Jägerites affected later. Hardie looked like an artist, and indeed in general his point of view was that of an artist. He was not the least of a politician, and he was simply thrown away in Parliament. He could not be disciplined into a party man, and no party could have retained him. In every respect, excepting in practical politics, he was superior to every one of the Labour members and to many other members of Parliament, yet in Parliament he was not a success. He did not and could not appear to advantage in a rôle for which he was ill-adapted by nature. Although his early education had been somewhat neglected, Hardie had the talent for letters which seems to be indigenous in Ayrshire. He was a creature of impulse. His impulses were always genuine, no matter how mistaken might be the judgments associated with them. The trade-union secretary and Labour member of his time fell very readily into the ways of living and the modes of thinking of the commercial and industrial stratum of the lower middle class with which they came into contact and unconsciously imitated. Hardie was quite different. He never fell into the habits of his fellows, but identified himself rather with the intellectual and artistic proletariat than with any faction of the middle class. This was no pose, but was the simple outcome of his nature. He was the only really cultivated man in the ranks of any of the Labour parties. I had not seen him for several years when one day, not very long before his death, he walked into my library in Toronto. It was very pleasant to hear again his broad Lowland accent and to talk about our mutual friends of thirty years before.

Among Scots men of letters of this period I feel confident that when the lesser figures are forgotten one name will stand out conspicuously as the name of a man of very fine genius and of very noble character. That is the name of Cunninghame Graham. Cunninghame Graham fell heir at an early age to an embarrassed property from which he derived a slender income. When he was about twenty years of age he went to South America, and there on the pampas he learned to become a superb horseman and acquired the enormous muscular strength which enabled him to perform such feats as are only to be accomplished by men of similar training. He learned also to speak Spanish, and became infected with an enthusiasm for Spain and Spanish literature which is shared to the same extent by no other Englishman save Fitzmaurice Kelly. Graham's love of adventure and his immunity from fear led him to disguise himself as an Arab and to penetrate Morocco, an enterprise which his horsemanship enabled him to perform with ease. The result of this adventure is *El Mogreb*, the only book about Morocco which is worthy of any serious attention. In his prime, as I knew him, Graham's slender form, his grace of movement, his latent strength of body and character, together with his refinement, suggested a figure such as Velasquez would have painted and called "Portrait of a Man," or such a personality as would have been drawn with sure hand by Cervantes. Examples of subtle humour overlying deep intention abound in all of his writings. No one of his generation could be more playfully serious or could better disguise a deep saying in a jest. Some years ago I read in the *Spectator* an exquisitely humorous review of a book on Spanish literature. The review began with an account of the book, taking it at its face value slightly exaggerated. This account is abruptly arrested by the entrance of a visitor. "What is that you are reading? I know. It is ——. Give it to me." The book is handed over, and is immediately thrown to the other end of the room by the visitor. Then follows what is really a masterpiece of erudite criticism put into the mouth of the visitor in which the shortcomings of the author are disclosed, interrupted by occasional mock appeals for mercy on the part of the reviewer. I thought I recognised in the visitor the person of Fitzmaurice Kelly. Within a few days I met Kelly at the Savile, and he acknowledged that in the narrative there was a foundation in fact, though Graham had really written the review.

While Graham was engaged in agitating for an eight hours' day I had a letter from him from Algiers written in his characteristically humorous vein. He said that he had gone to Algiers with the intention of promoting an eight-hour movement in that region of wage slavery. He found that an Arab agitator who proposed to increase the normal working hours from two and a half to three had been promptly assassinated. Propaganda for an eight-hour day was, therefore, out of the question. Graham also mentioned a curious meeting he had had with a Spanish gentleman in a café. Having been informed that Graham was a member of Parliament, and therefore a person of influence, this gentleman asked him to communicate with the British Embassy at Madrid and endeavour through it to induce the Spanish authorities to allow him to return to his native country, as he was suffering from nostalgia.   On Graham's asking what was the reason for his involuntary exile, he explained that he had had a little difficulty with a gentleman in Seville, but he did not explain, what Graham on further inquiry discovered to be the case, that the little difficulty had been in a measure settled by the gentleman now in exile having cut the other gentleman's throat. As a writer of short stories I do not think that Graham is excelled by anyone in English, or by any other excepting by Balzac, De Maupassant and Anatole France in French, and Leo Tolstoy in Russian.

Among my Scots literary friends of these days I should count William Renton, who in general lived at Ambleside, and made and polished there the small volumes of verse and prose he produced from time to time.   His features at this period bore an almost startling resemblance to those of a bust of Julius Cæsar in the British Museum. He was known among his friends as Jesus Renton, because on the back of an early book of his on *Jesus* the binder had omitted to leave a space between the title and the name of the author.   Renton had much not altogether inexact learning, and he had developed a quasi-systematic scheme for indicating graphically the relations of literary epochs to one another which would have given Henley convulsions had it come under his notice.   Renton elaborated this ingenious device one evening at Belyse Baildon's before Geddes and a number of others. I poked fun at the thing until I thought I detected a look of real pain in Renton's eye, and then stopped.   Renton's verse, though giving evidences of want of spontaneity and of over-elaboration, has un-doubtedly fine poetical quality.

I have already mentioned in another connection Miss Mary Hill Burton. Although so far as I am aware Miss Burton wrote nothing of importance, she was a cultivated woman. She assisted, perhaps in a minor way, her brother while he was writing his monumental history of Scotland. One of my most cherished Edinburgh friends was Miss Jane Hume Clapperton, authoress of *Scientific Meliorism*.   We used often to meet in the summer at the country house of the Manns on Loch Lomond. Miss Clapperton had a remarkable mind. I do not know that she had original or inventive genius, but she had the genius of orderly arrangement. She had not been brought up in the school of Comte, and yet the cast of her mind was Comtist. She was strongly impressed with the ideas of the unity of knowledge, and with the necessity of applying science to human life in such a way as to make for progress. The question of sex she grappled with delicacy as well

I—P

as boldness. Free as she was from aggressiveness, she had less influence upon the men and women of her time than she might have had, but during the nineteenth century not more than two women—George Eliot and Sonya Kovalevsky—gave evidence of more intellectual power, and neither of these had so sane and wholesome an outlook upon life as Jane Hume Clapperton.

What may justly be regarded as the most important demonstration of Scots genius during the last twenty years of the nineteenth century was not in the field of literature, but in the field of art. It must be allowed that almost none of the names I have mentioned as those of men writing especially within that epoch could be ranked alongside of their greater precursors among their fellow-countrymen or alongside some at least of their English contemporaries. It is different with regard to the artists of that period. Scotland of earlier times had produced at intervals individual painters of real greatness—Jameson (the Scots Vandyck), Raeburn, who might fairly be called the Scots Rembrandt, and Wilkie were each in his own way admirable artists; but at no time had there been any important group of painters, still less any such group as might fairly be regarded as a school. In the eighties conditions were quite otherwise; in Whistler's phrase, "Art was upon the town." In Edinburgh there were several notable painters, at the head of whom may be placed Sir George Reid, President of the Royal Scottish Academy—a portrait painter of great penetration. In Glasgow there was a large and growing group of painters who at the beginning of the period may be said to have worked together, and together to have attacked their problems in paint, solving them each in his own way, yet with an aim sufficiently common to challenge attention to the group collectively. This group came to be known as the Glasgow School, although they objected to the name on the ground that it implied a similarity of method and intention among the different members of the group which had no foundation in fact.

To appreciate adequately the importance of the service rendered by the Glasgow School of painters it is necessary to realise the situation in respect to art in Scotland immediately before their time. The early seventies may be held to represent low-water mark alike in public appreciation and artistic production. There was in Edinburgh the School of Art, managed by the Royal Scottish Academy, and there was in Glasgow the Haldane Academy or School of Art. In both of these institutions students were taught the elements of drawing, and those who desired to go beyond the elements were encouraged to do so; but in neither of these schools was there the atmosphere in which artistic effort might thrive. The consequence was that those who thought they had that within them by which they might become artists went elsewhere for their atmosphere—to London, to Paris, or to Antwerp. To one or other of these centres of artistic production they went to study, and many of them remained to paint; few returned to their native places. There was a good gallery in Edinburgh, and there was an important gallery in Glasgow, although the value of the latter was not then generally recognised. There were in the early seventies no collectors, or none who were either competent critics or were willing to permit themselves to be guided by such persons. There were, nevertheless, annual exhibitions, and a certain production of paintings and of sculpture; but only an easy-going eclecticism could recognise in these any of the qualities of works of art. They were conventional, and to those who were familiar with the works of the great artists of the past quite uninteresting. A change might have come about from many causes: gradually the growth of art elsewhere might have affected Scotland partly by its influence upon Scots artists abroad and at home, and partly by infiltration through the public mind of a knowledge of art. In my opinion, the change actually came about through the coincidence of increase in wealth and of the skilful exploitation of that increase on the part of two or three persons whose natural aptitudes and opportunities enabled them to seize the psychological moment. I have already noticed the magnitude of the industrial development of Scotland in the early seventies—the rapidity of the growth of the iron and coal trades, as well as of the industries ancillary to these. Wages, profits and rents all increased rapidly. Fortunes relatively great in respect to the past began to be made.

One Sunday in, I think, 1875 I went to the opening after re-decoration of a church in one of the suburbs of Glasgow. I had heard a rumour of the startling character of the decoration, and I was anxious to see what it was like. Undoubtedly the decoration was startling enough. Great masses of positive colour—red and blue, with figures of dense black—the motive was Egyptian and the design might have found a fitting place in a great hall of one of the Pharaohs. In an ecclesiastical building it was inappropriate; in any building in Western Europe the effect would have been bizarre; the design was out of scale and wanting in the repose indispensable in church architecture and adornment. Nevertheless, the decoration was bold and in its way original. I felt at once here at least is the work of a designer of brains and courage. I made inquiry about the artist, and found that his name was Daniel Cottier, a native of Dumbarton on the Clyde, and then designer or foreman, or both, in a firm of painters and decorators in Glasgow. Shortly after this occurrence I learned that Cottier had gone to London, where he had established himself in business as a designer of stained glass and as a dealer in pictures and antiquities. I think it was in 1877 or 1878 that Cottier took another step. He had become acquainted with a remarkable man of a character somewhat similar to his own, but lacking in skill of artistic handicraft and in pecuniary shrewdness, both qualities possessed in a high degree by Cottier. Cottier's friend was William Craibe Angus. Angus had been a shoemaker in Aberdeen, and had acquired a knowledge of literature and art by the process of self-education and by association with men of letters and artists. Cottier assisted in establishing Angus in the business of an art-dealer in Glasgow, enabled him to take not merely a large shop but also a large house, both of which were filled with more or less important works of the French and Dutch Schools. Cottier continued to buy in Paris and the Hague, and to send on to Glasgow a stream of the products of Corot, Millet, Rousseau, Diaz, Daubigny, the Marises, Mauve, Israels and others. At that time the prices of works of art were very moderate when compared with the prices of later years, but the existence of a society in which there were at least some men of substantial fortune was an indispensable condition of the sale of any of them. There were such men. Notable among them were R. T. Hamilton Bruce of Edinburgh and Forbes White of Dundee. Bruce was a landed proprietor who had made a fortune in milling, and White, who was not a proprietor, did the same thing. Other collectors of note of that and of the immediately succeeding time were Wm. Connal, Jnr., and Matthew Arthur,[1] both of Glasgow. I do not know that any of these collectors had any deep knowledge of art, but they had a liking for pictures and the means to obtain them. Undoubtedly they suffered themselves to be guided by men like Cottier and Angus, and indeed some of them principally by these very men. The consequence of these conditions was that within ten years—that is, between 1876 and 1886—a really large and representative collection of the works of the French and Dutch painters and their allies had found its way into private hands in Scotland, although as yet such works were not to be seen in the public galleries. This new condition became manifest when, under the auspices of Hamilton Bruce, a Loan Collection of these recent acquisitions was made and exhibited at the International Exhibition held at Edinburgh in 1886. Henley wrote the text of a catalogue of many of the leading pictures, admirably illustrated by

[1] Later Sir Matthew Arthur.

William Hole with etchings. This was undoubtedly an important event in the history of art in Scotland. The Loan Collection brought home to those who were hovering on the edge of artistic things that the conventional art of the immediately preceding time had ceased to be interesting, and whether or not the new methods were destined to be permanent, fashion in art had begun to change. The painters and their journalistic allies of the older dispensation felt their authority and even their living slipping away from them. They denounced what they called indiscriminately "impressionism," and this useful word was given a very wide extension. There were some amusing caricatures and some clever practical jokes. A shoemaker in an Ayrshire village, who had acquired enough dexterity with his brush and palette to paint landscapes sufficiently faithful to satisfy the simple requirements of his neighbours, had been in the habit of placing his paintings in the window of his little shop. These works were marked at such prices as secured a ready sale among his humble clients—five shillings, ten shillings, and the like. Beside these inexpensive luxuries there appeared one day a formless daub of primary colours obviously dashed on the canvas in a few moments. This was labelled "Impressionist Landscape, £300."

Shortly before the Edinburgh Exhibition of 1886, in fact in 1882, Robinson, H.M. Surveyor of Pictures, had, as I have mentioned in a previous chapter, reported upon the McLellan Collection in the Glasgow Corporation Galleries, and had drawn attention to its great importance. The ready accessibility of this collection to students of art in Glasgow undoubtedly enabled these students to profit. They became familiar with the works of the Dutch painters, as well as with those of the Italian and other schools. There was thus in preparation, at least from 1883 or 1884, the soil upon which a new art was destined to thrive. When the Edinburgh Loan Collection came in 1886 there was already a certain public by whom it might be appreciated. Moreover, the period of economical depression, which had followed that of the inflation of the early seventies, was in 1886 almost at an end. A rising breeze of optimism stirred the air. People were once again making money and spending it in luxuries. Nevertheless, public appreciation was slow in developing. The critics who were articulate enough to make themselves heard and lucid enough to make themselves understood had endorsed certain new painters, most of these being French and Dutch, and purchasers rushed to buy their works. Prices advanced rapidly under the pressure of this demand. It was not until this phase of the economic process had advanced that any reaction began to make its appearance in the direction of painters of English and Scots origin who had been influenced by foreign schools.

Meanwhile native painters touched by the new spirit found themselves in a quandary. They were not sought by conventional picture buyers who adhered to conventional artists, and they were not sought by collectors of the new art, because these had not yet made up their minds to hang domestic works of whose merits they were not certain alongside those paintings of the foreign schools which they had come to regard as masterpieces.

The new painters were young and energetic. If the connoisseurs would not come to them, they could appeal to the public; they could even challenge the public, and if needs must they could throw their glove in the face of the public. Under similar circumstances this very thing had been done before.

In, I think, 1888 the New English Art Club held its first exhibition. It was more than personal—it was egotistical. Yet this demonstrative egotism was a necessary part of the game. If the works of Corot and his brethren of the Barbizon School had an increasing public, this occurred not merely because of the merits of these works, great though these might be, but also because the Barbizon School had an expert group of *claqueurs* who apprised the public of these merits and keyed the public up to the pitch of acknowledging them. Even " Hernani " had not been launched without a *claque*. The New English Art Club invented what might be called the auto-*claque*. They endorsed one another with vigorous applause. They painted portraits of each other and engaged in very audible mutual admiration. These resources, undignified as they were, appeared to be successful in attracting public attention, and eventually in securing the favourable notice of the professional critics. The New English Art Club thus for a while became the mode, and it continued to occupy a prominent place in the public eye until it was obscured by other more recent groups, and came to be remembered only as an old-fashioned affair whose existence had served a purpose and had ceased to be of moment.

While the New English Art Club was struggling into notoriety, people who were interested in painting became aware that a wholly new set of names was beginning to make its appearance in the annual exhibitions of the Glasgow Institute of the Fine Arts. These exhibitions had been conducted for some years in an eclectic spirit. The Institute was predominantly a lay body. The painters who were members of it were not as such entitled to have their pictures hung upon the line or hung anywhere. Its walls were open to all comers, provided their works, in the opinion of the hanging committee, were fit to be hung. These new names were those of natives or residents of Glasgow, some of whom had gone to the studios of Paris and Antwerp, and had had the advantage of the criticism of the painters in these centres. Some of them had been in Spain, but I do not think that any of them had had experience of London. Several had not been abroad. It became slowly evident towards the end of the eighties that these names belonged to a group of men whose paintings placed them in a class by themselves. They did not paint all after the same manner, but there was sufficient similarity in intention to justify their being regarded as a group. This group did not begin by explaining itself or by employing any of the minor arts employed successfully at this time by the New English Art Club, it began quite unostentatiously to send its pictures to the galleries for exhibition. One day, however, one of its members threw down a challenge. This member was E. A. Hornel, and his challenge was "The Galloway Landscape." It was really a manifesto of the newly arisen school. Hornel had been at Antwerp, but there was no suggestion in the picture of the Antwerp group of that day. It was individual and undeniably vigorous. It was a landscape with a cow in the foreground, full of light and of masses of vivid colour. Had the joke been then in vogue, it might have been described by the critic as "Picture of a cow, heavily camouflaged." The critics pounced upon it, and abused it. According to them it was not only without merit, it was mischievous. The committee, with great good sense, had hung it on the line, so that the challenge could not pass without notice. The landscape was offered at a very moderate price—seventy pounds if I remember correctly—yet it was not sold, nor did it pass from the painter's hands until long after its first exhibition. Yet as a manifesto it served its purpose.

It was evident from that time henceforward that a new force of indisputable energy and of great talent had emerged in the field of art. The important names in these early days of the Glasgow School were James Guthrie,[1] John Lavery,[2] Macaulay Stevenson, Edward Walton, James Paterson, E. A. Hornel, George Henry, T. Corsan Morton and Alexander Roche, painters, and J. Pittendreigh MacGillivray, sculptor. Other names came later, but these were the first. Guthrie and Lavery developed into really great portrait painters, although it was "The Highland Funeral" that brought the former first into notice. Walton became also a subtle and sympathetic portrait

[1] Now Sir James Guthrie, President of the Royal Scottish Academy.
[2] Now Sir John Lavery.

painter. Morton early developed a talent for decorative landscape, and Roche, who was a very fine draughtsman, came to be noted for figure pieces of singular grace and charm. Henry's portraits of women became famous. Paterson devoted himself to landscapes possessing a tame beauty. He was averse from any riot of colour, and he cultivated chiefly the rendering of light in simple compositions. The landscapist of most considerable powers so far as the group was concerned was Macaulay Stevenson. In such a group there is always a spiritual elder brother who counsels and sometimes commands, whose criticism is valued more than any other, and who is always called in when a picture reaches a dead point and refuses to get itself advanced. Such a rôle was played by Stevenson. He could not write, but he could talk. Indeed, he was the most articulate painter I have ever known. He could explain, if sometimes in a weird and mystical manner, yet always at least nearly lucidly and sometimes brilliantly. While Stevenson had an original and fertile mind, his powers of production were limited by the fastidiousness with which he criticised his own work.

Some of those mentioned, including Macaulay Stevenson, knew the newer schools of French painting well—knew the painters who were struggling into notice in the seventies and eighties—Degas, Manet, Monet, Sisley and Renoir, for instance, as well as the Barbizon group of an earlier period. The Barbizon painters had achieved their mark, but the others had not. Only those of them who, like Manet, had means to fall back upon contrived to live otherwise than in a state of periodical vagabondage, in spite of the industry of many of them. I recall that when George Moore's *Confessions of a Young Man* was published, the Glasgow artists read it with great interest because it was infected with the new movement, and because it gave expression more or less articulately to the character of that movement. Visits to Paris, and to some extended residence there, gave vital touch between the Scotsmen and the Parisians. I do not think that it would be fair to say that there was even unconscious imitation on the part of the Scotsmen. Certainly there were in Glasgow no individual painters who could be fairly regarded as reflecting individual painters in Paris. At the same time, the contemporaneousness of the Paris and the Glasgow movements, although naturally enough Paris slightly preceded Glasgow, and the contact between them, inevitably contributed towards inspiring them with common aims although it did not give, and could not give, a common character. The temperaments and the available artistic materials differed. In general, the Parisians were original and audacious as well as thorough in threshing out their artistic problems; they had continuous advantage from the criticism of one another, and from the criticism of the older groups. These latter conditions constituted their atmosphere. The Scotsmen had slender advantages in respect to criticism and encouragement, and they were thrown upon their own resources. This induced reliance upon themselves, as well as a community of feeling by means of which they as a rule avoided the petty quarrels usual in such groups. It is true that they compromised more with convention than did the Parisians—but the convention of Paris is one thing and that of a centre of Scots Presbyterianism quite another.

A group of artists, however great their vigour may be, cannot continue to exist indefinitely without external encouragement. I have mentioned the existence of a school in which drawing and painting were taught, but where the absence of an atmosphere, such as was to be found in Paris, for example, was conspicuous. To some extent this absence was in the nature of things, but to some extent it might be qualified. In the early days of the artistic life of the artists whose names I have just mentioned, the Art School was conducted by a worthy drawing-master who was quite unacquainted with contemporary movements in art and quite uninterested in them. The equipment of the school was inadequate, even from the point of view of that day. The admirable gallery which I have mentioned was there to be seen, but it was little used in the work of the school. A great change came in 1888 with the appointment of a young and vigorous headmaster, who had been trained at South Kensington. I cannot say that at that time South Kensington stood very high in the estimation of the artists, especially those of the younger groups. But all who passed through South Kensington were not equally affected by the formalism which was its reputed characteristic. At all events, when Francis Newbery came to take charge of the Glasgow School of Art, he had competent professional knowledge and abundant enthusiasm for the encouragement of individual genius. He became at once an ardent ally of the young group of painters. He brought important lecturers on art from Paris and elsewhere, and he speedily transformed the relations between education in the elements of art and the superior practice of it. Under him the school became a vivifying influence, and from it there soon began to proceed a stream of painters and draughtsmen—both men and women.

In 1888 the small group which, in spite of their protests, had come to be known as the Glasgow School began to think that they should devise some means of explaining themselves to the public. I have already indicated that the usual intermediary between the worker and the public, viz. the journalist, was not a very competent intermediary. He was rarely, if ever, trained for such a purpose. The fact was then, as it still is, that the journalist as a rule is equally ignorant of science and of art. The workers in both fields are too much occupied in production and in expressing themselves through the media appropriate to these fields respectively to trouble themselves about interpretation to the non-professional public. Thus interpreters are necessary, and unfortunately they have very infrequently been forthcoming. Those who essayed the rôle of interpreters were still more infrequently accepted either by the artists or by the scientific people on the one hand, or by the non-professional public on the other. If they were accepted by one of these groups the other was almost certain to reject them. The Glasgow painters decided to interpret themselves by means of a monthly magazine. This idea took form in the publication of the *Scottish Art Review*.

I have already suggested the difficulties encountered by the founders of the *Scots Observer* and the initial mistakes which were made in their efforts to found it. Those who promoted the *Scottish Art Review* did not attempt to organise a staff of Scots dukes and earls, but they did attempt to publish a journal by means of a staff no less inadequately equipped for such a purpose. The dukes knew nothing about the business of writing and neither did the painters. The results were the same in both cases. After about three issues of the *Review* had made their appearance, the ink-wells of the amateur contributors ran dry, as they did about the same time in the other case, and for precisely the same reasons. The promoters of the *Review* then invited me to take charge of it. Had I been consulted before the *Review* was published, I should probably have counselled abstention, or at least delay. The reasons which militated against the probability of success in the publication of a literary journal in Scotland weighed even more against a journal of art. There were plenty of Scotsmen to write either journal, but they were not in Scotland. The primary motive of the publication of a monthly journal to demonstrate the artistic views of a new and small group was too sectarian to engage the attention of the wide public. The only condition upon which such a journal could be published was a condition in which a heavy subsidy could be counted upon until the purpose for which it was published had been served. However, the *Scottish Art Review* had been floated, and I took charge of it. I found it necessary at once to give it a tone more eclectic than had been intended, and naturally the interest in it of those who had originally promoted it began to fade. The artists were too much occupied with their own proper work to spend the time necessary to learn how to write, and in consequence, however interesting their essays might be to one another, they did not succeed in making themselves intelligible to the general public. It was thus necessary to draw into the field other contributors who might not know so much about the art of painting as the painters, but who knew a great deal more about the art of writing. The editing of such a review, under these circumstances, was a difficult task. I think I contrived to print in it some good material, and perhaps even to infuse into journalism of this kind a fresh note. The publication of the *Review* cost a good deal of money. It was not well managed on its business side, and in about a year the promoters became tired. I succeeded in inducing a firm of English publishers to finance it, and to continue its publication in Scotland under the new name which they insisted upon, of the *Art Review*. But this experiment did not succeed; and after the issue of seven more numbers it expired. I cannot leave the *Scottish Art Review* without endeavouring to pay a tribute to the man to whom such *succès d'estime* as it had was mainly due. This was Walter B. Blaikie, of Constable's. His skill made it a model of printing, alike in letterpress and illustrations, and his loyalty made the conduct of it an unfailing pleasure in spite of the conditions which rendered commercial success impossible.

It is clear that a systematic account of painting in Scotland has formed no part of my intention, therefore apology is not necessary for omission of names which some might regard as important. I have considered only those artists who came within the field of my personal acquaintance. Some of these I have, however, not yet noticed. Among the Edinburgh artists, in addition to Sir George Reid, were James Cadenhead, W. G. Burn-Murdoch, John Duncan, Hugh Cameron the water-colour painter, an interesting and attractive man, and D. W. Mackay, an oil painter of somewhat archaic manner and method, yet very sympathetic towards the younger men.

I think it was in 1892 that the art critic of the *Scotsman* remarked upon Mackay's contribution to the Royal Scottish Academy Exhibition of that year, that he was painting more thinly than was his custom. A few days after this criticism appeared, Mackay was at Lundin Mills in Fifeshire, where I was also staying. Lundin Mills was a favourite spot for painters. Cameron lived there, and at that time Newbery and others used to spend the summer in the village. The folk round about knew the painters well, and took a great interest in them and their work. Mackay was sitting on the roadside at his easel painting a landscape, *plein air*, when a farmer drove up. The farmer sat on the front of his cart and, as he passed Mackay, called out to him, "Dinna spare the pent, Mr. Mackay. They tell me you're sparin' the pent. Dinna spare the pent."

The principle underlying the salutation of the farmer may well be applied in general to Scots painting and other arts.

CHAPTER XVIII

LONDON CIRCLES IN THE EIGHTIES

Huge murmur from the throat of Babylon!
Illimitable leagues of piles confused,
Dome, tower, and steeple, stately palaces,
Islanded in a welter of dim street;
Mean habitations, warrens of dull life,
Tortuous, swarming; sullied, pale, cramped life,
With, in the midst, a large imperial River,
Turbid and troubled, the town's artery,
Spanned by tumultuous bridges; o'er them clang
Steam-dragon, chariot, horse and laden wain,
With hurrying people of the human hive.

The Hon. RODEN NOEL, London.

WHATEVER the reason, crowds appear to have for a time a stimulative effect upon the individuals composing them, and later a depressive effect. This may or may not be an unimpugnable dogma, but I believe it has the support of the biologists who devote themselves to the study of those creatures who, like man, live in groups. My friends who occupy themselves with such researches tell me that when they transfer one of the minute organisms belonging to some species in the category of social creatures from a small group to a larger one, the organism appears to be stimulated somewhat in proportion to the magnitude of the group and then to be subject to depression varying in some degree with the density of the crowd. Whether or not these observations are precisely paralleled by observations upon visitors to London, I am not aware; but of one thing I feel quite certain, and that is, that no one who lives continuously in London can possibly have a valid opinion upon the effect on his mind and body. To obtain an objective point of view, it is necessary to get away from London. On the ground of health, experience has shown that periodical change from the atmosphere of London is highly advisable, and that there is a close association between efficiency and such periodical change. The class which governed England for two centuries and still governs it, maintains its power by maintaining its health. While keeping its grip on the lever of London, this class gains the strength to manipulate the lever, not in London, but out of it. The country house, the

237

week-end, and vacations at Christmas, Easter and in late summer and autumn, keep the governing class up to the mark. Those who play at the game of politics have perforce to play it not merely in London but also elsewhere. A sound instinct impels Parliament to prorogue on 11th August, and to avoid an autumn session unless need for it is imperative. Whatever may be the social complexion of Parliament in future, and whatever class or group may acquire political power, this power cannot be retained without these or similar wholesome customs. Lord Lee's idea of providing a country house for the Prime Minister was thoroughly sound.[1]

London of all cities is least sufficient unto itself. Apart from obvious problems of food and water supply, London exists because of the network of which it is a member, and because the main lines of this network converge there. But London is as necessary to the network as the network is to London. If London were destroyed, it would be necessary in the interests of the rest of the world to re-establish it. We have seen three great capitals—Berlin, Vienna, St. Petersburg—isolated from the rest of the world for more than four years, yet the activities of the world went on. Isolation of London would have produced an entirely different order of consequences. The chaos brought about in Russia through dislocation of its commercial, political and social organisation would be spread over almost the whole world if London and what London means were eliminated. The destruction of London would be a decisive stroke against organised life in general.

Some years ago, long before the Great War brought Americans into sympathetic relations with Englishmen, my brother Henry stopped for a moment in St. James's Park opposite the Horse Guards. A man unknown to him came up and said:

"This may be very familiar to you, sir, but I want to tell you the impression it makes upon me. I am an American. I have recently arrived in England for the first time. I come here every day, and I have gotten to know these buildings—India Office, Colonial Office, Foreign Office, Downing Street, Treasury, Home Office, War Office, Admiralty—I know them all and I have been learning what they mean. I come here every day so that the sight of them may make the knowledge of them soak into me. I see now what the British Empire means—the modesty of it and the majesty of it. I tell you, sir, the British Empire is a tremendous fact, and I never understood it until now."

---

[1] The Countess of Warwick with equal sagacity has provided a similar retreat for the leaders of the Labour party.

The American had to go to London to understand it; but when he did, he saw it in more accurate perspective than any Londoner who had never been abroad could possibly have done.

The importance of London lies not so much in its magnitude, although, of a city as of a state, magnitude must be reckoned, nor in its character as the central ganglion of a great imperial system, but rather in its character as an inevitable world centre—of international finance, of international politics, of international relations of all kinds. The inevitability of London is its really significant characteristic, and this can be fully realised only by observations over at least some part of the vast network through which its international character is maintained; it cannot be understood by merely looking in London.

We must turn, not to the London of these days, enduring the strain of war with steadfast serenity,[1] but to the London of a generation ago, easy-going, apparently indifferent to its growing responsibilities and careless of the dangers to which by its very existence it was exposed.

The picture of London which I have assigned to the following pages has no pretensions to order or completeness. It must be taken for what it is—an impressionistic sketch, conveying those impressions of men and affairs which have remained most vividly in my mind, and including only those circles in which it has been my fortune to mingle. To anyone else the picture may appear distorted.

Of London in the seventies and early eighties I had only glimpses, chiefly as I passed through it on my way to the Continent. Indeed, I missed much through accident or want of design. I failed to see Carlyle because in a fit of shyness I turned from his door in 1874, when I might have entered it had I desired. Some years earlier I failed, through a trifling accident, to see Dickens. Carlyle very naturally excited the interest of the Scots youth more than any of his contemporaries. His election as Lord Rector of the University of Edinburgh in 1876 was a kind of national demonstration. Carlyle, like other Scotsmen of an earlier and a later period, turned his back upon Scotland and went to London. His earlier friends there had been Scotsmen like Edward Irving and John Stuart Mill, while he maintained a friendship with David Masson in Edinburgh; but his later friends were Englishmen like Tyndale and Froude. One man of no special note whose acquaintance I made, but whose name I have forgotten, knew Carlyle intimately. He spoke of Carlyle dropping into his house in the evenings and sitting literally beside the fire, on the floor, with

[1] Written on Cape Cod, Massachusetts, in the summer of 1918.

his back to the jamb of the mantelpiece, smoking a clay pipe continuously and talking in spasms. Curiously enough it was Jean Paul
who drew me to Carlyle, rather than Carlyle who drew me to Jean
Paul, for I had read *Siebenkäs* in 1870, before I read *Sartor Resartus*
or any of Carlyle's translations. It is little wonder that Richter
excited Carlyle's enthusiasm and in some senses gave a bent to his
mind and certain characters to his style. Both Richter and Carlyle
were by-products of mysticism—one of eighteenth-century German
and the other of eighteenth-century Scots.

While the Scots youth of my time were interested in Carlyle,
I doubt if they were influenced by him. His criticism of industrial
organisation, or rather his insistence upon the lack of it, had no practical effect upon the development of social ideas in Scotland, while
his worship of heroes was not exactly in accordance with the attitude
of mind of the Scots youth. They had a way of looking at heroes as
men of like passions as themselves—as being in all things altogether
as they were. Thus Carlyle's heroics amused but did not influence them.

At this period Dickens had a great popularity in Scotland. He
made a lecturing tour there; but I remember that the impression he
produced among my friends was that they preferred to read him.
They were disappointed in his want of poise and in his nervous anxiety
to produce a dramatic effect. In spite of the extent to which the
humour of Dickens appears to depend upon quaint turns of expression
and appreciation of his writings to depend upon knowledge of life and
character in the London of his time, Dickens has had for many years
a great vogue on the continent of Europe.[1] Some years after his death
I found myself under an obligation to Count Benyovsky, a Hungarian
nobleman, who had great enthusiasm for English literature. I asked
him if he would like me to send him some English books, and if so to
say what books he would prefer. The publication of Forster's *Life
of Dickens* had then just been announced, and he asked me to send
it to him when it was published. He said of all English authors the
one he most admired was Dickens. I found also that among English
authors Count Tolstoy had two favourites—Dickens and Ruskin. In
these cases, which I think are significant, what appealed in Dickens
was not his humour, which in spite of knowledge of the English
language, remarkably sound in both cases, could not possibly be fully
appreciated, but his humanity and, above all, his attitude towards life

[1] Of twenty-three plays and operas popular in Moscow in February 1919,
thirteen were by Russian authors, one by Maeterlinck, one by Saint-Saëns, two
by Molière, one by Shakespeare (*Much Ado about Nothing*), and three by Dickens.
Cf. Ransome, A., *Russia in 1919* (New York, 1919), p. 89.

and education. This attitude, rather than any literary qualities or artistic power in imaginative writing, attracted wide recognition of Dickens among cultivated people, especially, I believe, in Austria-Hungary and in Russia.

In 1886 I made the acquaintance of a circle which included many literary and scientific people of that time. The acknowledged centre was the house of Mr. and Mrs. W. D. Hertz. Mr. Hertz had been a manufacturer at Bradford; but he had lived on Campden Hill for some years when I first saw him. He and his wife were both of Jewish descent. They had for a long period been devoted adherents of Comte. Mrs. Hertz had translated a portion of the *Social Dynamics* into English. Through the marriage of their only daughter to George Paul Macdonell, they became related to a Scots family of unusual ability. The eldest of four brothers, James Macdonell was assistant editor of *The Times* under Delane; the second, Sir John Macdonell,[1] was Master of the Supreme Court; the third, George, was a barrister in Lincoln's Inn; the fourth, Paul, who was a singularly attractive young man, died early. The Macdonells were Aberdonians. The eldest, James, migrated to London and drew the others after him. All of the Macdonells added to great ability and enormous power of work, charm of manner and placid, cultivated character. Mrs. Hertz's sister had married Thompson, the inventor of the steam-roller; and, after his death, married Fletcher Moulton, who had fought the legal battles of the Thompson patents. Some years after her death he was called to the Bench.[2]

Mrs. Hertz had a remarkable personality. Her figure was *petite*, but her head was large and her features were marked by distinction. There was a legend to the effect that Leech had her in mind when he drew in *Punch* the receptions of Mrs. Leo Hunter; I suspect an anachronism, but whether the story be true or false, the suggested parallel was by no means apt. It is true that Mrs. Hertz surrounded herself with notable people; but they owed at least as much to her as she could possibly owe to them. Her insight into character was almost unerring; and her chief delight as well as a large part of her occupation was to discover young men of brilliant parts who needed help at the outset of their career, and to help them to the fullest extent of her power.[3] The charm of her conversation and her infinite tact brought about and kept about her many of the leading men and women

[1] He died in April 1921.
[2] During the war Lord Moulton rendered important services through his great technical knowledge.
[3] Fletcher Moulton was one of these.

I—Q

of her time. Apart from the Comtists—Frederic Harrison, Congreve, Bridges and Cotter Morison—what may fairly be called her circle included Browning, Goldwin Smith, Vernon Lushington, George J. Romanes, Felix Moscheles and Fletcher Moulton among the men, and Mrs. Clifford, Mrs. Sutherland Orr, Mrs. Lynn Linton and Mrs. Romanes among the women. All of these, excepting Browning, I met, some of them frequently, at her house. One evening Browning was to have come to dinner—a *partie carrée*—but to my lasting regret something prevented him, and I never had another opportunity. With the exception of Goldwin Smith, whom I knew intimately in later years, I think the most attractive personality was Cotter Morison, one of the Aberdonian contingent in London. He was a great master of the art of conversation. He knew how to glide from one deep saying to another better than anyone I have known. I was glad to notice that Lord Morley, in his *Recollections*, does justice to his memory. He had been Morley's tutor at Oxford. Morison was not a prolific writer; but he had a really profound knowledge of the Middle Ages and a singular sympathy for certain phases of religious feeling. Both are illustrated in his *Life of St. Bernard of Clairvaux*. Of the ladies, I saw more of Mrs. Sutherland Orr than of the others. She was a sister of Lord Leighton. When Browning was on his death-bed, she rushed to Italy to nurse him. She had been one of the most intimate friends of Browning and his wife.

Mrs. Hertz cultivated the society rather of literary, scientific and philosophical persons than of politicians; but Sir William and Lady Byles, who were dear friends of my own, were life-long intimates of hers, and she shared with them and Dr. Bridges an early enthusiasm for Home Rule. There was always a certain brisk quality in Mrs. Hertz's Sunday afternoons. Whatever was of importance at the moment was well talked over and the conversation went on in a vivacious stream, occasionally even flowing deep. To her conversational powers, Mrs. Hertz added great skill in the almost lost art of letter writing. I had many interesting letters from her. Characteristic examples of her correspondence are to be found in her letters to Goldwin Smith published after his death.

I have already indicated that in Scotland in the eighties there was a growing dissatisfaction with the existing political parties, and that this dissatisfaction afforded the soil where the seeds of various political and economic heresies grew and flourished. The same dissatisfaction was to be found in London, not among official and party groups, but among other groups in its complex society. Young men fresh from the universities, some of them touched with the enthusiasm of Arnold Toynbee, had thrown themselves into the Settlement movement under Canon Barnett, or, fired by *Robert Elsmere*, had frequented University Hall, about that time under the care of Dr. Philip Wicksteed. These latter were men of note. Canon Barnett was a shrewd, capable organiser of voluntary labour. He seemed to see that one of the immediate problems was how to satisfy the growing desire on the part of educated youth of the middle class to acquire the kind of knowledge of working people that was necessary to enable them to engage in effective administration. He seemed to see also that increase of elementary education among working people must inevitably produce discontent unless working people could be effectively guided towards the utilisation of their educational advantages in acquiring the kind of culture which had been supposed to be a monopoly of the middle class. Although I visited Toynbee Hall frequently I knew Canon Barnett only slightly, and I am not, therefore, in a position to say that the problems as I put them were those which chiefly presented themselves to his mind. Yet I do not think I am wrong in thus interpreting the Toynbee Hall movement. It seems to me to have been excellently intended, but directed towards the imposition upon working people of contemporary middle-class culture. Exhibitions of works of fashionable painters were organised in the East End, lectures upon literary and philosophical subjects were delivered, and personal advice was administered to those who desired assistance of this kind. It was all very sympathetic; but to some it had a flavour of dilettantism, while to others it revealed only the existence of a gulf wider than they had supposed between those who had inherited a desire and an aptitude for a cultivated life and those who had not. I have no doubt that the movement stimulated some to intellectual effort and brought to them the joy of life that that effort affords, while to others it conveyed knowledge of the real character of social problems which they might not otherwise so easily have obtained; but I doubt if the movement accomplished more. Yet this was something, and there are members of Parliament and of the London County Council, as well as many public officials, who owe much to what they learned at Toynbee Hall.

University Hall had a more definitely religious aim, although the religious feeling which inspired it was not of the orthodox variety. Dr. Wicksteed was a Unitarian—a man of a very deeply religious frame of mind. He had written upon Dante and upon Ibsen works of real scholarship. But here also was apparent an effort by certain members of one social group to impose its peculiar culture upon other groups whose life and habits would have rendered the imposition inappropriate, even if it could have been successfully accomplished.

Besides the communities of the Settlements, there were numerous small communities and isolated individuals who took up their abode in the East End of London, with the view of acquiring some knowledge of the life of the people there, either for the purpose of enabling them to become effective administrators or legislators, or for the purpose of formulating plans of social amelioration or of carrying out plans already formed. Most of these were young men from the universities reading for the Bar or in some other manner preparing for their future career. Very few of them were interested in any way in natural science. In general, their purely classical education predisposed them to look at the problems they encountered in a non-scientific manner, and thus these also incurred the reproach of dilettantism.

There was, however, one group which began about 1885 to examine the question of London poverty from a point of view which might fairly be called scientific. This group was collected round him by Mr. Charles Booth, who had just embarked upon the extensive researches which resulted in a monumental series of volumes. I became acquainted with Mr. Booth soon after he began these researches. I had myself been led (in 1884-85) to think of an exhaustive examination of the social problem by means of some adaptation of the method of Frédéric le Play, and had begun a preliminary inquiry involving the collection of family budgets and the intimate study of typical working families. I was somewhat astonished to find that Mr. Booth was not at that time familiar with the work of Le Play, or of the societies which, under his inspiration, had been founded in Paris; and that Mr. Booth's method was wholly original. This indeed was a great merit, although it rendered comparison of his results with those of Le Play rather difficult. Taken as a static view of the condition of London social life at the period when the inquiries were made, there is nothing to compare with the study of London by Mr. Booth and his collaborators. Industry, wealth, skill and sympathy were all in large measure expended upon the gigantesque research. Its full value cannot be realised until at some later and not too distant period a similar study is made for purposes of comparison. Mr. Booth's study was made during a period of low wages and low prices, and the most appropriate time to make a second study of the same kind would be during a period of high wages and high prices.

Quite dissociated from any of the movements described in this and in previous chapters, but nearly contemporary, was the movement of which the Fabian Society was the outcome. The history of this society has been written by itself. It is necessary only to interpret it. Among those who found themselves dissatisfied with the currents of opinion which characterised political parties after the Liberal victory and the Tory *débâcle* of 1880 were some who refused to share the prevailing optimism of the politicians, and yet were unable to accept without further inquiry the social specifics offered by the Land Nationalisation movement, or by the various Socialist movements that were beginning to launch their propagandas. These also were, in general, disturbed by the economical situation of the country during the Long Depression, and were not interested in the meagre Parliamentary programme of either party, or in the efforts, such as they were, of the Church and other agencies, then occupied with what was vaguely called "the social question." A small group of people, who had individually acquired this critical attitude towards the society of their time, formed themselves into the Fabian Society. The motto of Fabius was the motto of Joffre and Foch—"Wait, and when the proper moment arrives, strike." So far as waiting was concerned, the name was not unhappily chosen; but I am afraid that the original Fabians were not precisely fitted by temperament for striking, even when the moment might arrive.

Besides a motto, the Fabians possessed a postulate. This was the eighteenth-century postulate of the perfectibility of mankind. They supposed that what should be sought was the perfect way; perfection lay inevitably at the end of that way. From this there was no great transition to the idea that they had found the way and that the Fabians alone among mankind had attained perfection. This illusion, fascinating to themselves, gave colour to their political action as well as to their literary product. It showed itself in the policy of the Progressives as well as in the prefaces to his plays of George Bernard Shaw. The Progressives were fond of denouncing all other parties as reactionary and stupid, and of proclaiming theirs as the only enlightened group. In the same way Shaw found blemishes in every writer of plays but himself, and almost before he had cut his wisdom teeth as a playwright, he had talked disrespectfully of Shakespeare and had scoffed at every pre- and post-Elizabethan dramatist.[1]

For the Fabian, perfection was no distant aim, attainable only by prayer and fasting—no Holy Grail; but something easily achieved—

---

[1] The same attitude is to be found in Sidney Webb's *Decay of Capitalist Civilisation* (London, 1923). He denounces capitalists in general as "stupid."

wherefore *The Perfect Wagnerite, The Perfect Playwright, The Perfect Premier*, and the like.

There were among the Fabians convinced Socialists who did not see their way to attach themselves to any of the Socialist parties, although when the Fabian Society was formed these parties were, so far as England was concerned, in a merely embryonic state. In general, the Fabians were simply anxious inquirers looking for a gospel, rather than convinced gospellers who had one to preach. But many of them soon passed from that phase, and with sublime confidence in their own genius pointed the path by which they had themselves attained perfection.

The Fabians began early to bestow upon the public a series of tracts. These tracts had the freshness of extreme youth. There was nothing new or original in them; but they were clever and some of them were amusing. One of them, *An Appeal to Landlords*,[1] was written in a spirit of irony by no means delicate, but sufficiently masked to cause, as I was told at the time, the Liberty and Property Defence League, then recently established, to accept it as a serious contribution and to circulate it among its members. The most important tract, *Facts for Londoners*, was well done, and, together with other efforts, was influential in placing the members of the Fabian Society who desired to throw themselves into municipal affairs in a position to become candidates for the London County Council.

The early London County Council was variously composed. There were aristocratic politicians like Lord Rosebery, retired officials of great experience in high office like Sir Reginald Welby,[2] Socialist orators like John Burns, lawyers like Benjamin Costelloe, men of business and municipal politicians. Among these groups the Fabians made themselves felt. They had no experience in the conduct of large affairs, but they had intelligence, energy, and the power of applying themselves to serious study of concrete problems. Limited as was their outlook in certain important directions, it was nevertheless much wider than that of most of their colleagues. They applied themselves assiduously to study for debates, and they easily overcame the inarticulate mass of members whose examination of new problems was perfunctory, as might be expected of men without adequate educational preparation. The Fabians thus easily fell into the position of leaders; and it was natural for them to become confirmed in their sense of superiority. They became chairmen of important committees,

---

[1] Anonymous, but written, I believe, by George Bernard Shaw.
[2] Afterwards Lord Welby.

and they were soon in a position to suggest and to carry into effect the policies they had, during the few years of their existence, been formulating. They allied themselves with the Socialist elements and formed a Progressive party, which for a time dominated the Council.

The Progressive policy has yet to vindicate itself from the charge of being reactionary rather than progressive. A party whose policy involves increase in official control over the life of the people and increase in official control over the earnings of the people can only be materially justified of its works if both are more ample as a direct consequence of its policy. Its moral justification is another affair. The diminution of spontaneous action, and the threat involved in the policy of elimination of such action, may readily produce social confusion before the governmental machinery necessary to replace spontaneous action has been devised, or has been successful in functioning as effectively as that which preceded. In any case, the mere substitution of governmental action for private action of the same kind is not a demonstrable advantage. Only where private action is ineffective or absent is there a reasonable ground for the employment of the State forces. It may be argued that public opinion has settled that point. That is to beg the whole question. The assumption underlying the propaganda for certain forms of social legislation is that spontaneous action is always mischievous, while dominated action, even though taken by the same persons, is always beneficial. It is time that in the interest of the future of society a complete stock-taking and striking of a true balance be undertaken.

The whole question has assumed a new phase. Enough experiments have been made to enable an estimate of the net results of these to be formed. The economic life of society is an important, though not the only, basis of it, and we must ascertain what has been the net effect upon economic life of the experiments in collectivism which have been made. We are no longer concerned with the abstract doctrines of Marx. The Socialists themselves have riddled these to pieces, and they have long since passed into the limbo of discredited dogma. The problem is briefly—Is collectivism an economical system: does it result in a larger product and in such a distribution of the product as to ensure the continuance of increased production? The risks in case of failure are tremendous. Once individual initiative is destroyed in a nation there is little hope of its renaissance. To subject the national life to the bureaucrat thoroughly and completely may be to doom it to destruction. The real tragedy of Germany is the crushing of the national morale in the jaws of her own bureaucratic machinery; and the real tragedy of Russia is the imitation by the Revolutionary Government of the worst practices of the Tsarist régime.[1]

The success of some of their number in the municipal politics of London drew the Fabians from the wider political fields they might have occupied, and the literary success of others diverted them from political action. Thus the Fabian Society remained an interesting, but collectively an unimportant, group.

One of the most attractive of the Fabians was Graham Wallas. When I first met him in the eighties, he was working upon the diaries and documents of Francis Place. He rendered a real service to political history by publishing his account of early Radicalism in England. He became chairman of the Committee on Education in the London County Council and, free as he was from the bureaucratic tendencies of some of his colleagues, rendered in that position excellent service. His book on *Human Nature in Politics* is a highly original work written in a very fine spirit, and marred only by occasional lapses from lucidity.

I became acquainted with individual Fabians from time to time after 1884, when the Society was founded.

Sidney Webb I met for the first time in Newcastle in 1889. We had a controversy about Marx, Webb sustained Marx's thesis on value with knowledge and energy. Webb at that time was a clerk in the Colonial Office.

A group in some ways analogous to the Fabians emerged from South Africa after the Union was carried into effect. This group was known as the Round Table. Like the Fabians, they were afflicted with perfectionism; but, unlike them, they were concerned with imperial politics rather than with specifics for social change. Probably from the Prussian statesman Stein, through the medium of Seeley, they had become obsessed with the idea of unity.

To Stein unity certainly meant absolutism. To the Round Table it probably did not imply absolutism; but it certainly implied centralised oligarchy. A doctrine that runs counter to current tendencies of opinion is not on that account to be condemned; but a doctrine that runs counter to the actual progress of humanity cannot be justified.

---

[1] The actual working out in life of collectivist and communist ideas has brought about a change in the attitude of the leading Fabians, and perhaps age has mellowed them. Their recent writings show that they have not only less confidence than they had in the virtues of collectivism and bureaucracy, but they seem to have ceased to regard any fundamental change in the social structure as either inevitable or desirable.

The Union of South Africa may work well. Indeed it must, because the comparatively innumerous whites must unite to maintain their ground against an overwhelming black population. Union with them would, of course, be out of the question. Such a union would retard rather than promote human progress. But from a political union of closely related racial groups in South Africa to an imperial political union of very different races is a long step. If it could occur, the probable consequence would be political levelling down rather than levelling up. There is not much to choose between the formal unity through elimination of all but the proletariat advocated by extreme Social Democrats and the formal unity through ignoring the diversity of the constituent elements of the empire advocated by the Round Table.

The Fabians, who were the Young Englanders of their day, have grown older, and the hope may be cherished, wiser, if perhaps less consciously perfect; and the Round Table group, later in the field by a quarter of a century, is now growing older and perhaps also wiser. Even the Young Turks appear to have learned something, and perhaps also the Young Poles.

The tendency of modern social and political evolution seems to be towards increasing diversity rather than towards unity. In a half-conscious way this powerful tendency towards diversity—a chief concomitant of liberty—is the main factor in producing exaggerated outbursts of nationalism. Under the pressure of diversity as a disintegrating force in great States, we have seen in the first half of the nineteenth century rupture of the United Netherlands and quasi-separation of Austria and Hungary; and in the first quarter of the present century we have seen complete separation of Austria from Hungary, separation of Norway from Sweden, separation of Finland and Poland from Russia, quasi-separation of Ireland from Great Britain, as well as creation of numerous new relatively small States carved out of former great States.

The immediate occasion of the war was the attempt on the part of Austria to reverse the process of disintegration by annexing Bosnia and Herzegovina, and uniting these provinces to Austria-Hungary. In doing so Austria brought about, not consolidation of her own imperial system, but downfall of it; as well as downfall of three other imperial systems of which unification was a distinguishing characteristic. The observed tendency towards disintegration may be due to a passing phase of opinion, or it may be a tendency whose roots are deep in human society. In any case not unity but precisely its opposite is clearly the tendency of the moment, and this tendency appears to cohere with the theories of liberty upon which society in almost every country in the world has within recent times been basing its action.   There is an evident need for co-operation, not merely of the constituents of a non-unified or loosely coherent State, but of many States politically wholly independent; and such need remains.   But unity is another affair.   Even discussion of it might injure a State whose solidarity depends not on a formal document but on a state of mind.   Great danger may lie in the reduction of this state of mind to a formal document, because thus to polarise it is to promote stagnation or conflict.   The United States Constitution prescribed exactly in what union consisted, and yet it cost a Civil War to maintain the Union, and it costs now serious controversies whenever any political question of deep moment arises.   Unity is no safeguard against political conflicts.   Thus, in so far as formal unity is the propaganda of the Round Table, there seems little hope for it. I may be permitted to say that I saw the ineffectual consequences of the propaganda for unity from the beginning and did not hesitate to point these out to the Round Table group, excited as they were with enthusiasm over what to their inexperienced minds was a new idea.

I have elsewhere given an account of some of the Scots men of letters who lived in London during the period of which I am at present writing.   These did not form a specific group.   After the manner of their kind, they mingled with other groups according to their idiosyncrasies and some of them chose to remain aloof from literary society.   Of all of the Scotsmen in London, perhaps William Sharp was the most sociable.   Industrious as were his habits, he was on terms of amity with a wide circle.   In his earlier years he had known Rossetti and had written a life of him.   Theodore Watts-Dunton and he were on friendly terms, although I only saw him once with Sharp. One of the houses to which Sharp and I went frequently was that of Mrs. Mona Caird, the authoress of *Is Marriage a Failure?* Mrs. Caird was an Alison,[1] a cousin of the younger Alisons of Stranraer, who were the friends of my childhood.   She had married a Hampshire farmer, the son of Sir James Caird of Genoch, near Stranraer.[2] Caird the younger was a solid man of good practical ability but without intellectual interests, although he tolerated these in others.   He knew a great deal about sheep, and I had many instructive conversations

[1] Her father was John Alison, *cf. supra*, chap. iii.
[2] Chap. iii.

with him on that subject. I found a humorous incongruity in discussing farm management with Caird in a drawing-room filled with a
really brilliant circle composed largely of the advanced women whom
Mrs. Caird had drawn about her. Of those whom I met there I recall
especially Mathilde Blind, the daughter of Karl Blind, and Ellen Key,
the Swedish writer upon "the woman question," as at that time it
was called on the Continent. Both were very able women. One evening
I was introduced to a young lady by Mrs. Caird. We happened to
drift a little aside, and she said to me, "I have just come from South
Africa, where I have been for a long time, and this is very strange
to me. Are you learned and clever like the rest of these people?"
"Not a bit," I answered, "I am as stupid as an owl in daylight."
"Then," she said, "we can have some human conversation." I
interrogated her upon South Africa, and she gave me an account of
her life there with much intelligence and humour. On the same, or
a similar occasion, I felt a friendly grasp on my arm, and a deep
voice said in my ear, "How is Chimmie and how is Turk?" The grasp
and the voice belonged to Stepniak. He had stayed with us at Busby
in Scotland and he had made himself a friend of my small son (now a
professor of biology) and his retriever, Turk, who was his constant
companion and guardian. Sergius Stepniak, whose real name was
Kravchinsky, had been an officer in a dragoon regiment. He had
thrown himself into the *V Narod* movement,[1] and through it had come
to acquire revolutionary sympathies. Stung by attack upon and gross
ill-treatment of his mother, he had walked in broad day in the Nevski
Prospekt in St. Petersburg and shot through the heart the chief of
the Russian police, Menzentsev. Stepniak escaped to England and
remained there for the rest of his life. Whether or not because he had
mingled an act of private vengeance with a significant revolutionary
deed, and on that account felt some qualms of conscience, I do not
know; but this event appeared to cast a shadow over his mind.
He never referred to it. His writings showed that he took a much
more moderate and practical view of the revolutionary movement
in Russia than was customary among revolutionists at that time. So
far as I am aware, he never afterwards interested himself in any
revolutionary intrigues. He continued to write for many years
articles on Russian affairs for *The Times*. These articles are free from
violence and are filled with accurate and well-digested knowledge.
His books on the Russian peasantry and on the Russian Government
are real contributions to history. Circumstances rendered it necessary

[1] *Cf.* p. 159.

for him to make his living as a hard-working journalist; but his real destiny, if it could have worked out, was to have taken his place alongside of Turgenev as an interpreter, through works of the imagination, of the spirit of the Russian youth of his time. Turgenev had given an incomparable account of the spirit of the Revolution in 1848; but he had not been so successful in his attempt to portray the spirit of the *V Narod* period, and of the revolutionary movement which grew out of it. Stepniak could have done that, and he did do it to a not inconsiderable extent in his *Career of a Nihilist*. This novel is full of power. It is not merely a faithful account of a movement of great importance in the history of humanity, but it is a work of real literary art. Characteristically Russian it was; but it was written by a Russian upon a Russian subject. The novel was written in English,[1] and the style, though perhaps not precisely according to some English standards or rather fashions, is undeniably good. One of the things for which I find it hard to forgive Henley is the advice he gave to Stepniak. He told him that the *Career of a Nihilist* was not well written, and that in future, if Stepniak wrote a novel, he should write it in Russian and have it translated into English by another hand. I did all I could to counteract this preposterous nonsense, but Henley's influence over Stepniak was too strong. Stepniak became discouraged and never published another novel. Henley was quite incompetent to form a judgment on such a matter. He knew nothing about Russian literature or Russian movements, and he was altogether averse from sympathy with revolutionary ideas. . He was evidently unaware that no Russian-English translator at that time could possibly have rendered into English Stepniak's writings half so well as Stepniak could write in English himself; and he was evidently unaware that no English version of any Russian novels had up till then been other than disappointing. The piquant Russian flavour of *The Career of a Nihilist* was thoroughly appropriate. It is impossible to estimate what the world of letters has lost through Henley's discouragement of Stepniak.

Stepniak held views not at that time, or since, prevalent among Russian revolutionists. He was really a constitutionalist and a moderate. He told me, for example, that he anticipated a great change in Russia through the growth of religious dissent. During the *V Narod* period, the Raskolniki, or groups dissenting from the Greek Orthodox Church, were in general of a liberal frame of mind, and there

---

[1] Stepniak's *Underground Russia* (London, 1883) was originally written in Italian and afterwards translated into English and Russian (St. Petersburg, 1909).

was a tendency on the part of persons of liberal views to join dissenting sects partly for the purpose of utilising their organisation for promotion of political liberalism among the people. Yet this movement was by no means extensive, and many dissenting sects were characterised by enthusiasm for the less rational of the heresies of the early Christian Church and by mysticism rather than by any modernity in religious belief. To my mind, the cast of Stepniak's temperament was that of an artist rather than that of a political philosopher or that of a revolutionist. Yet I never met an artist who was so amiable and so gentle in his judgments. Stepniak's features were of strongly-marked Tartar type, not the type of the degenerate Tartars of the Crimea, but probably nearer that of the Tartars of Kazan. He had in his blood, no doubt, some strain of the free Cossack. Probably this circumstance induced him to choose "Stepniak" (one from the steppe) as his pseudonym.

Stepniak lived in Bedford Park, but he was not of it. His almost incessant labours did not, as I have already indicated, entirely deprive him of social pleasures, but they restricted these to comparatively rare occasions. He had little contact with the community among whom he lived. The community of Bedford Park was rather undeservedly scoffed at by the Londoner. Bedford Park at that time was a suburb consisting of villas occupied by people who had acquired a reputation for a special variety of culture. They had a theatre of their own, where they produced plays composed and acted by themselves. In a cultural sense they were self-sustaining and self-sufficient. They were supposed to live in an attenuated atmosphere and at a certain altitude above their neighbours. This was the external and envious point of view. In point of fact many of them were very cultivated, intelligent people, with distinctly fine views of life and abhorrence of commercial materialism. Among my friends there were Dr. John Todhunter, who wrote some charming plays with classical motives, and W. B. Yeats, who lived there with his father, who had been an artist. When I made his acquaintance, Yeats, who was then quite young, had already published his *Life of Blake*. His own mystical temperament had drawn him to Blake in his earliest years, and for a long time he had devoted himself to the study of his works. I think it was through Yeats that I was able to induce R. L. Nettleship of Oxford to send me, for examination, his collection of Blake's pencil and pen-and-ink drawings. In this very extraordinary series of imaginative works Blake endeavoured to express his mysticism in line as in another manner he had expressed it in prose and verse.

I had intended to reproduce these drawings in the *Art Review*, but the stoppage of that periodical prevented me from carrying out my intention.[1]

Among my London acquaintances at this time was Arthur Symons, who lived in the Temple with Havelock Ellis. Symons had a talent in verse like Degas in painting. He was extremely skilful, but it seemed to me that his intellect wanted momentum. Whatever he did was done with grace and elegance, but it lacked vitality. He was a good critic and perhaps hypercritical of his own work.

Sharp edited for Walter Scott, the Newcastle brickmaker, contractor and publisher, a little volume, *A Century of Sonnets*, and wrote otherwise for the series of books published by Scott. Mrs. Sharp also contributed a small book on musical composers. Sharp enlisted in the same service many of his literary friends, and in general contributed towards the formation of a group of younger men and women who were just beginning to devote themselves to letters. Scott, though an able man of business, was not familiar with literature or even with publishing. The printing and publishing business had, I believe, been acquired as the security of a bad debt, and was conducted by him for the purpose of saving his investment. I was told at the time that when his manager mentioned that he was about to publish a book of sonnets, Scott asked who was going to write it, and on being told said, "What can he know about sonnets? I know more about them than anybody else." It appears that a "sonnet" is a kind of brick.

The time seemed appropriate for the issue of books of a reasonably high standard at a low price. Paper was cheap, a younger generation of writers was springing up and their services could be procured at no great cost. The results justified the experiment. I saw, in 1889, in Scott's warehouse at Newcastle, tons of "Canterbury Poets" and "Camelot Series," packed in cases for shipment to Australia, where they had already obtained a large market. Such a business could not be carried on without the aid of brains, and the brains were provided, in the first instance, locally in Newcastle. Two young men, both living there, Ernest Rhys and W. H. Dircks, were really the moving spirits in the launching of the series of books which Scott published, including those I have mentioned as well as the "Contemporary Science Series" and the "Great Writers." The last-mentioned consisted of new works, many of them of high merit; the "Scientific Series" was composed partly of original works and partly of translations from French,

[1] I am not aware that these remarkable drawings have been reproduced.

German and Italian, and the "Camelot Series" consisted of reprints with new introductions. The series of poets, which alone consisted of a hundred volumes, contained new critical introductions as well as some volumes of new verse. To achieve these results in a short time was rendered possible through the activity and capacity for suggestion of Rhys and Dircks. They speedily enlisted a large number of writers, some of whom had not previously been known to the wide public. Among these were T. W. Rolleston, Havelock Ellis, Patrick Geddes and Arthur Thomson, the Rinders (friends of Sharp), and Marzials [1] (then a clerk in the War Office). Scott opened a house in London, and there Rhys and Dircks removed from Newcastle. I admired very much the conscientiousness, skill and energy thrown by these young men into the task of editorship. They were well qualified for it by eclectic and sanguine temperament, and both of them had a good sense of style and unflagging industry. Rhys, Rolleston and I occasionally regaled ourselves with steaks and ale at the " Cheshire Cheese," an antique hostelry off Fleet Street; Havelock Ellis I used to see in his chambers in the Temple, held under Ernest Radford, who was a barrister though he did not practise.

In 1889 or 1890 I mentioned one day to Emery Walker that I would like to make the acquaintance of Samuel Butler, in whose *Luck or Cunning* and *Life and Habit* I had been much interested because of his criticism of Charles Darwin and his effort to turn attention to Lamarck as well as to Erasmus Darwin. Walker, who was not interested in such matters, said that if I wanted to talk with Butler about them I should go by myself, and that I needed no introduction. Butler's chambers in Clifford's Inn were next door to Emery Walker's, so I went immediately. The door was opened by Butler's man, whose name I afterwards learned was Alfred. I was ushered into a comfortable room and soon Butler made his appearance. He was without a coat and was drying his hands, which were deeply stained, as I recognised, by nitrate of silver. He told me he had been developing photographs. I wasted no time, but told him the simple fact; that I had been impelled to call upon him unintroduced because of my interest in his biological views. At once he became cordial. He put on his coat, produced a box of cigars, and we sat down by the fire for a long afternoon. He made many sharp criticisms of Darwin, and I detected, although I did not probe, a certain personal animus. The causes of this have been fully explained in a little pamphlet by Butler's friend, Henry Festing Jones, and I need not develop them

[1] Sir Frank Marzials.

here. I suppose that Darwin really did not take Butler so seriously as Butler took himself, and that after a certain point Darwin did not trouble himself about him. The whole question has assumed a new phase owing to the development of scientific technique and to the co-ordination of physics and chemistry with biology, and therefore the quarrel between Darwin and Butler has ceased to have any but historical importance. That importance, however, it has. It was really an incident in the wider movement which at that time was beginning to take place towards more critical examination of the hypothesis of evolution as stated by Darwin. The position of Darwin in the historical development of biological theory is unassailable, even if his fundamental hypothesis may be proved to be invalid. Butler, untrained as he was in biological research, undoubtedly contributed to biological science, although his criticism of Darwin may be regarded as purely negative. That Butler had put his finger upon a serious defect in the Darwinian hypothesis seems to me to be evident from the direction taken by Weismann and others of the Ultra-Darwinian School.

From Lamarck and Darwin, Butler and I passed to Tabachetti and the sculptures of Varallo, of which he has given an account in his *Ex Voto*. I do not recall his talking about the *Odyssey*, which he thought was written by a woman; but he did talk at some length about music and musical composition, on which he was enthusiastic, speaking very warmly of his friend, Henry Festing Jones. Butler's conversation was characterised by the same dry humour which appears in his writings. Indeed, these writings err, if they do err, in being too conversational, in having too many elisions. In conversation with a person who is more or less familiar with the subject, elisions are a great saving of time; but in a permanent and systematic record they are apt to occur in such a manner as to mislead the uninstructed reader. There is, perhaps, no more humorous essay in our language than *Quis desiderio?* I saw in Butler's rooms the drawings which are now at Caius College, Cambridge.

I think it was in 1894 that I became acquainted with W. H. Stead. I had been interested in him because of his enthusiasm for Russia and because of his knowledge of certain phases of European affairs. We met first in London and afterwards in Paris. In later years he visited me at least twice in Canada, and I visited him in London. Stead was a man of extraordinary natural ability, not by any means fully developed, through his journalistic life and habit of skimming over things to get at what he thought was the gist of them. This apparent gist was, after all, only some of their more obvious and by no means their fundamental features. He had unbounded confidence in himself, in his capacity for work and in his powers of penetration. His really remarkable qualities lay, however, to my mind, in his invincible courage and in his sympathetic character, which enabled him to acquire the confidence and the affection of people, even while they distrusted his judgment.   Sir Charles Russell [1] told someone who told me that one evening he was alone at dinner when Stead bounded in upon him. Russell naturally asked him if he had dined. Stead answered that he had been too excited to eat for some time, and could not eat then. Russell pushed him a decanter of port and a jar of biscuits. While devouring these Stead told his story. He said that he had become aware of the traffic in young girls in London, and that he had determined to expose it in the *Pall Mall Gazette*. It was necessary to obtain indisputable evidence from the mouth of some witness whose words would attract universal attention and demand universal credence. He had decided that Russell should be that witness, and that he should obtain the evidence in a manner which Stead proceeded to describe. Russell was too good a lawyer and too cool a man to undertake such a task. Stead then intimated that it would be necessary for him to perform it himself. Russell endeavoured to dissuade him, but without avail, and Stead carried out his project on his own account. Undoubtedly he knew the risk he ran; but it appears to me that he thought his reputation and the obvious sincerity of his intentions would save him from serious consequences. They did not do so and he found himself in Holloway Jail. I do not think that he ever regretted his action, although this case and another in which he found himself involved brought him into association with a seamy side of life which was not wholesome for him. It appeared as though every wronged woman went to Stead for advice and assistance, and the burden of such affairs became intolerable even to a man of Stead's sympathy and patience. I waited for him one day for three-quarters of an hour while he listened to a tale of woe from some lady whose husband had neglected or ill-treated her. He threw himself into the Peace Movement, and by this means was able to free himself from what was rapidly becoming an incubus. His "War against War" was carried on actively for some time, and this led him into remarkable relations with the Tsar Nicholas II. I am not sure that Stead's powers of penetration were sufficient to enable him to distinguish between genuine advocates of international justice and the numerous

[1] Afterwards Lord Russell of Killowen.

I—R

adventurers, career-makers and political intriguers who were engaged in the exploitation of the Peace Movement to their own varied ends. I found Stead always interesting, and sometimes illuminating, on international affairs; but in these, as in other matters, he was too apt to jump to conclusions and to confuse the actual and the ideal. His self-regardlessness and disinterested enthusiasm were beyond question and above praise. He was the kind of man who does not truckle to the people, and who stands unabashed before princes. My conversations with him were in general upon foreign affairs, and therefore I did not come into contact with him in relation to spiritism, which, I understand, became in later years his principal personal interest. When the *Titanic* went down, she carried with her one of the finest, although by no means one of the most intellectual, spirits of our time.

About 1894 I became acquainted, through Robert Ross, with Oscar Wilde, Alfred Douglas, Count Steinbok (who was a ward of Benjamin Costelloe), Max Beerbohm and Aubrey Beardsley. Apart from Robert Ross, for whom I had a great affection, I was not attracted by this group. Several of them, notably Wilde and Beardsley, were men of genius. Almost a generation has elapsed since the melancholy incidents which marked the close of Wilde's career, and it is now easy to detach the products of his pen from the cloud which enveloped their author. Wilde's plays are witty and graceful, and his essays have the sparkle to be expected of one who was accustomed to regard himself as a "lord of language." Beardsley originated a new style in drawing, although his style may fairly be regarded as being derived from the French painters of the latter part of the seventeenth century and the early part of the eighteenth. Beardsley was rather learned in French literature and art of the sixteenth century and later.

The character and direction of the literature and art of England in the final quarter of the nineteenth century cannot be understood without taking into account the writings of Wilde and the drawings of Beardsley.

Apart from the Socialist circle that hovered about Morris, his most immediate friends were Burne-Jones and Faulkner. Unfortunately, I never met either. I went with Morris one day to his shop in Oxford Street, hoping to meet Burne-Jones; but I did not see him, and I had no other opportunity. Emery Walker and Walter Crane, of course, I knew well, and also, though not so well, Seddon the architect, who was one of Morris's most faithful allies in the Anti-Scrape,[1] Eric Magnusson, the Icelander, with whom Morris had

[1] The Society for the Preservation of Ancient Monuments.

translated some of the sagas, and with whom Morris travelled in Iceland, and York Powell, who had a singular resemblance in his features
to Morris, was also interested in Scandinavian literature, and was
on friendly terms with Morris. Powell was especially well informed
about French affairs and was in the habit of making frequent visits
to Paris. We used occasionally to meet at the Savile. In that club
also I used often to meet two Raleighs,[1] Ray Lankester, Frank Beddard,
the Prosector at the Zoo, Alexander Ross, Henry Higgs, then in the
Secretary's Department of the Post Office,[2] and Sir Alfred Greenhill,
of the Artillery College at Woolwich. On Saturday afternoons in the
early nineties Edmund Gosse, Rudyard Kipling, Andrew Lang,
George Saintsbury, William Hunt, W. J. Loftie and others used to
go for a pow-wow, while W. H. Mallock dined occasionally.

Here also I became acquainted with the celebrated American
specialist in nervous diseases—Weir Mitchell of Philadelphia. Up
till that time (1894) Mitchell had written little excepting professional
contributions to the medical journals. He told me with habitual
humorous exaggeration that his son had achieved success as a writer
of short stories and a novel or two, while his own efforts in the same
direction had been rejected by the publishers. Mitchell had an acute
mind and great tact in dealing with patients suffering from nervous
disorders. One of my friends, who put himself under his care in
Philadelphia, had as sole prescription an invitation to dine with
Mitchell two or three times a week. Mitchell had an inexhaustible
fund of amusing stories, with which he entertained his friends. He
is associated in my mind in this respect with Dr. Joseph Bell, of
Edinburgh, although Bell was a man of more refinement than Mitchell,
and his stories were shorter and more subtle than Mitchell's and were
better told. In the Savile also at this period I met Brander Matthews,
who lectured upon Dramatic Literature at Columbia University,
New York. Matthews had a curious hobby in the collection of stories
about conjurers. Of Houdin, the French conjurer, for example, he
had a number, which he afterwards published. Among the Americans whom I met at the Savile was Hennessy, a painter of note in
his time, who had been long resident in London. I met also otherwise Melville Dewey, an American artist whose landscapes have
a quiet charm.

[1] Sir Thomas Raleigh, Legal Member of the Indian Council, and his brother
Sir Walter, Professor of English Literature at Oxford.
[2] Afterwards in the Treasury and private secretary to Sir Henry Campbell-
Bannerman.

Sargent I never met, but Morris told me a story which reminds me of him. An American artist had lived for a time in Gloucestershire, in the neighbourhood of Morris's place, Kelmscott Manor. He was in the habit of riding about the country, and on one occasion took a short cut over a field of cabbages, the property of a farmer. The farmer met him and upbraided him sharply for trampling down his vegetables. I had been guilty of an exploit of this kind as a boy; but I took my scolding meekly, turned my horse about, picked my way carefully to the road again and nothing more came of it. The artist pursued the same course so far; but during the night he reflected that a free-born American should not have so meekly submitted to the reprimand of a British farmer, who had, no doubt, feudal ideas about the sanctity of land and sordid ideas about the value of cabbages. The artist determined that the farmer should be punished and that these offensive notions should be whipped out of him. Early in the morning, the artist took a stout riding-crop and rode over to interview the farmer. When he saw him he proceeded to administer a horse-whipping. The farmer, taken at disadvantage, suffered this; but within a couple of days the artist received a summons to attend the local court. The magistrate heard the evidence and sentenced the artist to pay a substantial fine or go to jail, saying that had the artist thrashed the farmer when he was stopped by him, he should have fined him only a guinea, on the ground that the assault was an impulsive action; but the deliberation overnight put the affair on another footing. It would not be fair, on the foundation of this story, to base a criticism of those works of art by which Sargent has made himself famous, yet I avow that his "Carmencita" in the Luxembourg and his "Judgment" in the Boston Public Library have both given me the impression of deliberate violence. They are, indeed, so aggressive that the paint might have been imposed by blows of a horse-whip. Less strident are his panels of the Prophets, also in Boston, but these have no relation whatever to mural decoration, and their use for this purpose seems grotesquely inappropriate. Some day perhaps they will be replaced by designs more in keeping with those of Puvis de Chavannes on the same staircase, and removed to a gallery of paintings where they might be exhibited to greater advantage. Sargent's portrait of Henry Irving, exhibited, I think, in the Royal Academy in 1889, might fairly be described as a caricature. It emphasises the weak points in Irving's character with great cleverness but without sympathy. One of Sargent's most important works, the portraits of four Johns Hopkins

Professors of Medicine and Surgery—Welch, Kelly, Halstead and
Osler [1] (later of Oxford)—challenges comparison with Rembrandt's
"Five Stallmeisters" and his "Anatomist." Beside these colossal
achievements Sargent's huge canvas looks stodgy, as if the strength
of the painter were of an order not quite equal to such a task.

In 1888 and 1889 the art of painting in Great Britain experienced
a kind of crisis. The Pre-Raphaelite movement had died with Rossetti.
Its interest and influence had been rather in topic than in technique.
When Whistler in jest advised Rossetti to take a painting out of its
frame and put in a sonnet, he uttered a pregnant criticism of the
Pre-Raphaelites, for they were rather men of letters than painters.
It may be that Whistler was no better draughtsman than Rossetti,
but he knew it and Rossetti did not. Whistler indeed had a fine
appreciation of line, although he probably never produced anything
of which he himself fully approved. Whistler's persiflage concealed a
real modesty and amiability. Although I have seen Whistler, I never
knew him; but young etchers of that time have told me of his extraordinary kindness and the helpfulness of his criticism. The affair
of the British Artists occurred at that moment, and Whistler shook
the dust of England off his feet and went to Paris. He thought that
British art had drifted into a *cul-de-sac*. Millais, who had been a
Pre-Raphaelite, had become a fashionable painter; Leighton, who
was an admirable draughtsman, painted sumptuous illustrations of
classical literature; Cecil Lawson, who was perhaps the greatest
English landscape painter of any time, had died, and no one of equal
importance had succeeded him. Traditional technique had reached
a high point. The moment was the end of an age. Acres of canvas
were delivered at the doors of the Royal Academy every year and
thousands of square yards were hung on its walls; yet it was evident
that the art of painting had become stagnant, so stagnant that the
slender wave of the New English Art Club appeared as if it were the
herald of a storm. The variety of method adopted by the new men
directed attention to technique, and even the experiments of the
Square Brush and other groups gave a wholesome stimulus. It was
evident that in the world of art there was still territory to be marked
"unexplored." Beside the extravagances of the cubists, and the
futurists of later days, the experiments of the New English Art Club
and other groups seem commonplace indeed; but they were new in
their time. To the best of my recollection, the first exhibition of the
New English Art Club was held in a house in Kensington belonging

[1] Sir William Osler.

to Dr. Wyld. I was taken to see it by Norman Wyld, his nephew, immediately after it was opened. There was, after all, nothing very startling; but it was interesting, because it disclosed the existence of a compact group of young painters who had had the courage to express themselves as they wanted and to defy the *dii majores* of the Academy. The early Christians had again launched themselves against the pagans, secure as these were with Olympus behind them. I soon made the acquaintance of some of the new painters. Francis Bate was secretary of the club. One day he was descending the steps of the National Gallery while Ruskin was mounting them. Struck by Bate's resemblance in his ample auburn hair and features, Ruskin muttered as he passed him, "Raphael." Of the group of new men belonging to the New English Art Club and otherwise I was particularly attracted by the work as well as by the personality of H. H. La Thangue and of George Clausen. There was something quite new and powerful in their painting—in the former a vivid sense of light and colour, and in the latter a decisive draughtsmanship which promised great things for the future, a promise which has not remained in either case unredeemed.

At that time the Scotsmen of the new school had not migrated to London; Scotland was represented there by David Murray, who belonged to the conventional landscapists, by Allan, who was a competent though not distinguished water-colour painter, and by Alfred East. I knew all of these, but East was the only one who interested me. He had left Glasgow before the new movement there began, and he had not been touched by it. There was nothing aggressively new about him, but he was a good landscape painter. In 1888 he had just returned from Japan. I think he was the first of the British artists to go there. He painted a number of landscapes in Japan, and on his return exhibited them in London. I reproduced a few of them in the *Scottish Art Review*. Many of them were very clever, those in which he sought to give the spirit of the Japanese landscape in the Japanese manner were conspicuously so, although I could not find any artistic value in imitation. East had a rather wider interest in and knowledge of the world than most of the artists of his time in London, and I liked him on that account.

Outside of the classical group at the Royal Academy, detached from any of the newly-arising schools, essentially individual in his character and his art, was John M. Swan. Swan was both sculptor and painter. He haunted the Zoological Gardens in Regent's Park, and studied assiduously the forms, gait and character especially of lions. He was familiar with the works of the great masters of the past who chose to turn their art to the same account. One day I was going into the British Museum; I met Swan coming out. I greeted him:

James Mavor. "Oh! ho! I know where you've been."

John M. Swan. "Well, where?"

James Mavor. "You've been spending an hour over 'The Hunt of Nasur-bani-pal.'"

John M. Swan. "Right you are. It is the greatest sculpture in the world."

This stupendous relief was one of the sources of Swan's inspiration. Swan's water-colours are very fine, but they are almost monochromes. He was not a colourist. He knew this very well and laboured over some of his more vivid oil paintings without ever getting them quite right. When he painted a lion, he modelled it beforehand and to some extent painted from the model. Thus, perhaps, he got into the way of looking at things as if they were grey in nature. Yet the landscapes in which he placed his animals were finely conceived, although they are sombre. So absorbed was he in his work, especially in the earlier days of his career, that it was told of him that during the months of July and August 1870 he worked in his studio in London without knowing that the French and the Prussians were at war. Swan was from the south of Ireland. He had none of the traditional spirit of the Gascons, and was as far removed as possible from Tartarin of Tarascon, yet he looked like a Gascon. He had a great shock of black hair and a powerful physique. Swan had a good knowledge of Japanese bronzes and had made a small but very fine collection. Like Rodin, Swan's great strength lay in his powers as a draughtsman. He drew copiously, with so decisive and vigorous a line that it seemed as inevitable as fate—that "thus and not otherwise," but always just as it was, it should and must be drawn. I have said that Swan was not a colourist. I do not think he was; but by this I do not mean that he was without appreciation of colour. He liked finely-coloured fabrics and knew much about colour; but in his painting his mind seemed to concentrate itself upon structure and upon rendering the flexure of the skin of his animals in such a way as to express the muscles and bones. He was not so concerned with colour, which in the case of the animals he chose to depict was rarely vivid. He stood alone in his time as a painter of lions.

Another animal painter of less note whom I knew at this time was Wolff. He was a German who had lived in London for many years.

While not a great artist, he had a very intimate knowledge of the habits of certain animals and a facility in making characteristic drawings. He surrounded himself with birds and other creatures set up on the walls of his studio, and lived in a rather eccentric manner.

Among my friends in London of these years, apart from any of the groups whom I have mentioned, was Gilbert Coleridge. Coleridge was Master in Chambers. He had a good knowledge of art and took a genuine interest in the newer movements. I remember his telling me a characteristic story about his grand-uncle. Hartley Coleridge had, as is well known, given rise to some anxiety on the part of his family, and it was resolved to hold over him a family council. On leaving the assembly, Stephen Coleridge was asked by a friend, "Well, what did you do about Hartley?"

Stephen Coleridge. "The fact is we never got to Hartley; Samuel began to talk philosophy and so we never reached him."

Friend. "Why did you not stop Samuel's discourse?"

Stephen Coleridge. "We could not. It was so splendid."

In Gilbert Coleridge's house he had some beautiful pencil drawings —portraits of various members of the family, by his grandmother, the wife of John Duke, brother of Samuel Taylor Coleridge.

I have given in this chapter a brief sketch of highly-cultivated circles composed of people almost all of whom have made important contributions to letters, philosophy, science, or art. I shall now try to sketch another circle—precisely of an opposite order, in which none of these pursuits have any place—in which, if they were found, they would be grotesquely misplaced.

In the East End of London there is a street running parallel to the canal known as the Limehouse Cut, distant from it about one hundred yards. From this street a series of *culs-de-sac* extend to the wall which encloses the bank of the Cut. These streets, during the period of which I am writing, were occupied exclusively by costermongers. Costermongers form a large and varied group, containing within it numerous smaller groups possessing characters sharply distinguishing them from each other. The main street in question ran north and south. In its northerly part at this point the street running to the Cut was occupied by well-to-do costers. Each family was the owner of the house occupied by it as well as of the barrows and donkeys used by its members in their business. On Sundays the amusement of the street was the aristocratic sport of cock-fighting. This sport was against the law; but no officer of the law ever ventured

into the street. Had any attempt been made to put a stop to the
traditional sport, all evidence of it would have been obliterated long
before the police made their appearance. The next street was occupied
by an inferior stratum of coster society. Here the costers rented their
houses; they possessed the barrows and donkeys they used. Here
also were Sunday sports. The means of this community did not permit
them to keep the expensive game birds which gave gladiatorial shows
in the adjoining street, they contented themselves with trials of
skill and strength between dogs—principally bull-terriers, these being
less expensive than game birds and less troublesome to take care of.

The next street was occupied by another group, inferior in means
to the last mentioned. The members of this group rented the houses
or portions of houses they lived in and they also hired the donkeys
they used, though they owned the barrows. They were unable to
afford either birds or dogs for the satisfaction of their appetite for
exhibitions of pugnacity, and therefore they were obliged to dispense
with the standing armies enjoyed by their neighbours. Yet they had
to fight, and so they fought one another.

Finally, the least prosperous of this series of communities resided
in a street parallel to the others, but occupied by a group of rather
dilapidated houses inhabited by costers who paid rent for them and
who hired barrows as well as donkeys. To engage in fights serious
enough to amuse the fastidious taste of a neighbourhood accustomed
to such displays is not an inexpensive form of Sunday amusement.
A black eye or a split ear, not to speak of occasional more severe
injury, may deprive a man of his earning power for several days;
therefore a community which habitually engages in this form of
sport must have some reserves. The group occupying the last street
in the series had no reserves; its members could not fight either
vicariously or personally; but they could compete otherwise—they
simply ran races with one another—the least costly, and on the whole
the most healthy of the varied sports in the neighbourhood.

Among these groups living in adjoining streets there were very
slender social relations. They did not customarily entertain one
another. They were not interested in one another's sports. They did
not either compete or co-operate in business. They rarely intermarried.
Each street was inclined to endogamy. Exogamy, when it did
occur, generally meant marriage altogether outside the series of
social groups.

The members of these circles, associated locally but socially separated by family tradition and by difference in economical resources,

were not wage slaves; they called no man master. They were, in fact, free and independent, and they made their livelihood by the ancient method of retail trading, employing their own slender capital and their own means of transport. Saving for supplies of goods they were independent. They did not customarily either give or take credit, and they hoarded their reserve cash rather than deposit it in any bank or invest it in securities. The Church never troubled them, they were aloof even from the Salvation Army, and the State represented by the police let them alone so long as they made no unusual disturbance within their own boundaries. These people were undoubtedly of mixed racial origin, although their general practice of endogamy prevented them from mingling freely with their neighbours. They may have had a generous amount of Spanish blood. Yet their characteristics were those of the English described with the vivacious and not altogether favourable pen of Froissart. In their paganism, their combativeness, their love of free society, their fondness for sports involving the conflict or the death of animals, their dislike of official and ecclesiastical interference, their endogamy, their ignorance of letters, of art, of science and of philosophy, their placid toleration of what to others would be material discomfort, their indifference to surroundings, their lofty contempt of their neighbours and their rigid interior social classification, they resembled a large group of aristocratic society in England that derived precisely this kind of culture from precisely the same post-mediæval period.

I think it was in 1889 that I paid a visit to a certain English country house. The original building had been built by Vanbrugh in the time of Queen Anne, but the greater part of it had long ago been destroyed by fire and it had never been re-erected. The family lived in what had been the servants' quarters. There were gathered those pieces of furniture and those pictures and other belongings that had been saved from the fire. The passages were littered with hunting crops and saddlery. Everywhere was disorder and everywhere were evidences of a free and careless life, evidently agreeable to the occupants, who bore a name once great in the history of the country. In all essential particulars their habits and customs were those of the costermongers, though they rode to hounds instead of riding on a barrow behind a donkey. Both made it a point to attend the Derby.

The groups I have described were by no means the only coster groups in London. There were many others. One evening I was prowling about East London, accompanied by a School Board officer, whom I often took as guide because he had an unrivalled knowledge of the people of the region. Sometimes, even when the streets were crowded, he was saluted by nearly everyone who passed us. His name was Kerrigan. On this evening we came to a street—a *cul-de-sac*—but not one of the series above mentioned, although it was also in Limehouse. This street was inhabited exclusively by costers dealing in fish. In the early morning they went to Billingsgate Market for their supplies, and they vended these in their accustomed routes. One of the families living in this street had numerous members and connections, the main branch of it being headed by an old man who was reputed to be well off. When we reached the street we discovered that every window in it was broken, and there lay scattered on the pavement the evidences of recent struggle. We went, indeed, to see a battle-field. On the previous morning the engagement had taken place, and everything was now peaceful and wrecked. The old coster discovered one day that during his absence his house had been entered and his money had been stolen. I think the amount was about one thousand four hundred pounds. He suspected strongly one of his neighbours, a relative, who lived directly opposite his house. The old coster had ventilated his suspicions, and soon the street was aware of them. Just before daybreak on the morning of the day before that of our visit, the accused man, with a small number of his friends, awaited, at the door of the old coster, the exit of the owner, whose custom it was to go to market at that hour. They were armed with pokers and other instruments of "cold iron" suitable for offensive purposes. When the old man appeared he was assailed. He raised an outcry, and he was soon joined by members of his family, who rushed to his assistance armed with what weapons were available. The sound of fighting soon roused the street; from every door there poured partisans of one side or the other in the quarrel. Men and women equally engaged in the struggle, which soon developed into a formidable battle. Missiles flew through the air, and everything breakable by them was broken. The partisans must have been almost equally divided, for the struggle continued with varying fortune for hours. It was not a struggle for territory, it was an affair of blood. Early in the morning the police appeared at the end of the street, but their numbers were not sufficiently numerous to enable them to enter. Had they done so, they would merely have drawn upon themselves the fury of the angry combatants, who would have united to defeat them and then fought out their own quarrel afterwards. It was expedient to permit the battle to reach a stage when the combatants were beginning to be exhausted and then to intervene in force. This stratagem was adopted. About two hundred policemen were mobilised and towards eleven o'clock in the forenoon, after the battle had been waging for six or seven hours, they succeeded in clearing the street and in driving the combatants into their houses.

Froissart was right. The English are a quarrelsome people, and they sometimes fight for the mere joy of fighting.

One night, after a ·long prowl with my friend Kerrigan in the underworld of the East End—in thieves' dens and cellars in which were lying on straw the most wretched of man- and woman-kind, and past opium dens—a painful and terrible journey—we had gone to the Old Stairs at Wapping, and to some other places which Dickens has made familiar. Midnight found us on our way home, when at a street corner we met Father Wainwright, who was out on some mission of mercy. We stopped to speak to him for a few minutes, when we suddenly became aware of a man furtively stealing along in the shadow of the houses. He looked warily in our direction; but seemed satisfied that we meant no harm, although he realised that we saw him. He stole past us and disappeared. Father Wainwright said, "I know that man. He has committed a murder and he is hiding from the police. I am trying to persuade him to give himself up. If he does so and confesses he may escape a death sentence. If he does not give himself up he must ultimately be caught, and then there will be little hope for him. Poor fellow, he is not such a bad sort."

St. Peter's, Wapping, under Father MacConnachie and later under Father Wainwright, with their devoted adherents, was rendering immense service to the people of that region.

I had met General Booth several times; on one occasion, for some days together, we were visiting a mutual friend. It is difficult to give a just account of the remarkable personality of General Booth. His aspect, as well as his manners and habits, were distinctly Hebraic. I was enormously impressed by his power over men. There is no doubt in my mind that he thoroughly enjoyed the exercise of that power. His administration of the Salvation Army was the administration of an autocrat; and incidents of autocratic rule were not wanting. One of his commissioners had acted as my guide in tours of night shelters and other Salvation Army institutions in London. After our tours were finished he asked me to write a letter to the effect that I had appreciated his attentions. I wrote as he desired and handed the letter to General Booth, re-enforcing its terms by word of mouth, as I supposed that this course would best serve the interests of my friend the commissioner. He waylaid me when I left the General and asked for the letter. I told him what I had done. He asked where the General had put the letter. I told him that the General had put it in a drawer in his writing-table. "That is the end of it," he said; "it will never be seen again. You have no idea how we are surrounded by ambitious people who are seeking every opportunity to advance themselves." As the man had really been attentive to me, I wrote a copy of my letter to the General and handed it to the commissioner. This incident suggested that the Salvation Army was by no means free from the personal intrigues common in other religious and political organisations. Even the Apostles quarrelled with one another over preferment. The autocracy of the General rendered the Army peculiarly liable to incidents of this kind. I found General Booth very businesslike and very hard. I had become aware that during a strike of brickmakers in the London district the Hadleigh Colony had supplied bricks to contractors who were inconvenienced by the strike, and had thus entered the field as strike-breakers. I mentioned this to General Booth, and pointed out to him that the Salvation Army might be very fairly criticised for using labour subsidised by funds subscribed for charitable purposes in such a way as to contribute to the breaking-up of a strike, whether the strike were justifiable or not. The General said, "I have nothing to do with that. I am a brickmaker; and whoever wants my bricks and will pay for them can have them."

I visited Hadleigh in 1892 and submitted a report upon it to the Glasgow Social Union. The impression it made upon me was not wholly favourable. It seemed to me an extremely expensive form of poor relief. The idea of setting unemployed on remunerative labour was undoubtedly attractive, but organisation of this labour at Hadleigh was so expensive that the enterprise was far from remunerative. It appeared to me that the work was largely done by paid workmen, for whom the colonists fetched and carried. When I was there a comparatively small number of paid workmen were employed, but this number had to be greatly increased. It became very evident that there must be some system by means of which unemployed who were capable of producing sufficient to maintain themselves must be separated from unemployed who were not, otherwise there would be a great waste of material as well as of supervision. Later this view impressed itself upon the whole system of dealing with unemployment with beneficial results. I cannot say that the Hadleigh experiment had any but negative value in this development.

I spent some time in examining night shelters of the Salvation Army in London in the same year. These shelters contributed to ameliorate a situation which had become desperate for a large number of people, but I am unable to regard them as desirable institutions in any serious sense. They offered food and shelter at a minimum of cost, but they tended to perpetuate the need for their subsidised provision.

CHAPTER XIX

HOLIDAYING IN ICELAND AND IN THE WEST HIGHLANDS IN 1890-91

I.—ICELAND

So hidden was that country, and few men sailed its sea,
And none came o'er its mountains of men-folks company.
But fair-fruited, many-peopled, it lies a goodly strip,
'Twixt the mountains cloudy-headed and the sea-flood's surging lip;
And a perilous flood is its ocean, and its mountains, who shall tell
What things in their dales deserted and their wind-swept heaths may dwell?
WILLIAM MORRIS, *The Story of Sigurd the Volsung* (1876).

ICELAND offers a limited but vividly interesting field to students of many sciences. The geologist, especially the specialist in volcanoes, the zoologist, especially the ichthyologist and the ornithologist, and the botanist, especially the specialist in Alpine flora, may find ample material for study. Nor are the interests of the island confined to those of the natural sciences. The student of comparative literature cannot afford to neglect Icelandic literature, still less can the student of economic history, of social development or of social psychology. Apart from science and literature, Iceland is a good holiday ground. It is remote from the rest of the world, in spite of its easy accessibility. Until the installation of wireless telegraphy, it was even immune from immediate contact with the mainland of Europe. The manners of its people are unspoilt by industrial prosperity, its air has the characteristic piquancy of the hyperborean atmosphere, its scenery is varied and sometimes very beautiful.

Several of my friends, William Morris, James Bryce and others, had made pilgrimages to Iceland, and in 1890 I determined to follow their example. My brother Sam and I sailed from Leith in the last week of June. There were few passengers; Dr. Anderson of York, an enthusiast in volcanoes, Dr. Johnstone of Naples, who had made some studies in the same subject, a rather boisterous person who was a farmer in one of the Midland counties, a son of one of the partners in the firm of Vickers at Sheffield, and a young man from Birmingham are all I remember. Our cargo consisted mainly of flour, coal, candles,

271

coffee, sugar and miscellaneous groceries, with some cotton and other textiles. Our fellow-passengers were not interesting, and the voyage was dull. The only amusement was afforded by the conduct of one of them who, under the influence of sea-sickness, made in loud wails a detailed confession of his wicked life. Eventually, in order to relieve the passengers of what was becoming a nuisance, the captain put him to sleep with a heavy overdose of champagne drawn from the ship's medical comforts. We steamed up the east coast of Scotland, rounded Rattray Head and traversed the Moray Firth, whose waters and coast had been very familiar to me from my early years. Then we made for the Pentland Firth. The tide flows through this comparatively narrow strait with tremendous force. When the tide is flowing in one direction and the wind is blowing in the opposite, the seas are perhaps more "choppy" than may be experienced anywhere else in the world excepting in the Bay of Fundy. The Pentland Firth is indeed one of the most turbulent of waterways, and a small vessel may be knocked about in it even when there is no unusual gale. This was our experience then as it was my experience on every occasion when I have sailed in these waters.

We lost sight of Dunnet Head on the evening of the second day out from Leith, and on the evening of the fourth we sighted the smoking peak of Hecla. Beyond Hecla, as night wore on, we saw away to the west, lit up by the sun now very low on the horizon, for the hour was about eleven, the white cone of Snaefell. This snow-covered mountain appeared isolated in the ocean, wholly detached from other land. Since the lower slopes were below the horizon, the pure white aspect of the mountain far out at sea in the fading light of the northern summer evening gave the impression of a phantom island. We found that it was ninety miles away. The south coast of Iceland is curiously composed of long narrow spits of lava rock or lava sand, stretching parallel to the main line of the coast and separated from it by lagoons. There was no sign of life excepting the blowing of a school of great whales which passed eastward between us and the land in full cry after fish. We ran close to the Westmanoë, and saw the sheep on the high table-tops of some of the group. These sheep are hoisted to their elevated pastures on the small plateaux in early summer, and are brought down to less exposed places on other islands when winter comes. We saw the houses of the few fishermen who occupy the small group of islands, but we did not stop. Like all such places, the Westmanoë are rich in legends. Here, it is said, came the Irish seafaring traders when, in the Middle Ages, there was traffic between Iceland and Ireland. The principal landing-place of these traders was appropriately called Patriksfiord on the mainland of Iceland due north of Westmanoë; but the Westmanoë group, otherwise unoccupied, presented a secure natural haven. Here, legend has it, there came four Irishmen in their ship. They brought with them four women ravished from their former husbands. They remained undiscovered for a long time; but eventually the four deserted spouses fitted out an expedition, sailed into the northern seas, and in a voyage like the voyage of Maeldun hunted for and found their wives and their abductors. A fierce battle was fought on the strand of one of the Westmanoë, the ravishers were killed, and the lost wives were brought back to their native country.

In the early morning we witnessed the gradual linking up of the snowy summit of Snaefell with the darker line of the coast, passed the recently disrupted rocks at Reykjanes, and then rounded the point into the harbour of Reykjavik. The contour of the hills round the bay is very fine, but the absence of trees leaves the landscape naked. Reykjavik, in spite of its simplicity, has somewhat of the air of a metropolis. It has a Government House, in which the Danish Governor of Iceland resided, three newspaper offices, at least two publishing houses, and a Latin school. The city, which at that time (1890) numbered about three thousand inhabitants, had the reputation among the country folk of sharing with other metropolitan centres in luxury and gaiety, as well as of offering to the provincial youths who were sent there for their education temptations from which they were exempt in their remote and austere homes in the Icelandic valleys.

The children of the little town came to a hall to which we were invited and sang for us "God Save the King," "Rule, Britannia," and other English songs. Readers of *High Latitudes* will remember the amusing speech delivered in Latin by Lord Dufferin on his reception at Reykjavik. I ventured jocularly to allude to this incident in conversation with one of the leading inhabitants; but he evidently did not appreciate the humour of Lord Dufferin, and gave me to understand that he thought the speech was not in the best taste.

I paid a visit to the publishing houses and bought some Icelandic books. When the parcel reached the hotel, I found that my purchases had been supplemented by gifts, civilly inscribed, from the publisher, who was also an author. Among the books were translations of Shakespeare into Icelandic and some volumes of poetry by living Icelandic poets.

I noticed in the streets of Reykjavik one or two copies of a large

I—S

poster advertising Stanley's *Darkest Africa*, which had recently been published, and I found everywhere evidences of keen interest in the affairs of the world.

I made at Reykjavik intimate acquaintance with the Icelandic pony. This extraordinary little horse, for it is rather inaccurately called a pony in England, is probably a diminutive Arab. I was told some years ago by Professor Cossar Ewart of Edinburgh, who is a mighty expert in the subject, that there are four species of Icelandic horses. I cannot discriminate these, but I found much individual variation. Some of the animals have the fine head and slender limbs of the typical Arabian breed, and some of them are uncouth and common-looking as if they came of less aristocratic lineage. Some of them are extremely clever, and some of them are extremely stupid. At Reykjavik and also in the north I found, as a rule, that they were skilful in detecting unsafe ground and very cunning in fording rivers. One day after a long ride, for the most part upon rather rough lava, I came upon a smooth sward of velvety green grass, and thought that this would be pleasant to canter over. My horse had different views and refused absolutely to set foot upon the sward. I dismounted, and looked more closely at the turf. Placing my foot carefully upon the margin of it, I found it easy to set the surface in billowy motion for some distance; and then I realised that the thin turf covered a wide expanse of mud into which both my horse and myself must have inevitably sunk had we ventured upon it. I came to the conclusion that my horse was wiser and more experienced than I was, and that I had better trust him in the future.

Most of the tourists who go to Iceland ride to the place where the Althing, or Icelandic Parliament, holds its biennial meetings, and at the same time visit the geysers. We decided to omit this excursion, much as I should have liked to accomplish it, and instead to go on in the ship to the northern fiords and to make a riding excursion in the north. After a few days' riding about Reykjavik, including a visit to neighbouring villages where we found fish curing and fish drying going on vigorously, we boarded our ship and sailed on our northern voyage. We regretted not to be able to enter Isafiord, but the superb views of the North Cape and of the great Dranga glacier in perfect conditions of weather afforded full compensation.

Denmark Straits, which separate Iceland from the ice-bound coast of Greenland, were like a sea of glass. These straits are only one hundred and eighty miles wide, and it is easy to imagine the hardy Norsemen either making their way across them by intention or involuntarily submitting to drifting, propelled by the wind and the currents. They told us in Iceland of the visit of Columbus, who had learned of the finding of Vineland, and desired to know if the Icelanders had any details of the voyages which might be of use to him. The saga of Eric the Red, meagre as it is, and Grœnlandingathattr in the *Flate-yarbok* were probably unknown to Columbus, for their importance was really first demonstrated by Thormond Torfæus in his *Vinlandia*, published in Latin in 1705. It is certain, however, that Columbus became aware of the tradition that the Norsemen had sailed to the west of Iceland and had found land, and that he desired to know more about the discoveries.[1] The subject has been from time to time investigated by Danish scholars, who have indicated the place of landing variously from Cape Cod in Massachusetts northwards.[2]

The North Cape of Iceland is a bold promontory at the extreme north-western angle of the island. Its precipitous face is white, not with snow, which could not lie upon it, but with the guano of the sea-fowl which rest upon it in countless numbers. These birds dived almost under the bows of the steamer and circled round it in the air. Eastwards from the North Cape there extends the Dranga glacier, sending its ice foot into the sea, and shedding miniature icebergs into it from time to time. We coasted along the northern shore until we came to the wide arm of the sea, the Hona Floi. This we entered, and towards the round head of it arrived at the mouth of the Blonda or White River. This river, white with the mud of the glaciers brought down from the distant mountains in which it has its source, colours the waters of the inlet to a distance varying with the tide. Our vessel dropped anchor off the mouth of the river and we rowed ashore. About the point where the milky stream meets the darker waters of the sea our boat was surrounded by seals, who bobbed their cat-like heads out of the water and examined us inquisitively, as if they regarded us as intruders upon a domain over which they claim exclusive jurisdiction. I suppose that the Icelanders do occasionally

[1] Adam of Bremen had in the eleventh century spoken of the discovery of previously unknown countries to the south and west of Iceland, and Italian writers in the Middle Ages also took notice of such discovery. See the monumental work of Fridtjof Nansen, *In Northern Mists* (London, 1911), vol. i. *passim.*

[2] The most recent and the most interesting of these researches has been made by Professor N. P. Steensby of Copenhagen. He has given an account of his investigations in *The Norsemen's Route from Greenland to Vineland* (Kjøbenhavn, 1918); reprinted with alterations from *Meddelelser om Gronland* (Kjøbenhavn, 1917). He proposes to demonstrate that the Vineland of Eric's saga was in the neighbourhood of the site of the village of St. Thomas on the south shore of the St. Lawrence, about seventy miles below the city of Quebec.

kill them, because I have seen sealskin tobacco pouches and the like in Iceland, but as a rule the Icelanders have no liking for killing anything; their laws against killing birds, *e.g.*, are particularly stringent. The seals evidently felt secure against attack, and their attentions were almost impudent. We landed upon a spit of black sand—the triturated lava which forms the banks and the bed of the milky river. Here our vessel discharged part of her cargo. It was piled upon the sand out of the reach of the tide, to be taken away by the farmer customers who came down from their valleys for the purpose. Here also we found the horses we had engaged some time before, waiting to carry us into the interior. We formed a respectable cavalcade. In addition to the purchasing agent of the steamship company, who intended to buy ponies in the pony market of Vithimyri, we had a member of the Icelandic Parliament, one of the passengers who desired to join us, and there were also my brother and myself, as well as the owner of the horses, who was to accompany us to look after them and to bring them back when our use for them had ceased. Each rider had two horses. We rode one in the morning and the other in the afternoon. There were, in addition, horses for the baggage, including tin chests containing about £2,000 in gold for the purpose of paying for the horses proposed to be bought, with spare horses for these burdens. In all we had fourteen horses.

Late in the forenoon we cantered off up the valley of the Blonda—known as the Langadale, and mentioned in several of the sagas. We rode steadily on all day, the only signs of life we saw were in the flights of sea-swallows which came so near us that we could have struck them with our riding-whips had we been expert enough. The birds were clearly as resentful of trespass as the seals were in their element. Towards evening, although in the long northern day it was not dark, we reached a farm-house where we were to spend the night. When we rode up to the door, we waited, according to Icelandic etiquette, for the appearance of our host, who had, of course, no knowledge of our intention to encroach upon his hospitality. In a few minutes the farmer came, and courteously invited us to dismount. We entered the house. The passage was also the harness-room, and was littered with saddles and bridles. We were shown into the *solar* or parlour to the right of the entrance, and in a few minutes more the wife of the farmer entered, carrying a tray upon which was coffee with its accompaniment of cognac in the exact number of cups necessary for our party. The fact was that the farmer had seen us riding up the valley, had surmised our intention to pay him a visit, since his was the only house for many miles, had counted our number, and had advised his wife accordingly. She had immediately put on coffee beans to roast, had ground them, and placing them in a woollen bag had boiled coffee sufficient and no more than sufficient for the party. When we arrived, the coffee was ready to serve.

The farmer had inherited his land from his ancestors, who had held it since the taking of Iceland in the tenth century. Their names were to be found in the *Landnamabok*. He had never been out of Langadale, yet he spoke English well, had read English books, and he had an intelligent understanding of the things of the external world. His family was growing up, and he felt that one day the time must come when he should send his boy to Reykjavik to the Latin school. He dreaded that moment, because he knew that in the great cities there are many temptations, and that the moral strain upon the country youths who went there was likely to be severe. The farm area in acres was probably about five or six hundred, but the area was not expressed in terms of acres. The customary Icelandic measurement is by the hundred, and the hundred is a measure of annual value and not a measure of area. There is great sense in this, because much of the farm land was covered with perpetual snow, while some of it consisted of hills too high for pasture and too rocky even for the growing of grass. Area, therefore, by itself meant nothing. A hundred meant the value of a hundred yards of *wathmal* or native Icelandic woollen cloth, and its equivalent was a ewe and six sheep. A farm was thus measured by its sheep-bearing capacity. At that moment (in 1890) a sheep was worth about two shillings in English money.

We dined frugally but amply on cold mutton cured in *skir*, or the whey of sheep's milk, and whale-flesh also cured in the same manner. At night we were accommodated in beds made like boxes rather too short for the taller members of our party. After we were comfortably ensconced in these boxes, the farmer's daughter, a buxom damsel of seventeen, came to tuck us in and to see that we were well settled for the night. In the morning before we rose she brought us coffee and cognac. Our horses had been turned loose, and had been wandering in the hills during the night. Some time had to be expended in finding them, and during this time I occupied myself in climbing the hill behind the farm "bye" in order to obtain a view of the valley.

It was a more difficult enterprise than I had counted upon, very steep with an awkward cornice of rock near the top. However, I negotiated it without misadventure, and came down after a climb of

an hour and a half to find the farmer much puzzled to account for
my conduct. He could understand, he said, going up a mountain to
hunt for lost sheep or lost horses, but the idea of going up merely
to see the landscape and then to come down again seemed to him
very eccentric and unreasonable.

Sometime in the forenoon we were able to start. In spite of the
size of our party and of the draughts we made upon his resources,
the farmer could hardly be persuaded to accept any payment. When
we insisted, he charged us at about the rate of two shillings each.
A long ride that day, still up Langadale, brought us to the church and
the horsefold of Vithimyri, where the horses were brought to market.
There were a great many farmers who came in from the surrounding
region with their wives, bringing the horses they wanted to sell. These
horses had been loose on the hills all winter and had made their living
by scraping the snow from the grass with their hoofs. The grass of
Iceland is extraordinarily good. It seems to have been like the horses,
imported, for it bears a strong resemblance to Italian rye grass.
Farmers literally shave the fields, dotted as they are by hummocks
about eighteen inches high. They save every blade they can in order
to provide food for those of their animals that they require to keep
near the house for use in the winter.

Every traveller pays a small local tax for grazing, and grazing-
places at frequent intervals are provided and looked after. The horse
fair was a really fine sight. The young animals, fresh from the hills,
were full of fire and were running about like wild creatures. Our
purchaser bought about two hundred of them. These animals were
driven down to Sautherkrokr on the north coast, shipped on board
the steamer, and taken to Leith. Here they were placed on a farm in
order to recover from the effects of the voyage, and then were subjected to examination. They were paired in respect to size and colour,
broken to harness or for riding, and the best of them sold for these
purposes. Those that turned out not to be suitable for luxurious uses
were sent to the mines, in whose depths they were destined to spend the
remainder of their lives until some mechanical means of locomotion
by electricity or otherwise might be devised.

In course of time we made our way from Vithimyri to Sautherkrokr,
where we found our ship. Sautherkrokr is a pleasant village, occupied
by Danish fish merchants and their employés. It almost touches the
Arctic Circle, and it therefore has the distinction of being one of the
most northerly of permanent human settlements. In the house of
one of the Danish merchants we found an English ivy growing in a

pot, and sending its tendrils upwards to a frieze along which it was trained on each wall of the room—an intelligent piece of decoration.

At Sautherkrokr we met with two incidents in Icelandic life. One was the dispensation *plein air*, literally on a log, of justice by a sheriff on his annual visit to the district. The process of law was brief and simple. Another was a domestic quarrel between an elderly man and a much younger woman to whom he had been "handfasted." That is to say, they had according to agreement lived together for a year on the understanding that if they chose to marry after the expiry of the year they could do so, but marriage was not binding upon either party. The result of this connection, which at that time (1890) was said to be not uncommon in Iceland, was a child. The woman, for some reason, did not want to marry; but she did want to have the custody of her child. The father did not appear to care whether the woman married him or not, but he also wanted the child. The woman came on board our steamer, followed by the man, who continued to demand the child. After the dispute had gone on for some time, the captain, on the eve of our sailing, ordered a couple of sailors to put the man in one of the harbour boats which was just putting off. The next moment the ship was under way. Whether or not the dispute was resumed subsequently I do not know. "Handfasting" under one form or another has been practised in every country in Northern Europe. That it has been widely prevalent, and has been retained for centuries in some places, suggests at least a suitability to certain conditions and to the psychology of certain people.

Near the entrance to the fiord, at the head of which is the village of Sautherkrokr, there is Grimsoë, the island where Grettir the Strong secluded himself. Grimsoë is just inside the Arctic Circle, and is the most northerly part of Iceland and its satellite islands. We called at Seythisfiord, a fishing village at the head of a small but fine fiord, where we had the luxury of getting halibut and other fish direct from the sea into the pot, the only really luxurious method of cooking fish. Hall Caine, in his novel about Iceland, makes a curious mistake regarding Seythisfiord. He speaks of going in a cart from that village to Reykjavik. The thing was impossible; even in 1890 there was no road, and the bridle trails could not be traversed by a cart.

From Seythisfiord we returned to Leith, having a distant and dim view of the Faroes shrouded in fog.

II.—THE WEST HIGHLANDS, 1891

I hear the sea-song of the blood in my heart,
I hear the sea-song of the blood in my ears;
And I am far apart,
And lost in the years.
FIONA MACLEOD (WILLIAM SHARP), *The Divine Adventure* (1900).

These lines of William Sharp are placed here not merely because they express with precision my feelings as I look back upon these now distant occasions when I wandered in the West Highlands, but because my journey there in 1891 followed upon an attack of grippe contracted in London while I was staying with Sharp, and through which I was nursed with the greatest kindness by his wife. The writings of Fiona Macleod, a name under which Sharp chose to mystify the world, are remarkable feats of imagination. Sharp was not really familiar with the atmosphere of the Highlands, yet either from the Celtic strain in his blood or from the sheer force of his genius he reproduced the characteristic flavour of Ossian, and he gave it a touch of modernness which he took care was not discordant. I was recovering slowly from the attack of grippe when my friend, now long dead, George Handasyde Dick, Indian merchant and best of good fellows, came to me and said that his yacht, a yawl of about a hundred tons, lay at Oban, waiting for me to be sufficiently well to make the railway journey from Glasgow. In about a fortnight I was assisted one morning by two sailors from the railway carriage to the captain's gig, and was able feebly to step on board the yacht. So invigorating is the air of the sea and of the West Highlands—not to speak of the nourishing influence of the wine of the country—that the same afternoon, while running up the Sound of Mull, the wind having freshened and brought up a shower, I stepped gaily on deck well equipped in oilskins, and from that moment felt, after weeks of dilapidation, my own man once more.

About fifteen years had elapsed since I had sailed up the sound in the company of John Stuart Blackie and my lifelong friend James R. MacColl, one long dead and the other the master spirit of huge industries in Rhode Island. The company on the yacht was different but congenial—Dick himself, his nephew and Mr. Cornes of London. The latter was head of an important firm in the Chinese and Japanese trades. He had a house in Yokohama, and dealt in the tea of the region round Shizuoka, shipping it from Japan to the United States. In his earlier years he had been on the China coast, in the employment of the great firm of Jardine, Mathieson and Co.

We dropped anchor in the evening in the Bay of Tobermory. This bay is justly celebrated for its beauty. Enthusiasts compare it with the Bay of Naples. The scale is not the same; it may be more fittingly compared with other Highland inlets, and among them it must take a high place. Here one of the ships of the Armada found a haven and a grave. The late Duke of Argyll, better known as the Marquis of Lorne, conceived or supported the idea of searching the bay for the sunken vessel. After much laborious sounding and diving, the hull of the vessel was found and relics of the great adventure were recovered from it. Some of the families of the west end of Mull count among their ancestors Spanish sailors who were in the crew of this or other ships of the Armada lost on the Highland coasts. From Mull we sailed in a leisurely way north towards the Sound of Sleat, passing the islands of Muck and Eigg, and seeing in the distance the forbidding heights of Rum. We ran up Loch Hourn, and having the luxury of a steam tender, we boarded her and went into waters where the yacht could not go. When late in the afternoon we reached again the entrance to Loch Hourn, the whole aspect of the weather in the Sound had changed, black clouds and a driving south-westerly wind were bringing up a storm. We had the choice of returning to the secure harbour of the upper loch or running for Skye and the shelter of one of its ports. Our captain elected the latter course, reefed to the last reef, stowed everything comfortably, left the tender behind to follow us next day, and sailed out beyond the headland. The wisdom of his precautions became evident whenever we came into the Sound. A squall struck us sharply, and every stay seemed to be strained to the last point. We ran across in the night under almost bare poles, and in pitch darkness came under the shelter of Skye into smooth water. The darkness was so impenetrable that it was no easy matter to determine exactly where we were, and it was still more difficult to pick up in the dark off Armadale a mooring to make us safe for the night. Our captain was equal to the occasion, and we rode confidently till the morning.

The day broke fine, and we sailed in gorgeous weather through the narrow straits at Kyleakin into the Inner Sound separating Skye from the mainland. Then past Raasay we sailed into the harbour of Portree, where we remained for several days. On one of these days we drove to Uig on Loch Snizort, on the west coast of Skye. This beautiful place was the scene of a curious episode which shortly before our visit had been brought before the Scots law courts. My friend John Murdoch, the editor of *The Highlander* and an ardent advocate of the crofters during the movement which began in the seventies and continued even after the Crofter Commission of 1886, had published in his newspaper from time to time attacks upon the Laird of Uig, the state of whose crofters was said by Murdoch to be especially bad. The laird died, and he was buried in the churchyard of Uig. This churchyard is situated on the bank of a stream which in spring becomes a turbulent torrent. The enclosure is protected by a stone wall, but on occasion this wall is damaged by the spring freshets. The house of the laird is situated on the bank of the same stream some distance below the church. Shortly after the death of the laird, the melting snows and heavy rains made the stream unusually high and turbulent. The waters undermined the churchyard wall, and made a wide breach in it. Through this breach the waters poured and tore up the earth in the graves. Among these graves was that of the laird, and his recently interred coffin was torn from its resting-place and washed, through the breach in the churchyard wall, down the stream. This was strange enough; but, according to the story published by Murdoch, the further journey of the dead man was stranger still. The stream carried him down and deposited him upon the table in his own dining-room, the rising waters having flooded the house, and the wreckage carried by them having broken the windows. In a region where the people are customarily credulous where supernatural agencies are alleged to be concerned, this startling episode induced inevitably the interpretation that the return of the laird was a judgment upon him for his treatment of the crofters. This interpretation was explicitly made by John Murdoch, who was genuinely infected with the Celtic superstitious habit of mind. He published an article in *The Highlander* describing the event in detail, and saying that the judgment of Heaven was evident. Somehow the idea does not seem to have struck him that the return of the laird might just as well have been interpreted as a judgment upon the crofters. The laird had his own opinion of their conduct during his life and he might have returned to warn them to mend their ways. Had John Murdoch ventured upon this interpretation nothing would have happened, excepting perhaps scepticism among the crofters, who would have found the interpretation little to their liking. Unfortunately John chose the other interpretation, with the consequence that the family of the laird sued him for libel. The case was argued at length, much evidence was called, and the court held that in announcing that the judgment of Heaven had fallen upon the dead laird John Murdoch had libelled him and must therefore pay the costs of the suit. I have forgotten whether or not he was obliged to pay pecuniary damages; but I recall that the suit altogether cost him four hundred pounds. This marked the end of *The Highlander*. John Murdoch afterwards ran for Greenock in the election of 1885 in the interests of the Land Restoration movement. His expenses were paid by two enthusiastic old ladies. In spite of the assistance of Morrison Davidson, who contributed during the campaign a series of lively and humorous articles, Murdoch received only a few votes. There was a legend, and I believe a true one, that from his earliest youth Murdoch had worn the kilt, and that he had never desecrated his legs by clothing them in the trousers of the oppressive Sassenach.

We saw the wall of the graveyard and we saw the house of the laird, but we found no other evidence of the episode.

At Portree in the evening we were serenaded by songsters in a boat, who sang to us across the waters of the harbour "Over the Sea to Skye" and other locally appropriate melodies.

From Portree we made our course northwards to the Gair Loch, landed and drove to Loch Maree, a beautiful inland water. Then we returned, sailing southwards to Oban, having spent three delightful and health-giving weeks among the Scots fiords.

CHAPTER XX

> Came they that kept our England's sea-swept hem,
> And held afar from her the foreign fear.
> After them came
> They who pushed back the ocean of the Unknown
> And fenced some strand of knowledge for our own
> Against the outgoing sea
> Of ebbing mystery;
> And on their banner "Science" blazoned shone.
>
> FRANCIS THOMPSON, *The Victorian Ode* (1913).

THE British Association meeting at Manchester in 1887 coincided with the Manchester Exhibition of that year. Although since then I have been at many meetings of the British Association, I have always looked back upon this one as in many ways the most interesting. There was a great assemblage, not only of British men of science, but also of foreigners. Perhaps the science best represented by the latter was biology. The most important foreign biologists were Weismann of Freiburg and Hubrecht of Utrecht. Weismann came to expound his theory of the continuity of the germ-plasm. He did so in German to a large audience, and Ray Lankester followed with a summary in English. There was some debate, but everyone was more interested in hearing Weismann expound his doctrine in person and in witnessing his dogmatic manner than in criticism of the doctrine itself at that moment. Even in 1887 there were many who refused to regard Weismannism as the final word, and who saw in his ultra-Darwinian statement of the doctrine of evolution a contribution to discussion rather than an unimpugnable contribution to knowledge. Since that day even the word "evolution" has fallen into the background, the fashion of science has changed, and attention is now directed to the chemico-physical processes of life, and to heredity merely in so far as it throws light upon these processes.[1]

Sir William Thomson (not yet Lord Kelvin) was there of course.

[1] A new interest in inheritance of acquired characters, and therefore a revival of Lamarckism, has been introduced by the researches of Professor Pavlov of the University of St. Petersburg.

284

At that time he was sixty-three years of age and in the prime of his amazing activity. I dropped into Section A (the Mathematical and Physical Section) frequently. Not only did he speak on almost every paper, but in general he was able to say that he had touched the special subject of it, in some paper of his own, twenty or thirty years earlier. It was as true of Kelvin in science as it was of Morris in art, that he never touched anything without in some way changing its history.

The popular lecture was given by Sir Robert Ball, who, though not a great man of science, was an accomplished humorist. I recall the dexterity with which he gave a humorous twist to recondite things. Sir Frederick Bramwell, in proposing a vote of thanks, gave an account of his experiences on the switchback railway, which he had apparently seen for the first time at the Manchester Exhibition. Those who remember the enormous bulk of Sir Frederick can imagine the delight of his fellow-passengers, qualified by anxiety lest the railway should break down under the unusual strain.

At Manchester I dined for the first time with the Red Lions, receiving from the Jackals my invitation as a cub. The fun was good; I think it was on that occasion that Harold Dixon, Professor of Chemistry at Owens College, made some amusing chemical demonstrations by way of taking off papers read at the Chemical Section.

The British Association met at Bath in 1888. I stayed with Cedric Chivers, well known as a bookbinder. Chivers had married a friend of our Stranraer days, and he had therefore asked me to stay with him. Among the foreigners was P. J. C. Janssen, who established the observatory on Mont Blanc. Janssen was lame and heavy. Like Campbell, the blind alpinist, he had to be carried up the mountain on a chair by numerous porters. I spent several evenings in his company and found him a copious talker. My old friend John Brown, F.R.S. (of Edenderry), was there, so also were Herbert Foxwell and Henry Sidgwick. The Economic Section was enlivened by a paper read by George Bernard Shaw upon economic history.[1] Like all Shaw's economic writings, the paper was amusing and superficial. The years 1886–88, as may be gathered from other passages in these memoirs, marked the moment when many students of economics, who for the previous ten years had been much influenced by Marx, were beginning to find out the deficiencies of his reasoning and to call in question the particular aspects of the materialistic interpretation of history upon which Marx had founded his predictions regarding the future of society.

[1] The paper is to be found in *The Fabian Essays*.

These years also marked the moment when some of the Fabians, who had affected to be merely students and had disclaimed propaganda, discarded the rôle of students and became avowed Socialists. The difficulty of public adherence to a propaganda is that a much greater amount of courage is required to leave than was required to enter a movement. The demands of an active propaganda permit few opportunities for serious study, and very rapidly there arises a disposition to reject any evidence and every argument that may seem to militate against the interests of the propaganda. The ecclesiastics have no monopoly of intolerance. Indeed, of all groups of men in modern times probably the Marxists are the most bigoted, the most contemptuous of opinions about society and its problems other than their own. At this period Shaw had recently espoused Marxism, and had publicly taken the vows of a convert. To him the new gospel afforded an adequate explanation of the past as well as guidance to the future worthy of implicit obedience. Had Shaw been otherwise than he was he would have been by so much the less effective as a propagandist. He was quite in earnest so far as he went; if he had been able to place Marx more justly in relation to his time, Shaw would not have been so much in earnest. His thesis was, of course, intended to be a destructive criticism of the system of private property, and of all that that implies. Discussion would have been futile. Henry Sidgwick, with his customary urbanity, took the paper seriously; and in his inimitable and delightful stammer said, "Under no circ-c-cumstances c-c-could I c-c-c-consent to a g-g-gospel of p-p-public plunder." I afterwards went off with Shaw and had some tea. He came from London to read his paper and returned by the afternoon train, taking no interest in any other proceedings.

Among the people at the Bath meeting was George Jacob Holyoake, then a very old man. I had some walks with him and tried to draw him out about Robert Owen. I was aware that Owen had looked upon Holyoake as a rather light-weight, and I was interested to find out how Owen appeared to him after the lapse of more than forty years since they were allies. Holyoake spoke of Owen as arbitrary and domineering. I was quite prepared for this, for I knew that at least on one occasion Owen had snubbed Holyoake in public. Holyoake had mellowed into a pleasant old man. He had seen many of his early enthusiasms become widely influential. The Co-operative movement, of which he was the earliest although not the most critical historian, had come into its own; and if the country had not adopted secularism as its credo, it had become so widely secular in its practice that secularist propaganda had almost ceased to have any field to work upon.

The Newcastle meeting of 1889 brought to my mind tender and sad recollections, for I had not been on the Tyne since 1885, when I spent some time at Low Walker with my brother Ivan, who was then manager of the shipbuilding yard of Hawthorne, Leslie and Co., Jarrow.

At this meeting I met old friends like Edgeworth,[1] Foxwell,[2] Cunningham,[3] and Patrick Geddes. Cunningham and Henry Sidgwick had a bout at the Economic Section, in which the old quarrel of economic theory and economic history practically petered out. Sidgwick, in his address as President of the Section at the Aberdeen meeting of 1885, had offered a sharp criticism of the attitude of the economic historian who abjured theory and devoted himself to the task of recorder. He had also attacked vigorously the article on Political Economy in the *Encyclopædia Britannica*, written by Dr. J. K. Ingram.[4] He said what was perfectly true, that to ask Dr. Ingram to write this article was equivalent to asking Professor Huxley to write the article on the Bible. Illuminating as Ingram's article was, his summary dismissal of much of the current discussion of economic doctrine as *contestations steriles* was hardly just, and was, moreover, rather apt to lend support to less well-instructed critics. These were prevalent enough at the time, and they were disposed to regard lightly all laborious efforts to grapple with the difficulties inherent in all economic problems. While Ingram was right in insisting that economic discussion should not degenerate into hair-splitting comparable only with the scholastic disputations of the Middle Ages, he was wrong in so far as he appeared to discourage the application to economic problems of scientific methods universally employed in other sciences. Yet he only, after all, appeared to do so. His central philosophical position—that of a Comtist—would alone have prevented him from really falling into the error of discrediting sound scientific method.

The quarrel had really arisen through the influence of German economic historians, of whom Roscher was the most conspicuous, who went so far as to insist that the formulation of all economic theories should be suspended until a much greater quantity of data had been collected. This was equivalent to saying that data should be collected

[1] Professor of Political Economy at Oxford.
[2] Professor of Political Economy at University College, London, and Fellow of St. John's College, Cambridge.
[3] Rev. Wm. Cunningham, Fellow of Trinity College, Cambridge.
[4] Professor of Greek, Librarian and afterwards Provost of Trinity College, Dublin.

blindly without definite direction or purpose, and that after a long period had elapsed it might be permissible to look at the collection to see what was in it. The facts are that in so far as collections of this kind are made they are useless, and that no historian of the first order can possibly proceed in this manner. Even Roscher was constantly theorising. Given, however, the necessity of dividing labour in a vast field, there are some whose *métier* lies rather in collecting data than in formulating doctrine, and others whose *métier* lies in the latter task. Both are necessary for scientific advance. This was in effect the outcome of the discussion.

There was no great turn-out of economists at the Edinburgh meeting in 1892; but I think Nicholson[1] and Smart[2] were there, and Dr. Ingram came over from Dublin. I had become known to Ingram through Geddes some years earlier, and he had sent me for comment the proofs of his book on Political Economy which grew out of the *Britannica* article above mentioned. Ingram was a man of deep and wide learning. He was not a professed economist; but from his point of view he knew the literature and the development of the subject as thoroughly as anyone. He had been a member of the Young Ireland group of 1848, and had been on friendly terms with William Smith O'Brien and others of that period; and he was the author of the stirring verses, "Who fears to speak of '98?" In later years he changed his opinion on the Irish Question and announced his hostility to Home Rule. *Punch*, in a single line, chaffed him on this *volte-face*: "'Who fears to speak of '98?' Dr. Ingram."

The meeting was attended by an unusually large number of foreign men of science. The Frenchmen came in force. They were naturally attracted in large measure by the remembrance of the ancient close alliance, social, political and dynastic, between Scotland and France. While England was the enemy of Scotland it was convenient for Scotland to have a powerful ally. The influence of French art and the work of French craftsmen of the sixteenth century are still very manifest in Old Edinburgh. Many of the houses in the High Street were built either by French architects or under their influence. The fine diaper ceilings of such houses as Bailie Waddell's, and the mantelpieces of many other houses from Holyrood to the Castle, are clearly of French origin in design, if not actually of French workmanship, for the social association between Scotland and France outlived the

---

[1] J. Shield Nicholson, Professor of Political Economy in the University of Edinburgh.
[2] William Smart, Professor of Political Economy in the University of Glasgow.

conditions that determined the political alliance.   Externally Old Edinburgh is a replica of parts of Old Paris.   The latter has within living memory almost disappeared, while fortunately Old Edinburgh, in its essential features, remains as an architectural monument of unrivalled beauty.

Among the Frenchmen who came to the meeting was M. Edmond Demolins, the author of *A quoi tient la supériorité des Anglo-Saxons* [Paris (c. 1894)]. Indeed, this vivacious book appears to have been the outcome of the visit of the author to Edinburgh.   It is not strange that it was in Edinburgh that M. Demolins derived a favourable impression of England, many foreigners have done the like; but it was strange that of the people with whom he was mostly intimately associated during his visit, and from whom it may be supposed he derived the impressions which constituted the data for his book, few could with fairness be placed in the Anglo-Saxon category.   Most of them were Celts, some of them were Scandinavians, others Norman-French, only one, viz. Dr. Cecil Reddie, about whom, no doubt, a large part of the book is written, can be described as belonging to the stock now regarded with some shyness as Anglo-Saxon.   I do not know why M. Demolins, who had undoubtedly the scientific spirit, employed this expression instead of the simpler and truer word British.   There is no reason why the British people should be called by the names of two tribes who certainly do not constitute the bulk of their parent stocks.   There is at least as much of Norse and Norman blood in the British Islands as there is of either Angle or Saxon, and there is probably quite as much Celtic as any other.   The origin of the word English has lost its original and temporary significance; and British is the truer and sounder expression in an ethnographical sense, because it was upon the already complex British stock that the Saxons and the other comparatively recent invaders and immigrants were grafted, even if we admit a high degree of fertility to the Danes, the Angles, the Saxons, and the eleventh-century Norman-French who bestowed themselves upon us.

The indisputable fact is that, so far as personal and immediate impressions were concerned, M. Demolins derived his knowledge of the Anglo-Saxons whose superiority he so generously acknowledges from Highland Scots like Patrick Geddes and Lowland Scots like Miss Rose Hill Burton, and not from Englishmen, with the already-noticed exception of Dr. Cecil Reddie, of whose admirable and original school at Abbotsholme, in Derbyshire, M. Demolins gives so glowing an account, although he had not seen it.   I must not, however,

I—ʊ

leave the impression that M. Demolins was a loose and inaccurate literary worker.   He was, on the contrary, an investigator most careful and competent, possessing an acute and penetrative intelligence. For many years he continued the systematic social researches begun by Frédéric le Play. I am convinced that to the acute mind of M. Demolins his observation of the idealism and intellectual fecundity of Geddes's genius and the practical sagacity and common sense of Reddie, coupled with his courage in innovation which enabled him to embark confidently upon a revolutionary educational method and to succeed in establishing it, and the opportunities M. Demolins had for studying both of these remarkable men very closely through his intimacy with them, first caused the mental illumination by means of which he understood the English character.   This character he was perfectly right in concluding, although the instances which were the basis of his deduction were few, owed its strength to the compound of idealism and practical sagacity.   It may appear strange that his instance of common sense should be found in an Englishman and his instance of idealism in a Scotsman.   Yet even here his diagnosis will be recognised by the impartial and instructed critic as wholly sound.

Among the foreigners at the Edinburgh meeting was Helmholtz. It was destined that he should not long survive; but his fine physique gave no suggestion then of approaching decay.

One of the customs of the British Association is the delivery of a popular scientific lecture to working-men on one of the evenings during the week of the meeting. At Nottingham, in 1893, the lecture was delivered by Sir Victor Horsley, whose death in Mesopotamia, in the service of the Empire and in the prime of his life, was so great a loss to science.   The rule of the Association is that, unless the hall where the meeting is held is of sufficient dimensions to admit all comers, the members of the Association refrain from attending.   An exception is made in favour of a few members who are specially invited to accompany the lecturer to the platform. The chair is usually taken by the President of the Association.   The President of the Nottingham meeting was Sir Burdon Sanderson, whose sardonic aspect was a mask for a singularly simple-minded and gentle nature. I had often heard, in Oxford, stories of Sir Burdon's absence of mind, of his going to his room to dress for dinner, and instead of dressing going to bed; of his being roused on such an occasion, and of his dressing and going to the drawing-room, where he shook hands with his guests, bidding them good-night instead of accompanying them to the table. I was not, however, prepared for the extraordinary instance of abstraction of which I was a witness. The small group of persons who were invited to accompany the chairman and the lecturer to the platform consisted of Sir Frederick Bramwell, who was the father-in-law of the lecturer, Sir Douglas Galton and myself. The platform was approached by a narrow staircase on one side and by a similar staircase on the other. The chairman, Sir Burdon Sanderson, led the way to the platform; he was followed by Sir Victor Horsley, who in turn was followed by Sir Frederick Bramwell. Sir Douglas Galton and I brought up the rear. When Sir Douglas and I reached the platform we found Sir Victor Horsley and Sir Frederick Bramwell both seated, but the chair appointed for the President was vacant. Although he had mounted the stairs in advance of the others, he was nowhere to be seen. The idea of what had occurred came into both of our minds at the same moment. Sir Douglas and I did not sit down, but immediately crossed the platform and went down the other stair which led to the anteroom we had just left. There we found Sir Burdon calmly putting on his overcoat. He had bowed to the audience and instantly disappeared at the side of the platform opposite to that by which he had entered. Sir Burdon received from us without discomposure the intimation that the lecturer and the audience were waiting for him, returned to the platform and introduced the lecturer. Each of the persons on the platform found on his chair a bundle of anti-vivisectionist literature, which the Secretary of the Anti-Vivisection Society had caused to be placed there as a counteractive to any knowledge that might be imparted by the lecturer and derived by him from those experiments upon animals by means of which he was able to promote, as he did, the science and art of surgery.

During these years (from 1886 till 1893) I attended a number of meetings of scientific and professional associations other than the British Association, e.g., the Institution of Mechanical Engineers at Dublin (I think in 1886), at Sheffield in 1890, the Institution of Naval Architects at Glasgow, and elsewhere. When I was in Dublin in 1886 I unfortunately missed Dr. Ingram, who was from home, but I saw a good deal of Dr. Traill, both of whom were afterwards Provosts of Trinity, and I saw something of Dr. Samuel Haughton. My experiences of Dublin were such as led me to believe that the Irish lived in an atmosphere of moisture. I was never anywhere else called upon to endure quite so copious libations. The history of one afternoon will suffice. After a generous luncheon at Trinity College, Dr. Haughton proposed to me to visit some of the notable places in Dublin.[1] The notable places were all either factories like Guinness's, in which alcoholic stimulants were manufactured, or laboratories in which various alcohols were blended. It was a point of honour to sample the products everywhere. After a couple of hours of amusing conversation and rather trying absorption, I was seized by a reporter of the *Freeman's Journal*, who proposed to show me the town from his point of view. We went to St. Meighen's Church, in whose crypt there are some celebrated coffins in which lie defunct nuns and alleged crusaders. This gruesome expedition required, of course, immediate counter-irritants. Then we went to see the spot in Phœnix Park where, about five years before, Lord Frederick Cavendish and Mr. Burke were murdered. Once more we had to apply remedies. For some hours we passed from some historical place to the nearest place for refreshment, and when dinner-time came I was glad to call a halt. After dinner, which was at the Mansion House, I was asked by a friend in a mysterious manner to follow him. He took me along some passages and eventually arrived at a door. We passed into a small room, where we found a large gentleman in white stockings, plush breeches and a gorgeous coat, sitting at a table with a bottle and glasses before him. This gentleman was Mr. White, the factotum of many successive Mayors of Dublin. The Mayor at that time was Mr. Sexton, but he was in London attending to his parliamentary duties. Mr. White was evidently acting in his absence. He entertained us hospitably with the wine of the country and stories of the Mansion House until an hour in the morning that I have forgotten.

I had arranged to meet Dr. Traill at the railway station to go with him to the Giant's Causeway. The train left at six o'clock in the morning. To achieve it was not easy, but it was done. Dr. Traill's subject was graphic statics, but he was perhaps better known for his graphic stories. During the early part of our long journey he entertained me with an account of his experiences in promoting and constructing the electric railway from Portrush to Bushmills and afterwards on to Giant's Causeway. I am under the impression that this railway was the first electric railway, but I am not certain. There was another similar line in the south of Ireland, and there was an electric railway in the neighbourhood of Berlin. Both of these were constructed about the same time as the Bushmills Railway, and either of them may have antedated it. At all events Ireland, not by

[1] Among his other contributions to knowledge, Dr. Haughton wrote (in 1846) a paper upon the equilibrium of solid and fluid bodies.

any means remarkable for mechanical progress, was one of the pioneers, if not absolutely the pioneer in electrical transport, and its first electric railway was to a distillery.

The current was generated at the Bushmills Falls by means of a turbine, I think of Swiss manufacture, and was conveyed to the car by an iron brush in contact with a side rail. This rail was an ordinary T-iron with the flat side uppermost; it was raised about two and a half feet from the ground on wooden posts erected close to the ditch on one side of the public road. The spaces for cross-roads were simply left vacant, the impetus of the car being sufficient to carry it over the short distance. The overhead trolley had not then been invented. The farmers in the neighbourhood objected to the line on the ground that the raised side rail was dangerous for their horses. A farmer's horse had, indeed, been so unfortunate as to come into contact with the rail and had, according to the farmer, been killed by the current.

The first section of the line, between Portrush and Bushmills, having been successfully constructed by the small company promoted by Dr. Traill, and having secured sufficient traffic to demonstrate its utility, the company decided to apply to Parliament for powers to continue the line from Bushmills to the Giant's Causeway. The farmers opposed this extension and, if I am not mistaken in my recollection, employed Mr. Bidder, who was at that time a celebrated parliamentary counsel, to appear for them. Dr. Traill had as witnesses Sir William Thomson (afterwards Lord Kelvin) and Sir Frederick Bramwell. Dr. Traill gave me an amusing account of his cross-examination before the Parliamentary Committee. Mr. Bidder began by demonstrating the position of the line upon a plan which was hung on a wall of the committee-room. After he had gone on for some time, he turned to put a question to Dr. Traill, who said:

"If, sir, you will be good enough to have the plan of the Wexford waterworks, upon which you have been demonstrating, taken down and the plan of the Bushmills Railway hung up in its place, I will be glad to show you how it runs."

This was point number one against Mr. Bidder. The cross-examination proceeded, and as it drew to a conclusion Mr. Bidder said, "Now, Dr. Traill, you have said that the raised side rail of your line is so placed that it is not dangerous; how do you account for the fact that a horse was recently killed through coming into contact with it?"

Dr. Traill. "My information is that what you have stated is not a fact. The facts are, as I understand, that a very old horse did come into contact with the rail and that the invigorating current he received kept him alive for an hour or more after he otherwise would have been dead."

This was rather audacious; but on general grounds the utility of the line was recognised by the Committee, the Bill was eventually passed, and the extension was constructed. When I was there it had been opened but a short time.

I can testify to a certain amount of probable danger from the side rail, for while Dr. Traill was standing by I carelessly put my umbrella upon it and received a slight though distinct electric shock. I do not now recall the voltage of the current, but it must have been pretty low.

We spent the night at the Causeway, and the morning among the fine columns of basalt of which it is composed. I ran across a local landlord who inveighed against the Home Rulers with much bitterness, spoke of Ulster volunteers, arming, civil war and the like. I thought at the time that he was talking wildly, and that civil war was unlikely to happen even in Ireland. We have seen in this very neighbourhood, thirty-five years later, a condition fairly to be described as one of civil war.

CHAPTER XXI

"SETTING THE POOR ON WORK"

GERMANY IN 1892 AND 1893: FRANCE, BELGIUM AND HOLLAND IN 1893

> Foil'd by our fellow-men, depress'd, outworn,
> We would leave the brutal world to take its way,
> And, *Patience!* *in another life,* we say,
> *The world shall be thrust down, and we up-borne.*
>
> And will not, then, the immortal armies scorn
> The world's poor, routed leavings? or will they,
> Who fail'd under the heat of this life's day,
> Support the fervours of the heavenly morn?
>
> No, no! the energy of life may be
> Kept on after the grave, but not begun;
> And he who flagg'd not in the earthly strife,
>
> From strength to strength advancing—only he,
> His soul well-knit, and all his battles won,
> Mounts, and that hardly, to eternal life.
> MATTHEW ARNOLD, *Immortality* (1868).

IMMEDIATELY after the close of the meeting of the British Association in Edinburgh in August 1892 I sailed from Harwich to Hamburg. I had three companions, Professor Wright, who occupied the Chair of Agriculture in the Glasgow and West of Scotland Technical College, Mr. John Speir, farmer at Neilston, near Glasgow, and Mr. James R. Motion, Inspector of Poor at Glasgow. We were asked to go to Germany for the purpose of visiting and reporting upon the German labour colonies as a means of providing work and subsistence for the unemployed. The report was to be made to the Glasgow Social Union. The idea of such a commission originated with Mr. D. M. Stevenson,[1] who had visited the labour colony at Bielefeld, and had been much impressed by the idea it embodied.

The years from 1878 until 1886 had been years of trade depression and of consequent unemployment. Although by 1892 the acute stage of the depression had passed, there was still unemployment, and there

[1] Afterwards Lord Provost of Glasgow and now Sir Daniel M. Stevenson, Bart.

was prevalent a desire to find, not a temporary remedy, but some self-acting means of providing employment in such a way as to avoid the necessity of temporary remedies. The idea of a colony in which beggars and other poor persons should be welcomed, or to which such persons might be sent by public authorities, is not new. The plan was fully set forth in an Act of the reign of Elizabeth, and was actually in operation in England for three hundred years. I have given an account of the history of the plan elsewhere.[1] Apparently without knowledge of the previous existence of labour colonies in England, the adoption of them was urged by the Rev. Herbert Mills in a remarkable little book called *Poverty and the State*. Mr. Mills carried on an active propaganda, and in consequence public attention was directed to the experiments in labour colonies which for some years had been going on in Germany, and to the much older institutions of a similar character in Holland. Some brief reports had been made upon these continental colonies, but it was thought advisable that some of those persons who had been interested in the relief of the unemployed in Glasgow should have a personal opportunity of investigating the working of the system.

The commission therefore went to Germany. On our arrival at Berlin, we met, through the British Ambassador, the then Minister of the Interior, Count von Ehrenberg. The Count had evidently taken an interest in the subject, for he told us much about it and advised us to go to Rickling in Holstein, and offered to instruct the governor of the district to meet us there and facilitate our inquiries. He also arranged for us to see the town labour colony in Berlin. Our stay in Germany could not be a long one, and we therefore confined ourselves to the adoption of these suggestions, going in addition only to Reppen, in the province of Posen.

On our arrival at Oldesloë in Holstein, we met the Governor of Kiel, Herr von Heinze, who accompanied us to the colony of Rickling. He was most kind and helpful. The colony was established at Rickling for two purposes: one was to reclaim a morass, and the other was to reclaim the men who had for one reason or another failed to secure or to retain employment. The colony was open to all comers, but it was remote from a town and once in it was difficult for a colonist to get out, unless he was prepared to tramp for some miles, with the risk of being arrested as a vagrant. Since, however, the German law of settlement rendered a parish liable for the maintenance of poor persons who had resided in it for two years, any colonist whose domicile was

---

[1] See article "Setting the Poor on Work," *Nineteenth Century*, 1892.

outside the parish in which Rickling was situated was obliged to leave the colony before the expiry of that period. This ejection did not, however, prevent him from immediately obtaining entrance to another colony in another parish. Since there were twenty-four colonies throughout Germany, it was quite possible for a man to be a permanent colonist, provided he changed his colony once every two years. This colony, like the other German colonies, was supported by public subscription. There was an offset to the expenditure in the increased value of the land, for the labour of the colonists was redeeming the marsh. Redemption was effected by drainage, and by bringing sand from a neighbouring elevation by means of a light railway. There was no pretence that the labour of the colonists was efficient. The process of land redemption could have been accomplished by ordinary hired labour at less cost. Yet, if their labour were not organised in this or in some other manner, the men who were colonists would have had to be supported at the public charge. The results of their labour in land redemption recouped the administration of the colony for a portion at least of their maintenance. In so far as the unemployment experienced by them had been due to depression of vitality from dissipation, illness or other causes, the fresh air of the country and strictly enforced sobriety, with regular and ample food, might be expected to render at least a certain proportion of the colonists capable of entering once more the ranks of regularly employed labour, assuming that at the time there was demand for their services. Under certain conditions, therefore, and with due regard to the limitations of the scheme, we came to the conclusion that there was a place for colonies of the Rickling type in any comprehensive plan for dealing with unemployment. The Rickling experiment clearly did not interfere with local employment, for apparently the land which was being redeemed by the colonists would not have been redeemed at all unless it had been redeemed by them, and since the product of their labour, so far as it had gone, consisted entirely in preparation for future yield from the improved land, and not at once in produce competing in the market with other produce yielded by labour under ordinary conditions, competition with labour external to the colony did not for the time enter into the question. When the land was redeemed and the cultivation of it began, then of course the subsidised product of the colony must enter into competition with the unsubsidised product of external labour.

The town colony of Berlin presented a different problem. There we found the colony in the throes of a dispute with external labour. The colonists had been set to various industries. Some of them made

clothes for themselves and others, but they were not all tailors, and
if they had been they could have made more clothes than were required.
Some of them were set to make shoes. When these rudimentary requirements and others of the same character had been met, it was
found to be necessary to set the remaining colonists to production of
goods for sale. They were therefore set to the making of cases of
wood for the packing of tinned commodities. The moment that the
colony obtained a contract for a large quantity of these cases from a
local manufacturer of canned articles, the firms by which these cases
had previously been supplied and their workmen felt themselves
aggrieved, and complained. "Here," they said, "you are relieving
unemployment with one hand, and producing it with the other. What
you have done is to take the bread out of our mouths to put it into the
mouths of men who have been unable to get it for themselves, and
who have shown themselves unworthy of regular employment." In
this *impasse* the administration of the Berlin colony was not alone.
It is the experience of all such attempts to deal with unemployment.[1]

Although the difficulties and weaknesses of the labour colony
plan "sprang into the eyes," I felt the advisability of further and more
minute investigation, and I was therefore very glad when in the
summer of 1893 the Board of Trade, through my friend Llewellyn
Smith,[2] asked me to make such investigation, not only in Germany,
but elsewhere. I made arrangements to spend the summer upon this
task. I procured the necessary authorisations through the Foreign
Office and went to Bonn early in the summer. Procuring all the available literature on the subject, including reports and statistics of all
the colonies in Germany, I spent some weeks in digesting these, as
well as in making myself acquainted with the regulations of the police
and with other matters bearing upon the question of unemployment
and upon the question of labour in general.

I had been led to believe that one of the merits of the German
labour colony system, with its ancillary shelters for working-men
both in town and country, was that these institutions offered an open
door to the poor, and even to the destitute. I felt some doubt as to
the reality of this offer, and I resolved to test it. Dressing myself
shabbily, I presented myself one night at a workman's shelter in Bonn
—one of the institutions in the system. I found a severe-looking person
in charge. On my asking for a bed, he demanded my papers. I knew

[1] The detailed results of our short investigation are contained in a Report
published in Glasgow in 1893.
[2] Now Sir Hubert Llewellyn Smith, K.C.B.

very well what he wanted. He wanted my workman's book stamped
by the police. I answered him quite truthfully that I had no papers.
"Then," he said, "you can get no bed." "But," I remonstrated, "the
hour is late. I may not be able to get a bed elsewhere. I am willing to
pay for it." "It does not matter," he said, "without papers no one can
sleep here." I told him what I had been told was the purpose of the
institution. "Get out," he said, "if you don't go at once, I shall call
the police." I felt quite satisfied that my doubts were very reasonable,
and I went.

Next morning, otherwise habited, I went to the same place and
presented an order from Berlin instructing keepers of such places to
allow me to inspect them. I was received with great civility by my
friend of the night before, who did not recognise me, and I was shown
over the establishment. The shelter was neither better nor worse than
similar shelters I have seen elsewhere.

The German police system, with its hard-and-fast regulations,
renders it possible for the labour colony and the shelter system to
exist as it does. Its door is open, it is true, but every person who enters
it must be known and his movements must be kept on record.

Later I went to Bielefeld. Bielefeld is an extraordinary place. There
a remarkable man has founded a circle of institutions stamped with
the stamp of his own personality. This man is Pastor von Bodelschwingh. He is one of those who signed the denunciation of England
at the outbreak of war. Very unfortunately during my stay at Bielefeld
the pastor was taking the waters at Ems, and I did not see him. I was
received by his principal assistant, Pastor Mährchen, and by Fräulein
Heidseck, matron of the hospice.   They made me welcome, and I remained in their very delightful society for some weeks. The hospice is
maintained for visitors and for the nurses employed in the institutions.

The central institution is the great hospital for epileptics. It
housed about 1200 inmates. An attempt was made to segregate the
more serious cases from others, but this segregation was not carried
very far, only the violent cases being kept really separate. Great stress
seemed to be laid upon two remedies—bromide of potassium and
religious exercises. The atmosphere was highly charged with piety.
Genuinely devout as were most of the clergymen, divinity students
and others whom I met at the hospice, their attitude of mind could
hardly be counted as modern. Their conversation and mode of life
recalled very vividly the atmosphere of early nineteenth-century
Germany as indicated in the autobiography of Heinrich Stilling and
other books of the same period. I cannot say that the piety was

obviously pushed to an unhealthy extreme; but in the case of some it was ecstatic, while in all it seemed to breed a peculiar credulity, not merely in matters of faith, but as well in matters concerning the administration of the institution. Criticism was impious in the presence of devotion and benevolence. In addition to the asylum for epileptics, there was an orphanage. The entire community attended service in the church of the institution, a large edifice, in which there were more than a thousand in the congregation on Sundays. A seizure of epilepsy occurred at the average rate of one every ninety seconds throughout the service. These seizures were dealt with promptly and silently by the nurses, no notice was taken of them by anyone else.

The institution of most interest to me was the labour colony, about nine miles from Bielefeld, founded by Pastor von Bodelschwingh. After staying for some time under the hospitable roof of the hospice, and learning much of the labour colony system as a whole from Pastor Mährchen, I drove out one day to the colony. There, in the house of the director, Herr Meyer, I remained for three weeks. Instead of going from one colony to another, and of having snapshot impressions of each of them, I decided to stay long enough in one colony to become acquainted with its actual working, and with the life of the colonists.

The results of the inquiries I was able to make have been given elsewhere,[1] here I need only set down a few incidents not otherwise recorded.

I occasionally had a meal with the colonists; but I found the experience very depressing. They were not allowed to talk at meals on the ground that they would make too much noise. The silence of the tables where several hundred men were sitting seemed unnatural, and suggested indeed the restraint of a prison. Although the directors who presided talked to me during the meal, all around was oppressive and obviously envious silence. I therefore preferred, after a few experiences, to have my food in the house of the director. There the director's wife was very kind and supplied my needs to the extent of her power. Her larder was limited in variety. There was plenty of *schenken*, plenty of *schwarzbrod*, and a few other foodstuffs of which the Germans are fond; but there were no eggs, there were no fowl, there was no such bacon as may be had in Yorkshire or Wiltshire or Ireland, there was no mutton; in short, there were none of the articles of food upon which I had been accustomed to sustain myself. I had

---

[1] *Agencies and Methods of Dealing with Unemployment*, Parliamentary Paper, London, 1894.

vainly supposed that a good digestion was equal to anything; but about ten days of *schenken* and *schwarzbrod* convinced me to the contrary, or convinced me that my digestion was not good enough. Indeed, I became rather seriously ill. I had no drugs and there was no doctor, not even any apothecary within nine miles. Under these circumstances I employed the simple and natural remedy of copious draughts of warm water. The concern of my friends the director and his wife was touching; they felt themselves responsible for my well-being, and they were seriously disturbed. So soon as I was able to eat they decided upon a great sacrifice. They had no farmyard fowl, but they had a number of tame pigeons. These, in spite of my protests, they served to me day after day, until when I took my departure I had more than decimated their dovecots. It was a fine attention conceived in the best spirit, worthy of the Count who served his falcon to his mistress.

The Meyers gave me a very favourable impression of the rural life of Germany. The conditions were, of course, unusual, and Meyer was an exceptional man, but he was a product of German peasant life, and he would have been regarded as a good product in any country. Very placid, with great experience of the character of the submerged man, and inexhaustible patience in dealing with him, Meyer was clearly *the* man for his position. The colonists were a curious set of people. There was a count, sent to the colony on the ground of incurable dissipation and kept there simply to keep him from brandy. He was an amiable and well-mannered fellow, not without intelligence, but I doubt if he was being benefited by the society in which he found himself, although regularity of life and fresh air were, no doubt, doing something for him. There was a murderer who had served a long sentence of penal servitude, and who had found it impossible to get employment outside the colony. I had long talks with him, carefully avoiding reference to his past history, and found him apparently purged of violent intention. The foreman carpenter of the colony was himself a colonist. He was given to periodical bouts of drunkenness, and in order to accomplish these he escaped from time to time. Sometimes a fortnight elapsed before he was discovered and brought back, or was inclined to return of his own accord. During these periods of absence the carpentry work of the colony was at a standstill, and the carpenters were then employed in the fields. Notwithstanding his weakness he was an excellent workman. He superintended all repairs, as well as the erection of all new buildings.

I had free access to the books of the colony and to the police and other records of the colonists, and I spent much time in examining these. It thus came about that in the absence of the director or of the colonist who acted as clerk, I was often the only person in the office. One day, while I was alone, a strongly-built young man presented himself and asked for admittance. I demanded his papers, and catechised him about his history. He had been a farm labourer, and in constant employment. He had quarrelled with a companion, they had fought, and the other had been severely injured. The young man had been arrested, and sentenced to a term of imprisonment. When he was released from prison, he was looked upon as a jailbird and was refused employment. He had no recourse but to tramp to the colony. I found the police docket of this young fellow, and it confirmed his statements. Very many of the colonists had been in jail, either because of crimes of violence or because of theft. Many of them had long been separated from their wives and families, and many of them had spent years in the labour colonies. Some of them had been in the habit of migrating from a northern to a southern colony in the winter, and from a southern to a northern colony in the summer. A comparatively small number of the colonists returned permanently to normal employment. There was, however, one peculiar exception to this general rule. The brickmakers of Lippe-Detmold made good wages during nine months of the year, and during three months in winter they were in enforced idleness because the brickyards were closed. Before the establishment of the labour colonies, these brickmakers were obliged to save enough out of their wages during the period of employment to maintain them during their period of idleness. The rate of wages had in the nature of the case to be high enough to enable them to live even during the season of unemployment, otherwise the district might have been denuded of brickmakers. When the colonies were established, they offered an opportunity to the brickmakers of employment during the winter months. This opportunity was utilised, to begin with, by unmarried workmen; but gradually the less thrifty of the married workmen drifted to the colonies during the winter. The habit then began to grow in Lippe-Detmold, among the brickmakers, of spending the whole of their wages during the brick-making season, and of relying upon the colonies for their maintenance during the period of unemployment. Soon the employers seized the opportunity of reducing the wages at the brickyards. Here was an unexpected and undesirable reaction of the labour colony system. While relieving unemployment it reduced wages.

There were other reactions; for example, in the neighbourhood of the colony the farmers were quite willing to employ the colonists after they had been under the discipline of the colony for a short time; but with the understanding that the wages to be paid them were less than the customary wages. Their labour, they argued, was less efficient than normal labour, otherwise they would never have had to resort to the colony; moreover, the employment of them was more or less of a charitable act, and the amount which any farmer could dispense in charity was limited.

After visiting the German colonies, I went to the single French colony which corresponded to the German type—the colony of La Chalmelle, near Epernay on the Marne. The colony is small and is not characterised by any exceptional features. On my way there I stopped at Epernay, having reached that town by way of Metz and Luxembourg. I arrived late in the evening, and jumping into a cab at the station told the driver to take me to the best hotel. The aspect of the place to which he took me was so uninviting that I told him to take me to the next best. This one had even less to recommend it, and I asked to be driven back to the first. When I entered, I found that the *salle à manger* was dismantled for the night, the chairs being piled on top of the tables, and that the hotel was shrouded in darkness. I found someone to attend to me, however, and I was taken to a room to which access was obtained by an external stair in the courtyard. The room was fairly clean, and tired as I was after a long journey, I went supperless to bed.

In the morning I rose early, to find the *salle à manger* still unprepared for its office, and I left the hotel to ascertain whether or not there was a restaurant in the neighbourhood in which I might have at least first breakfast. Nothing of the kind was visible, and I prolonged my walk through the town. After passing streets of indifferent character, I suddenly found myself at one end of the Rue Commerciale. From squalor I came at once into regal magnificence. This street is without doubt one of the finest streets in the world. Every building in it is a palace, and every palace bears a familiar name. The street is dedicated to champagne, for here are the principal offices of the great champagne houses. They are all imposing edifices, built predominantly of grey stone, with large quadrangles embellished with flowers. These great houses extend from the street to the edge of an abrupt precipice which rises from the plain, and at the base of this precipice are the entrances to the *caves* in which the champagne is stored.

I spent some time in admiring this magnificence, and then returned to my inn. Here was a transformation. The *salle à manger* was open, and was occupied by a number of gentlemen who were breakfasting. With serviettes tucked into their collars they were attacking their viands in eloquent silence. I joined them at once, and had reason to withdraw any aspersions I had been induced to make upon the hospitality of Epernay. From Epernay I went to Rheims, and then to Paris, which I had not visited since 1881. After a few days at the Hôtel Corneille, during which I visited some of my friends, I went to Laon, a city whose acquaintance I had often desired to make. Laon is a very remarkable place—alike on account of its situation and on account of its history. The city occupies the whole of an almost crescent-shaped eminence, rising abruptly out of and commanding the level plain stretching on all sides—on the south towards Rheims, on the north towards the Belgian frontier, on the west towards the coast, and on the east towards the Ardennes. It is little wonder that in the Middle Ages Laon became an important military, administrative and ecclesiastical centre. The citadel, the walls, and the gates of the city are the tangible evidences of the first, and the bishop's palace and the cathedral of the second and third. The Bishops of Laon exercised territorial jurisdiction over the surrounding country.[1]

At the date of my first visit in 1893 the city walls were rather dilapidated, the gates had not been repaired after having been blown up in some mediæval siege, and the cathedral exhibited symptoms of neglect. The town had an air of depression. Within a few years this was destined to be altered, but the story of the change must come in its proper place.

From Laon I went to St. Quentin, and spent a while examining the curious stone columns of the Hôtel de Ville, upon which mediæval humorists had expended their ingenuity; from St. Quentin I went to Brussels. There I saw Sir Frank Lascelles and Mr. Conynghame Green[2] at the British Embassy, and they arranged for me to have an opportunity of visiting the penal colony at Merxplas, near Antwerp. This huge colony, the largest of the kind I have seen anywhere, was established for the purpose of receiving beggars who were consigned to it by the courts throughout Belgium. It was designed exclusively for men, there being other colonies for women and a colony for boys.

I observed on my visit to Belgium in 1874 the prevalence of begging,

---

[1] A picturesque account of Laon is to be found in Eugene Sue's *History of a Proletarian Family*.

[2] Sir Conynghame Green was afterwards at Pretoria and later at Teheran and Tokyo.

both in the cities and in the country villages. The improvement in the economical position of Belgium which had taken place in the seventies and eighties had at once rendered begging less necessary and more discreditable. In the late eighties the question had been resolutely forced upon the attention of the Belgian Chamber. Stringent laws against mendicancy were passed, and as a corollary institutions for the reception of beggars were established. Here the problem was not the relief of temporarily unemployed persons, but was the elimination of a hereditarily mendicant class. If it were possible to redeem any of the beggars, they might be redeemed and passed into the ranks of normal labour; but if they could not be redeemed, they were to be kept permanently segregated from the rest of the community in the hope that hereditary pauperism might be extinguished, and the begging habit effectually cured. I found Merxplas an immense farm, with thousands of men working in the fields under the eyes of armed guards, while hundreds of other men worked in trunk-making workshops and in factories for the manufacture of stationery for the service of the different departments of the Government. The place was a huge prison, where the prisoners were exercised in a useful manner. The intelligent official to whom I was consigned confided to me that the task of dealing with the convicted beggars who were sent to the colony was a very uncongenial one. He had an extremely unfavourable opinion of the view that any but a small fraction of the convicts could possibly become useful citizens; yet he thought that Merxplas was a good place in which to concentrate these people, and thus to prevent them from continued mendicancy. The individuals, he thought, were irredeemable, but by sentencing every convicted beggar to Merxplas, begging as a system might be stamped out.

I had not been in Antwerp for twelve years, and during that period enormous changes had been in progress. The new docks were finished, and the expansion of German foreign trade, as well as the growth of Belgian industry, had made Antwerp one of the great ports of the world.

My duties next led me to Holland, which country I should have visited in the first instance had I been studying the labour colony system in its historical sequence. It was in Holland that the poor colony was first organised on an extensive scale.[1] A Dutch planter in Java who had made a great fortune determined on his return to his native country to eliminate pauperism by inducing paupers to go into colonies, taking their whole families with them. He did not hope much

[1] Although the system had been tried in Hamburg at an earlier period.

I—U

from the parents, but he did expect that discipline and education would enable their children to take a useful place in the world.

I went from Antwerp to Rotterdam, where I had not been since 1878, and found that the modernisation of the city had been carried to a great length during the nineteen years that had elapsed since my first visit in 1874.

Causes similar to those which had modernised Antwerp had affected Rotterdam. Both of these ports had profited by the vigorous German trade movement and the trade in Dutch bulbs had grown to profitable dimensions, while in addition there was the important trade in spices, etc., from the Dutch East Indies. The prosperity of Holland was obvious. There seemed to be little occasion for benevolent enterprises to provide for the poor.

I went on at once to the Hague, where I intended to examine into the administration of the poor colonies, and to make my plans for visiting them. When I arrived at the Hague I reported myself to Sir Horace Rumbold, who received me with great kindness. Sir Horace may be said to have belonged to the old school of diplomatists. His *Reminiscences*, published late in life, abound in indiscretions, but at the time I knew him he was discretion personified. Perhaps his experiences in Vienna had something to do with opening his lips. There are certain types of diplomacy which must have that effect upon the most discreet of men. Sir Horace was good enough to bring me into contact with several members of the Dutch Cabinet. Among these, those who impressed me most were Mr. Tak van Poorvliet, Minister of Justice, and Dr. N. Pierson, Minister of Finance. The former gave me much information on the special subject of my inquiry, and his introductions afterwards facilitated my movements. The latter gave me an interesting account of his attempt to introduce into Holland a progressive income tax. If I am not mistaken, Mr. Pierson was the first responsible statesman to formulate and introduce this important method of taxation. His measure was defeated in 1893, and he resigned his office. Later he was carried into power as Premier by a large majority, and his measure was passed. Holland was, indeed, the first country to adopt the plan of increasing the rate of taxation by sharp graduations with the increase of income. Mr. Pierson had been Professor of Political Economy in the University of Amsterdam, and he had also been President of the Bank of Amsterdam. To the knowledge of an accomplished economist he added the experience of a financier in an institution of wide international consequence.

It was inevitable that an income tax should occupy an important place in the Dutch system of finance. A large part of the annual earnings of the Dutch people came to Holland in the form of net income derived from commerce in the Dutch colonial possessions. If a Dutch Finance Minister were to rely upon indirect taxes by means of import duties, upon excise duties or upon a land tax, the Government must necessarily be permanently poor, even although a large proportion of the population might be rolling in wealth. Although Holland expended very little upon military services, the national expenditure was of necessity very heavy. The country had to be kept free from the inroads of the sea on its northern and on its western boundaries. Carelessness or neglect in the maintenance of the dykes might have as consequence the submergence of at least half the land. The annual budget was indispensably large relatively to population and area, and it had to be balanced under the economical conditions of Holland by an income tax.

I had decided to go north to the poor colony of Fredericksoord, near Assen. Knowing this, Sir Horace Rumbold asked me if I would mind having a fellow-traveller. He said that Mr. Thayer, the American Minister at the Hague, had been four years in Holland, that he had not travelled through the country, and that he was about to return to America. He therefore asked me if I would take him with me on my little expedition. I dined the next evening with Mr. Thayer, who lived at my hotel, the Oude Doulen, and we arranged to travel together. I found Mr. Thayer an amusing and agreeable travelling companion. He was a lawyer from Minneapolis, not very copiously informed upon international affairs. He made no secret of his want of knowledge, and told me that very little occurred during his period as Minister to demand any diplomatic skill. When anything did occur, he went over to Sir Horace, and talked it over with him.

We arrived at Assen in the afternoon, and drove over the moor to Fredericksoord. There we spent the night. As my time was limited, I asked the authorities to let me have access to the books of the colony from the beginning of its history, and to allow me to work upon them until the morning. My labours were well rewarded, for I was able by means of the entries in the books to follow the family history of the colonists sometimes for three generations. I need not give the details here, but I found that so far from having been able in all cases, although it was possible in some, to educate the youth of the colony in such a way as to make them useful citizens independent of charitable relief, the colony had experienced a tendency on the part of the boy colonists to marry girls also colonists and to return to the colony after having spent a short time in endeavouring unsuccessfully to make their living in the outside world. This was of course not always the case. The boys were educated in the agricultural school of the colony, and some of the least unpromising were sent to Java. There a certain proportion of them did well. Of those who were sent from the colony to employment in Holland some succeeded, but many returned to the colony to spend there the remainder of their days, in the same way as their parents and grandparents had done. I found also that the average number of children in the colony family was somewhat higher than the average number of children in Holland generally at that time.[1]

Having some private business to attend to, I had to go to Utrecht the next day; but in a few days I returned to Fredericksoord, and at greater leisure made the acquaintance of the colonists, their families, and the schools in which their young people were taught. On my way to or from the colony I spent a night at Assen, and was amused to find in the inn a number of Frisians talking in a dialect which I found little difficulty in understanding, owing to its resemblance to that of Aberdeenshire.

---

[1] Details of the results of this examination of the books of the colony are to be found in *Agencies and Methods*, cited above.

CHAPTER XXII

CANADA IN 1892

Keep us, O Thetis, in our western flight!
  Watch from thy pearly throne
Our vessel, plunging deeper into night
  To reach a land unknown.
          JOHN DAVIDSON, *Scaramouch in Naxos* (1889).

ON my return from Germany in September 1892 I rejoined my family at Lundin Mills, in Fifeshire. I found myself in a colony of another variety. Here the colonists also laboured, but in a different field and with a different outlook upon life. Lundin Mills is near Largo, celebrated as the reputed birthplace of Robinson Crusoe, of whom there is a statue in the main street. Largo is a fishing village of some antiquity, and even now of importance. The Bass Rock looms up in the distance seawards, and eastward and westward by land are the links which in an almost unbroken line extend round the coast to St. Andrews. The colony at Lundin Mills was a colony of artists. Among these were Frank Newbery, the headmaster of the Glasgow School of Art,[1] and Hugh Cameron, a Scots painter of note. Newbery had asked me to sit for my portrait, and he had finished it when I was called to Oxford to see W. J. Ashley,[2] who had just resigned the Chair of Political Economy in the University of Toronto in order to go to a similar position in Harvard University. Shortly afterwards I was appointed his successor at Toronto.

I sailed from Glasgow for New York in the middle of October. Although I have crossed the Atlantic many times since then, my first voyage was by far the worst. About the twentieth of the month we passed into the region of a storm. This storm was known afterwards as the Bermuda Hurricane. Never in any ocean have I experienced anything like it. The ship, the *Furnessia*, was of about five thousand tons, but she was tossed like a cork in the tremendous seas. For two days we made almost no progress. Hatches were fastened down, and there was no access to the deck. The captain was on the bridge continuously, and on Sunday he sent me a message asking me to take

---

[1] *Cf.* p. 233.   [2] Now Sir Wm. J. Ashley of Birmingham University.

309

prayers for him in the saloon. I held on to a post and managed to get through the service. Very few of the passengers emerged from their berths. On the third day of the storm I was able to go on deck, and with great difficulty made my way by holding on to a rope to the chart-room. It would be difficult to exaggerate the height of the waves. When we were in the trough of the seas they seemed to tower above the funnels and threatened to overwhelm the ship. To avoid the centre of the storm vortex we had to go out of our course, but when we came to the banks of Newfoundland we passed out of the hurricane into comparative calm and shallow, smooth seas. We reached New York a couple of days late. I did not tarry there at that time, but went on to Boston, where I found Ashley already installed at Harvard. He was very kind and helpful, and I spent a few days with him, meeting several of his colleagues, *e.g.* Dr. Dunbar, veteran of Civil War days and head of the Economic Department, Taussig, Hart, and others. We called upon General Francis A. Walker, the head of the Massachusetts Institute of Technology, known not only as economist but also as diplomatist. The talk fell on the silver situation, for Walker had a hereditary interest in currency, his father, Amasa Walker, having written many years ago an important book on the subject. Speaking of the demonetisation of silver resulting from the action of Germany in calling in her silver coinage after the Franco-Prussian War, Walker said that he believed this action was determined upon by Germany in order to demoralise the financial system of France, and thus to retard or prevent her economic recovery from the exhaustion occasioned by the war. This explanation was new to me. Writing about it afterwards to Foxwell, I found that he also entertained the same view. I did not, however, feel convinced by the argument. In the first place there were other causes for the demonetisation of silver—notably the increase in production which had begun to manifest itself in the early seventies and the condition of the silver coinage of the different States of Germany, which necessitated recoinage as well as a reorganisation of the currency system of the new empire. The fact that the demonetisation of silver would injure France as well as Italy, Switzerland, Belgium, the United States, and India, and through India Great Britain, was no doubt foreseen; but it is hard to believe that the currency policy of Germany was determined by that consideration. I am inclined to believe that the German Government was indifferent to the consequences of its monetary policy excepting as concerned Germany.

I found Boston much more like an English city than New York.

The streets were narrow and winding. The deadly directness of the New York thoroughfares was absent. At that time (1892) the street railway ran on the surface of Tremont Street alongside the Common. At the so-called "rush hours," when people were going home from business, between five and seven o'clock in the evening, the cars were crowded to suffocation inside, and along the footboards as many people as were able to obtain a foot- and hand-hold clung to them outside. Ere long the rails were to be removed from Tremont Street, a system of subways was to be made, and overcrowding was to be prevented by rigorously enforced regulation.

When I arrived in Toronto the street cars were drawn by horses, as they were in Glasgow when I left it; but a fortnight after my arrival the electrical system, which had been in preparation for some time, was inaugurated. Electrical power was generated by means of steam engines; these were some years later to be replaced by the turbines of Niagara.

I had been struck by the beauty of the autumnal foliage in Boston, and on the way from that city *via* Albany and Buffalo. In Toronto the foliage was very fine. Horse chestnuts, lining many of the streets and avenues and affording a delightful shade, were becoming rusty; but the maples were superb. In the parks and gardens the maples gave a note of gorgeous red and yellow, while in the suburbs the shumac shrubs were brilliant scarlet. There is a peculiar pungency in the air of North America in the fall, which may perhaps be attributed to the change of the leaf. From an eminence like the tower of the University, or the higher tower of Upper Canada College in the north of the city, Toronto looked like a settlement in a forest. When the trees were in leaf they concealed all but the high buildings, and in 1892 there were no buildings more than about sixty feet in height. Now there are many "sky-scrapers," and these have changed materially the aspect of the city.

The growth of a lake town inevitably acquires a character peculiar to its position. Toronto was situated between two rivers—the Don and the Humber—at the points where they flow into Lake Ontario. The original settlement was extended along the lake shore for a short distance west of the mouth of the Don. Gradually the settlement grew northwards, sometimes jumping over long distances, and established itself sporadically on the thoroughfare from Toronto into the interior. This thoroughfare, Yonge Street, extends from the lake northwards to Lake Simcoe, a distance of about forty miles. From the end of the eighteenth century settlers established themselves upon it. There still remain a few of the adobe or sun-dried brick houses and barns of these early inhabitants. I have elsewhere given an account of the attempted settlement about twenty miles north of Toronto of French *émigrés*, under the leadership of the Comte de Pousaye.[1] A group of French ladies and gentlemen reached their intended settlement in a sadly bedraggled condition, and after a struggle against adverse Nature sold or abandoned the land that had been granted to them by the British Government. The only important survivor of this ill-fated enterprise was a youth called Quetton, who came as a servant and lived to buy out his masters. He took the name of St. George, lived to a great age, acquired much land, and bequeathed a large estate to his descendants.

While sporadic settlement took place northwards, the population of the town settled in the arc of a circle, the chord being the lake shore. This arc has gradually extended until now the city extends beyond both rivers and northwards for many miles. The country to the north of Toronto is broken by the valleys of the two rivers and those of their numerous tributary streams. These valleys are sometimes narrow and form ravines, many of which remain, bridges over them having enabled the population to spread beyond them. Natural parks of great beauty have thus been plentifully provided.

Coming as I did from closely built towns, and familiar as I was with congested districts in these, the most striking feature of Toronto was the wide area over which the population was spread. The city presented the aspect of a rural village on a large scale. Even the smallest houses had garden space, and the larger houses had from a quarter of an acre upwards in all parts of the city, there being even some of these in the very heart of it surrounded by factories and business premises. Mr. Goldwin Smith's house, for example, in 1892 was in the heart of the city and yet was surrounded by a demesne of about seven acres. There were several houses in its neighbourhood with demesnes of from one to five acres. These wide spaces were valuable from an æsthetic as well as a sanitary point of view, as were even the smaller lots upon which less imposing dwellings were built. Yet this generous distribution of land involved distance between the houses, distance between the houses involved streets of an extent very great in proportion to the numbers of persons inhabiting them, and these conditions involved relatively heavy municipal expenditure for the maintenance of the streets and for the provision of public services, such as water supply, sewerage, lighting, and transport. For this

[1] In my forthcoming *Economic History of Canada*.

reason municipal debt was mounting rapidly, and municipal taxation had already become very high. Whereas the municipal taxes in a city like Glasgow were, in 1892, not more than twelve and a half per cent. of the annual value of the premises, those of Toronto were at that time about forty per cent. of the annual value. Amplitude of land is a costly luxury.

When the Canadian Pacific Railway was finished to the Pacific Coast, in 1886, a furore of speculation broke out over a great part of Canada. It was supposed that immediately upon completion of the railway a stream of immigration would set in and that this stream would result in immediate increase of trade, and therefore of population. Two cities were influenced by this furore of speculation more than other places. These cities were Winnipeg and Toronto; the first because it was the trading centre of the North-West, and the second because it was an important distributing centre for goods both from Great Britain and from the eastern States of the Union. In Winnipeg the price of land within the municipal boundaries advanced rapidly, not because there was actual demand for the use of it, but because demand was anticipated. Toronto had the same experience. Unused land was offered for sale at high prices, and the farmers whose land was within or bordering upon the city limits ceased to cultivate it and sold it to speculative companies which divided it up into building lots and by way of inducement to purchasers ran wooden sidewalks on open fields or along avenues cut through standing timber. A belt line of railway designed to serve the new districts was built beyond the arc of the curve of the city boundary. The boom lasted for about three years, from 1886 till 1889; then it collapsed. There was no demand to justify it. The immigration into the North-West and into the country as a whole was insufficient to produce trade to sustain and employ so great an increase of population as the speculation in land implied. The effects of the boom lasted longer than the boom itself. When I arrived in Toronto in October 1892 the city was still suffering from the boom and its collapse. Within a few years a large quantity of the land that had been bought during the boom by people of small means was sold for the taxes that according to the system prevalent in Canada were allowed to accumulate as a charge against the property upon which they were levied. There was even a decline in population. People who came into the town during the fictitious activity induced by the boom left at the close of it for other towns or for the United States. In some districts whole streets of shops were left vacant, and over all there was an air of depression.

I arrived in Toronto in the end of October, and found that there was still to be expected a full month of fall before the winter began. It was a tradition that no snow lay on the ground for more than a day until the first snowfall after Christmas, and then it remained on the frozen surface—remained until everyone was weary of it. Towards the end of April it was sometimes washed away in violent torrents of rain.

I found the sudden variations of temperature interesting but trying. One evening I went out to dinner; I walked back to my rooms in the college in a light unbuttoned overcoat, the night was balmy and pleasant, and the moon was shining over the green *campus*. The hour was eleven. At two in the morning-I was wakened by a loud rumbling noise. I rose and went to a window looking out upon the quadrangle. What had happened was evident. The temperature had suddenly dropped, and at the same time snow had fallen heavily. The grass of the quadrangle was covered by it to a depth of some inches, and the snow was sliding down the roofs of the college buildings. It was by this that I was aroused. In the morning I called at the meteorological observatory, and found that between eleven and two the thermometer had fallen twenty-six degrees.

On another occasion I had a curious experience of the consequences of a rapid fall in temperature. I had decided to take a Japanese print from my portfolio and hang it above my mantelpiece. The print was by Toyo Kuni II.; it represented a fierce combat in an arena round which there was a crowd of Samurai and retainers eagerly watching the duellists. The print arrived from the framer, and I proceeded to put it in its place. After I had placed it, I glanced at the total effect. I have an antique bronze Buddha from Tibet of which I am particularly fond, and am therefore inclined to give it the place of honour in the centre of my mantelpiece—a place it has held, indeed, for more than thirty years. The new arrangement brought this scene of Japanese violence immediately above the Buddha. I fancied that the finger of his right hand (the figure represents "the teaching Buddha") was raised as if in solemn admonition and I remarked to him, for I was accustomed to talk to him in familiar fashion, "I have put this picture above you. If you don't like it, you can let me know." I sat by a blazing fire, for it was a cold evening. At a late hour I retired. A colleague occupied rooms below mine, otherwise no one lived in the same college building. About three in the morning I was aroused by what appeared to be the violent smashing of a pane of glass. I sat up in bed; immediately a door opened in the passage below, and I heard the voice of my colleague—Professor Baker, Professor of Mathe- matics—calling, "Mavor, are you awake? Someone is breaking into the house." I answered, rose, lighted a candle, and my colleague and I explored. We found the windows intact; unable to explain the occurrence, we returned to bed. Next morning I discovered that the Buddha had smashed the glass of the newly-framed picture. He had evidently adopted this method of making me aware that he dis- approved of scenes of violence. I have told the story as it occurred; if anyone is inclined to offer a materialistic explanation of the pheno- menon, I have given all the relevant data. I refuse to spoil the story myself.

In the beginning of December I was invited by Mr. E. B. Osler, one of the directors of the Canadian Pacific Railway, to go with him to Montreal in order to meet the other directors, as well as the general manager of the line, Mr. William C. van Horne. I spent a very inter- esting day with them, meeting also for the first time Mr. Shaughnessy, who was then assistant general manager.[1] Among the directors was General Thomas, who represented the shareholders in the United States. Mr. Boissevain, who represented the Dutch interests in the line, at that time very large, and some of the members of whose family I had met in England, was not present. Thus began a friendship with Van Horne which lasted for twenty-three years until his death in 1915.[2]

During the Christmas vacation I decided to see something of the smaller towns in Ontario, and also something of the life on the Indian reserves in that province. My colleague, H. R. Fairclough,[3] brother- in-law of Grant Allen, undertook to guide me in the first enterprise, and Oronhyateka, the most remarkable American Indian of his time, invited me to his place at Desoronto, where there is a reserve of the Mohawks, to which nation Oronhyateka belonged.

With Fairclough I visited Hamilton, London, Brantford and St. Catharines, and saw something of the society of these provincial towns.

At that time these places had not been touched by the vigorous trade movement of 1900–12, nor had they experienced the invasion of foreign labourers which took place during these years. They were rather stagnant. Industry in most of them was conducted on a small scale. They were inhabited by the descendants of settlers who had

---

[1] The president of the line at that time was Lord Mount Stephen, but he was not present. Mr. Osler afterwards became Sir Edmund Osler, Mr. van Horne Sir William van Horne, and Mr. Shaughnessy Lord Shaughnessy.

[2] See vol. ii. chap. xxxvii.

[3] Now Professor of Latin in Leland Stanford University, California.

taken up their land by grant or by purchase between about 1790 and 1840, together with immigrants arriving in small groups or individually at more recent dates, and the families of these. Each of the towns had a history and a *milieu* of its own. The most important among them was Hamilton, originally settled predominantly by Scotsmen. There was already the beginning of what later grew to be an important industry; but at that time this industry had not developed and the town wore a sleepy air. Its commerce depended clearly upon the farming country about it, and very largely upon the fruit farms of the Niagara Peninsula. London had been settled by English people, who called their river the Thames, and their streets Piccadilly and other names reminiscent of London. The adoption by a rural town in Ontario of the name of the great metropolis has necessitated the use of the convention London, England, and London, Ontario, in speech and writing. James Bryce [1] told me while he was visiting Goldwin Smith in Toronto he addressed a letter to Sir Edward Grey, Foreign Office, Whitehall, London. The letter went to London, Ontario, passed through the Dead Letter Office, and only after some delay reached its destination. London has been for a long time the educational centre of what used to be called Canada West. There Bishop Helmuth founded a school which grew into a university, and as well a theological college. Brantford was even at that time (1892) a flourishing centre of the trade in agricultural implements. One of its establishments was united with another in Toronto, and its chief development occurred in the latter city because of the greater plentifulness of labour; but sufficiently important establishments remained in Brantford to carry on until labourers found their way there in abundance.

From Brantford we drove up the valley of the Grand River, passing a celebrated stock farm which had fallen upon unprosperous days owing to the growth of ranching in the North-West, and came to a large Mohawk reserve, with a school and a church founded there by the New England Company in the reign of Queen Anne.

Brantford was the home of Alexander Graham Bell, the inventor of the telephone, who began there on the farm of his father the experiments which eventually led to his great invention. Years after my first visit, I went to Brantford for the celebration (in 1917) of the fiftieth anniversary of the invention of the telephone. Dr. Graham Bell was there, and in the account which he gave of the development of the telephone he said that "it was conceived in Brantford, and born in

[1] British Ambassador at Washington, afterwards Lord Bryce.

Boston." A very fine symbolic sculpture by my friend Walter Alward was unveiled in Brantford on that occasion.

St. Catharines (I have been unable to discover the origin of the peculiar spelling) was founded by United Empire Loyalists, who came from the United States after the successful revolution in 1776. The treatment of these people by the Revolutionary States is not a creditable episode in American history. They were despoiled of their property and actually or practically forced to leave the country. One American historian at least, Mr. W. R. Thayer, has had the courage to tell the truth about the episode. St. Catharines was the terminus of the so-called "underground route," by means of which negroes who had escaped from their plantations were enabled to find a refuge from capture by the Legrees of the period before the abolition of slavery. The descendants of these negroes remain in St. Catharines as a material portion of the population. In 1892 there were still some who had themselves escaped by the "underground route."

I made the acquaintance of the society of the provincial towns I have mentioned. The people were exceedingly hospitable and kind to me, yet I derived an impression not altogether favourable of the effect upon them of residence in small communities. Very few of them were reasonably well educated, hardly any of them had intellectual interests of any kind. I found that in the previous generation it had been not unusual for well-to-do parents to send their sons to England for their education; this practice had altogether fallen into abeyance.

Before the close of the year I found myself in Desoronto on a visit to my Indian friend Oronhyateka. This remarkable man had as a youth attracted the attention of Sir Henry Acland, who was in the suite of the Prince of Wales, afterwards King Edward VII., during his visit to Canada in 1861. In an unguarded moment Sir Henry had said to the bright-looking Indian boy whom he saw at the Grand River Reserve that he hoped he would be able to carry on his education, and, no doubt facetiously, added, "One day we may expect to see you at Oxford." I have no doubt that Sir Henry was extremely surprised when he was taken precisely at his word. One day Oronhyateka walked into his rooms. Sir Henry did what he could. Oronhyateka was given some educational facilities—I do not know exactly what they were—but somehow the air of Oxford did not agree with him, and ere long Oronhyateka returned to Canada. He afterwards went to the United States, where he obtained a medical degree. The practice of medicine afforded too restricted a field for his ambition; but it brought him into relations with a friendly society—the Independent Order of

Foresters—and he found a sphere in which his extraordinary organising powers might be developed. Long before I knew him he had succeeded in building up a great mutual insurance association on an assessment basis. This plan of varying assessments came to be discredited, but by means of it he made his society a huge affair. At the time I speak of he was in enjoyment of a very large salary, as well as of commissions of considerable amount. He was, moreover, complete master and autocrat of his organisation.

I had travelled from Toronto with Oronhyateka, and when we stepped from the train at Desoronto we were met by a handsome sleigh, comfortably furnished with buffalo robes and drawn by four horses, each with a tall red plume on his head. We drove off in great style to his place some miles off along a winter road. A winter road in Canada cuts not only across country, but cuts also across lakes and rivers on the ice. Wrapped in buffalo robes, we defied the wind and thoroughly enjoyed the drive. Oronhyateka's house was extremely commodious. He had a large and very plain living-room, but the great room of the house was the drawing-room. Never had I, nor have I since, seen such an amazing apartment. There were collected everything that barbaric taste and ample means could provide. Oronhyateka had travelled widely, and had accumulated on his travels the things that struck his fancy. He had a replica of the Coronation Chair, upholstered in velvet and lavishly decorated with gold. He had extraordinary pictures on the walls, which were covered with the thickest of embossed papers in brilliant red. He had the most dreadful of modern vases in marble and bronze, the sophisticated barbarism of Birmingham harmonising surprisingly with the untutored barbarism of Desoronto; and dominating everything, a life-sized statue of Oronhyateka himself in plaster painted to look like life. I found that it was a copy of a bronze belonging to his Foresters.

In spite of this gaucherie he was extraordinarily kind, and his conversation was full of interest. He took me next day to the village which is the centre of the Mohawk reserve, and introduced me to several of the people. I found them simple country folk. They were living in comfortable houses, and all of them were well clad and prosperous-looking. One woman with whom I had a long conversation asked me if I had been to any of the great cities, and she mentioned specially London, Paris and New York. I told her that I had visited these places. Then she added, "They tell me that there are savages there, perfect savages." "Yes," I said, "you were told quite correctly. There are savages in these places, perfect savages."

On New Year's Day Oronhyateka took me to the house of one of his kinsfolk, where all the family connection were to have dinner. About twenty-four persons sat down to table. To say that the table was loaded with viands would convey no accurate idea. It was loaded and emptied and loaded again. Geese were brought and consumed, and more geese were brought and consumed until a fair-sized flock had been sacrificed. Oronhyateka explained to me that an Indian must eat until he can eat no longer, and that this was a surviving trait of his nomadic and uncertain life. The strongest beverage was tea; because under the Canadian law no Indian might be served or supplied with alcoholic liquors. The rationale of the regulation was that as an Indian does not know when he has had enough food, he shares with many of his white brothers a reluctance to stop drinking when he has had enough.

There were speeches and much reasonable and pleasant jollity. One or two of the guests had come from a distance. One was a mechanic from Rochester, in the State of New York. All were Mohawks, and all were of Oronhyateka's family. Oronhyateka claimed through his mother descent from Joseph Brant, a celebrated chief who fought on the side of the British in the Revolutionary War.

Oronhyateka regaled me in the evenings with Mohawk stories, which he told very well. Some of these stories were variants of Indian legends of wide prevalence. One of them varied so much from similar creation stories that I venture to set it down here.

"In a settlement" (many of Oronhyateka's tales began with this phrase, equivalent to "once upon a time") "there was a great hunter. This hunter had a sister, who often went with him on his hunting expeditions. Once after a long absence they returned, and shortly afterwards the women began to make scornful remarks about the sister of the hunter. Then there came an open charge that she had broken the law of the settlement. The young woman was tried by the elders, and being found guilty was sentenced to death. The manner of her death was this. A tree was uprooted, she was placed in the cavity and left there. So soon as the people of the settlement had gone, the earth in the cavity sank and the girl sank with it. She fell for an indefinable time, first through land, and then through water. Her fall was observed by the marine creatures, who were perturbed by it and consulted among themselves in order to determine what should be done. They decided that the tortoise should go beneath the falling woman so that she might rest on its back. When she did so the water subsided, and she found herself floating on a great waste of waters.

On the back of the tortoise she gave birth to two boys. They speedily grew, and one of them gave evidence of good nature, the other of evil nature. The good boy with his finger formed the floating dust on the surface of the water, and the wicked boy attempted to frustrate his efforts; but the good boy persisted and gradually succeeded in making out of the floating dust mountains and valleys, leaving the water in rivers and lakes. Thus the world came into existence." [1]

The folklorist may compare this tale with that of Nanibozho (or Nenabōj, the cheat), a tale current among the Chippeways.[2] This tale was told to me by Oronhyateka as a Mohawk tale. Nanibajou (this was the Mohawk form of the name) and his brother lived in a secluded hut in a forest. Nanibajou was a great medicine man, and his brother was a great hunter. The brother had seen and hunted a white deer in the forest, but the deer escaped him, and he was obliged to return. A few days later he determined to set out to hunt for this deer, and he left the hut. After some days his brother Nanibajou became anxious and went into the forest to look for the hunter, feeling certain that he had met with some accident. As he went along a hunting trail, he overtook a bull-frog, who was leaping along in a great hurry carrying a medicine-bag on his back. "Where are you going?" said Nanibajou. "The King of the Sea-lions is sick," said the frog, "and I am going to give him medicine." Nanibajou killed the frog and, taking his skin and his medicine-bag, continued to penetrate the forest. Soon he came to a lake, and looking out upon its waters waited for some sign which might guide him to his brother. A little kingfisher chirped on a branch. Nanibajou listened to his song and heard, "I know where Nanibajou's brother is. I see Nanibajou's brother." In a short time the waters of the lake began to be disturbed, and Nanibajou saw the heads of sea-lions emerging on the surface. He promptly changed himself into the stump of a tree and watched the sea-lions. They came up on the beach, and played about upon it. One of the old sea-lions came up to Nanibajou and looked at him suspiciously. "This is a new stump," he said. "How did it come here?" The young sea-lions said, "Why, it has always been here." "I don't think so," said the old sea-lion. "Let us see whether it is a real stump or not." The sea-lions then rushed at

[1] This is the legend, or is apparently derived from the legend, of the Algonkins, in which "a virgin mother bears a white and dark twin, the former of whom becomes the tribal culture hero and demiurgic deity." *Cf.* Brinton, D. G., *The Lenape and their Legends* (Philadelphia, 1885), p. 132.

[2] About the same time (in 1892) the Nanibozho myth was recounted to me by my friend Dr. W. H. Ellis as narrated to him by a Chippeway. The versions differed very slightly, and I may have mingled them in the version I have given as Oronhyateka's.

the stump and endeavoured to knock it over, but Nanibajou extended his roots firmly down into the earth, and held his own against them. "We told you so," said the young sea-lions. "This is a real stump all right." "No, there is something suspicious about it," said the old sea-lions. They left the beach and returned to the lake. Then the little kingfisher began his song again, "I know where Nanibajou's brother is. I see Nanibajou's brother." This convinced Nanibajou that the sea-lions had to do with his brother's disappearance, and he determined to follow them. He transformed himself once more, putting on the skin of the frog, and carrying the medicine-bag on his back he plunged into the lake after the sea-lions. He followed them to the cave of the King of the Sea-lions, and when he came to the entrance he saw his brother's body hanging over the side of the door like a curtain. He took no notice of it, and passed in to the chamber where the king lay sick, saying to the guardian that he had been sent for to attend the king. The chamber was crowded with sea-lions. He insisted upon their leaving the cave because, he said, "I cannot give the king medical attention while this crowd is here." So soon as he was rid of the sea-lions, he killed the king, and then going out rapidly he seizea the body of his brother, and made his way with all speed to the beach. When the sea-lions found the dead king, they pursued Nanibajou, who swam valiantly towards the shore. He gained land before his pursuers, and ran into the forest. When the sea-lions reached the beach, Nanibajou was already out of sight; but they continued their pursuit. Then the waters of the lake rose with them and began to flood the country. Nanibajou fled to a neighbouring hill-top, but still the waters rose. Nanibajou set to work to make a raft, upon which he and his brother might escape. He succeeded in finishing his raft, and when the hill-top was submerged by the water he floated off. Breathing upon the body of his brother, Nanibajou brought him to life. He found that they were not alone upon the raft. Several animals had taken refuge with them. Among these were a loon (the Great Northern Diver) and a musk-rat. This little group were afloat upon the waste of waters. There was no sign of the waters subsiding, so Nanibajou said to the loon, "Will you dive and bring me up ever so small a mouthful of mud? If I have this I can make dry land." The loon dived. After a time it floated up near the raft—dead. Nanibajou took it, and breathing upon it, brought it to life again. Then he turned to the little musk-rat and said, "Will you try?" The little musk-rat dived and came up—dead. Nanibajou breathed upon it and brought it to life again. Once more the little musk-rat dived and came up again—dead. A third time the

I—X

little musk-rat dived and came up—dead; but between its forepaws, which were tightly clasped together, Nanibajou found minute particles of mud. He breathed upon the little musk-rat, brought it to life again and took the particles of mud from its paws. Placing these particles in the palm of his hand, he dried them carefully until he had a small quantity of powdery dust. This he threw upon the water, and gradually the particles extended in a wide circle round the raft. Then Nanibajou traced with his fingers in the water and there were formed rivers and lakes, and valleys and mountains soon made their appearance. Thus the world began. Out of gratitude for the service rendered him by the little kingfisher Nanibajou gave him a topknot of brilliant red, for his head had previously been surmounted by a topknot of ashen grey.

The Indians of Canada are wards of the Government. They are endowed with land reserves, and when as sometimes happens these are surrounded by white settlements, portions of the reserves are purchased from the Indians, and the funds so provided are invested for the benefit of the particular community whose lands are taken. The community enjoys the income of these funds. In addition, each registered Indian is entitled to a subsidy, not great in amount, but sufficient to prevent him from sinking into want. The Mohawks are fairly good farmers, and many of them have shown themselves capable of energetic competition with white men in many fields. The Mohawks of Desoronto, like those of the Grand River, to whom they are related, are Anglicans. I found in both reserves a curious strain of devoutness. Many of them, including Oronhyateka, were members of Orange lodges.

The country in the neighbourhood of Desoronto was at one time a great lumbering region, and in 1892 lumbering was going on at no great distance from the town, where in large mills timber was cut and dressed for domestic use and for export. We had many drives through the woods over the winter roads. The temperature was very low.[1] One day, while walking in the Mohawk reserve, an Indian came up to me, stooped, and taking up a handful of snow, applied it to my ear, saying, "Sir, your ear's froze."

The movement of the Ontario farmers and their sons to the North-West, to Manitoba first and later to the Prairie Territories, began about 1876, became increasingly vigorous towards 1890, and by 1892 had seriously affected the towns which were dependent upon the farming community for their existence. The towns had been distributing

[1] One day 26 degrees below zero F., or 58 degrees of frost.

rather than industrial centres, and thus until industries were established in them it was inevitable that the depletion of the farming
population meant decline and eventual ruin. Protection to industry
thus became the cry of the towns. Indeed, it was in Hamilton that the
policy of protection was first agitated. But protection by means of
a tariff upon imports is a slow remedy. The towns were obliged to
adopt more immediate measures of their own to protect themselves
against decay. They adopted the expedient of offering exemption from
municipal taxation, and even cash bonuses, to manufacturers to
induce them to establish industries. By means of protection on the
one hand and these inducements on the other, industries were established in the towns. But this process had certain reactions. Growth
of industries drew to towns people who otherwise would have remained
on farms, and thus still further accelerated depletion of the rural
population. Moreover, it drew from rural districts workmen who had
carried on rural industries—masons, carpenters, blacksmiths, and the
like. Rural skill declined, and the farmer became more and more
dependent upon urban industry. The effect upon production was
equally important. Rural manufacture had produced goods made
to order and made to endure, urban manufacture produces goods made
to sell, whether they endure or not. Even the farmer who was handy
enough to be his own craftsman, and to do his own saddlery, his own
carpentry work, and his own building, either ceased to perform these
labours, which had rendered him, so far as they went, independent of
the movement of prices or of wages, or migrated to the towns, where
he became a manufacturer on a small scale or a workman.

Protection thus had the following important effects. Production
was increased in quantity and diminished in the quality of durability.
Rural districts were depopulated and urban districts were increased
in number and in population. The self-contained character of the
rural districts passed away, and these as well as the urban districts
became more and more dependent upon external markets.

An efficient industrial system cannot be created to command or
in a hurry. Movements of population are often so rapid that neither
spontaneous nor governmental organisation can cope with their
reactions. Thus the processes which have been described brought
about a certain confusion. The people in the towns were disappointed
at the slow growth of industry, and clamoured for more protection
or for State subventions to specific industries. The farmers had made
for themselves the simple and effective machinery they employed;
but they had abandoned this method, and had become accustomed to

the more complicated though better-finished machines turned out by
the factories. They now clamoured for free trade in these machines.
There thus grew up a divergence of interest between town and country,
a divergence that was destined in later years to produce real conflict.
The effect of these movements upon the society alike of the towns
and of the country was very manifest. People became restless; they
demanded more assistance from the Government; they demanded
expenditure in their districts of public money. Where this money was
to come from they regarded as no concern of theirs. Government
might borrow it and might charge the interest of the loans upon the
railway companies, upon the banks, upon corporations of one sort or
another, upon any group of persons excepting upon those who demanded the expenditure. They meant to resist any form of direct
taxation by means of which they should be themselves compelled to
pay for benefits they were receiving. Anyone might pay so long as
they were not obliged to do so. Under the pressure of this attitude,
useless canals were dug, useless public buildings were constructed,
and avoidable debt was piled upon debt.

The process of industrialisation of Ontario had not, however, gone
very far in 1892, the life of the province was still predominantly an
agricultural and rural life. Meanwhile the economic movement in
the United States had completed the industrialisation of the East;
many farms were abandoned there, partly because high industrial
wages drew men to the towns, and partly because competition of new
land in the Middle West against exhausted land of the East handicapped the eastern farmer. The railway system had been widely
extended in obedience to popular clamour for improved transportation,
and every new railway brought in its train reactions alike upon the
rural district and the town. Anticipations of easily acquired wealth
were sometimes realised, but more frequently they were found to be
illusory. The very agency upon which hopes had been built was cursed
for falsifying these hopes. People clamoured for State control of the
railways in order that rates might be determined by political and not
by economical considerations, hoping that by this means the economical
power of the railways might be diminished, and that of merchants
and manufacturers, and perhaps also that of consumers, might be
increased. But the political control of the railways through Federal
and State Commissions did not merely diminish their earnings, it
destroyed their credit. Extensions became impossible, and even
maintenance of the existing lines was jeopardised. The railways had
been built largely by foreign capital, of which the main portion was

British. The furore against the railways was intensified by the knowledge that foreign capital was largely concerned. Pressure against the railways induced the collapse of some of them, and the combination of groups of lines in order to buttress their credit. Soon the furore against the railway companies was extended to all corporations. As attempts on the part of the politicians and the public to control these corporations increased, the corporations became fewer in number and relatively stronger. Simultaneously the method of conducting corporation business became more unscrupulous, politicians were bought, and the public was alternatively bullied and cajoled.

The consequence of these movements in the United States was a decline in domestic and foreign credit, and eventually a financial crisis. This crisis occurred in 1893. The collapse of foreign credit meant collapse in foreign exchange, and disorder alike in stock and commodity markets. The banking system of the United States, devised to promote competition and to prevent monopoly, had also prevented the concentration of capital necessary to enable financiers, public and private, to deal with financial crises.

The industrialisation of Canada had not proceeded far enough to draw Canada to any material extent into the network of international commerce or finance; and thus the crisis of 1893 in the United States affected Canada very slightly. Exchange turned sharply in favour of Canada, and that was all. Timorous people in Canada began to realise their securities and to accumulate ready cash, but this process was not widely extended.

In 1892 the Conservative Party was in power at Ottawa, although the death of Sir John Macdonald in 1891 had left it without competent leadership. Rival ambitions within the party were destined to ruin it within a few years. In 1892 Ontario was governed, as it had been for about twenty years, by the Liberals, who were fortunate in having as leader and Premier Sir Oliver Mowat, an exceedingly skilful politician and a very able constitutional lawyer. He had collected about him a Cabinet most of whose members were also able politicians. Although the names Liberal and Conservative can hardly be regarded as conveying any very definite indication of the policies of the respective parties, they served as slogans at elections and they assisted in maintaining the party organisations.

The working of the British North America Act, especially during the first twenty years after Confederation, had developed a series of disputes between the Dominion Parliament and the Provincial Legislatures. In these disputes, as the champion of the interests of Ontario,

Sir Oliver Mowat had played a leading rôle. Either because he was never in the wrong, or because he was always able to convert the Judicial Committee of the Privy Council to his point of view, he invariably succeeded in his appeals to that body against the decisions of the Law Officers at Ottawa. It is little wonder, therefore, that political traditions were somewhat slenderly regarded, and that he was able to maintain his Government in power.

On the day of my arrival in Toronto I was introduced to Sir Oliver and to several members of his Cabinet. Sir Oliver asked me some questions about political affairs in Great Britain, and among these asked me what progress was being made in Home Rule for Scotland.

James Mavor. "None at all."

Sir Oliver Mowat. "Why?"

James Mavor. "Because everyone knows that if there were Home Rule in Scotland the government of the country would fall into the hands of a few Edinburgh lawyers."

Sir Oliver Mowat. "Would that be a bad thing?"

James Mavor. "The rest of the country apparently thinks so."

I then realised that Sir Oliver was himself a lawyer, and that nearly all his Cabinet were lawyers also.

Towards the end of the eighties there was a more or less influentially supported movement in Ontario having for its object annexation to the United States. This movement did not originate among the commercial classes, but it was conceived from commercial rather than from political motives. So far as I was able to diagnose it from the fragments surviving in 1892, it had its origin in the trade depression to which I have alluded. The contemporary trade movement in the United States was vigorous while that in Ontario was stagnant, and after the collapse of speculation due to exaggerated anticipations of the rapid development of the North-West, decidedly depressed.

Mr. Goldwin Smith had given the annexation movement the weight of his authority, and had written copiously in its favour.[1] Symptoms of returning trade activity had by 1892 caused the movement to lose impetus, and the crisis in the United States in 1893 for the time being gave it the *coup de grâce*.

The general impression which the society of Toronto made upon me during the first few years of my residence in that city was that which might be supposed to be derived from any provincial town in England or Scotland, excepting that in Toronto the impression was that of a more rather than less provincial region. There seemed to be

[1] *Cf.* vol. ii. chap. xxxii.

little contact with the world at large, and even little contact with the rest of the huge country to which the city belonged. Comparatively few of the leading people were accustomed to travel widely in Canada, and very few of them travelled abroad. Of those who did so, few had the fundamental education necessary to enable them to benefit by foreign travel. Defective education thus produced the same effect as insularity, although Toronto is in the heart of a continent. The people were hospitable and friendly, yet they had slender intellectual interests, and suffered under the illusion that the movements, political, industrial, intellectual and other, of the rest of the world did not concern them, and that there was no need to trouble about them. The tendency towards economical self-containedness which I have noticed extended into fields other than those exclusively economical—into the field of letters, for example. The general public were disinclined, or were supposed to be disinclined, to interest themselves in any country but Canada. There were few Canadian magazines, and these studiously refrained from printing anything about any other country. A story must have its scene laid in Canada. Every article must have the Canadian "view-point." Efforts must be made to develop "sturdy Canadianism" and the like. In this attitude towards the rest of the world, including of course Great Britain, which to most of the people was an unknown and foreign country, Toronto society resembled the corresponding society in the United States, excepting that in the latter the attitude towards Europe was influenced by a certain hostility to Great Britain, a feeling which was not to be found in Toronto or elsewhere in Canada. The most strongly marked difference between the two societies lay precisely in the more intimate contact with Europe, and especially with Great Britain, which Canadian society maintained.

CHAPTER XXIII

> Masters, for that learn'd *Cecil's* skill is deep,
> And sore he doubts of Bacon's cabalism.
> I'll show you why he haunts to *Hatfield* oft;
> Not Doctors, for to taste the fragrant air,
> But there to spend the night in Alchemy
> To multiply with secret spells of art,
> Thus private steals he learning from us all.
>
> ROBERT GREENE, *The Honourable History of Friar
> Bacon and Friar Bungay* (1594). (Slightly adapted.)

THE meeting of the British Association was held at Oxford in 1894. Lord Salisbury, Chancellor of the University, was President. His address was one of the most remarkable of any which have been delivered from the conspicuous rostrum of his position. I had the good fortune, as a delegate bearing an invitation for the Association to visit Canada in 1897, to have a place given to me immediately below the small group on the platform of the Sheldonian. Beside Lord Salisbury there sat Lord Kelvin, and next to him Professor Huxley. It transpired that Kelvin was to move the vote of thanks and Huxley was to second the motion. The incident, not without painful memories, has already been somewhat fully described in the *Life of Huxley*, by his son ; but I may here record my own impressions. Everyone knew of Lord Salisbury's interest in science. He was reputed to be something of a chemist, and to be not unacquainted with electricity, especially on its practical side in the development of electrical engineering in estate management. In short, he was supposed to have what most of the statesmen who have enjoyed the advantages of an Oxford education have conspicuously lacked, a scientific attitude of mind. It might readily have been anticipated, therefore, that he would give in his presidential address a summary of the recent advances in those branches of science in which he was particularly interested, and with which he was generally regarded to have a more than superficial acquaintance. The custom of the presidential chair prescribed a course of that kind. Very rarely, if ever, had a President of the British Association ventured upon ground with which he was not at least as familiar as any of those in the highly expert audience he was addressing.

In the earlier part of his discourse Lord Salisbury was on sure and non-controversial ground. He gave an excellent summary of the main points of the phase of development in chemistry and chemico-physics to which the researches and speculations of Mendeléef and Herz in particular had brought these sciences, remarking with justice that the latter had not brought the problem of the meaning of the complementary forces of negative and positive electricity any nearer to a solution than Franklin had a hundred and fifty years before. Lord Salisbury might with equal justice have mentioned Faraday as the real originator of modern electrical developments, for it is the simple truth that in Faraday's *Experimental Researches* are to be found the germs of all the important developments in electro-physics up till the time when Lord Salisbury spoke.

Had Lord Salisbury stopped at that point all would have been well; but he seemed to be inspired by a curiously perverse humour. He proceeded to revive a controversy which, if not dormant, had been at least quiescent for several years—a controversy which, so far as published evidence went, had not been within the sphere of his imme-diate interests. Using as his text a statement of Weismann, who was more Darwinian than Darwin himself, he proceeded to demolish it after the manner of the ecclesiastics of thirty years before.[1] When he came to this passage in his address, I observed him turn, with what I took to be a mischievous twinkle in his eye, towards Huxley, apparently desiring to enjoy the effect upon him of the attack. Huxley could not disguise his uneasiness; he evidently knew what was coming. Lord Salisbury, with a kind of malice prepense, quoted Kelvin against Darwin, another irritant to Huxley because he must have considered Kelvin a non-expert witness on a biological question. Experienced polemic as Huxley was, the fire had burned out of him. He was emaciated and obviously ill. Gradually, as the speaker proceeded, a remnant of the old vigour seemed to return so that he might meet the grievously disappointing situation. After thirty-five years of hot controversy, in which the opponents of Darwin from the theological standpoint had been so far defeated that evolution was announced in nearly every pulpit, here in Oxford, in the British Association for the Advancement of Science, there appears at the very head of that Association, and before a scientific audience drawn from all parts of

[1] I had heard Weismann develop his thesis fully at Manchester in 1887, and had not been convinced by him. Although the subject is not mine, I distrusted Weismann's dogmatic insistence upon the completeness of his premises. This circumstance does not affect my view of the invalidity of the grounds of Lord Salisbury's attack.

the world, an attitude of extreme obscurantism. The labour of years seemed to have passed for nothing. It was clear that Huxley was profoundly affected. He did not seem to realise that in the first place Lord Salisbury was not speaking *ex cathedrâ*, although he was in the chair of the President, and in the second, that he was attacking rather Weismannism than Darwinism. When Lord Salisbury concluded Lord Kelvin moved the vote of thanks. He did so with perfect honesty. Biology was not his subject. He saw great difficulties from a physico-mathematical point of view in reconciling the Darwinian hypothesis of evolution in biology with the physical data which he had in his mind, and besides, being a devout man, he was reluctant to abandon the idea of design. He therefore undoubtedly was justified, scientific man though he was, in expressing general approval of Lord Salisbury's point of view. It was otherwise with Huxley. Since the publication of *The Origin of Species* in 1859, he had been the chief protagonist of Darwinism. He had imbibed the pure milk of the Darwinian word, and the growth of his reputation as a polemic had been due to its nourishing qualities. When he rose to second the motion, he was clearly suffering from both physical and mental strain. For some moments he controlled himself admirably. He made the complimentary remarks appropriate to such an occasion and then, for a brief space, he let himself go. He did not say much; but what he did say sufficiently indicated the direction of his thoughts and feelings. It was said, not in pessimistic acceptance of destructive criticism, but in vigorous defiance. I thought at the time, and remarked to my friends, "That is the last flicker." It was; Huxley died within two months.

From the reference to the incident in the *Life of Huxley*, by his son, it appears that the day before the delivery of Lord Salisbury's address, a copy of it was sent to Huxley, after he had agreed to second the motion for the vote of thanks. He had, of course, agreed as a matter of course, without being aware of the subject of the address. Huxley spent an anxious night deliberating whether or not he should implement a promise made without knowing what the performance of it implied. He decided that he must implement it as best he could. Had Huxley been younger, he could easily have given an effective answer to the attack; as it was this was impossible.

Looking back upon the incident, I am unable to see that Lord Salisbury made any real contribution to the controversy on one side or the other. Probably both he and Huxley overestimated the import-ance of mere dialectics in scientific discussions. While I do not think that Lord Salisbury shone in such adventures, unless we regard the accomplishment of a *tour de force* with ephemeral effects as shining, I should yield to no one in admiration of his political sagacity, amounting sometimes to very fine genius, and to the capacity he had for taking large and long views, although occasionally he was apt to emit a phrase conveying a contrary, though on the whole wrong, impression.

Among many agreeable memories of the Oxford meeting I recall that at the close of one of the forenoon sessions of Section F, my revered teacher and friend, Edward Caird, Master of Balliol, came into the room to find and carry me off with him for a talk. We picked up Benjamin F. C. Costelloe, who had been a fellow-student of mine, although he was a little older. He was a Snell Exhibitioner. After he left Oxford he was called to the Bar, and later became a member of the London County Council. He wrote the extremely interesting introduction to the *Report of the Markets Rights and Tolls Commission*. We strolled into New College Garden and sat there for a long while talking, chiefly Costelloe, about the London County Council. As it was then a new institution, the Master was much interested in Costelloe's account of the actual working of it. The conversation was entertaining enough; but as it was the last long conversation I had the opportunity of having with Caird I regretted then, as I do now, that it was not steered into other channels.

A dinner at Dr. Charles Lancelot Shadwell's, who then occupied Frewen Hall, at which Professor Edward Newton, the zoologist, and others were present, remains in my mind as a most pleasant recollection. The talk ran chiefly on dialects. Several of those present were extremely well up in the dialects of the southern counties, especially Somersetshire. We had, in long narrow glasses, audit ale—an enchanting and stimulating beverage. Frewen Hall is built on the site of St. Mary's College—where Erasmus studied while he was at Oxford. The walls of the hall literally embrace portions of the ruins, for these are contained in the brick walls of the house, the brick being applied like veneer on both sides of the remains of the ancient building. On that or on some similar occasion I met at Dr. Shadwell's his brother Lancelot, who had written a remarkably original book on economics. He was blind, and not long afterwards he met with a tragic end through an accident due to his blindness. On his election later as Provost of Oriel, Dr. Shadwell left Frewen Hall to reside in the college.

One day during the Oxford meeting, I was asked by the Committee of Section F to introduce the discussion upon a paper contributed by a member upon a subject of which I was supposed to have

some special knowledge. The paper appeared to me to be very superficial. I must have admonished the author rather severely, because
as we walked out of the meeting together, Henry Sidgwick said to
me in a tone of gentle remonstrance:

"You sh-sh-should not have d-d-done that. There was no n-n-need
to k-k-kill the m-m-man. You sh-sh-should just have s-s-said, 'My
g-g-good f-f-fellow, you know n-n-nothing about the s-s-subject.'"

It is possible, after a fashion, to suggest a stammer; but it is
quite impossible to reproduce the charm of Professor Sidgwick's. It
lent a piquancy to everything he said. The rebuke was no doubt
merited; but I have heard Professor Sidgwick himself give the *coup
de grâce* in an argument, which left little breath in the body of his
opponent. No one, I think, excelled Sidgwick in delicious fun when
he had a mind to it. He had been persuaded to write an article on
"Luxury" for the *International Journal of Ethics*; and his principal
example of excessive and inexcusable luxury was the accumulation
of books by one of his friends. He may have had in his mind Lord
Acton, or a still more flagrant offender, Professor J. E. B. Mayor,
because the first had a large and the second an enormous library;
but it was supposed by some that he had especially in mind H. S.
Foxwell, of St. John's. Whether that be so or not, I do not know;
but that he was poking fun at them all is highly probable.

One day, long after the period of which I am at present writing,
I met Professor Sidgwick turning into Whitehall from Downing Street.
I remarked to him that there had been great doings at Cambridge
over the Stokes celebration.

Henry Sidgwick. "Yes, we h-h-had to do something f-for p-poor
old Stokes."

James Mavor. "I have heard that you gave him a good dinner."

Henry Sidgwick. "Yes. We had to g-g-give a g-g-good d-d-dinner
or the G-G-Germans wouldn't have come."

One of the smaller functions of the Oxford meeting was a dinner
given by the Provost and Fellows of Oriel College to the foreign
economists. There was a goodly company. In the common-room,
before dinner, I was standing by Henry Sidgwick, when he drew my
attention to an exceedingly tall figure, taller by a full head than
anyone else in the room.

Henry Sidgwick. "Who is that man with the extraordinarily
able-looking head?"

He was Richard Lodge, afterwards Professor of History at
Edinburgh.

At Oxford I enjoyed the hospitality of Professor Odling, and there at dinner one evening some of my earliest recollections were excited by meeting Admiral Sir Erasmus Ommaney. My mother had come up to Oxford from Scotland, and with one of my sisters was present at this dinner. The Admiral's two sisters had been friends of my mother's early youth, and the Admiral had been a frequent visitor at North-West Castle, Stranraer. He had been a captain in one of Parry's Arctic expeditions.[1] The day after this dinner I parted from my mother to keep an engagement at Cambridge, and shortly afterwards to sail for Canada. I never saw her again. She died at Dunblane two years later.

II.—CAMBRIDGE IN 1894

> Ah, Granta! Shall it ever be
> That I once more shall visit thee?
> Once more admire King's turrets tall
> Down-looking upon fair Clare Hall?
>   " J. G.," in *Cambridge University Magazine*, 1840.

After the close of the Oxford meeting of the British Association, my friend John S. MacKenzie,[2] whom I had known in Glasgow days, was kind enough to invite me to spend two or three weeks with him at Trinity College. This great kindness enabled me to see old friends —Ridgeway,[3] Foxwell,[4] Cunningham,[5] Jebb [6] and Dodds [7]—and also to make some new friends. The experience was a great delight to me. I worked in the University, or in the College Library, or in my rooms, where books were brought for me, during the day, and in the evening dined with the Fellows at Trinity, or at St. John's with Foxwell or

[1] Sir Erasmus Ommaney commanded the small British fleet which during the Crimean War entered the White Sea. The only exploit accomplished by it was firing some round shot into the Solovietsky Monastery. On visiting the island in 1899, my brother Sam was shown some of the shot embedded in the wall of the monastery.
[2] Then Fellow of Trinity College, Cambridge, afterwards Professor of Philosophy, Cardiff.
[3] Then recently transferred from Cork, where he had been Professor of Greek, to Cambridge, where he became Disney Professor of Archæology. Now Sir Wm. Ridgeway, F.B.A.
[4] Herbert Somerton Foxwell, Fellow of St. John's College, Cambridge, and Professor of Political Economy in University College, London.
[5] Wm. Cunningham, D.D., Fellow of Trinity, author of *The Growth of English Industry and Commerce*.
[6] Sir Richard Jebb, formerly Professor of Greek at Glasgow, in 1894 Professor of Greek at Cambridge.
[7] G. M. Dodds, Senior Tutor of Peterhouse.

Stout.[1] Sometimes I joined the Fellows at combination and sometimes I played chess with Stout in his rooms or elsewhere. Ridgeway's archæological researches had interested me for many years, and I often went out to Fen Ditton to spend the afternoon with him, and occasionally I spent some time in Foxwell's library at John's. This library, the most important collection of economic works in existence, was accumulated with enormous labour by Foxwell. Sidgwick's joke was a clever *jeu d'esprit*. Perhaps there is a point at which the accumulation of books, like the accumulation of anything, becomes culpable; but the collection of books upon a special subject, and the careful classification of them, is a real service to mankind. I doubt if the self-sacrificing labours of Foxwell will ever be acknowledged to the full extent of their value. He began to collect economic tracts and books at a fortunate moment. The economical changes of the seventies resulted in dispersal of many libraries which had been buried unused in country houses. These libraries often contained documents of priceless value for the economic historian. If Foxwell or someone else who might have pursued the same method had not collected them, they would in all probability have been destroyed as useless lumber, and the economic material they contained would have been irretrievably lost. It may be quite true that the collection of an individual may far exceed his own powers of digestion or use; but the value of a collection cannot be determined by such a criterion or by the estimate placed upon it by laymen who know nothing of the subject which gives the collection its character. It is often argued that great collections should be public property. This may be, but public officials are rarely competent to make special collections. These can only be made by private enthusiasts. If the intelligent formation and classification of a special library is a vice, it deserves to be called a splendid vice. Its victims are few.

III.—CAMBRIDGE IN 1904

The meeting of the British Association for 1904 was held at Cambridge. During the meeting I enjoyed the hospitality of Clare College. Chrystal, Professor of Mathematics at Edinburgh, was there also, and we had many *causeries* in the Fellows' Garden after dinner. I dined occasionally at John's with Foxwell, and at Caius with Ridgeway. I have noticed in the first part of this chapter the address of Lord Salisbury

---

[1] Then Fellow of John's, now Professor of Logic at Oxford.

as President of the British Association at the Oxford meeting of 1894. The address of his nephew, Mr. Arthur Balfour,[1] as President of the Association, at Cambridge in 1904, was not less remarkable. Mr. Balfour is probably in general regarded as a more intellectual man than his uncle; but his intellectual pursuits have been rather in a philosophical than in a scientific direction. I have noticed that Lord Salisbury undertook an excursion in a field with which he was not known to be familiar, and that with a kind of sardonic humour he rode roughshod over the biologists and especially over the Darwinians. By 1904 the question of evolution had assumed a fresh phase, and the old controversies had died a natural death. Attention had come to be directed rather to the physico-chemical discoveries of Lord Rayleigh, Sir William Ramsay and the Curies than to the variation of species by natural selection or otherwise. It was appropriate, therefore, for Mr. Balfour, in his *résumé* of scientific progress, to take account of the new discoveries. He certainly did not do so in a commonplace manner; he was bright and amusing, but there was here also a spice of sardonic humour. Certain passages of his address were extraordinarily clever pieces of caricature. The exaggeration of them was so subtle that not immediately did it dawn upon the audience that they were listening to an elaborate joke. Doubtless upon some of the audience it did not dawn at all. I walked to my rooms with Sir William Ramsay, who modestly said that he did not understand that part of the address which referred to his particular subject. If it had been intelligible undoubtedly he would have understood it, for no one knew more about the subject than he did. Mr. Balfour is much too intelligent a man to make an unintelligible statement otherwise than consciously and with a purpose. He had the model of his uncle's elaborate joke before him, and he evidently determined to have one of his own. The joke was, of course, not at the expense of either Lord Rayleigh or Sir William Ramsay, but at the expense of the audience which customarily attends such addresses. Such audiences are usually composed of persons who know only one science and of persons who know no science. It is not easy to bamboozle a man in his own field, but it is quite easy to bamboozle him in someone else's field, while those who have no field are still more easily bamboozled. Mr. Balfour was addressing a few physical chemists upon a physico-chemical subject which was out of his range, and he was addressing a larger number of persons who knew no more about physical chemistry than he did himself. He therefore allowed

[1] Now the Earl of Balfour.

his fancy to play about the subject and amused himself in the invention of portentous phrases which were intended to be mere spinning of words—spinning, however—and here was the sting of the affair—which was quite good enough for his audience.

The only excursion connected with the meeting, which I attended, was a visit to Woburn Abbey, where we saw the experimental farm and the wonderful zoological garden of the Duke of Bedford. We were received by Mr. Prothero, the commissioner and the historian of the estate. The experiments at the farm relate principally to the breeding and growing of fruit, but necessarily they include many of general horticultural or agricultural bearing. I was particularly interested in the experiments upon the toxic properties of some grasses, as I had encountered this problem in the Canadian North-West. The zoological collection at Woburn is unique. No animals of a ferocious character are kept; but there are whole herds of each known species of deer, there is a herd of Prejevalski's primitive horse, herds of the four varieties of Icelandic horses, and rare animals of like character. Enormous numbers of aquatic and other birds are kept in freedom or in quasi-freedom, as are all the animals. They are not confined in houses, but have whole parks wherein to range. The zoological collection occupies many hundred acres. In the house there is one of the most remarkable collections of pictures in England. To the best of my recollection there were fourteen Holbeins of the first order in one row in a long gallery. There was by far the finest example of the work of Ferdinand Bol I have seen anywhere, and there were numerous other treasures of distinction.

CHAPTER XXIV

THE NORTH-WEST OF CANADA AND BRITISH COLUMBIA IN 1896

The boundless ineffable prairie;
    The splendour of mountain and lake
With their hues that seem ever to vary;
    The mighty pine forests which shake
In the wind, and in which the unwary
    May tread on a snake;

And this wold with its heathery garment—
    Are themes undeniably great.

. . . .

C. S. CALVERLEY, *Fly Leaves* (1872).

Two circumstances gave an impetus to an economic movement in Canada after the period of depression indicated in a preceding chapter.[1] These were the beginning of an immigration movement from Europe and from the United States and the discovery of new gold-fields in British Columbia. These circumstances occurred almost simultaneously in the summer of 1895. Early the following summer I went westwards in order to visit the localities principally affected by the new tide of immigration and by the gold discoveries.

I have already noticed the boom in the North-West which followed the completion of the Canadian Pacific Railway in 1886 and the subsequent collapse of the boom. Winnipeg had recovered from this collapse, and ten years later the optimism of the West exhibited its customary resilience. I spent a short time in Winnipeg, which impressed me as having been built upon prospective rather than upon realised economical conditions. The agricultural population of the North-West could not at that time support by any production which it might accomplish a city planned on so generous a scale. This invincibly sanguine atmosphere had its invigorating effect. I found an astonishing amount even of intellectual energy in many of the people whom I met. Compared with the sleepy and self-satisfied East, the West had at least the merit of vigour. Yet Winnipeg had clearly been built on credit; and the East had interposed its credit

---

[1] Chap. xxii.

to support it. I found evidences everywhere of the presence of Scottish capital, furnished through the agency of Toronto and Montreal financial houses. By means of this capital the farms of Manitoba had been brought into cultivation and stocked, and by means of it Winnipeg had been built. Even so, it was a raw city; the prairie trails came to its borders; Indian tepees were visible at St. Boniface across the river; and in the heart of the town the wide Main Street was as yet unpaved. On a wet day the mud of it, the so-called "gumbo," was impassable, and there were tales of horses and waggons being lost in its unfathomable depths. Nevertheless the land offices were busy, settlers were coming in, and everybody was confident that the country was going ahead. I travelled through Manitoba by Glenboro, an important Scots settlement, to Souris, and back by Morden and Morris to Winnipeg. Everywhere I found signs of comfort and prosperity, even in some places of luxury, and always evidences of industry. I had an introduction to a member of the Manitoba Legislature in one of the Southern constituencies. When I called upon him I found him painting a wheelbarrow. I presented my letter. He told me that he was too busy to talk to me, and that I had better come some other time. People who are so industrious must thrive. I found later that this man had a capital of not less than fifty thousand dollars. I drove through the Mennonite settlements. Although these people were thrifty and were comfortably settled in good houses, I found their land rather indifferently cultivated. They seemed to be satisfied with a standard of life somewhat lower than that of their neighbours. The Mennonites had migrated from the United States to Manitoba in 1876, aided by their co-religionists in Ontario. Although they were not communists they had a strong sense of communal life, and maintained the traditional character of their community. Their material affairs were regulated by a kaiser and their spiritual affairs by a bishop. They retained their language, which is a corrupt German derived from their ancestors, who migrated from Holland to Germany and from Germany to Russia. The Canadian settlers or their parents had migrated from Russia to the United States. The more conservative of the Mennonite communities had adhered closely to the tenets of their prophet Mennon, from whom they derived their name; but there had been many defections, and groups had separated from the parent stock, bearing with them some, but not all, of their traditions, while individuals had separated themselves wholly from the communities and had been absorbed in the general population. As a group the Mennonites, with their separate language, their separate educational system, and their separate religion, constitute an *imperium in imperio*, a community within the greater community of the State. I shall have occasion in another place to consider the effect upon the North-West of such enclaves.

The general impression which I obtained from this journey through Southern Manitoba was of a country naturally extraordinarily fertile —a large area of the land consists of rich black soil comparable only with the so-called black soil zone in Russia—but indifferently cultivated. The cattle everywhere were very poor stock. At that time very slender efforts had been made to improve it by the introduction of well-bred animals.   Nature was so bountiful that the farmers were disinclined to assist her.

From Winnipeg I went northwards, on what was then the Manitoba and North-Western Railway, to Minnedosa.   At Gladstone I saw the beginning of the Dauphin line, which afterwards grew into the Canadian Northern Railway system. Here were the first important evidences of fresh immigration. Immigrants from Galicia, of whom I shall have more to say hereafter, were pouring in. This migration, destined within succeeding years to assume formidable dimensions, began in 1895. In 1896 the stream became considerable, and these immigrants furnished the labour which built the railways of the North-West from that time onwards.   From Minnedosa I travelled by a small railway, which rejoiced in the grandiloquent name of the Great North-West Central, to a village equally grandiloquently named Rapid City. One day it may be destined to assume municipal importance, but then it consisted of but a few houses. One of my students was about this time in charge of the school at this place.   He told me that on his arrival at his post he visited the only merchant, who kept a "general store." On one of the shelves he found a number of books. These consisted of about a dozen copies of Kant's *Critique of Pure Reason* in the English translation.   He asked the merchant why he had so large a stock of so recondite a work. The merchant told him that there were many Germans in the neighbourhood, and that some bookselling agent had recommended Kant as a German author of note.   The investment had not been remunerative, since no purchaser had been attracted.[1]   From Rapid City I drove, late in the evening, across country by prairie trail to Brandon.

[1] "The *Critik der Reinen Vernunft* was published about five years before the French Revolution, but lay unnoticed in the publisher's warehouse for four or five years" (De Quincey, *Logic of Political Economy*, Edinburgh, 1863, p. 116 n.). If this is true, we need not be surprised that the circulation of Kant's most important book should have been no speedier in Rapid City, Manitoba, than in

Some miles from Brandon we stopped at a farm-house. The hour was about eight in the evening. All was dark; the family had evidently gone to rest. With much good-nature, however, the farmer and his wife rose and prepared supper for my driver and myself. At that time there was a generally diffused habit of hospitality in the North-West. The population was thinly spread over a vast region, distances were great between settled areas, places of public accommodation were widely separated. Movement about the country would have been impossible unless travellers could count upon being hospitably entertained by the settlers when need arose.

Brandon was an important wheat-shipping centre, and there were many elevators at the station. The hotel, the best in the place, was almost unendurable.

At Regina I began to realise the meaning of one of the most serious of the problems of the western prairies. The year 1895 had been a dry year—i.e., a year in which the rainfall is less than the evaporation from the surface over a given area. Such years may be counted upon to occur periodically. When two or three dry years come together, and when the grain crops are parched and the grasses withered, the farmers become discouraged, "pull up stakes," and go away. South of Regina, in the immediately preceding years, the district of Weymouth had been settled and emptied, and was in process of being slowly settled again. The evidences of long-continued drought were everywhere. There were cracks in the blue clay subsoil to the depth, sometimes, of several feet. The soil had not moisture enough to hold it together. The surface of the earth seemed to be undergoing the process of frying.

I found that an ecclesiastical conference was going on at Regina, and that all the missionary bishops of the North-West and beyond were present. I met them at dinner at Government House. The Archbishop of Prince Rupert's Land—the early name for the greater part of the region now forming the provinces of Manitoba, Saskatchewan and Alberta—Dr. Machray, and Dr. Reeve, Bishop of Mackenzie River, were there, as well as other bishops of regions less remote. Both Dr. Machray and his son were Sidney Sussex (Cambridge) men.

The Lieutenant-Governor of the North-West Territories in 1896 was Mr. Charles Macintosh, a genial and hospitable man. After

Königsberg, where Kant was born, and where he was a professor in the University. But De Quincey's story is faulty. The first edition of the *Pure Reason* was published in 1781, eight years before the French Revolution. It may be that its sale was impeded by the censorship upon other writings of Kant's; yet a second edition was published in 1781.

dinner with the bishops and a game of billiards with my host, I went to the house of Mr. Haultain,[1] the head of the Territorial Government. Here I met Colonel Perry, afterwards Commissioner of the North-West Mounted Police, and Mr. Insinger, a member of the Territorial Assembly. These gentlemen had very kindly convened themselves at the only hours at my disposal, and they devoted them to instructing me upon the affairs and prospects of the Prairie Territories. I was much impressed by their breadth of view and by the intelligence with which they were evidently grappling the problems presented by a new and sparsely settled country. They had all resided in it for many years, and they were all familiar with every part of the wide region and apparently with almost every person in the country. Mr. Insinger was a Dutchman, connected through his mother with the celebrated Scots-Dutch family, the Hopes, who had been settled in Amsterdam for two hundred years. Mr. Insinger had come to Canada for his health and had settled on a ranch near Yorkton. He represented in the Territorial Legislature the district in which he lived. I found that he had made a serious study of municipal administration, and that he was chiefly responsible for the legislation concerning local government in the Ordinances of the North-West Territories.

The question of the erection of the territories into provinces, and of endowing the people with provincial rights, had not yet been recognised as falling within the field of practical politics, although it was destined very soon to become hotly discussed. Mr. Haultain told me that he was in favour of dividing the territories into provinces, but he thought that a long time must elapse before division would be an act of wisdom. In any case, he said, whenever the provinces are erected, the provincial governments will greatly increase the cost of administration, and in order to avoid the unpopularity of increased taxation must inevitably plunge the new provinces into debt. He prophesied with accuracy, for no sooner were the Prairie Provinces brought into existence, as they were soon afterwards, than both Saskatchewan and Alberta were in the market for money for the provincial governments and for the municipalities, whose powers of borrowing were now unrestrained.

I am convinced that it would have been a great advantage if the erection of the new provinces had been deferred for ten or fifteen years, until a larger population had settled in them and a greater number of experienced men of affairs had come to be available for the conduct of the administration. Under the territorial system the

[1] Afterwards Sir Frederick Haultain.

country was governed with economy and intelligence by competent and conscientious men. Under the provincial system these were promptly got rid of and replaced by men, in general, without education and without experience. The result was as Mr. Haultain anticipated. We talked over the climatic and administrative difficulties of the country until the time came when I must go to the train. Early in the evening Mr. Insinger had decided to go west with me, and we reached the station in time to catch the train about six o'clock in the morning. Mr. Insinger and I travelled together for several weeks in Alberta and British Columbia. At Calgary we were hospitably entertained at the Ranchmen's Club, then pleasantly housed in a modest cottage, and we were driven out to visit the irrigation farm of Mr. Hull, some miles from the town. For the first time I saw irrigation on the grand scale. We drove through a field of mixed brome and timothy grass the general height of which was fully nine feet. The field was being harvested and we saw the novel mechanical appliances which were necessary to manipulate the enormous weight of the crop. Here also we saw a herd of fine Hereford steers, and lunched with the cowboys at a table with a large revolving centre, upon which were placed the dishes, from which we helped ourselves, spinning the table until the dish we wanted was within reach. The gargantuan vegetables were, of course, grown under irrigation. The first experiment in this method of agriculture in the Calgary region was conducted by my friend William Pearce, of the Canadian Pacific Railway Land Department, upon his farm, then in the outskirts of Calgary. His example was followed by Mr. Hull, and later by others. Afterwards the Canadian Pacific Railway Company constructed a large dam upon the Bow River, and provided for the irrigation of a part of their dry lands in the Calgary region.

From Calgary we went to Banff, where we made an excursion to Devil's Lake and climbed Tunnel Mountain. Then we went on to Revelstoke through the mountains. The grandeur of the Rockies and their subsidiary ranges must be seen; I cannot undertake a description. Comparison with Switzerland is to my mind fruitless. Each region has its peculiar beauties and its own magnificence. In sheer beauty of individual peaks, like the Jungfrau, the Matterhorn, the Aiguille Verte and the Aiguille de Dru, Switzerland is probably incomparable; but if magnitude be regarded as the criterion, then the Rocky Mountains easily excel, while there are a few individual peaks of fine mountain form like Mount Donald or Mount Stephen. In the Rockies, and even more in the Selkirks, the glaciers are impressive; but I did not find those I saw more so than the Swiss ice fields.

From Revelstoke we went to Arrow Lake, and embarked on the steamer for Nelson and Traill. The night sail on the Arrow Lakes and the Columbia River was a wonderful experience. At frequent points on the horizon we saw the glare of forest fires and realised the fearful handicap suffered by British Columbia in the destruction of timber these involved. A recent commission found that out of twenty-four trees in British Columbia which must annually be deducted from the forest resources, twenty-two are destroyed by fire, one is destroyed by disease, and only one is utilised. This is one of the tragedies of British Columbia.

Our vessel was navigated in the night by means of a powerful searchlight. There were no stationary lights on the lake shore or the river banks. The prow of the vessel was wedge-shaped, so that when it was desired to make a landing at a place where there was no wharf or other landing accommodation, the nose of the vessel was simply run up on the bank of the lake shore. The navigation was not easy. Large logs were frequently met with floating on the stream, and sometimes an uprooted tree had floated and sunk in such a way as to leave its roots resting on the bottom and the trunk rising many feet out of the water.

During the night we stopped at many places where there were scanty signs of settlement. Occasionally a rough board nailed upon a tree on the bank announced that the place was Maryville or Pine City, or the like; and sometimes there was near this board a wooden shack and a tent, the only signs of habitation. Now and again we stopped at a point where even these signs were absent, but where a trail emerged from the forest. At such a place a prospector would land with his horse and his equipment, consisting of a bag containing the flour, bacon, tea, sugar and tobacco by means of which he proposed to subsist during his solitary expedition in search of gold or silver ore. Robson was the terminus of a railway, and was therefore in the enjoyment of a wharf. In the morning we came to the rapids of the Columbia, and we were piloted with great dexterity through the swirling currents past jagged rocks that projected themselves in mid-stream. Traill had been founded the previous year, but the stumps of the forest trees which had been cut down to make an open space for the town were still standing, the streets were of the crudest order, and some of the people were living in shacks; a large number of the more recent settlers were living in tents. I saw in a

shop an announcement to the effect that shares in the Keble Mine
were for sale. Inquiry revealed the fact that an Oxford undergraduate,
prospecting, had found what he thought was a mine, and had endowed
it with the name of his college. The Traill smelter had been established,
I think, in October 1895, but I did not visit it.   The same afternoon
I took the switchback railway from Traill to Rossland.   The little
train was crowded and we had to accommodate ourselves as best
we could in the caboose or baggage waggon.   The distance was seven
miles and the fare was one dollar.   In a mining camp the cost of
living does not count, everybody is supposed to be rolling in money,
and everyone wants to get ready cash for his needs by discounting
the future by selling mining stocks at a base fraction of their nominal
value.   Such documents were often used, when they could be used, as
a form of currency.   Rossland, although scarcely a year old, was a
busy little town.   There was a good hotel and a long main street,
upon both sides of which houses, shops and brokers' offices were
being built.   I saw a large safe being put into a shack which had
been prepared for it—the agency of the Bank of Montreal.   There
were numerous saloons.   There was a public dance-hall.   The main
street was not yet graded.   In the centre of the eastern end of it there
was a high rock which occupied almost the whole width of the street,
and the traffic had to find its way round it.   At the west end of the
street, and in the middle of it, a miner was working a claim.   The
town was full of prospectors coming and going from the mountains,
registering their claims and raising money upon them, or reporting
their finds to the speculators who "grub-staked" them, or provided
them with funds to support them while prospecting, and also agreed
to pay them wages while they were searching for gold.   All night
long voices in the streets were heard talking of gold—gold—always
gold—as if nothing else in the world mattered.   Samples of the ore
were handed about, people bought mining stocks at one end of the
street and sold them at the other.   In the hotel champagne flowed
freely when promoters of mining deals came into the town.   There
was a long street occupied by houses of ill-fame; and there were, no
doubt, disorderly elements.   These were kept under sharp control by
one policeman—a certain John Kirke—who was the solitary representative of the majesty of law.   A very efficient representative he
was.   He tolerated much, but he would not tolerate any violence.
One day a miner from the United States, accustomed to the free use
of the revolver in the camps across the border, drew his weapon in
the street in Rossland.   The heavy hand of John Kirke came down

upon him. He was charged with carrying arms without a licence, and shipped at once to the jail at Yale, about three hundred miles away and many miles from any mining camp. He would probably be sentenced to a month's imprisonment, and then discharged in a place in which there was no employment, and out of which he would probably have to walk for many days before he could get near any goldfield. The distance of the jail at Yale was a great asset in the business of maintaining order at Rossland.

One of the characters of the region at that time was the Rev. Mr. Irwin, universally known among the miners as Father Pat. He was a clergyman of the Church of England, but he had no definite charge. He wandered about the mining camps, slept in the miners' shacks, and undoubtedly ministered to the miners in his own way.

The only means of getting about the mountains was on horseback. There were a few roads to the mines that had begun to be developed; but otherwise only bridle-paths or the roughest kind of trail led from the town to the prospects in the hills. The horses, known as cayuses, had been brought from the prairies; but they had already learned the trick of mountaineering. The new conditions may have stimulated their intelligence. Some wiseacres in horseflesh insist that the horse is naturally a stupid and timid animal. The cayuse is not. He has wisdom beyond his years. He is as expert in going down a steep slope as he is indefatigable in going up one. I have seen exhibitions of cavalry in many countries; but such evolutions as were performed in these were performed every day in the mountains by cayuses under much less nimble riders. I was riding one day along an extremely narrow and uncertain path on the face of a mountain and on the edge of an abrupt declivity of about three hundred feet. A tumble meant death both to man and horse. My cayuse slipped and came down on his knees. Instead of struggling to rise, a proceeding that might have been fatal, he remained perfectly still. I dismounted and went to his head. He then rose with deliberate caution.

The whole country round Rossland was staked out in mining claims, and parties were being every day organised to visit more or less distant prospects, which were being boomed by the discoverer or by people who had purchased his prospect from him. There were amateurs in the business of mining, and there were experienced miners who had pursued their calling in the mining camps of the United States, of South Africa and of Siberia. The call of gold had been heard by them in the most distant places. There was even a man with a divining-rod who was seeking gold by means of it. This man had been known as a water-finder, and he was trying his skill on metals. I am not aware that he found any gold; but one day there was an alarm in the camp that he was lost himself in the mountains. Search parties were organised, and late at night the diviner was discovered in an exhausted condition.

I made the acquaintance of an old miner who had been a "forty-niner," *i.e.*, he had been mining gold in California during the mining boom of 1849. He had come to the Rossland district before Rossland was, and, I think in 1894, had, along with two other experienced miners, explored the region, and had made the first discoveries of gold. If I am not mistaken, they had come from the Pend d'Oreille mining camps, and they had been struck by the similarity of the diorites of British Columbia to those of Idaho. There they had always found gold-bearing veins underlying the diorite, and they found that the same formations occurred in British Columbia. Their search for the veins was prolonged. They had exhausted their resources, and had not the wherewithal to pay the necessary fees to the Government for the registration of their claims. They were able to convince the official of the value of their discoveries, and he undertook to provide the funds on condition of his being given an interest in the claims to the extent of one-quarter. Out of these discoveries and this transaction there grew the well-known Leroy and Centre Star mines. My friend whom I have mentioned, whose name was Durant, had somehow been able to acquire from his partners complete control of the Centre Star claim, and he proceeded to work it on his own account, driving with his own hands, and with what labour he was able to procure, the drifts which enabled him to ascertain the probable total value of the mine. When I made his acquaintance he was living alone in a log shanty at the mine, and he was still engaged in driving his drifts. I often visited him; he took me through the mine, which was even then very extensive. He told me that the only way to conduct gold-mining profitably was by the exercise of the most rigid economy. "Look after the candle ends," he said, "and the mine will come out all right." He told me the value at which he had estimated the ore already disclosed by his operations, and the price which he intended to ask for the mine. "I will keep the mine and work it," he said, "until I get my price." He kept his word, and about a year after I saw him he sold the mine at the price he had mentioned. Whether or not the purchasers realised their anticipated profits or even recovered their expenditure I do not know, but Durant received his money. While he was at Rossland he evidently lived with the greatest frugality. He had developed his mine on credit and had to borrow upon the security it gradually came to represent. When at last he found himself in funds he discharged his obligations, and then, taking with him a relatively large sum of money, he went to New York, where I was told he enjoyed—or supposed he enjoyed—three glorious weeks. He was by no means a young man, and he had more than once had similar although less remunerative mining adventures; but the rebound from poverty and debt to affluence carried him, for the moment, off his feet. He returned to his home in the Western States and, I have no doubt, lived happily ever after.

The experience of Durant was, I believe, the experience of at least a few of the pioneers in the gold-fields of Southern British Columbia; but of the speculators and of the general economic effect upon the country another story must be told later.

After two or three weeks in and about Rossland, we went to Nelson on the Columbia River. Here we found an older and less crude mining camp. The Hall copper mines had established there a smelter, to which the copper was brought by an overhead gravitation system of transport on the Lartigue plan, which had many years before been advocated by Fleeming Jenkin.[1]

From Nelson we went to Kaslo, a small camp in which, so far as external appearance went, there seemed to be congregated the roughest of mining populations. Every man looked like a bravo of Venice, and conducted himself with unexceptionable propriety. In the evening we took a box at the "Grand Opera House." The pit was occupied by small tables, round which the audience sat, smoked and drank, waiters being kept moving about replenishing their glasses. The play, the name of which I have forgotten, was a sentimental domestic drama, in which sorely-tried virtue was finally triumphant. The actors were an itinerant troupe of the feeblest sort, and their wardrobe evidently differed not at all from that of their audience. If they carried any properties with them they did not use them on the stage. I have no doubt that had a modern problem-play been offered to them the miners would have hissed; they were perfectly familiar with the shady side of life, and they wanted something to which they were unaccustomed. Presentation of the domestic virtues suited their mood precisely.

Kaslo had had its moment of magnificence, and like many another more ancient city had fallen from its high estate. The particular circumstances which led to its rise and to its fall are not of moment

[1] *Cf. supra*, chap. v.

to record here. The fall was sudden. It came like a bolt from the blue. One morning the local newspaper printed across its first page in the largest letters its limited founts of type afforded, "Bust! By Gosh!" This calamity occurred shortly before our visit, and the empty houses and shops and the deserted street afforded tangible evidence of decline. When a collapse of this kind strikes or even threatens a mining camp, the prospectors, miners, and camp-followers desert the place at once, and, abandoning it to its fate, seek another field for their speculative energies.

From Kaslo we went by a small and shabby mountain railway to Sandon, a mining camp in a narrow gorge. The line passed through forests devastated by fire. Excepting in an area in which every living thing is demolished by heavy artillery bombardment, it is impossible to conceive anything more desolate. Hundreds of square miles of burnt timber, the remains of tree trunks standing gaunt and blackened, and everywhere fallen timber half reduced to charcoal by the flames, made an indescribable scene of desolation. At one point in the line a large tree had fallen across it. The crew of the train decided to return; but on attempting to do so, it was found that another tree had fallen behind us. Our train therefore returned to the first-mentioned obstacle, and in course of time it was removed by means of saws and axes.

We had passed from the region of gold into that of silver; for the mineral at Sandon was galena, and the lead and silver were both recovered on the spot. Sandon was confined within the narrow limits of a gorge, but it was a prosperous little place. The galena was plentiful; the lead was easily recovered, and the silver concentrates were shipped to Helena or Butte, Montana, for reduction. There was more of an industrial than a speculative atmosphere. A neat little club indicated a society less uncultivated than we had seen at Kaslo.

From Sandon we made our way once more to the Arrow Lakes and to Revelstoke, from which we went on to Vancouver. At that moment Vancouver had scarcely begun to feel the stimulus of the gold discoveries. The city owed its existence and what prosperity it enjoyed to the fact that it was the terminus of the Canadian Pacific Railway and the centre of a great lumbering industry. The forest still impinged upon the city. The short electric line between Vancouver and New Westminster ran through a dense mass of enormous trees. I saw a single log being hauled by sixteen horses. Lumbering was, however, not a prosperous business. Wages were high and labour was difficult to procure. There was a comparatively slender demand for timber. Some of the largest lumbering companies were in the hands of liquidators for the benefit of their shareholders and creditors. New Westminster had been rebuilt after a fire which had reduced the town to ashes, and owing to the salmon fisheries its canning establishments were briskly occupied. In both places Chinese and Japanese were extensively employed, the Chinese chiefly in the canning factories and the Japanese in the lumber yards. Both, but especially the Chinese, were also employed in domestic service. In the neighbourhood of Vancouver, as also at Nelson and other places, the Chinese had become extensive market gardeners. The trade unions were powerful enough to insist upon restriction of Oriental immigration and upon the imposition of a heavy poll-tax upon Chinese immigrants.

The sail across the channel and through the Canal of Haro to Victoria was very fine, and the view of Puget Sound and the distant mountains of Washington Territory [1] was magnificent.

Victoria owed its existence to the fact of its being a Hudson Bay post. The Hudson Bay Company had gone beyond the territory defined in its original grant, and had established a post there in order to facilitate its trade with Alaska, which it had carried on during a large part of the period of Russian possession of that country. During the Crimean War Russia had not interfered with the Hudson Bay Company, in spite of the fact that it was subject to Great Britain; and at the close of the war offered to sell the region to the company for, I believe, one million pounds. The company, however, declined to entertain the offer, on the ground that it was too large an enterprise. When Alaska was acquired by the United States, the Hudson Bay trade on the coast declined. Discoveries of gold were made in British Columbia early in the fifties, and the gold dust and nuggets were purchased by the company at its post at Victoria. From that post also the company supplied the miners and prospectors. The attention of the directors of the company was thus attracted to British Columbia, and certain individual directors, among whom was the late Lord Strathcona, made extensive purchases of land on the island of San Juan da Fuca and elsewhere, forming a separate company for the purpose. The remoteness of the colony and the length of the voyage round Cape Horn, the only practicable route by which it could be reached until the railway was stretched across America, retarded its growth, and settlement increased very slowly. The construction of the Canadian Pacific Railway, which was completed

[1] Now the State of Washington.

in 1886, gave the mainland and the island of Vancouver a great impetus. The geniality of the climate and the beauty of its surroundings attracted to Victoria many Englishmen of means, who formed the nucleus of an agreeable society. But a society of this kind is apt to lack vigour, and in the absence of other immigration is inevitably destined to meet with economical discouragement. In 1896 Victoria was rather stagnant. It was the port from which the Canadian Pacific liners sailed for Japan, China and Australia, and that was all. The naval station of Esquimalt, in the immediate neighbourhood of the city, was still in the hands of the British Admiralty, and a cruiser was generally stationed there; but while this circumstance brought naval men to the port, it meant little for the prosperity of the community.

Yet the society was extremely pleasant, many notable persons having their houses in or near Victoria. Clive Phillips-Woolley [1] and Warburton Pike,[2] for example, both lived at no great distance. Both had been in their earlier years adventurous travellers, and both were first-rate sportsmen.

Under the guidance of some official persons we visited Chinatown in Victoria. This quarter did not at that time differ from similar quarters elsewhere. Warren-like houses, such as I afterwards saw in Fuchow and elsewhere in China, were occupied almost to suffocation. We found the Chinese playing their own gambling games and their own musical instruments. In a restaurant we found four men sitting round a table, upon which there was a savoury ragout in a bowl in the centre. Each man had a spoon and they all ate from the common dish. They courteously allowed us to taste their dish; we found it very good. Each man had a bottle of Chinese wine made, no doubt, from rice; but of this we felt incompetent to judge the merits.

The Chinese problem in British Columbia, like that in California, is very complicated. I had a long conversation on the subject with a leading trade-unionist in Victoria. His principal objections to the Chinese were that they taught the white youths to smoke cigarettes which contained a little opium and that they used in their market gardens human excrement as manure. Of the really important issues he did not seem to have any idea. He disclaimed at once the notion that the Chinese were objected to because they were willing to work for lower wages than Europeans.

It is very obvious that if British Columbia be regarded, not primarily

---

[1] Sir Clive Phillips-Woolley was the author of many books on sport, *e.g.*, *Savage Svanetia* (on hunting in the Caucasus), and of some fine patriotic verse.
[2] Warburton Pike was the author of *The Barren Lands*.

as a place of residence for Europeans attracted by the geniality of
its climate and the opportunities it affords for sport, but rather as
a country rich in natural resources awaiting exploitation for the
general service of mankind, the exploitation of these resources is
the first consideration. If the migration to British Columbia from the
other provinces of Canada suffices to carry on this exploitation, the
population of the province will be homogeneous; if there is immigration from the United States, from the British Islands, or from Continental Europe, the population will be less homogeneous, but it will
still be predominantly European. If, however, this immigration is
either inadequate in numbers or in industrial activity to meet the
contemporary demand for the products of British Columbia, either
the economical prosperity of the province must be compromised,
as well as the prosperity of other countries, or non-European
labourers must be admitted to share in the exploitation.

.The Chinese have been admitted; but under certain conditions.
These conditions are that only by permission not easily obtained are
Chinese women allowed to enter the country, and that Chinese men
must pay a heavy poll-tax. The social reactions of the first condition
can readily be imagined, the reactions of the second are not less
disadvantageous. The poll-tax on entry was, in 1896, five hundred
dollars. This sum, an enormous one for a Chinese labourer in China,
is customarily paid for him by a company organised for the purpose
of conducting the business of Chinese emigration. This company
advances the steamship fare and the entry tax for selected emigrants.
When these men arrive in Canada they are thus heavily in debt.
Repayment instalments and interest absorb, for a time, the whole
of their surplus earnings, and they must perforce live with the utmost
frugality. During the period of this debt dependence the Chinese
are, in effect, peons or slaves of the company. If the entry tax is
increased in amount the period of peonage becomes longer. There
is no difficulty in obtaining the necessary funds in China for emigration, because the profits of the exploitative trade in emigrants are
very great.

On the side of China the real difficulty will arise when the Straits
Settlements, to which Chinese migrate in vast numbers, are over-
populated. Up till now the Malay Peninsula has been the reservoir
into which the surplus population of China has been pouring. When
this reservoir is full, the congestion in China must become insupport-
able or other reservoirs must be found. British Columbia, and not
less Australia, must thus encounter a grave dilemma. They must find

the exploitation of their resources restricted or they must open their doors, either widely in obedience to external pressure or in some guarded fashion, through peonage, as under the present system in British Columbia, to greatly increased Chinese immigration.   In either of the two last-mentioned cases, these countries must experience the social difficulties encountered in all systems of slavery or quasi-slavery, where the proletariat consists largely or exclusively of races recognised as inferior to the dominant race.

The case of the Japanese is on a different footing. Although the people of British Columbia do not habitually discriminate between different Oriental races, the treaties between Great Britain and Japan involve special treatment of Japanese migrants. The immigration of Japanese is restricted, but so also is the emigration from Japan. Although the population of Japan is increasing rapidly, and although emigration has become almost a necessity, the problem is by no means so urgent or likely to be so grave as the problem of China.[1]

Among the important resources of British Columbia is coal.   In the eastern part of the province there were beds of anthracite which have now been almost exhausted; in the south-east and in the north-east parts there are beds of bituminous coal. The principal mines in Vancouver Island are the bituminous mines at Nanaimo, about eighty miles north of Victoria, on St. George's Channel. I had the good fortune to go down one of the pits.   These mines extend for several miles under the waters of the channel, the coal being brought from the more distant chambers of the mine by means of an electric railway actuated by a trolley. We had a weird journey on this line, crouching low in the waggon in order to keep clear of the trolley, which was only a few inches above our heads. The mine was a thousand feet deep, and at the foot of it there was a lofty and wide chamber, off which there were stables for horses, these being used, as well as electricity, for transport. I noticed that, while all the miners were Europeans, the men who manipulated the hutches of coal as they reached the pit-head were Japanese.   The activity and muscular strength of these Japanese labourers impressed us very much. The labour laws of British Columbia did not permit Oriental labourers to work underground.

In the afternoon I called at the office of Mr. Bray, the Gold Commissioner for the Nanaimo district, which at that time had a very large area. While I was in his office four men came in to register mining claims. In the evening Mr. Bray told me that these men had

[1] For Chinese and Japanese migration see vol. ii., chaps. xxxviii. and xxxix.

come to register the first claims upon the Stewart River in the extreme north-western part of Canada. The discoveries of these pioneers led to the opening-up of the celebrated mining field known as the Klondyke. Within a few months the rush into the Klondyke began.

In general, British Columbia gave me the impression of a country whose economical conquest must encounter great difficulties. In spite of the improvement of the means of transport, it must always lie at a relatively enormous distance from the centres of population, and therefore from the great markets. The very magnitude of its timbers and of the area covered by forests render the clearing of the land impossible without labour and capital on a huge scale. The labour required was of the roughest and most strenuous character, even when it was facilitated by machinery. But few of the immigrants into the colony were either inured to or inclined for strenuous labour, and perhaps the climate is not conducive to great exertion. The indigenous inhabitants of the coast, the Siwash Indians, are probably of all the Indian races the least energetic.

During the gold fever of 1895–98 people from all parts of Canada, and indeed from many remote parts of the world, were drawn into British Columbia to look for gold, either by prospecting for it or to get it by some means out of the hands of successful prospectors. Farmers rented or even abandoned their farms in Prince Edward Island, in Nova Scotia, in Ontario and in the Prairie Territories, and set out for the new El Dorado. These men sometimes endured enormous hardships, many of them lost their lives; yet these hardships were not undergone in productive labour, but in toil to reach a scene where they might take part in a game of chance. This invasion of British Columbia and, through British Columbia, of the Klondyke brought a certain amount of trade to the merchants of Vancouver and Victoria, and to the railway and shipping companies; but the discoveries of gold drew the whole population into the network of speculation and brought about a contempt for the slow and arduous labour of normal industry. Since it was supposed that anyone might equip himself in an hour for the business of prospecting, and since people of the most diverse occupations embarked upon it, wages in general came to be based upon the wages of prospectors. The gold-fields drew off labourers and those who remained in their customary occupations demanded the same pay as the gold-seekers. The market for labour was thus demoralised, and the market for commodities inflated by the demand for supplies for the mining camps. Meanwhile

I—Z

capital was being drawn into the province from the East, and through the East from Great Britain and the continent of Europe as well as from the United States. It is difficult to form any estimate of the total amount of external capital invested at this time in machinery and in management and wages in anticipation of gold yields which were expected to enable the speculators to refund their capital with handsome profits in addition.

The Northern British Columbia gold areas, which had been exploited somewhat sporadically since about 1850, were known as placer areas. The gold was present in the river gravels and in the sandy beds of the rivers. The gravels were washed in the earlier years by simple means, and later by formidable "monitors" which threw jets of water with great force upon the river banks. The gold thus recovered was almost pure. In the southern gold-field of British Columbia the gold existed in chemical combination with other substances. The process of reduction was difficult and expensive. Materials for fluxes were rarely readily available and some of the ores were insusceptible of being economically reduced unless they were mingled with less refractory minerals. Only certain ores could, therefore, be reduced in British Columbia, and the refining of almost none of the ores was possible in the neighbourhood of their exploitation.

It is almost quite certain that the value of the total yield of gold from the workings in Southern British Columbia has fallen far short of the total amount of external capital which has been invested in the enterprises. Technical difficulties, together with the difficulty of procuring labour at a price which the enterprises could afford, rendered the greater number of the prospects abortive. Meanwhile, the more stable industries were compromised through the effect of the gold mania upon wages. There was an inundation into the country of ready money through the supply of external capital, spasmodic growth of mining towns and of distributing centres from which they drew their supplies, advances in the price of land in these places —and in the course of time discouragement, disappointment and collapse. While the gold discoveries drew attention to British Columbia and while they gave a temporary stimulus to the country, it is doubtful if they can be regarded as otherwise than harmful to its serious development.

There are certain advantages in local autonomy, but when it comes to handing over to a small number of persons an area which they are unable to utilise in spite of their legally monopolistic powers, the disadvantages become apparent. The province of British Columbia had, in 1896, the area of a huge state and the population of a moderately-sized town.

While I was in Regina, Colonel Herchmer, then Commissioner of the North-West Mounted Police, was kind enough to offer to arrange for me an excursion under the auspices of his force to enable me to visit the ranches in Southern Alberta. When I returned to Calgary I made my plans in such a way as to avail myself of this generous offer. I intended to begin with the Stinson ranche, which was well known because of the remarkable personality of the owner. When I arrived at High River, where I had arranged for horses to meet me, I was prevented from carrying out my purpose by a heavy storm of rain and sleet. I therefore went on to Macleod, the principal Mounted Police post on the western prairies. Here I found Colonel Steele,[1] who furnished me with a waggon, horses, and a mounted escort. The day after my arrival was a fête-day at Macleod. On that day were held the annual races and steer-throwing and bucking-horse competitions. The races were a remarkable spectacle. At no great distance from Macleod is the large reserve of the Blood Indians, and not far away are the Sarcee and Peigan reserves. The Macleod races are the great festival of these peoples. They enter their ponies for the races, and they come almost *en masse* as spectators. All morning the Indians were riding over the prairie towards the race-course. I saw a powerfully-built Blood squaw riding a large horse which drew a travoy upon which rested a cradle bearing her papoose. The travoy consists of two poles, one end attached to the saddle gear and the other trailing on the ground.

When the races began the Indians lined up at the railing, all mounted. I doubt if in any races in any other part of the world are the spectators all on horseback. The Indians are very fond of betting; they bet their money, their blankets and their horses. They prepare for the races by training their ponies and their youngsters as jockeys. There is never any difficulty about starting. They line up their horses with the greatest dexterity and they customarily ride with the utmost fairness. The steer-throwing by cowboys was an amazing performance. The range animals of that period were very large, and an unusual combination of strength and skill was necessary to rope and throw them. Co-operation of horse and rider was remarkable. The lariat or looped rope was thrown over the horns of the steer, sometimes after long pursuit. The steer was fatigued by being kept in motion

[1] Afterwards Sir Sam Steele. General Officer in command of the Military District of Kent during the later years of the war.

continually until, by a sudden forced movement, the animal lost his balance and fell. Then the cowboy dismounted, while his horse, with the lariat attached to the saddle, held the steer, keeping the rope taut and watching every motion. The cowboy proceeded to tie the legs of the steer and thus render him powerless. The bucking competitions afforded not less interesting exhibitions of skill and endurance. A horse which had showed in his youth an extreme reluctance to allow himself to be mounted was permitted to spend his life on the prairie, roaming at will over its vast expanse. Every year this horse was caught by pursuit and lariat, and brought to Macleod for the bucking competition. He was a genuinely wild animal, for although he had been born of domesticated parents, he had quickly reverted to the primitive life of his ancestors. The first to attempt to mount him was a good-looking young half-breed. He was not absolutely sober although he was by no means drunk. He came on the field nonchalantly smoking a cigarette, and vaulted on the back of the bucking cayuse. He was thrown immediately, and he rose from the ground still smoking his cigarette. This performance was repeated several times; the moment he was in the saddle he was off again, the horse playing with the precision of a good pitcher at a baseball match. Then came another competitor. He was a celebrated cow-puncher. I think his name was Stewart. He succeeded in keeping the saddle; the horse reared and plunged, jerked and wriggled, now his forefeet were in the air, and now his head was between his forefeet and his hind legs were in the air. The struggle lasted a long time; but the man conquered, and rode the bucking horse, now subdued, round the lines.

In the afternoon I went into the Hudson Bay Store, and there learned of an Indian snake-charmer who had come into town to attend the races. Upon my expressing a desire to see this man, another Indian who was in the store undertook to fetch him. He took from a tray exposed on the counter a small circular mirror from a stock of such mirrors, there being a sale for them among the Indians. Taking this mirror to the door, he heliographed to the other end of the street; in a short time the snake-charmer made his appearance. He immediately produced from his breast and from his pockets several small snakes, which he fondled with ease and a certain grace.

Next day we set off on our round of the ranches. The first ranche at which we stopped was about thirty miles from Macleod towards the foothills of the Rocky Mountains. The drive was very interesting. We passed through great herds of Herefordshire steers browsing on the open prairie. Lying unnoticed among them were frequently to be seen coyotes or prairie wolves. These animals are about the size of a large English collie. They are known occasionally to kill isolated calves, but they are too timid to attack grown cattle, or even to attack calves in their presence. Apart from gophers and an occasional skunk, there was little life observable on the prairies. The skunk was indeed a nuisance. When we set off from Macleod we were followed by a dog—a greyhound which attached itself to us; later we found ourselves attended by other dogs of various breeds, so that after some hours we had a veritable pack. The morning was not far advanced when we saw at some distance on the rolling prairie a small animal whose body appeared to be about the size of a large cat. Down the vertebral column there was a broad riband of white fur, otherwise the fur was black. The legs of the creature were very short, and it moved slowly with a waddling gait. The dogs recognised their legitimate prey, and made for it. Our mounted policeman at once attempted to get near enough to shoot it with his revolver; but the dogs were swifter. Whenever the attack began the creature employed the means of defence with which it had been endowed by nature, and the consequence was that we were strongly tempted to shoot the dogs. They had, indeed, to be kept at a distance until the horrible odour they had contracted had become less pervasive. As it was, the odour of the skunk hung about our waggon and about our clothes for a couple of days.

We did not see any timber wolves, nor did we even hear them at night. Perhaps the reason was that just before our visit to the foothills the ranchemen had been much troubled by losses of young stock from attacks by wolves, of which there appeared to be very numerous packs. They therefore made a contract with a band of Kootenay Indians to come over the mountains and to hunt down the wolves. The Government paid a bounty upon each wolf destroyed and the ranchemen added to this, and provided besides for the maintenance of the Indians. My recollection is that in three weeks they killed about seven hundred wolves in the foothills between Calgary and the international boundary.

The ranche for which we were destined was a horse ranche. Upon it there was bred the Canadian Clydesdale, descended from the celebrated Clydesdale stock, but rather lighter than the heavy Clydesdales of the Glasgow district. The Canadian animals were probably hardier than their parent stock, for they were able to make their living on the prairie and in the foothills during the winter. In case of exceptionally deep snow, they were able, unless they happened to be browsing at too great a distance, to procure hay at certain places at which it was stacked for their use. When we arrived at the ranche, we found that about sixty animals had been rounded up for shipment to London, where they were destined for the vans of Pickford. The ranche house was similar to that of Mr. Hull, which I have already described, and the table was furnished in a similarly ample manner. We were invited to lunch and we sat down with the cowboys. Another drive of about thirty miles brought us to the Cowley ranche, belonging at that time to my friend Frederick Godsal. We were driving towards his house in the evening, when we saw approaching us on the prairie a couple of horsemen with ropes hanging from their high Mexican saddles. When they came nearer, we found that one of them was the proprietor of the ranche. He received us cordially and showed us into a comfortable parlour, the centre table being covered with magazines. Our host excused himself while he changed from his riding clothes, and I picked up the current number of the *Nineteenth Century*, in which I found an article contributed by him.

We spent the night at the Cowley ranche, and then next morning went on to Pincher Creek. A line of railway had been projected from Macleod into the mountains, and a portion of its embankment was visible, but the line had been abandoned, and it was not for some years afterwards that the Canadian Pacific Railway constructed what was known as the Crow's Nest Pass Line.

In spite of the absence of railway communication Pincher Creek had become an important place. Situated under the mountains and sheltered by them from all winds, excepting the dry easterly winds from the prairies, Pincher Creek enjoyed a genial climate and a relatively long summer. It became famous for its vegetables notwithstanding its distance from a market. These vegetables found their way into the neighbouring mountains, where already there were beginning mining camps, including camps for the incipient coal-mining, within a few miles from the town of Pincher Creek. There we spent the next night. From Pincher Creek we had a long drive—some fifty miles—to the Cochrane ranche. This great ranche, the largest on the Canadian side of the line, had at that time, so far as I remember, some fourteen thousand head of cattle. In a field near the ranche house we saw four hundred Herefordshire bulls, many of them being highly-bred imported stock. The ranche house was more imposing than any we had visited, for it was occupied as a permanent residence by Mr. and Mrs. Cochrane. Mr. Cochrane was the son of Senator Cochrane, of Montreal, the owner, and was the superintendent of the ranche. The isolation of the ranches may be surmised from the long distances which I have indicated as separating them. The Cochrane ranche was about fifty miles south of Macleod, and Macleod was the nearest town. In the event of sickness the inconvenience, and even danger, of so great isolation may be imagined. In the spring preceding my visit workmen had been brought to make some improvements in the house. One of these workmen became sick, so also did the only domestic. The lady of the house had to nurse both of them. A doctor had to be brought from a distance of fifty miles, and a professional nurse could not be procured at all. The sick workman died in spite of the utmost care possible under the circumstances. Such incidents were by no means infrequent on the prairies at that time.

The ranching system was inaugurated in the western plains of Canada about 1884, when the methods in use in Montana were adopted by Englishmen like Staveley Hill, who agreed with the Government for the payment of a sum for grazing rights over a certain area. The whole country to the south of the Canadian Pacific Railway and between the boundary of Manitoba and the Rocky Mountains was open. There was no settlement and no enclosed land. The cattle could thus range over an immense area. They were found actually to range about one hundred and fifty miles from west to east. The practice in Montana of branding the cattle belonging to a particular ranche with a regis-tered brand was followed in Canada. So also was the plan of rounding-up the cattle in the spring, and of branding the calves. The round-up was performed in this manner: Cowboys from all the ranches whose cattle were upon the ranges collected at a given point to the number of about two hundred. They were equipped with horses, waggons and supplies for a two weeks' expedition. The farthest eastward limit of the range of the cattle being determined, they rode to that point and spread themselves out northwards in a line extending from latitude 49° N.—the international boundary. They then rode west-wards, rounding-up the mothers and their calves. The calves were branded with the brand of the cows with which they were running. When calves were found without mothers, and therefore without indication as to their ownership, they were known as "mavericks." These "mavericks" were exposed for sale at the end of the round-up, and the proceeds applied towards the expenses of the round-up. In the autumn an expedition of the same kind was organised, but for a different purpose. The cattle which the various ranches intended to ship were rounded-up and taken to the nearest railway station in order to be entrained.

The ranching system was in full vigour in 1896; there was very little settlement, and such as there was, was concentrated at one or two places.

From the Cochrane ranche we drove to the Blood Reserve. Here we spent the night at a Mounted Police post at "Stand-off," near where a battle had been fought between the Bloods and the Peigans. The officer in charge of the post, Captain Jarvis, entertained us hospitably. In the evening, while I was talking with Captain Jarvis, the door of the sitting-room at the post suddenly opened, and there entered an Indian, well armed and dressed in a kind of uniform. He had ridden up to the post, dismounted, and walked silently across a verandah, which creaked under the slightest pressure from a European foot. He was one of the Indian scouts attached to the North-West Mounted Police. His advent caused me to ask my host by what name the Indians knew him. Captain Jarvis was good enough to give me the bedroom usually occupied by him. In the early morning I was awakened by the feeling that there was someone in the room. I opened my eyes and saw, standing at my bedside, another of these Indian scouts. It was evident that he had entered the post unobserved. He pronounced Captain Jarvis's Indian name and I directed him where to go. The incident illustrated at once the confidence of the police in the loyalty of the Indians and the extraordinary stealthiness of their movements.

There was a serious topic of conversation among the Indians of the Blood Reserve. They had become aware of the Venezuela incident, and of the consequent dispute which had arisen between Great Britain and the United States. The possibility of a war in which Canada might be involved at once occurred to their minds. They were, I was informed, seriously considering on which side they should throw their military force. They could probably have given a thousand men to either side, but of course none of these men were trained in modern warfare.[1]

We drove on to Lethbridge. As we drove eastwards on the prairies, the view of the Rocky Mountains became more extensive—in the foothills we were too near them. Gradually the mountain range within sight became longer, until, before the mountains sank beneath

---

[1] Many Canadian Indians volunteered for the Great War. Among the small tribe of Micmacs remaining on Prince Edward Island thirty-five per cent. of the able-bodied men volunteered.

the western horizon, we saw from Chief Mountain in the United States northwards for nearly two hundred miles. The view of the Rocky Mountains from the plains is more impressive than the view of their details afforded by traversing them.

At Lethbridge there are deposits of coal. These deposits consist of lignite, not high in carbon, but sufficiently so to be readily combustible. The seams are extremely narrow, and the cost of mining is therefore relatively great. The population of the small town is very diversified. Representatives of nearly every nation in Europe were to be found within its borders. Most of the foreigners were working in the coal mines. There was at that time the feeble beginning of settlement in the "bench" lands, or the lands on the prairie in which the rivers—the Old Man, the Belly and the St. Mary— had cut more or less deep gorges. The prairie level was thus high above the water-courses, and therefore dry. From Lethbridge we drove back to Macleod, and went from thence by rail to Calgary and then on to Edmonton.

Edmonton, like Macleod, had originated in a period before settlement. It was a Hudson Bay trading post, and when the monopoly of the Hudson Bay Company came to be invaded by free fur-traders, some of these established themselves here. Although there was a small Mounted Police station at Edmonton, the principal post of the district was situated at Fort Saskatchewan, about twenty miles from Edmonton up the North Saskatchewan River. Edmonton, as it was in 1896, was wholly on the north bank of the river. On the south bank there was the small town of Strathcona, which was the terminus of the Calgary and Edmonton Railway. There was no bridge over the river. In the evening, on our arrival, we stepped into a stage-coach drawn by four horses. We drove by a winding road down the high bank, and then we seemed in the darkness to be about to be plunged into the waters of the river. At a great pace, with admirable dexterity, the coachman drew up his horses on a raft which floated at the foot of the declivity. By means of this raft and a chain we were drawn across the river, and the coach was driven at a good pace up the steep road on the other side. In a short time we were at the door of the hotel. Among our fellow-passengers were Bishop Young of Athabasca and Bishop Reeve of Mackenzie River. The first-mentioned had with him his daughter and the second his wife. They were on their way to their respective dioceses. Athabasca Landing is on the Mackenzie River, about ninety miles north of Edmonton. It was then reached only by stage-coach. The diocesan centre of

Mackenzie River was at Great Slave Lake, about twelve hundred miles north of Athabasca Landing. In the beginning of June a steamer, belonging to the Hudson Bay Company, leaves Athabasca Landing for the mouth of the Mackenzie, conveying supplies for the Hudson Bay post situated on the river; but at other times the only means of performing the journey is by an open boat. Bishop Reeve had hired such a boat, and intended to perform in it his long journey. He hoped to accomplish it in about two months from his leaving Athabasca Landing.

At Edmonton I reached my farthest point and turned my face homewards. I arrived at Toronto in the beginning of September, having been absent about three months.

The impression derived from the North-West in 1896 was that of a huge undeveloped country. However rich in natural resources it might be, these resources could not be developed without increase in population and without the expenditure of a great deal of capital. Immigration had been proceeding slowly, and therefore capital had been coming in slowly also. This relatively slow rate of progress seemed to me to be due to the variability of the climate. For some years together the rains might be excessive; storms of hail even in the summer were not unusual. I had seen cabbage leaves pierced by hail as if they had been riddled with bullets from a machine-gun. This condition had been met in Manitoba by a hail insurance system organised by the Provincial Government, and individual losses were thus avoided. When the melting of the snows and the heavy spring rains raised the level of the rivers and flooded the prairies, especially in the valley of the Assiniboine, the effects were calamitous. Not less so were those of the years of deficient rainfall, when the prairies were parched and the soil cracked from sheer absence of moisture. A succession of such years sometimes caused abandonment of whole regions, the farmers throwing up their homesteads, on which with the most unremitting labour they could raise nothing, and on which for that reason they could raise no money.

These were grave drawbacks, yet neither the excessive drought nor the excessive moisture was a constant phenomenon. In spite of their occasional, and in some districts even frequent, occurrence, farming in Manitoba and in some parts of the prairies was on the whole a profitable enterprise. As much land as a man could cultivate with his own labour was to be had for nothing, and he could acquire additional land at a small cost. No-rent land, when fruitful, has its advantages. But no-rent land implies the absence of hireable labour.

No labourer will work for another if he can get land of his own for nothing. Every labourer is not, however, a good farmer, and thus no-rent land, or land of extremely low price, implies a low average of production. This was very amply illustrated in much of the land I saw. The farmers were making a living upon it for themselves and their families, but the living was often at a very low standard of comfort.

Yet I saw sufficient to lead me to believe that, if a stream of immigration of more or less skilled cultivators by some means took place, the productivity of the country would increase rapidly, and that the farmers would be able to some extent to overcome, and in any case to provide for, the inequalities of the seasons. I thought that as immigration increased the price of land would advance, and that the necessity of increased production would be brought home to the farmers, if only through the diminution in the external prices of their product through increased production.

When I returned to the East I communicated these impressions to some of the leading financiers. I pointed out that the application of capital to the North-West would facilitate immigration, and consequently would contribute to the increase of the area under cultivation. To my surprise I was met by the utmost scepticism. The country was quite undeveloped, they said, when it is developed it might be worth their attention. Some of them paid a visit for the first time to the North-West soon after, and this visit led to modification of their views of the country and its prospects. Yet caution has always been necessary in financing the West. The enthusiastic optimism of many Westerners did not afford a basis of security sufficiently tangible to permit the investment of funds held in trust for others.

CHAPTER XXV

CANADA IN 1897-1901

Where the blindest bluffs hold good, dear lass,
And the wildest tales are true,
And the men bulk big on the old trail, our own trail, the out trail,
And life runs large on the Long Trail—the trail that is always new.

   .   `   .   .   . .

The Lord knows what we may find, dear lass,
And the deuce knows what we may do—
But we're back once more on the old trail, our own trail, the out trail,
We're down, hull down on the Long Trail—the trail that is always new.

RUDYARD KIPLING, L'Envoi.

THE excitement about the gold discoveries in Southern British Columbia in 1895 was as nothing to the fever which spread with vigorous contagion when, in the autumn of 1896, the discoveries on the Klondyke came to be known. In British Columbia the gold was buried in mines in chemical combination with other metals and in refractory ores. It could not be recovered without arduous labour even when the gold-bearing ore was actually in hand. In the Klondyke all was different. A stroll by the river produced a fortune in pure gold. To stoop down and pick it up was the easiest thing in the world. Not only the spirits of avarice and gambling were excited, the spirit of adventure was stimulated, as it had been in 1849. The gold trail was an old trail, but the trail for gold which led to the frozen North was a new trail. The wildest tales might be true. The gold lay to be picked up at the end of the trail. What did it matter if the trail were long and dangerous? So much the more adventurous the journey. The first discoveries were registered in August 1896. In the following spring the rush into the Yukon began. Adventurers from all parts of the world poured into the country, some of them seeking gold, others seeking to prey upon the gold seekers.

There were two principal routes to the Yukon—one by steamer from Seattle up the coast of British Columbia and Alaska, then up the Yukon River to Canadian territory; the other by the Stickeen River and over the White Pass to the Stewart River, on which were the Klondyke claims. Some adventurous persons attempted to go by another route, by that, indeed, which had been recommended to me the previous year by the Hudson Bay Company, viz., the route by Edmonton, down the Mackenzie River, and then across the mountains to the Stewart River. This proved a very disastrous route, and many gold seekers lost their lives upon it. The reasons for the disasters which attended those who attempted this route were probably that the gold seekers were not experienced in travelling in wild countries, that they had insufficient resourcefulness, and that they went in too great numbers to avail themselves of the expert means of transport—namely, by Indians across the mountains.

The other routes were more readily adapted to the pressure of numbers, but the main rush was by the White Pass. Unfortunately I was unable to see this remarkable sight. I should have liked to do so.

The effects of the new gold discoveries upon the general economic situation in Canada were the stimulation of local trade in the centres nearest to or in communication with the mining regions, this stimulation reacting upon the supply centres in the East, and the outbreak of a mania for speculation in mining shares. Farmers utilised their reserves and townspeople devoted their savings towards the purchase of stock in mines, of which they knew nothing and could know nothing. Capital which might have been invested in agriculture or in industry was frittered away in fatuous attempts to discover gold. Mining in the Yukon was carried on, to begin with, in a costly way by amateur miners. A few fortunes were made by rich finds, more were made by selling supplies at high prices to the mob of prospectors and miners who thronged into the camps. By far the larger number of these returned disappointed. Gradually the mining assumed another character. Companies with large capital worked the fields systematically, and some of them were for a time able to pay good dividends. In later years the advance of prices and the increase of wages in the industrial centres rendered gold mining less profitable. Only the richer fields could yield sufficient to induce either labour or capital to venture into them.

On the whole, the gold discoveries in the Yukon, as well as those in Southern British Columbia, bestowed an evanescent and doubtful benefit upon the country.

The beginning of an important immigration from Central Europe in 1895 has already been noticed. This movement proceeded at an accelerated rate in 1896 and 1897. The immigrants came for the most part from Galicia and Bukovina, then provinces of Austria. The chief reason for this movement was the congestion of the peasant population in Galicia. The great plain which lies immediately to the north and east of the Carpathian Mountains is occupied by people of Ruthenian extraction, speaking Little Russian and belonging to the Uniate Church. This church is composed of those members of the Orthodox (or Greek) Faith who adhered to the short-lived reunion of the Eastern and Western Churches never fully authorised by ecclesiastical authority. The congestion of population on the Galician plain resulted in depression of wages for agricultural labour and in the rise of rents for the peasants' holdings. An active propaganda carried on by the railways and the steamship companies informed the Galician peasants of the existence of no-rent lands in the Canadian West, and the offer of extremely low rates for transport to these lands induced them to embark for them. The peasants were very poor, many of them had little more than sufficient to pay for their passage, but they were industrious and frugal. If it did not connive at the emigration the Austrian Government did nothing to impede it. The congestion was indeed troublesome, the people were of a race different from that of the bulk of the people of Austria, they occupied a frontier province, and they might soon become discontented with Austrian rule. It was better to allow a certain number of them to go; those who remained would be better off than they were before the emigration, and better off than they could be without it. Thus for several years the Galician immigration into Canada numbered from 4000 to 6000 per year. Ere long the effects of the emigration from Galicia began to manifest themselves there. Wages increased and rents declined. Then the Austrian Government began to interpose checks upon emigration. Meanwhile some 40,000 Galicians and Bukovinians had emigrated to Canada. They came at an opportune moment.

New railways were being projected in the North-West, and these people were available to build them. Employment upon railway construction was an advantage to them. They saved the greater part of their wages, devised spontaneously a system of co-operative credit, took out homesteads, bought stock and agricultural machinery, and established themselves with incredible rapidity. The system of co-operative credit organised by the Galicians was very simple. When a Galician was ready to begin work upon his homestead, he obtained the signatures of forty or fifty of his friends who were already established. These signatures on a folio sheet of paper were appended to a note for one or two hundred dollars, drawn at three or four months. Such notes were readily accepted by the banks. They were discounted, and the proceeds employed for the purchase of seed. The first crop was generally potatoes. These were planted about the third week in April. Before the end of June the potatoes were ready for digging, and before the note for the seed was due the potatoes were sold and the funds were deposited. The implement makers also accepted these joint notes for machinery and the merchants for supplies, and thus, by means of frugality and punctuality on the one hand and credit on the other, Galicians immigrating without means quickly established themselves. I was told by bankers that the notes of the Galicians were always met.

The Canadian and British settlers clamoured for Government credit instead of organising for themselves a joint credit system. The consequence was that by means of political pressure a system of Government credit was instituted with priority of lien for advances. Liens were piled upon liens until these became so numerous that even when a settler had established himself he was unable to borrow in the open market because owing to these liens his credit was gone. He became thus entirely dependent upon Government credit, and in course of time the investment of private funds through the banks was discouraged.

When the Galicians began to arrive, and for eight or ten years after the beginning of the migration, they were too poor to build houses, and they therefore adopted an expedient not unknown in some of the impoverished regions of Eastern Europe. They made dug-outs for themselves. I have seen many of these dug-outs in the North-West, and I have been in some of them. They were customarily about five feet deep on a slight rising ground, with a trench round them to prevent their being flooded. The walls of the dug-out were usually neatly squared off, shelves being sometimes cut out for household utensils. The roof was composed of poles cut from any standing timber in the neighbourhood. These poles were placed close together, and then covered with clay in such a manner as to make a watertight roof. The Galician families lived in these makeshift abodes until they were able to build houses upon their homestead lands. When they were able to do so, they obtained permits to cut timber on areas owned by the Government, unless there was suitable timber on their own homesteads. They went in groups to the timber areas, cut their logs, and hauled them to the sites of their houses. Although the Galicians have a strong sense of the advantages of individual ownership, and have therefore no idea of becoming communists, they have an equally strong sense of the value of co-operation.

I received from an authentic source the story of a Galician family.

In its essential features the story is by no means unique. In the spring of 1896 or 1897 there arrived at the then insignificant settlement of Rosthern on the Regina and Prince Albert Railway a Galician family, consisting of a man, his wife, and five children. When they alighted from the train they had no money, and when the woman looked round upon the open and unoccupied prairie, almost destitute of even a shrub, she went into hysterics. Then she fainted. A kind-hearted official went over to the inn and procured a glass of spirits, which he forced the woman to swallow. This brought her to her senses, but did not relieve her mind. Here she was with her young family in a desolate place without resources. She was a powerfully-built woman, accustomed to hard farm labour, but the conditions seemed to her hopeless. A farmer who was on the platform offered to take the whole family to his place. He did so, and found that the labour of the family was very ample to compensate for the cost of their subsistence. Within a week it was evident that they were worth much more than their food and shelter. He arranged with them for the wages customary in the neighbourhood. They remained with him about three months, and then found other employment. In the spring of the following year the man entered for a homestead for himself, and for another for his eldest boy. I visited this family five or six years after these events. I found that in addition to the homesteads they had acquired by purchase a whole section, or six hundred and forty acres, which they were bringing into cultivation. There was a good house thatched in the neat Galician manner. Very large barns and implement sheds indicated care and prosperity. I saw the mother of the family standing in her doorway looking with pride upon her extensive possessions.

In 1896 I had met upon the prairies numerous "prairie schooners" or hooded waggons, in which families belonging to the Western States were touring the country in search of suitable land. At that time many of these intending settlers were returning to their homes in the United States without having been able to find what they wanted. They were, in general, frightened by the visible evidences of drought. In 1897 and in the immediately subsequent years the weather conditions improved, a dry cycle seemed to have passed away, and a wet cycle seemed to have come.

Agents of the Canadian Immigration authorities were active in Nebraska and other States in which land had advanced sharply in value. Farmers were able to sell their lands in the United States for relatively high prices, and then to cross the line with ready cash and obtain for nothing their share of homestead lands, while if they chose they could invest a part of their capital in additional land. It was necessary for them to cultivate their homestead lands, but it was not necessary for them to cultivate their purchased land. They could keep it until an advance in price rendered sale expedient. Thus the American invasion began. Many of those immigrants from the United States who came between 1897 and 1904 were possessed of means. They often brought great quantities of stock, farm implements, and household effects with them. Their migration was caused by a combination of circumstances—the coincidence of demand at high prices for land in Nebraska and the existence of a large area of land of at least fair quality available for homesteads practically gratuitously in Canada. These American farmers were, in general, readily absorbed into the mass of the agricultural population. There were some cases in which absorption was slow and difficult.

All the American farmers who migrated into Canada were not of either American or British extraction. Many of them had come either directly or indirectly from various parts of Europe. Among these European immigrants who had come *via* the United States, having resided there for a longer or a shorter time, there was a large group of German Catholics from the Rhenish provinces. Persuaded by the plausible tongues of agents, they had migrated in a large group and had purchased land.

In 1899 I made my second trip to the North-West, visiting especially the Yorkton region and the Qu'Appelle Valley. In the first part of this trip my principal interest was in the Doukhobors, and I have devoted a separate chapter to them. In the second part of my trip I visited particularly the Swedish and Finnish settlements.

In 1896 I had witnessed the effects of drought, I now saw the effects of excess of moisture. The whole of the plains in the neighbourhood of Portage la Prairie were under water. Haystacks appeared as if they were floating, and the farmers in those cases in which they did not abandon their houses altogether, lived in upper storeys and went to and fro in boats. The elevators were also under water; in many of them the grain had been soaked and become swollen, and the distorted elevators had burst. The waters of the Assiniboine had become uncontrollable. On the Saskatchewan, Swan and White Sand Rivers bridges were down, and communication by railway, and even otherwise, was interrupted.

I had arranged to drive into the Qu'Appelle Valley from Whitehills, a station on the Canadian Pacific Railway west of Brandon. I took with me a Swedish interpreter who knew the district. My principal

I—2 A

object was to see the Finnish settlers before my departure for Finland.
I arrived at Whitehills early in May. Our journey involved crossing
the Qu'Appelle River, about thirty miles from Whitehills. When we
arrived at the river the whole valley seemed to be under water, the
bridge over which we had expected to go being covered to a depth of
nearly three feet. It was inadvisable to attempt a crossing, the chief
risk being at the end of the bridge where the approach might be washed
away. We procured a farmer who undertook to ride across the bridge
before us and report upon the conditions on the other side. All went
well, and we accomplished that stage safely. Our next experience was
not so easy. Some miles from the bridge and on the north bank of the
river we encountered a tributary creek through which the trail passed.
There was no bridge. Our driver proposed to ford the stream at the
trail, but I did not like the look of the high banks and the torrential
stream that was surging between them. I suspected that the bed of
the stream, which normally was at no great depth, had been scoured
into a V shape, and that if the horses once got their heads down
nothing could save us or them. I decided to wait at the crossing, because I knew that the Finnish farmer whom we were going to see
expected us, and that, being in all probability an intelligent man, he
would be aware of the state of the crossing, and would be anxious
about our passage. In that case he would be likely to ride out to meet
us. Our driver became impatient, and insisted upon attempting to
cross the stream. I warned him that the stream was in a dangerous
condition, and told him that I should not be answerable for the consequences if he made the attempt. He was, however, very headstrong,
and although I refused to enter the waggon, he went on. He had no
sooner gone down the bank than he realised his mistake, the horses
lost their footing, and horses, waggon and man were washed down the
stream into still deeper water. Fortunately the horses swam, while
the man, although much frightened, kept his head and maintained
his hold of the reins. He sank up to the neck, lost his footing upon the
waggon, and floated helplessly, the horses meanwhile struggling to
gain the opposite bank. At that moment the farmer came up and
assisted the unfortunate man to land. My interpreter and I afterwards
crossed the stream upon a hayrack, sitting upon the topmost bar.
The water at the ford was not less than ten feet deep.

Our Finnish farmer had been the manager of a factory at Helsingfors. The owners of the factory became insolvent, and his means of
livelihood disappeared. He had saved a little money, and he determined to emigrate with his family. He had built himself a house, and

PROFESSOR AND MRS. MAVOR IN LIBRARY AT UNIVERSITY CRESCENT

From a photograph (1907) by J. W. Mavor

had stocked his farm. He had several horses, and had no reason, he said, to regret that he had become a farmer. With his family the case was otherwise. This family consisted of his wife and a son and daughter. The latter were a healthy and capable couple; but they had been accustomed to the life of a capital city not without gaiety, and they found the isolation of the Qu'Appelle Valley little to their mind. They did not object to the hard work of the farm, but the isolation distressed them. They had gone into Winnipeg in the winter, and had found employment there; but it was necessary to remain on the farm in the summer, and during that time they found it very lonely. They told me that the next farm was twenty miles off, and that they did not like to go so far for a dance. I tried to explain to them that these conditions would in all probability soon be altered, and that as settlement increased loneliness would diminish. No doubt, they said, but this would take time.

I have narrated these incidents because they illustrate the risks and inconveniences of settlement in an unorganised country, where the struggle against nature is incessant, and where the sparseness of settlement makes it difficult to keep young people upon the farms. This is especially the case where the settlers have been accustomed to the social life of a large community.

The British Association visited Canada for the first time in 1884, when the meeting was held in Montreal. This was also the first occasion of its meeting outside the British Islands. In 1893 the Canadian Institute decided to invite the Association to visit Toronto at as early a date as might be arranged. Grants were obtained from the Dominion Government and from the Provincial Government of Ontario, and an invitation was sent. As I happened to be attending the meeting at Nottingham in 1893, I was asked to convey the invitation and to ascertain when it was likely the visit would take place, the arrangements of the Association being generally made some years in advance. No definite response was made in 1893, and I was again instructed to repeat the invitation at Oxford in 1894. The arrangements were completed in 1895, and the meeting took place in 1897. It was a great pleasure to be able to welcome many of my oldest friends—Lord Kelvin, Gerald Fitzgerald, Oliver Lodge, James Bryce, Henry Higgs, and many others. Above all, I had the great pleasure of having with me during and after the visit of the Association my friend Prince Kropotkin, whom I had been able to induce to make the meeting of the Association an occasion to visit Canada. Among the foreigners were Penck, the geographer from Vienna, and Dr. Magnus, the botanist from Berlin, and among the visitors from the United States Simon Newcomb, the astronomer, who by birth was a Nova Scotian.

An excursion to the Pacific Coast was arranged through the kindness of the Canadian Pacific Railway. A large number of the members took advantage of this excursion. Among these was Prince Kropotkin, who afterwards wrote his impressions in an interesting article in the *Nineteenth Century*.

The Toronto meeting of the Association came at an opportune moment. The immigration movement was just beginning, and undoubtedly the meeting advertised the country and gave an impetus to immigration, especially from Great Britain. It also contributed to accelerate the influx of capital from Great Britain which began shortly afterwards to be noticeable.

In 1897 the exploitation of the water power of Niagara Falls had been going on for some time on the American side, but there had been as yet no development on the Canadian side. The reason was that in the United States there was an increasing amount of capital seeking investment, and increasing credit available for utilisation; it was, therefore, easier to procure in the United States than in Canada the large amounts of money necessary to embark upon the development of water power. The activity on the American side, resulting in the building of factories and the growth of a large industrial town, in contrast to the absence of any such activity on the Canadian side, struck some of the visitors very forcibly. Some of them, notably Mr. Bryce, felt convinced that sooner or later the Canadian side must share in the general movement. The exploitation of the American Falls had, however, to some extent vulgarised them. The beauty of the scene was compromised by the clumsiness with which the earlier utilisation of water power had been effected. This had been so obvious that a movement had been promoted both in the United States and Canada to prevent the commercialisation of the Niagara Falls, and to preserve their beauty from destruction by industrial enterprises. This movement led to the acquisition of land on both sides by public authorities belonging to the respective countries. The United States authorities secured some islands and a portion of the mainland in the neighbourhood of the falls, and converted these into a public park. The Ontario Government also acquired a large area on the Canadian side and made a public park, placing the administration of it under a commission. At the same time, by international agreement, the amount of water which could be taken from the falls for industrial purposes was limited. Not until some years after 1897 was there any important development on the Canadian side. When this development did occur, it was first encouraged and afterwards hampered by political interference. The water power of Niagara might have been utilised without destroying the scenic beauty of the falls had the Ontario Government adopted an intelligent plan, and had it given reasonable and consistent facilities for the investment of capital in hydraulic enterprises. The policy of successive Governments vacillated from extreme concession to extreme restriction, and ended by expropriation of the enterprises that had been developed under Government concessions. The result was the discrediting of all private enterprises in water power, and for several years complete absence of development by the Government. An extensive governmental scheme is now (1922) in process of realisation, but the success of it from a financial point of view is as yet undetermined.

While the gold fever undoubtedly diverted capital from agriculture and industry, it rendered capital mobile which otherwise might have been inert, and it drew into the country capital which might not have found its way there excepting for enterprises promising large returns. Much domestic capital was lost to the owners of it, and much was wasted in utterly unproductive prospects; but some of it was effectual in establishing certain businesses and in enabling others which otherwise might have succumbed to carry on their affairs until normal times came round again. The same was true of external capital.

When the immigration movement of the late nineties took place, it came before the gold fever had spent itself, and the real demand for land and commodities involved in immigration produced a vigorous trade movement. This movement was probably facilitated by the increased mobility of capital induced by the gold mania. Thus the gold discoveries, disappointing as they were in direct tangible results, may have played a part in the general economic improvement which was observable in Canada in 1899 and 1900. There was an increased demand for labour, together with an increased supply of it. Wages did not rise, but the aggregate amount paid in wages was much larger and employment was more regular. These conditions expressed themselves in demand for more houses in the industrial centres. Rents advanced sharply in 1901, and then began the development of suburban areas which Toronto and other towns experienced. This development constitutes a unique chapter in the history of civic growth. Farms in the neighbourhood of towns that had been affected by the boom of 1886-89 were once more the scene of speculative activity. The provision of houses for working-men did not offer sufficient inducement to the speculative builder, but the prospect of selling large areas of land at a relatively low price attracted the attention of land agents. They did not trouble about making streets, about water supply, sewerage, or conveniences of any kind. They simply staked out the land, and sold it for very small prices. Large areas were bought by working-men at about $4 per foot frontage. This meant about $100 (£21) for a lot 25 ft. by 80 to 100 ft. Even this small sum was not usually required to be paid in cash. A payment of $10 and $5 per month afterwards constituted the usual arrangement. Workmen bought these small lots, and for $40 or $50 they bought enough lumber to enable them to build houses by means of their own labour. Thus for an expenditure of about $150 (£31) a workman could provide himself with land and a house—not very permanent or comfortable and not very safe, because the houses were constructed wholly of wood and tar paper, yet passable as a makeshift. If a workman chose to do so, he could fund the amount customarily paid by him in rent, and within two or three years he could save enough to enable him to build and pay for a brick house upon his land. This is what actually happened in general. In many cases the owners of these small lots were able to sell the land to advantage under the influence of the rise in the price of land which occurred between 1901 and 1912. In Toronto alone upwards of 10,000 wooden shacks of the sort described were built by workmen for themselves in 1901 and 1902.

CHAPTER XXVI

I.—LONDON IN 1899

Rise up, thou monstrous ant-hill on the plain
Of a too busy world!
WILLIAM WORDSWORTH, *The Prelude* (1799–1805).

As I expected to be for a short time in London in 1899, I was asked
by the then recently formed Authors' Society in Canada to undertake
negotiations regarding the simultaneous passing in the British and
Canadian Parliaments of an amendment to the Copyright Acts, which
would enable the Canadian publishers to import in sheets books printed
in Great Britain and would at the same time bring the British and
Canadian Copyright Laws into harmony. I had many conferences
with the leading English publishers, and especially with Mr. John
Murray and with Mr. F. R. Daldy who had for many years devoted
himself to the copyright question. I also had conferences with the
members of the legal department of the Colonial Office. Above all,
I had the great privilege towards the close of his life of meeting frequently Lord Thring, who had been for forty years parliamentary
draughtsman. Through Lord Thring I was invited to give evidence
(both in 1899 and in 1900) before the Lords' Committee on Copyright.
At this Committee also I made the acquaintance of Lord Monkswell
and Lord Welby. The copyright question had long been a bone of
contention between the Law Officers of the Crown in England and the
Law Officers of the Crown in Canada. The latter had long held the
view, confirmed by successive Administrations, that the British North
America Act endowed Canada with complete autonomy regarding
copyright. The English Law Officers held equally firmly that such was
not the case. For years the matter remained in an *impasse*, and no
change could be effected. Whenever the subject was broached copyright was lost sight of altogether, and the discussion became concentrated upon the constitutional question of the powers of Canada under
the British North America Act. Under these circumstances some of
us proposed to try to secure simultaneous legislation to the same effect
in both Parliaments, in order that the question of relative powers
should not arise. I need not recite here the tedious negotiations

extending over two years. They resulted in the Canadian Parliament passing the Act of 1900, and in the Lords' Committee recommending similar legislation in Great Britain. The Lords' Bill of that year was thrown out in the House of Commons; but later an Act was passed in effect homologating the Canadian legislation, which in any case had survived the period of two years after which it could not be disallowed. In the course of these negotiations I saw a great deal of Lord Thring. He was then over eighty years of age, but full of fire and energy. I was staying with him at Englefield Green, near Windsor, when one evening, in his library, pointing to a long row of folios which contained the texts of the Bills he had drawn, he said, "As these Bills were when I drew them, they were, I think, pretty consistent, at all events their consistency was very carefully considered. After they had passed through the hands of Parliamentary Committees and amendments upon amendments had been made upon them, I am afraid that consistency was not their strong point."

Lord Thring was a great admirer of Mr. Gladstone. Curiously enough, I met at his house one of his friends who was not. He was Canon Lonsdale of Lichfield. Canon Lonsdale had been at Eton shortly after Mr. Gladstone left Eton for Oxford. He had many curious stories of the Eton of his day. The Headmaster was Dr. Keate. Dr. Lonsdale thought Keate a great humbug. He gave as a characteristic note about him that he said to the boys, "Love your enemies, boys, love your enemies; if you don't, I'll flog you." Among other friends of Lord Thring whom I met were Admiral Sir Edward Fanshaw, a very fine old sailor, and Rowntree, who wrote the book on poverty in York, after the manner of Mr. Charles Booth's *London*.

I met at lunch at James Bryce's, E. I. Godkin, the editor of the *New York Evening Post*, and Brunetière, the editor of the *Revue des Deux Mondes*. I found Brunetière very precise and dogmatic, Godkin well instructed in European affairs. The talk ran chiefly on the United States. Brunetière's impressions of that country were rather clear than deep.

One of my summer tasks for 1899 was a study of the working of Employers' Liability and Workmen's Compensation for industrial accidents in Great Britain and the Continent. The new Acts had excited interest in Canada, and the Ontario Government had asked me to report upon their operation. The provisions of these Acts in Europe implied a phase of industrial development more advanced than that attained by Canada, and I therefore advised the Government to refrain from adopting the principles embodied in the German Acts and to adopt with caution those of the British Acts. The question of workmen's compensation remained in abeyance for ten or twelve years, when agitation arose and a commission of inquiry was appointed which led to the adoption of a modification of the German system, which had been introduced in the State of Washington. Like many other legislative experiments, the Workmen's Compensation Acts have proved to be extremely expensive to the community, although they may have been of some benefit to certain groups of workmen and to certain groups of employers, and especially to those groups in which, through carelessness or otherwise, the number of accidents was above the average in the industries in question.

In London at this time I made the acquaintance of Julius Reuter,[1] of Westermarck, author of *Human Marriage*, and of Yiro Hirn, who had written with originality and learning upon æsthetics. Both are Finlanders, and both were excited about the Finnish constitutional question, which was then in an acute stage. Westermarck spent most of his time in Morocco, which he found an excellent field for sociological studies. He had been on friendly terms with Rasuli. I spent an evening at the Authors' Club, where I saw G. W. Steevens[2] and Max O'Rell, and at the Garrick, where I met H. B. Irving and Toole, now in his dotage. The poor old fellow, who had in his day been one of the greatest comedians and one of the most active and jovial of men, sat silent and lugubrious. Among my old friends of whom I saw something were Frank Beddard, prosector at the Zoo, John M. Swan, John A. Hobson, J. M. Robertson, Alexander and Robert Ross, and of course Kropotkin, with whom I stayed for a while at Bromley.

II.—GERMANY, AUSTRIA, ITALY, SWITZERLAND, DENMARK
AND SWEDEN IN 1899

Heights castellate,
Quaint towns, fair farms, and morn-illumined sails,
Mid carolling of birds, while thro' the vale
Of vineyards flows the river. . . .
BENJAMIN DISRAELI, *The Revolutionary Epick*
[(1834) 1864].

Early in 1899 Mr. Clifford Sifton,[3] Minister of the Interior, asked me to undertake a study of the possibilities of emigration from the continent of Europe to Canada, and to report to him on the subject. After

[1] Then studying in the Library of the India Office, now Professor of Oriental Languages in the University of Helsingfors.
[2] Steevens went to South Africa. He was shut up in Ladysmith, where he died.
[3] Afterwards Sir Clifford Sifton.

some preliminary studies in the North-West in order to bring my knowledge of parts of that immense region down to date, I sailed for Europe in May. I was detained for some weeks in London. I reached Berlin in June, and almost immediately went on to Cracow, where I had an appointment to meet Dr. Oleskow, of Lemberg. Dr. Oleskow was a professor in the Technical and Agricultural College at Lemberg, and he had a few years before paid a visit to the North-West. Although the emigration of the Galicians to Canada from 1895 onwards had been due to several general causes, Dr. Oleskow had been influential in assisting to direct the emigrants towards Canada, for he had written pamphlets and disseminated information about the country. I was, therefore, instructed to see him in this connection. The ancient city of Cracow, at one time the capital of Poland, lies in the great plain which extends northwards from the northern slopes of the Carpathians. The mountains form the southern horizon looking from Cracow. The population of the city is largely Polish, but there is in it a considerable proportion of Jews. In the Jewish quarter a traveller steps into the Middle Ages. He meets the mediæval Jew everywhere.

Having transacted my business in Cracow I hurried back to Berlin, where I had to make inquiries into the working of the German Workmen's Insurance System. In the course of these inquiries I had to see a number of officials and, as well, a number of German labour union leaders. Although all of these received me with courtesy, I felt in the atmosphere a suggestion of hostility to Great Britain which I had not felt when I was in Germany six years before. The moment was indeed critical; the controversy between Great Britain and the Transvaal was becoming acute, in fact it was marching to war. The impression I received from general conversation was deepened by meeting some Englishmen who resided in Berlin, and who occupied positions which enabled them to form considered judgments of the currents of opinion.

At that time there was not observable any demonstrative hostility, although there seemed to me to be a certain subdued ill-will. This ill-will probably had its beginning, not in commercial rivalry as some suppose, but in the discovery by the Germans that in any quarrel between the United States and a European Power, Great Britain would be found on the side of the United States. This discovery was made during the Spanish-American War. Then there came the attempt, partially successful as it was, on the part of the Government of Kruger to enlist sympathy for the Transvaal in the struggle against Great Britain.

From Berlin I went, *via* Dresden, Saxon Switzerland and Leipzig, to Vienna. There I made inquiry into the working of the Austrian Workmen's Insurance System, and also into the question of emigration from Austria. I made up my mind that the fundamental reason for the emigration from Galicia was the pressure of population in that province, and that the inducement of free homestead land in Canada was of itself quite sufficient to cause the continuance of the stream of immigrants which had already been flowing for four years. I therefore advised the Canadian Government to suspend altogether the payment of commissions to agents and steamship companies for immigrants into Canada from Central Europe. Had this advice been accepted, the discreditable incidents connected with the promotion and operation of the Atlantic Trading Company could not have taken place. The existence of the commissions led to the transactions in which this company took part, and led to exposure and discredit. I do not believe that any immigration of consequence resulted from the proceedings of the company, while the cost to the Dominion was very great. The immigration would in all probability have taken place had the company never existed.

From Vienna I went *via* Venice and Milan to Genoa, where I pursued my investigations into emigration from the north of Italy. The emigration from South Italy did not concern me, because that was chiefly to the Argentine Republic and the United States, the climate of Canada being in general too severe in the winter for the Mediterranean peoples. I found it expedient to spend several days at Chiasso, on the Swiss-Italian frontier. In this little Swiss village, a couple of miles from Como, there were no fewer than five emigration offices. The *contadini* who found themselves inspired with a desire to emigrate had no difficulty in getting over the frontier, at that time and in that place very perfunctorily guarded. The regulations concerning emigration from Italy were enforced with some rigidity at the seaports, but the emigration by railway was at that time ignored. The Swiss and German railways and the shipping companies from Antwerp were carrying peasants in great numbers from Piedmont and Lombardy to the United States and Canada.

I was not travelling for pleasure, but these days in Northern Italy were very enjoyable. Venice was a delight. In the Academy I spent a good deal of time, much of it being devoted to the drawings of Leonardo. One hot day in July there was a *festa* of some kind, and the peasants and townsfolk filled St. Mark's completely. The gay shawls of the peasant girls harmonised with the Byzantine decoration of the cathedral, although the colour effect was subdued by the mists exhaled by the perspiring bodies of the congregation. One or two steamers disturbed the waters of the Grand Canal; but the motor-boat had not yet made its appearance, and it was possible to float lazily through the city in a gondola.

When I left Chiasso I had hoped to visit Prince Khilkov [1] at Ascona, near Bellinzona; but at Chiasso I had a telegram from his wife saying that he had gone to Geneva to see Paul Biriukov.[2] As I was anxious to meet him again, I pursued him to Geneva. There I found Biriukov's family in a charming house looking out upon the Salève, but Biriukov and Khilkov had both gone to Lucerne. I had no leisure for further pursuit. From Geneva I went to Winterthur, for the purpose of seeing Herr Forrer, the well-known advocate, who afterwards became President of the Swiss Republic. My purpose in seeing him was to learn about the movement in Switzerland for workmen's insurance, of which he had been for a long time the most active promoter. I found that the working of the Referendum in Switzerland had the effect of paralysing all such movements. Again and again the Swiss Chamber was convinced of the expediency and timeliness of certain reforms, and again and again the conservatism of the people, expressing itself through the Referendum, prevented these reforms from being carried into effect.

From Winterthur I hastened northwards to Berlin and then to Warnemunde, from which port I crossed to Denmark and went to Copenhagen. Here I expected advices about appointments in Finland which had been made for me; but these advices were slow in coming, and I spent a few days in visiting. I saw Professor Westergaard, the incumbent of the Chair of Political Economy in the University of Copenhagen, and the leading authority in Europe on population. I found his suggestions very helpful in the study of migration of people, which is indeed a part of the larger question of population; neither of these questions has of late years had the attention of economists that it deserves. If they were important in the eighteenth century when Malthus wrote his incomparable treatise, they are still more important now, when the greater magnitude of population brings every day fresh aspects of the problem.

One of the sights of Copenhagen is the Thorwaldsen Museum. It is a pity that Denmark should have had only one sculptor, but it is still more of a pity that the solitary sculptor should not have been an artist. Nothing could be more naïve than the frescoes on the

---

[1] *Cf.* vol. ii. p. 6.   [2] *Cf.* vol. ii. p. 70.

exterior of the building, nothing more deadly uninteresting than the mechanical figures in the interior. One day it may be hoped that the Danes will have the courage to take the whole museum and sink it in the Sound.

From Copenhagen I crossed to Mälmo and went by rail to Stockholm. The Swedish railways have the smartest and most comfortable sleeping-cars in Europe. Their *coupés* are a real luxury after the close and dusty compartments of the German railways and the primitive Pullman car of America. At Stockholm a fête was in progress, the country folk had come in and the streets were full of peasant costumes. The collection of pictures in the Royal Palace is interesting, although the gallery does not rank among the finest.

END OF VOL. I

INDEX

Lightning Source UK Ltd.
Milton Keynes UK
UKOW06n1933070617
302922UK00012B/91/P